D1594952

CURRICULUM

Design and
Development

CURRICULUM

Design and
Development

David Pratt

Queen's University

HARCOURT BRACE JOVANOVICH, INC.

New York   San Diego   Chicago   San Francisco   Atlanta
London   Sydney   Toronto

ISBN: 0-15-516735-9

Library of Congress Catalog Card Number: 79-92130

Printed in the United States of America

*Copyrights and Acknowledgments appear on pages 487–90, which constitute
a continuation of the copyright page.*

Preface

Curriculum is, and will always be, a major concern of the professional teacher. Whenever teachers seek clearer purposes or better strategies for their teaching, they are reflecting on curriculum questions. Curriculum thinking is therefore as old as education itself. But for most of its history curriculum thought produced little clear guidance for the practicing educator. Only in the twentieth century has curriculum emerged as a subject for systematic study. And it is mainly in the past decade that the field has begun to produce a substantial body of validated principles for developing curricula. Some of these principles, such as mastery learning and criterion-referenced measurement, have become well known. Others, for example those relating to needs assessment, management of aptitude differences, and curriculum evaluation, deserve wider discussion in the educational community. In this book, these and other issues are examined in relation to the overriding question, How can we develop more valid and more effective curricula?

Much of the curriculum research of the past decade points to the paramount need for design. Time and again logical analysis and empirical experiment have shown that if education is to be effective and creative, all aspects of curricula must be designed with care and with imagination. This book outlines the curriculum decisions confronting educators, starting with the consideration of significant human needs and ending with the implementation of curriculum innovation in the classroom. At every point the conceptual and research basis for the principles and procedures

v

is described to provide clear, step-by-step guidance for curriculum practitioners, whether they are designing curricula for individual classrooms or for entire school systems.

Curriculum: Design and Development addresses these major questions: What basic needs can education meet and how can priorities be established? How can designers organize their work to increase their chance of success? How can the overall purpose of a curriculum best be expressed? What are the specific intended learning outcomes? How can their attainment be assessed? What characteristics will learners bring to the learning situation? What is the optimal organization for instruction? What human, material, and administrative resources will be needed? What strategies can be used to evaluate the curriculum and to install the program? The material has been arranged to correspond with the order in which a curriculum designer would face such questions, but the chapters are sufficiently self-contained that the sequence in which they are read may be varied. Instructors, students, and other readers will also be able to determine without difficulty which chapters are critical for their particular purposes and which may be treated as supplemental reading.

This book is intended for educators involved in curriculum; that is, for practicing teachers; for teachers in training; for administrators who evaluate, implement, or supervise curricula; and for curriculum developers, coordinators, consultants, and managers in school systems and other educational and training contexts. It has been written for educators working in all subjects and at all levels.

Curriculum: Design and Development is especially appropriate for use in curriculum courses at undergraduate and graduate levels. The substance and the approach of the book have been tested in many such courses for several years. Education students in their initial training gain confidence from design skills that are directly applicable in the classroom. Graduate students value the enhancement of professional expertise founded on a firm basis of established knowledge. The text is supplemented by questions for self-evaluation and suggested activities at the end of chapters. With its growing stature as a field of study, curriculum has inevitably developed a terminology of its own; an appendix provides a glossary containing definitions of the specialized terms used in the book. Additional appendixes provide sources of information on instructional materials and equipment, a specimen curriculum, a model of a curriculum design system, and answers to the end-of-chapter questions.

To pay adequate tribute here to all those who have contributed to the development of this book would be impossible. My colleagues at Queen's University provided counsel and support during the five years the book was in preparation. Many of them read and criticized chapters in early drafts; their comments were invaluable in improving style and substance. Queen's University provided a year's sabbatical, which was generously supported by the Canada Council. During that year, the Department of Educational Studies at Oxford University was a considerate and stimulating host.

I owe much to the painstaking chapter reviews by Russell L. Ackoff, The Wharton School; Lorin W. Anderson, University of South Carolina; Leslie J. Briggs, Florida State University; I. K. Davies, Indiana University; Arthur W. Foshay, Columbia University; Jack R. Fraenkel, San Francisco State University; Robert M. Gagné, Florida State University; Norman Gronlund, University of Illinois; Mauritz Johnson, State University of New York at Albany; Edmund V. Sullivan, Ontario Institute for Studies in Education; Decker F. Walker, Stanford University; Ian Westbury, University of Illinois at Urbana-Champaign; and Belle Ruth Witkin, Alameda County Office of Education, California. The defects surviving the scrutiny of these authorities are my own.

Curriculum: Design and Development would not have been written without the contribution of the more than 6,000 undergraduate and graduate students, teachers, and administrators with whom it has been a pleasure to work in curriculum courses over the past eight years. Their insights and observations and their reports of experiences in applying curriculum principles in school situations have helped in many ways to clarify my own thinking on curriculum issues.

It has been a pleasure to work with the book's staff at Harcourt Brace Jovanovich. I am especially indebted to William J. Wisneski, Elizabeth Holland, Juliana Koenig, Kay Ellen Ziff, Steve Saxe, and Tracy Cabanis. Their work improved the text immeasurably, while their advice and encouragement were invaluable.

Only a writer's family knows the true cost of authorship. My warmest appreciation to Peggy, Kathy, Rosemary, and Jonathan; it was in their free hours that this book was written.

D. P.

Contents

3 The Curriculum and Human Needs   43

Part Two   PRELIMINARY STEPS IN A CURRICULUM PROJECT   77

4 Needs Assessment   79

11   Selecting Instructional Strategies   297

12   Managing Aptitude Differences   331

13   Logistics   369

1

Prologue: Design in Education

Design is the core of all professional training. It is the principal mark that distinguishes the professions from the sciences.

—Herbert Simon (1969, p. 55)

The Nature of Curriculum

People build and create before they think about principles of design. When their undertakings are successful, perceptive observers begin to recognize underlying principles. Then these principles are used to build and create better things. At least until this century, this was the pattern of human progress. It was the way in which agriculture developed, as did metallurgy and architecture. Education also followed this pattern. Schools have been organized, pupils educated, and teachers have debated what to teach and how for millennia. But it is only in the last sixty years that educators have systematically sought general principles for the design of

3

all aspects of the effort to help people learn: to guide, in other words, the design of curriculum.

When intuition, folklore, and conventional wisdom give way to operating principles supported on the one hand by validated theory, and on the other by evidence of practical effectiveness, what emerges can properly be described as an applied science. Its practitioners can be termed professionals or applied scientists. This book endeavors to outline curriculum design as an applied science and a field of professional expertise.

Our first step must be to define curriculum. There are many competing definitions, and failure to arrive at agreement has frequently diverted important discussion into semantic dispute. The common element of almost all usage of the term is agreement that curriculum has to do with planning the activities of learners. The definition used in this work incorporates but goes beyond that popular meaning: *A curriculum is an organized set of formal educational and/or training intentions.* The scope of the term varies from a curriculum for a small unit within a single subject to a multi-year sequence that includes several academic subjects.

The implications of the above definition need to be made explicit. (1) A curriculum is intentions, or plans. They may be merely mental plans, but more commonly exist in written form. (2) A curriculum is not activities but plans, or a blueprint, for activities. The word *program* will be used to refer to learner activities that result from the implementation of a curriculum. (3) A curriculum contains many other kinds of intentions, such as what learnings students are to develop, the means of evaluation to be used to assess learning, the criteria according to which students will be admitted to the program, the materials and equipment to be used, and the qualities required of teachers. (4) A curriculum involves formal intentions, that is, intentions deliberately chosen to promote learning; it does not include random, unplanned, or nonlearning activities. (5) As an organized set of intentions, a curriculum articulates the relationships among its different elements (objectives, content, evaluation, etc.), integrating them into a unified and coherent whole. In a word, a curriculum is a system. (6) Both education and training are referred to in the definition to avoid the misunderstanding that occurs if one is omitted.

The Nature of Design

Numerous terms are used to describe the activities that result in the production of curricula. The terms *curriculum making* and *curriculum construction* were preferred in the early years of the field but were somewhat inappropriate for describing products that were conceptual rather than material. *Curriculum planning* and *curriculum management* are frequently used terms. Both are somewhat restrictive: planning normally refers to prespecification of actions, and management to direction and operation of a system but not to determination of its purposes. For many years *curriculum development* was the term most frequently encountered. More recently the activities of curriculum workers have been increasingly referred to as *curriculum design*. Clearly there is a wide overlap between these two terms, and it would be pedantic to explore the distinction between them at length. Development has connotations of gradual evolution and growth; in the curriculum context it has the advantage of familiarity. Design implies a greater degree of decisiveness and precision, and the concept of design is used and understood fairly consistently by people who work in various applied sciences. Both terms, curriculum development and curriculum design, are used frequently and to an extent interchangeably throughout this book.

Design is the appropriate term to introduce a discussion of some basic principles. Design may be defined as a deliberate process of devising, planning, and selecting the elements, techniques, and procedures that constitute some object or endeavor.

Most of us live in an environment dominated by human design, much of it inadequate. We are all familiar with the child's toy that breaks the day after purchase, the gadget that fails to meet its promise, the automobile that is recalled to correct design defects. At a deeper level, social critics point to industrial processes whose design overlooks effects on natural and human ecosystems; to health care designed not to maintain health but solely to treat illness; or to a criminal justice system that incarcerates amateur criminals in institutions from which they emerge as dedicated professionals. This is not to imply that defects are deliber-

---

Myopic Design

In Malaysia some time ago, in an effort to kill off mosquitoes, American technologists sprayed woods and swamplands with DDT. Result? Cockroaches, which ate poisoned mosquitoes, were so slowed in their reactions that they would be eaten by a variety of tree-climbing lizards which, sickened in turn, could be eaten by cats, which promptly died of insecticide poisoning. The cats having died, the rat population began to increase; as rats multiplied, so did fleas: hence the rapid spread of bubonic plague in Malaysia. But this is not all. The tree-climbing lizards, having died, could no longer eat an insect which consumed the straw thatching of the natives' huts. So as Malaysians died of plague, their roofs literally caved in above their heads.

—Peter Gunter (1977, p. 93)

ately designed into these systems; rather that they are not deliberately designed out.

Disappointment with human design leads some people to distrust the very concept of design. But a rejection of design implies a rejection of deliberation as the prelude to action, and hence a rejection of responsibility itself; for responsibility entails the idea of behavior guided by consideration of its consequences. Design is itself ethically neutral; it may be applied to worthy or to unworthy ends. But in the absence of design, worthwhile ends can be achieved only by accident. The cure for bad design is better design.

Art and Design

Many educators have reservations about applying the concept of design, with its implications of technique and prespecification, to the human and creative enterprise of teaching. The argument is often stated that education is essentially an art; as an art, it is something necessarily intuitive and spontaneous, to which design and technique are inappropriate.

This is a serious concern that deserves to be addressed seriously. Its fundamental weakness is that it rests on a misconception of the nature of art. No matter what art is examined, one finds that it is not intuition and spontaneity (though both have a place) but design and technique that are crucial. The great painter, the sculptor, the architect, the dancer, the actor, the musician, the poet: all of them spend years developing technique; design is the cornerstone of all their work. One thinks of Michelangelo laboring for ten years on his last, unfinished work, the *Rondanini Pietà*; of Dylan Thomas writing a hundred drafts of a single poem or Hemingway rewriting the ending to *A Farewell to Arms* forty times; of the many ballet dancers who have written in their autobiographies that they had no childhood because their early years were consumed in the effort to master the technique of their art.

What is art? "Art" is the stem of such words as *artificial* and *artifact*; etymologically, art means something contrived. If ceramics is an art, does it cease to be one when a potter like Wedgwood uses scientific techniques of experiment and industrial techniques of mass production? Does the Parthenon cease to be a work of art when we find its design based on immensely complex and sophisticated mathematics? Is Leonardo's *Last Supper* less artistic because his brilliant perspective rested on his extensive scientific research in optics? If we call a sculptor an artist, can we call a surgeon an artist? Definitions seeking to separate art and design are self-defeating; a much broader definition is needed, perhaps Louis

Dudek's "Art is anything that people do with distinction" (Colombo, 1976, p. 17).

Wishful thinking gives rise to the belief that the essence of art is spontaneous inspiration. In the same way, some teachers maintain that to be creative, teaching must be unconstrained by planning and design. But no musician ever complained of being constrained by the score; it is through the score that the musician expresses his or her creativity. In similar fashion, by planning those elements of a learning situation that are best determined in advance, curriculum design can liberate the creativity of the teacher.

The relationship of art to design is reciprocal. Design is an important element in the arts; art is also a part of design. Many aspects of design are technical, notably those in which alternatives are selected on the basis of established criteria. But the generation of alternatives and the creation of initial conceptions cannot be reduced to technique but require the imagination and creativity of the artist. It is therefore perfectly legitimate to speak of the art of curriculum design.

Nature and Design

If curriculum design is indeed an art, and if art is "artificial," does this make design unnatural? On the surface, this conclusion would appear to be inescapable. Both instinct and logic suggest that design is essentially unnatural, because its intent is always to control, change, or improve on nature. Nevertheless, the desire to find better ways of doing and making is a "natural" human tendency. The intellectual history of homo sapiens is the history of the quest for improved design. But humanity is not in this respect antithetical to the natural world, for the pursuit of improved design is not only the nature of humanity; it is the nature of nature.

From the pogonia orchid to the Douglas fir, and from the bottlenose

---

The half-baked Rousseauism in which most of us have been brought up has given us a subconscious notion that the free act is the untrained act. But of course freedom has nothing to do with lack of training. We are not free to move until we have learned to walk; we are not free to express ourselves musically until we have learned music; we are not capable of free thought unless we can think.

—*Northrop Frye (1963, pp. 42–43)*

dolphin to the snowy owl, the creatures of nature are designed, not sim
ply in their general form and function, but down to the last cell and
molecule. They are designed by the most rigorous process that we know,
which is millions of years of biological evolution. Biology, notably biological system theory, provides an understanding of the ways in which
organic systems absorb energy from the environment and use it in the
course of their development to create greater complexity, organization,
and integration (Bertalanffy, 1968). Consider, for example, one of the
most complex systems known, the human brain. One hundred billion
cells are ordered and integrated in the brain, each cell containing one
million constantly changing molecules and maintaining one hundred
thousand connections with other cells. "Could you actually believe,"
asks Weiss, a cell biologist,

> that such an astronomic number of elements . . . could ever guarantee to
> you your sense of identity and constancy in life without this constancy
> being insured by a superordinated principle of integration? . . . Despite that
> ceaseless change of detail in that vast population of elements, our basic
> patterns of behavior, our memories, our sense of integral existence as an
> individual, have retained throughout their unitary continuity of pattern
> (Weiss, 1970, p. 13).

The significant contribution of system theory to the scientific
thought of this century has been to show that the organic world is a
world of systems. In systems, subordinate parts are articulated into a
structure organized in reference to a goal. Living systems develop in the
direction of increasing elaboration and organization. Only death and inorganic matter are characterized by randomness and disorder.

System theory shows that design is at the core of nature. The unity
and coherence that characterize natural systems provide a model for the
often fragmented field of curriculum, while subfields such as cybernetics
provide theory that is immediately applicable to the design of instruction
(Pratt, 1978). For education the basic implication of the study of design
in nature is this: A humane and natural education will be one that faithfully reflects the essential characteristics of nature and of humanity. One
characteristic of both is the constant evolution of improved design.

Design in Education

A systematic approach to curriculum aims at improved design of learning
situations. To complex activities such as education, design can make a

number of specific contributions. Of the benefits of design that follow, the first four apply to almost all intentional human activities, including education, and are drawn from Hall's classic text on systems engineering (Hall, 1962, p. 78).

1. *Design focuses attention on goals.* Specification of purposes is a necessary first step in design. Explicit statement of goals helps to ensure that goals are worthwhile and that they are clearly understood by participants.

2. *Design increases the probability of success.* Potential problems can be anticipated and costly delays prevented. In an unplanned operation, managers have to respond to criticism by making decisions on the basis of expediency; thus the critics rather than the management will control the operation and will either slow down its progress or subvert the entire operation to different goals.

3. *Economy of time and effort is improved by design.* Poor alternatives can be eliminated before they are implemented. Planning is more likely than ad hoc decision making to reveal the best routes to the objectives.

4. *Design facilitates communication and coordination of projects.* Actions can be synchronized and sequenced to make the best use of time and resources. Competition among groups and individuals pursuing independent goals is reduced.

5. *Design reduces stress.* This is particularly true in teaching, which is a stressful activity. Researchers have found that a teacher's pulse rate will often double during a lesson. The same research shows conclusively that unstructured and unplanned teaching is much more stressful than planned instruction (Doe, 1975).

These practical functions make design the hallmark of the professions and distinguish them from the pure sciences. The distinction is worth exploring.

Science and Curriculum Design

The function of the pure sciences is the development of theory, and the purpose of theory is to explain phenomena. Curriculum design, like education as a whole, relies on the explanation of phenomena that theory provides, but is not itself theoretical. The terms *educational theory* or *curriculum theory* can be employed only through a loose and nonscientific use of the word "theory." At its most scientific, curriculum design is an applied science; like medicine and engineering, it draws on theory from the pure sciences, but itself develops not theory but operating principles to guide decision making in practical situations. It deals not with propositional questions, but with procedural questions, and its criteria are reasonableness and practicality. As Hilgard and Bower argue, applied science, or technology, uses what works, regardless whether it has yet been supported by theory:

> Applied science cannot wait for the answers of pure science to come in: crops have to be planted and gathered, the sick have to be treated, and children have to be taught with whatever tools and knowledge are now available. It is natural that in the early development of the relevant sciences the applied users, the technologists, will tend to be eclectic, picking up a plausible idea here and there, and using it somewhat inventively in the practical situation (Hilgard and Bower, 1966, p. 565).

But a curriculum designer is ideally more than a technologist. The technologist's job is only to solve problems; the role does not entail commitments to values or people outside of the immediate problem situation. Nor is the technologist required to make decisions about which problems to solve. The curriculum designer, on the other hand, must develop priorities to guide the selection of tasks to be performed, as well as be able to perform them; and these decisions are guided by value commitments to society in general and learners in particular. For this kind of role there is another term: the professional.

Educational Technology

Educational technology can be understood as meaning the development of a set of systematic techniques, and accompanying practical knowledge, for designing, testing, and operating schools as educational systems. Technology in this sense is educational engineering. It draws upon many disciplines, including those which design working space, like architecture; those which design equipment, like the physical sciences; those which design social environments, like sociology and anthropology; those which design administrative procedures, like the science of organizations; and those which design conditions for effective learning, like psychology. In technology, these disciplines are not pursued for their own sakes, but rather for the purpose of solving practical problems through the kinds of engineering efforts known as design and development. In connection with such efforts, there grows up a collection of know-how information, more or less generalizable to other problems in other settings, that deserves the name technology.

—*Robert M. Gagné (1974, p. 51)*

The Curriculum Professional

The curriculum professional—specialist, supervisor, or teacher—combines the interest of the scientist in knowledge with that of the technician in action. MacDonald and Clark borrow from Paulo Freire the value-laden terms *intellectualism*, meaning reflection without action, and *activism*, meaning action without reflection. They point out with some accuracy that

> Activism (or mindlessness) would seem to characterize much of the traditional curriculum patterns. Intellectualism (or "ivory towerism") would appear to have produced much of the curriculum theorizing (MacDonald and Clark, 1973, p. 1).

They use another of Freire's terms, *praxis*, to mean action with reflection. Praxis defines reasonably well the role of the professional.

Reflection implies independent thought, and professionals are accordingly distinguished by a degree of autonomy in their decision making. They themselves participate in the definition of their responsibilities, and in discharging them are not heavily dependent on specialists or superiors. This independence implies a corresponding degree of personal accountability for the decisions they make and their consequences. As A. L. Adams puts it, "Being in a profession means ultimately being accountable."

We could hardly use the term professional to describe a teacher whose responsibility is strictly confined to merely delivering the instruction prescribed in detail in a curriculum designed by a state, school district, or publishing company. This point is forcefully made by a British educator, Sir Alec Clegg:

> I have no time whatever for any system which recruits high-powered thinkers to contrive and foist a curriculum on the schools. This cannot work unless we believe that the teacher of the future is to be a low-grade technician working under someone else's instructions rather than a professional making his own diagnosis and prescribing his own treatments (Clegg, 1968, p. 9).

This possibly overstates the case. Society has some legitimate expectations of all professionals, and decision making that is entirely delegated to the individual leads to gross duplication of effort. But there is an important implication of Clegg's thesis: that teachers (and administrators) will be professional to the extent that they are provided with the scope, the authority, and the competence to make independent curriculum decisions.

> The professional draws upon the knowledge of science and of his colleagues, and upon knowledge gained through personal experience. The degree to which he relies upon the first two of these rather than the third is one of the ways in which the professional may be distinguished from the layman.
>
> —*Douglas McGregor (1960, p. 3)*

Such terms as *art, science,* and *technology* have too often been captured by antagonistic schools of educational thought and used as slogans in a war of words. The concept of professionality is capable of bridging the gap between the two main traditions in education which may be broadly termed the classic and the romantic. The professional shares with classic form what J. B. Priestley called "that touch of iron, that suggestion of the chisel"; a commitment to order and economy and a reliance on established data. But the professional pursues economy because wasted resources are wasted life; the basic allegiance is that of the romantic, to human values, to people, their needs, and their capacity for achievement.

Education is shaped by its practitioners. The best teachers have, for three thousand years or more, been amateurs in the original sense of the term: people distinguished not so much by special skills as by dedication to their work, to their students, and to the value of what they taught. The professional shares the dedication of the amateur but possesses in addition the technical expertise of the applied scientist. The evolution of the curriculum field has brought it to the point where a significant body of such expertise is available. This expertise gives credibility to the central role of the curriculum specialist, whether designer, manager, evaluator, or teacher of curriculum. We may anticipate that in the years that lie ahead, the schools will increasingly be shaped by the calibre and competence of their curriculum professionals.

References

Bertalanffy, Ludwin von. *General system theory.* Rev. ed. New York: Braziller, 1968.
Clegg, Sir Alec. In J. Stuart Maclure, *Curriculum innovation in practice: Report of Third International Curriculum Conference.* London: Her Majesty's Stationery Office, 1968.
Colombo, John Robert (ed.). *Colombo's concise Canadian quotations.* Edmonton, Canada: Hurtig Publishers, 1976.
Doe, Bob. Shape of a lesson. *Times Educational Supplement,* December 5, 1975.
Frye, Northrop. *The well-tempered critic.* Bloomington, Ind.: Indiana University Press, 1963.

Gagné, Robert M. Educational technology as technique. In Elliot W. Eisner and Elizabeth Vallance (eds.), *Conflicting conceptions of curriculum*. Berkeley, Cal.: McCutchan, 1974, pp. 50–63.

Gunter, Peter A. Quoted in Donald A. Read, *Looking in: Exploring one's health values*. Englewood Cliffs, N.J.: Prentice-Hall, 1977.

Hall, Arthur D. *A methodology for systems engineering*. New York: Van Nostrand, 1962.

Hilgard, Ernest R., and Gordon H. Bower. *Theories of learning*. 3rd ed. New York: Appleton-Century-Crofts, 1966.

MacDonald, James B., and Dwight F. Clark. A radical conception of the role of values in curriculum: Praxis. Paper presented at the Annual Meeting of the Association for Supervision and Curriculum Development, Minneapolis, March 1973.

McGregor, Douglas. *The human side of enterprise*. New York: McGraw-Hill, 1960.

Pratt, David. System theory, systems technology, and curriculum design. *Journal of Educational Thought*, 1978, 12, 131–152.

Simon, Herbert A. *The sciences of the artificial*. Cambridge, Mass.: M.I.T. Press, 1969.

Weiss, Paul A. The living system: Determinism stratified. In Arthur Koestler and J. R. Smythies (eds.), *Beyond reductionism: New perspectives in the life sciences*. New York: Macmillan, 1970, pp. 3–42.

2

TURNING POINTS

2

Curriculum Development:
An Historical Perspective

What seest thou else in the dark backward and
abysm of time?

—William Shakespeare, The Tempest, act 1, scene 2

Curriculum and Its Past

The curriculum field has a history but has often lacked a historical perspective (Kliebard, 1970). Curriculum writers have on occasion represented as novel ideas that were introduced, explored, and forgotten generations previously. In the brevity of their memories, they share the ahistoricism of the culture and differ little from specialists in many other fields, or from politicians, journalists, and the general public. The function of the study of curriculum design is to enhance decision making and as such is necessarily oriented toward the future. With their eyes fixed on the path ahead, it is understandable that curriculum thinkers rarely

15

look behind. Nevertheless, to leap into the future requires a firm footing in the present. And an appreciation of where the field is now is strengthened and illuminated by an understanding of its evolution from the past.

A review of the history of curriculum in the space available in this chapter can hardly claim to be comprehensive. Only the barest outline can be given of some of the events that have shaped curriculum thought. The summary restricts its attention to the influences that were important in the West, particularly in the English-speaking world. In the twentieth century, attention is focused on the United States, where curriculum design emerged as a distinct field of educational inquiry.

The Ancient World

Curriculum design is usually considered to be a development of the last hundred years, but this is a somewhat misleading simplification. The question Who was the first curriculum designer? is not unlike the question Who was the first psychologist? Shakespeare and Sophocles explored and chronicled the interior life long before the word *psychology* was invented. In a general sense, curriculum design is a matter of deliberate thought about the nature of education and instruction. Individuals have recorded their thoughts about education for 2500 years, and we cannot assume that, even before that, people did not think about education merely because they left no record.

It seems unlikely, however, that nonliterate societies devoted much energy to abstract thought on questions of education. Where a common recognition of what children need to know and be able to do is shared by the child and the community, little deliberation about ends can be expected, and methods change infrequently from one generation to the next. Typically the child learns skills from a relative or an elder in the home or in the practical situation in which the learning will be used (Kneller, 1965).

The nature of education in the literate societies of the ancient world also suggests that tradition was more influential than deliberate thought. In the scribal cultures of China, Egypt, and Syria, the aristocracy consisted of the literate priests, civil servants, and administrators who conducted the business of government. Education was extremely formalistic, with primary emphasis on passive memorization of sacred writings and national epics, often written in an archaic language. In military cultures, on the other hand, such as Sparta or Arabia, the aristocracy was a class of warriors. Their education emphasized training in martial skills, physical strength and endurance, and military virtues. It would change primarily in response to changes in military technology; hence, as heavily armed infantry began to replace the individual warrior-hero, the education of Spartan youth became more collective, with service to the state replacing individualistic ideals of prowess.

Greece and Its Legacy

By the fifth century B.C., Athens had established its cultural leadership among the Greek city-states. Although the Homeric warrior ideals of duty, glory, and self-sacrifice continued to influence the upbringing of the young, education had lost its basically military character. A balance emerged among moral, athletic, and aesthetic education. By the time of Socrates, Athenian boys of the upper class received their education at private day schools, learning to read and write, to recite poetry, to sing and play the lyre, to practice the rudiments of mathematics, and to perform athletic exercises.

While formal schooling was well established in Athens by the end of the fifth century B.C., the method of teaching employed by Socrates belonged to an older tradition: a tradition in which a young nobleman was entrusted to an older man for training and the educational relationship was one of love and inspiration (Marrou, 1956). Socrates' disciple, Plato, was also interested primarily in the training to be given to the elite, to whom, he considered, the affairs of state should be entrusted. But while aspects of their approach to education belonged to the aristocratic tradition, the educational thought of Socrates and Plato was essentially radical. Their primary concern was with the question What should be the ends of education? To this question, they replied unequivocally that education should lead the pupil to moral discipline, spiritual perfection, virtue, and truth. All aspects of education were rigorously examined with reference to their contribution to these ultimate ends. In their persistence in questioning traditional curricula and in giving educational ends priority over instructional techniques, Socrates and Plato established a model of inquiry that has been emulated by philosophers of education ever since.

But an elite model of education was unable to meet the educational demands of the Athenian middle class, whose economic and political importance expanded in the fourth century B.C. Changes in method and in curriculum became inevitable, and a new school of educators emerged: the Sophists.

The Sophists are the first people who can confidently be labeled professional educators. They would undertake the entire postelementary education of a youth for a fee, concentrating largely on useful knowledge and all-round education for life and for political leadership. Speculative and metaphysical questions did not greatly concern them; they were interested in practical problem solving and persuasion. They developed eloquence and argument into the fine art of rhetoric. Their method was group tutoring, and their aspiration was to reduce every area of learning

> For the free man there should be no element of slavery in learning. Enforced exercise does no harm to the body, but enforced learning will not stay in the mind. So avoid compulsion, and let your children's lessons take the form of play.
>
> —*Plato,* The Republic, *vii, 536*

to an exact science. In the Sophists we can see the first sustained effort to discover basic principles of instruction; they might also be termed the first educational technologists. While the contribution of Socrates, Plato, and Aristotle to the philosophy of education was profound, Sophists such as Protagoras and Isocrates, in the long run, probably had more influence on the development of Western education.

The effects of the Sophists on education necessarily make one wonder whether it is wise to trust education to the technicians rather than the philosophers. Many of the early Sophists aimed at providing a well-rounded education, in which the value of a study was judged by its contribution to civilized life and in which general learning was preferred to specialized training. But it was largely as a result of Sophist influence that Greek education, by the end of the fourth century, had become singularly joyless. It was almost entirely literary and specialized in rhetoric. Music and athletics, previously considered valuable for their influence on moral development, were viewed as irrelevant to vocational competence and had declined. Heavy emphasis on rote learning was accompanied by reliance on corporal punishment as the primary incentive. The school of love had been replaced by the school of pain. The effects of this tradition and this antithesis are still with us today.

Roman Education

Literary education, which has always been powerful, came to the fore in Rome in the third century B.C. The archaic Roman education, with its emphasis on the family, tradition, emulation of one's ancestors, the ideal of duty, and the peasant virtues, increasingly adopted the literary curriculum in which memorization of the poetry of Homer, the rules of grammar, and the conventions of rhetoric predominated. Roman education became bilingual and remained so for six centuries; a network of publicly supported schools spread classical education throughout the Empire. The significance of rhetoric in Roman education is indicated by the titles of the two major Roman works on education: Cicero's *Orator* (46 B.C.) and Quintilian's *Institutes of Oratory* (c. 95 A.D.). But while both Cicero and Quintilian viewed literary studies as the foundation of education, both advocated a more general preparation for life than was normally provided in Roman schools. Cicero, a lawyer, statesman, writer, and philosopher, believed the curriculum should include such studies as geometry, astronomy, music, physics, history, civil law, and philosophy. Quintilian was an academic, a professor of oratory, and his main importance lies in his legitimate claim to the title of the first educational psychologist. He advocated variety in the curriculum and in the daily timetable to maintain student interest; the use of games, competition, and praise, rather than punishment, for motivation; the use of modeling as an instructional technique; small classes; peer tutoring of younger by older students; and attention to individual differences in aptitude and disposition (Pounds, 1968).

The serious deliberation they devoted to questions of educational content and methods entitles Cicero and Quintilian, as well as a number of lesser-known writers, to be called curriculum thinkers. They provide some relief from the general picture of Roman education, in which the prized academic virtues were memorization and imitation, schoolmastering was a despised and meanly paid occupation, and brutal floggings were so pervasive that St. Augustine declared that death would be preferable to a return to childhood (Marrou, 1956).

Preindustrial Europe

It is less surprising that the narrow educational model of Hellenistic Greece was adopted by Rome than that it was also adopted by medieval Europe. The Christian church was initially distrustful of the pagan content of classical education, but in the social chaos that followed the disintegration of the Roman Empire in the West, the monasteries became the sole guardians of learning. In Eastern Christendom, the monasteries generally refrained from involvement in education, but in the West they developed an educational interest that was formalized in the Rule of St. Benedict (c. 525). The dependence of the monasteries on reading and writing led them to adopt the bookishness of classical education without the saving grace of its poetic content. For many centuries Latin, especially the mastery of grammar, dominated the school curriculum. The curriculum of the universities that began to develop in the twelfth century consisted largely of study and exposition of the scriptures and writings of the Church Fathers and theological disputation; classical Latin authors received increasing attention with the passage of time.

The separate development of European states during the Middle Ages helped to produce considerable variety in education. This was increased by the Renaissance and the Reformation. The Renaissance took many scholars back to the roots of the classical tradition in fifth-century Greece; the humanist ideal of the versatile individual was rediscovered, but its influence on education was limited to the slow expansion of Greek in the curriculum. The Reformation, by fracturing Christendom, gave a severe blow to the unifying power of the Church in education. At the same time, the Protestant idea of individual interpretation of scripture gave impetus to the development of literacy, a movement that was further stimulated by the invention of printing. The Counter Reformation in turn produced new educational patterns, such as the rigorous and systematically planned curriculum defined in the *Ratio Studiorum* of the Society of Jesus (Binder, 1970).

Generalization is made hazardous by the variety prevailing within each country. In sixteenth-century England we find independent grammar schools as well as schools under the jurisdiction of cathedrals, collegiate churches, university colleges, almshouses, craft guilds, and (before the dissolution of the monasteries) monasteries and chantries (Leach, 1911). Most of these schools admitted pupils who had already learned to read and write. Elementary education was conducted variously by individual parish clergy, in endowed free schools, by private tutors or schoolmasters, and in remote areas by traveling pedagogues who would appear every three or four years in a community, work a few weeks for a pittance by teaching the local children the rudiments of reading and writing, and then move on (Wedgwood, 1954).

But while institutions varied, the curriculum throughout the Middle Ages was relatively uniform. Elementary education consisted of learning to read and write, and sometimes to cast accounts; the curriculum for girls, where they were educated at all, would often be restricted to reading and needlework. Vocational education was conducted outside the schools, usually by apprenticeship under the aegis of the craft guilds. Secondary education concentrated almost entirely on studying Latin grammar, writing Latin prose and verse, and reading and translating Latin authors. Universities admitted students in their mid-teens; although several faculties of law and medicine are found by 1600, throughout the Middle Ages university education was generally synonymous with classical studies.

Occasionally a critic would question the value of this curriculum. Peter of Blois inquired in the twelfth century:

> What does it profit a student to spend his days in these things which neither in the army, nor in the Cloister, nor in politics, nor in the Church, nor anywhere else are any good to anyone—except in the schools?

But most critics accepted the content of the curriculum and merely challenged the methods of teaching. Although Erasmus, one of the most brilliant men of his time, championed the study of Greek in addition to Latin and vehemently supported classical studies, he criticized teaching approaches. In about 1515 he wrote:

> I have no patience with the stupidity of the average teacher of grammar who wastes precious years in hammering rules into children's heads. For

it is not by learning rules that we acquire the power of speaking a language, but by daily intercourse with those accustomed to express themselves with exactness and refinement, and by the copious reading of the best authors (Binder, 1970, p. 141).

Like Erasmus, John Comenius, a Czech bishop of the Moravian Church, advocated the direct teaching of languages. But he was well ahead of his time in supporting, in his *Didactica Magna* (1632), education in the vernacular, inclusion of science in the curriculum, adapting instruction to the intellectual level and disposition of the individual child, making ideas intelligible through relating them to concrete objects in the environment, use of the senses particularly through illustrations, constant attention to the use of what was taught, and equal educational opportunity for women.

But despite curriculum thinkers of the stature of Comenius, the classical literary curriculum remained firmly entrenched. As at the present day, but in that age on a monolithic scale, the force of tradition was inimical to the development either of curriculum thinking or of a design approach to education. The continuities between European education in the eighteenth century and education in Greece in the third century B.C. are far more striking than the discontinuities. It would take a redistribution of political power, the Industrial Revolution, and emigration to the New World to produce a radical change in the school curriculum.

The Victorian Debate

Education in the English-speaking world today draws its principal ethos from the dual traditions of Britain and the United States. Until the late eighteenth century this was a single tradition; by 1900 the direction of education in the two countries had diverged significantly.

Elementary education expanded rapidly in Britain in the nineteenth century. Each of the Parliamentary acts extending the franchise was followed by legislation expanding provision for elementary education. The major controversy of the period, however, concerned the curriculum of secondary education.

By mid-century the discoveries of scientists were having a profound effect on intellectual life in Britain. The curriculum in the schools and universities was still almost entirely classical. In 1860 Herbert Spencer published his essay "What Knowledge Is of Most Worth?" (Spencer, 1911), in which he attacked the dogma of classical studies. The scientific dogma he proposed as an alternative was less convincing than his criticism. Spencer's importance in curriculum thought is twofold. First, his attempt to formulate a rational hierarchy of priorities among areas of study signified a real advance in curriculum thought. His "classification

What Knowledge Is of Most Worth?

If there needs any further evidence of the rude, undeveloped character of our education, we have it in the fact that the comparative worths of different kinds of knowledge have been as yet scarcely even discussed . . . the need for it seems to have been scarcely even felt. Men read books on this topic, and attend lectures on that; decide that their children shall be instructed in these branches of knowledge, and shall not be instructed in those; and all under the guidance of mere custom, or liking, or prejudice; without even considering the enormous importance of determining in some rational way what things are really most worth learning. . . .

In education, then, this is the question of questions, which it is high time we discussed in some methodic way. The first in importance, though the last to be considered, is the problem—how to decide among the conflicting claims of various subjects on our attention. Before there can be a rational *curriculum,* we must settle which things it most concerns us to know; or, to use a word of Bacon's, now unfortunately obsolete—we must determine the relative values of knowledge.

Our first step must obviously be to classify, in the order of their importance, the leading kinds of activity which constitute human life. They may be naturally arranged into: 1. Those activities which directly minister to self-preservation; 2. Those activities which, by securing the necessaries of life, indirectly minister to self-preservation; 3. Those activities which have for their end the rearing and discipline of offspring; 4. Those activities which are involved in the maintenance of proper social and political relations; 5. Those miscellaneous activities which make up the leisure part of life, devoted to the gratification of the tastes and feelings.

—*Herbert Spencer, 1860 (1911, pp. 5–7)*

of activities" into survival, economic viability, parenthood, social and political life, and recreation and the arts still merits attention by curriculum thinkers. Second, he stimulated a curriculum controversy that ultimately led to radical changes in the curriculum in English schools. The debate involved many of the leading thinkers of the time, including the scientist T. H. Huxley, the classical educators Moberly of Winchester and Farrar of Harrow, the poets and classicists A. E. Housman and Matthew Arnold, the artist and critic John Ruskin, and the philosopher John Stuart Mill.

In a brilliant essay on this debate, Kazamias (1960) pointed out that both the scientists and the classicists relied on the doctrine of faculty psychology, or mental discipline: the belief that certain kinds of study "trained the mind" in general ways. Neither this premise, nor the claims of the protagonists that their favored discipline trained the mind more effectively than others, was put to empirical test. The debate was carried out by assertion and counter-assertion. Royal commissions on the schools affirmed the role of education as "the general cultivation of the intellect" and rejected the idea that schools might "prepare boys for special employments." Science, modern language, and mathematics, at first disdained, were gradually admitted on the grounds that they were liberal and human, rather than practical, studies (Kazamias, 1960, p. 316). But the classics did not make room for the new areas of study to provide the student with a broader education. Instead, the new subjects were introduced as alternative specializations. In the century following Spencer's essay, English education in the major secondary schools and universities became so specialized that by 1959 C. P. Snow could talk of "two cultures," populated by scientists and liberal humanists incapable of communicating with each other (Snow, 1962).

Although new patterns of schooling emerged in twentieth-century Britain to accommodate increased numbers of students staying in school until their mid-teens, English ideas and policies in curriculum remained shaped by a nineteenth-century aristocratic ideal. The characteristic product of the English school system was still envisaged as the cricket-playing, Virgil-quoting Christian gentleman with a private income. Although the economic infrastructure of the British Empire that had supported this ideal in the nineteenth century had weakened by 1918 and collapsed by 1945, a priori conceptions of what constituted a proper education remained the predominant influence on curriculum thought and practice. These conceptions were exported to the rest of the Empire, where they took vigorous hold.

The persistence of traditional ideals notwithstanding, England has produced important ideas and movements in education. In the 1960s, for example, English ideas on elementary-school environments had a considerable vogue in North America. But for the origins and main lines of development of curriculum design as a field of study, we must turn to the United States.

The American Tradition

Education was important in American society from the beginning: Harvard College was founded only sixteen years after the arrival of the Pilgrims at Cape Cod. A Massachusetts law of 1647 provided for the establishment of elementary schools and Latin grammar schools. The influence of the classical model of education began to weaken in the eighteenth century. Leading universities such as Columbia, Harvard, Princeton, and William and Mary broadened their programs to include liberal studies, professional schools, and the principle of electives.

Writing in the *Pennsylvania Gazette* in 1749 on "Proposals relating to the education of youth in Pennsylvania," Benjamin Franklin urged that

> Art is long, and their time is short. It is therefore proposed that they learn those things that are likely to be most useful and most ornamental, regard being had to the several professions for which they are intended (Binder, 1970, p. 271).

In advocating a secular and practical education, aimed principally at the development of knowledge that could be used in the service of society, Franklin was ahead of his time. The Academy he founded in 1751 eventually developed into the University of Pennsylvania, but not before it had succumbed to the classical tradition.

The nineteenth century vindicated the perception of Franklin and his fellow thinkers. Education in the United States began to diverge significantly from its European origins, establishing traditions that were to provide the background for the emergence of curriculum thought in the twentieth century. At the secondary-school level, private academies based on Franklin's model spread rapidly for the first half of the century. The evolution of the public high school during the same period was paralleled by a decline of the Latin grammar school, which was unable or unwilling to respond to the demand for a functional curriculum. Rapid economic development and settlement of the West made an effective and flexible educational system essential. Responsibility devolved on the schools to generate skilled manpower and to assimilate the children of the immigrants pouring into the United States. By 1890 basic elementary education was being perceived as the norm for all classes, and some 300,000 students were attending secondary school, two-thirds of them in public high schools (Krug, 1964). Professional schools continued to develop in the universities in the nineteenth century, and vocational instruction was further stimulated in 1862 by the Morrill Act, which provided the states with federal land for building colleges that would offer agricultural and mechanical arts.

The social need for improved public education was reflected in the nineteenth century by improved organization of schools. Until about 1840 school attendance tended to be irregular; teachers were untrained, transient, and largely unsupervised; and the school year often depended on the funds available to pay the teacher (Tanner and Tanner, 1975, p. 154). During the middle years of the century, support of schools was placed on a firm tax basis, and an organized structure of superintendency emerged. In Massachusetts Horace Mann, secretary of the State Board of Education from 1837 to 1848, founded the first normal school for training teachers, improved communication between the schools and the public, and raised the standard of instruction, facilities, and equipment in schools. His contemporary Henry Barnard introduced similar reforms in

Connecticut and Rhode Island, especially with respect to inspection of schools and the quality of textbooks and teacher training.

Considerable breadth came to characterize the curriculum of American schools in the nineteenth century. From a narrow focus on reading, writing, the classics, and religious instruction at the beginning of the century, many new subjects, including algebra, astronomy, chemistry, botany, surveying, and philosophy, entered the curriculum. Rugg reported that seventy-five new courses were introduced into the academies between 1825 and 1828 (Rugg, 1926a, p. 20). Science expanded rapidly in the second half of the century, so that by 1890 it constituted part of the program of almost every secondary-school student.

In few parts of the country was this diversity of subject matter matched by a diversity of instructional methodology. The prevailing mode of teaching toward the end of the century emphasized rote learning and memorization. Textbooks, often written from a formal academic viewpoint, tended to determine the curriculum. English teaching stressed grammar, analysis, and rhetoric. The literature program was dominated by the classical English works of Eliot, Goldsmith, and Tennyson. Traditional textbook teaching had an influential defender in William Torry Harris, superintendent of the St. Louis schools in the 1870s. To Harris, textbooks contained the accumulated wisdom of the species in its most accessible form. In opposition to this point of view, Colonel Francis Parker, superintendent of schools in Quincy, Massachusetts, was at the same time implementing the ideas of Froebel, Pestalozzi, and Herbart regarding active perception and exploration of the environment by the child, natural methods of learning, integration of different fields of knowledge, and application of learning to life. Harris, a scholar in his own right and an authority on Hegel, was the intellectual leader of the educational conservatives. Parker's ideas, developed and elaborated by Dewey, evolved into the philosophy of Progressive Education; and, at least until the 1950s, Progressive Education was regarded in the rest of the world as the unique contribution of America to educational thought and practice.

By 1890 American students who proceeded beyond elementary school were exposed to a broad curriculum with a strong practical and vocational element. Although only 7 percent of the age group attended high school, the principle of free public secondary education was firmly established. The curriculum was secular and intended to serve the social needs of the population as a whole.

But what of curriculum design? It is not much of an exaggeration to say that it still awaited birth. The curriculum debates of the nineteenth century rarely went beyond questions of content and the methods of instruction. W. T. Harris, his conservative views on teaching notwithstanding, was a pioneer, though a forerunner rather than a founder. His rationalization of the structure of the schools in St. Louis was accompanied by reorganization of the curriculum. The curricula he promoted were unique for their comprehensiveness and detail. He recognized the importance of careful design of courses of study, of instructional materials, and of assessment of achievement. Despite his advocacy of a narrow pedagogy, we see in Harris the development of the idea that curriculum design was a field of endeavor calling for special skills and procedures and requiring consideration of a wide range of factors that affect learning. Not without reason does Cremin (1971) consider Harris the inaugurator of modern curriculum thought.

The Curriculum Committees

Most curriculum design at the present day is carried out by curriculum committees. Unlike many educational practices that developed gradually and unobtrusively, the committee approach to curriculum made an abrupt and impressive entrance with the establishment by the National Education Association (NEA) of the Committee of Ten on Secondary School Studies in 1892. The committee owed its origin to Charles Eliot, the influential and reforming president of Harvard, who was appointed to chair the committee after he read a paper to the NEA in 1888 on the subject "Can school programs be shortened and enriched?" The committee was a blue-ribbon panel of academics, half of whom were college presidents.

Two features of American education in the 1890s were causing the colleges concern. One was the diversity of school curricula, which complicated the definition of eligibility for admission to college. The other was the successful opposition of schools to certain college entrance requirements, such as Greek, which raised the specter of the schools dictating admissions policy to the universities. The Committee of Ten dealt with both of these threats, establishing firm control of secondary school curricula by the universities for a generation.

Is is ironic that while Eliot's 1888 paper urged greater flexibility and individualization in the organization of school programs, the committee he chaired recommended in its 1893 report an extremely rigid and uniform program for secondary schools. All secondary-school students were to study a common curriculum of nine subjects: Latin, Greek, English, modern languages, mathematics, physics and chemistry, biology, history and politics, and geography. Detailed programs of study were drawn up, showing the amount of time to be devoted each week to the study of each subject. The idea of differential curricula or teaching methods to meet individual needs was rejected as undemocratic.

> Every subject that is taught at all in the secondary school should be taught in the same way and to the same extent to each pupil so long as he pursues

it, no matter what the probable destination of the pupil may be or at what point his education is to cease (Rugg, 1926b, p. 40).

Several important trends were initiated or reinforced by the committee, in addition to its introduction of the practice of curriculum policy making by national committees. (1) By rejecting art, music, physical education, and practical subjects as devoid of disciplinary value (early Greek educational ideas did not appear to have influenced these educators despite their classical training), it established the superiority of "academic" subjects in the curriculum. (2) The impossibility of agreement among different subject specialists regarding priority led the committee to place the nine subjects on an equal footing; Latin and Greek lost their traditional ascendency. (3) The committee initiated what Rugg (1926b, p. 41) called "curriculum-making by college entrance." (4) The rationale for the subjects chosen lay in the theory of mental discipline, or faculty psychology; all of them were thought to "train the mind" in significant ways. (5) The committee established the precedent of curriculum design by subject-matter experts, and its corollary, the assumption that curriculum design meant simply organization of subject matter. (6) The committee launched a tradition of ex cathedra pronouncement on school curriculum by eminent college presidents. This tradition was subsequently maintained by such luminaries as James Conant of Harvard and Robert Hutchins of Chicago.

The Committee of Ten was followed by a number of other influential committees. The Committee on College Entrance Requirements, appointed in 1895, made exact recommendations regarding the number of credits required in different subjects for college entrance, and in so doing firmly established the idea of the unit credit. The Committee of Fifteen on Elementary Education, also reporting in 1895, emphasized the central place of reading, writing, spelling, grammar, arithmetic, history, and geography in the elementary school curriculum.

Later committees of the NEA, and some of the committees established by such subject associations as the National Council of teachers of English, rejected the a priori academic assumptions of their predecessors. The Committee on Economy of Time, appointed in 1911, attempted to determine the curriculum by a curiously facile analysis of contemporary practice; for example, selecting historical content on the basis of how frequently particular persons and dates were mentioned in books and newspapers.

The most influential of the later committees was the Commission on Reorganization of Secondary Education, appointed by the NEA in 1913, which reported in 1918. To a great extent, this commission shaped the form and the curriculum of the American high school for several decades. Its philosophical distance from the Committee of Ten a generation before is indicated by the basic premise it adopted:

> Secondary education should be determined by the needs of the society to be served, the character of the individuals to be educated, and the knowledge of educational theory and practice available (Commission on Reorganization of Secondary Education, 1918, p. 7).

Heavily influenced by Dewey's view of education as the expression and guardian of democracy, the report emphasized the role of education in social integration, effective citizenship, and individual development. It announced seven "cardinal principles" for education: health, command of fundamental processes (of communication and numeracy), home membership, vocation, citizenship, worthy use of leisure time, and ethical character. There are marked similarities between these seven principles of 1918 and Spencer's hierarchy of activities of 1860. Twenty-six years later the Educational Policies Commission, chaired by Harvard President James Conant, would publish another similar inventory, the "ten imperative educational needs of youth" (Educational Policies Commission, 1944).

During their heyday the national committees had a substantial effect on the nature and substance of school curriculum. But they were of relatively little importance in the development of curriculum design. Their members were recruited not for their expertise in curriculum planning, but usually for their prestige or academic eminence. The committees' major long-term impact was to establish three conventions: (1) the idea of central determination of curriculum policy; (2) the practice of curriculum planning by committee; and (3) the reliance on university subject specialists to formulate curricula. These conventions were to be of particular importance in the 1960s. But in the years immediately after the First World War, the actual advances in thought about curriculum design were taking place elsewhere.

Curriculum Design Is Born

The period from 1900 to 1920 was one of considerable ferment in educational ideas. The child study movement, gathering strength from the developing field of psychology, demanded that schools focus on the developing needs of the individual child. Experimental methods applied to educational questions by Thorndike and other psychologists had essentially discredited the theory of mental discipline, which had been a cornerstone of educational thought for two thousand years. The idea of efficiency, promoted in industry by such writers as Frederick Taylor (1911), was being adopted by child-centered educators, who urged that the pupil's time should be viewed as a precious commodity.

The belief that every field of endeavor could be reduced to an efficient technique, characteristically American in its straightforward optimism and essentially Puritan idealism, was applied to curriculum by several educators, including C. R. Allen, David Snedden, W. W. Charters, Franklin Bobbitt, and Harold Rugg. To this group and their colleagues education owes the immediate origin of curriculum design as a distinct field of educational thought and practice. Of the group, Bobbitt and Rugg were probably the most influential.

Bobbitt published *The Curriculum* in 1918, a work that, according to Walker (1975, p. 264), is "generally acknowledged to be the first book devoted solely to curriculum in all its phases." In it, Bobbitt ascribed his conversion from a conventional approach to curriculum to his experience on a committee designing a curriculum for the elementary schools of the Philippines in 1901, in the early years of the American occupation.

> We assembled upon a table in the committee-room copies of the American textbooks in reading, arithmetic, geography, United States history, and the other subjects with which we had been familiar in American schools. We also assembled such American courses of study as we could find; and without being conscious of it, we mobilized our American prejudices and preconceptions as to what an elementary-school course ought to be.... We needed principles of curriculum making. We did not know that we should first determine objectives from a study of social needs.... We had not learned that studies are means, not ends ... that anything which is not effective is wrong, however time-honored and widely used it may be (Bobbitt, 1918, pp. 282–283).

Bobbitt's aim was a worthy one: to replace the "shortage concept of education" by education for personal and social proficiency. The ideal graduate, to Bobbitt, was the autonomous, cultivated, and useful citizen. But he was not entirely successful in persuading the educational community that the catalogs of life-activities that he published while professor of education at the University of Chicago, as a result of a study

---

Dewey on Efficiency

The subject announced for today was "Waste in education." . . . It deals with the question of organization, because all waste is the result of the lack of it, the motive lying behind organization being promotion of economy and efficiency. This question is not one of the waste of money or the waste of things. These matters count; but the primary waste is that of human life, the life of the children while they are at school, and afterward because of inadequate and perverted preparation.

—*John Dewey (1899, p. 77)*

of people who were expert in "high-grade living," formed a comprehensive basis for the curriculum.

> Ability to care for the teeth; ability to care for the eyes; ability to care for the nose, ear and throat; ability to care for the skin; ability to keep the heart and blood vessels in normal working condition . . . ability to sharpen, adjust, clean, lubricate, replace worn or broken parts, and otherwise keep household and garden tools and appliances in good order and good working condition (Bobbitt, 1924, pp. 14, 28).

Taken out of context, such inventories, along with the factory analogy that Bobbitt espoused, are easily satirized and have been repeatedly ridiculed by educational historians (Callahan, 1962; Kliebard, 1971).

More significant was Bobbitt's insistence that "curriculum making" was a field of study requiring special skills and procedures. Curriculum planners "should be primarily specialists in life itself, not in any special subject . . . generalists in education and not specialists in some portion of it" (Bobbitt, 1926, p. 52). And, "It is more important that our profession agree upon a *method* of curriculum-discovery than that we agree upon the details of curriculum-content" (Bobbitt, 1918, pp. 284–285). This was Bobbitt's main contribution, "to bring to professional awareness a new specialization—curriculum making" (Seguel, 1966, p. 101).

Harold Rugg, an engineer by training, had a broader vision and a more articulated social commitment than Bobbitt. A professor at Teachers College, Columbia University, he advocated the integration of history, geography, and civics in the schools, and in 1920 cofounded the National Council for the Social Studies. He shared the faith of Bobbitt, Charters, and their contemporaries in an emerging "science of education," but to a greater degree than most of them emphasized an education that would enable children to grapple with the problems of the future in a changing society. In his curriculum writing he stressed the need for a common vocabulary and the importance of cooperation among specialists and professionals from different areas, including classroom teachers, materials developers, measurement experts, administrators, psychologists, sociologists, and subject specialists. The difference between Rugg's approach and that of Bobbitt is shown in the following quotation:

> The purposes of education, the great guiding outcomes, are ultimates in life. They are discovered by thought and feeling. They are personal, subjective, and individual. . . . Social analysis merely gives us the techniques and knowledge we should have on tap. For the basic insights and attitudes we must rely, as we do for the statements of the goals of education, upon human judgment (Rugg, 1926c, pp. 80, 82).

In 1926 the National Society for the Study of Education (NSSE) published as its Twenty-sixth Yearbook a two-volume work entitled *The*

Foundations and Technique of Curriculum-Construction. The book was the work of a twelve-man Committee on Curriculum-Making, chaired by Harold Rugg. The committee included Franklin Bobbitt, W. W. Charters, George Counts, Charles Judd, and William Kilpatrick. The aim of the NSSE was to compose a consensual statement on the nature of the new field of curriculum planning. In this it largely succeeded. Although almost all the members wrote supplementary statements, substantial agreement was reached and recorded in a composite statement (some extracts from which are shown on pp. 31–32). What had been achieved was recognition of curriculum design as a specialized field of educational endeavor. This was a promising achievement. But the promise was not fulfilled.

Years Of Hiatus

The quarter-century from 1926, when the NSSE published its Twenty-sixth Yearbook, to 1949, when Ralph Tyler published *Basic Principles of Curriculum and Instruction*, were dry years for curriculum design. Education did not stand still, but in the field of curriculum planning few advances were made, and the work of previous years was largely forgotten. What happened?

State of the Art in 1926

In the selection and validation of curriculum materials expert analysis must be made both of the activities of adults and of the activities and interests of children. The data from adult life go far to determine what is of permanent value; the data from child life go far to determine what is appropriate for education in each stage of the child's development. . . . The ultimate test, therefore, of the value of an organization of curriculum-materials is the effectiveness of child learning. . . .

Curriculum-making includes three technical tasks of major importance: the determination of the ultimate and immediate objectives of education; the experimental discovery of appropriate child activities and other materials of instruction; and the like discovery of the most effective modes of selecting and organizing activities of the respective grades of the school. . . .

Curriculum-makers are obligated to consider definitely the merits and deficiencies of American civilization. . . . The chief aim will not be to reach final solutions for such problems—still less to establish any prior chosen position—but to build in the children methods of attacking controversial issues and increasingly to develop attitudes of open-mindedness and sympathetic tolerance. . . . In this connection, we respectfully suggest that it is not the function of legislative bodies to prescribe the detailed contents of the school curriculum. The people, through their legislative representatives, may properly formulate a general statement of aims and purposes of education. The task, however, of discovering appropriate materials of instruction through which to achieve those aims and purposes, is a technical one of great difficulty, demanding special professional preparation. . . .

The curriculum should provide for individual differences. In so far as possible under the administrative handicaps of large classes and a wide range of abilities, curricular provisions should be made specifically for several levels of ability. . . .

That part of the curriculum should be planned in advance which includes (1) a statement of objectives, (2) a sequence of experiences shown by analysis to be reasonably uniform in value in achieving the objectives, (3) subject matter found to be reasonably uniform as the best means of engaging in the experiences, and (4) statements of immediate outcomes of achievements to be derived from the experiences. . . . Education is progressively adopting the methods of science. Curriculum-making, correspondingly, is creating a progressive demand for specialization and for professional, scientific training, and experience. . . .

In local school systems it is particularly important that adequate central machinery be created for the continuous study of the school curriculum. In this work, the cooperation of experienced teachers should be secured, together with that of specialists in curriculum-making. The Committee heartily commends the practice of releasing efficient teachers from active class work to participate in the study of the content and organization of the curriculum materials within their chosen fields of work. . . .

This Committee condemns emphatically the evaluation of the product of educational effort solely by means of subject-matter types of examinations now prevalent in state and local school systems. We have reference specifically to the rigid control over the school curriculum exercised by those administrative examinations which over-emphasize memory of facts and principles and tend to neglect the more dynamic outcomes of instruction. . . .

—The Foundations of Curriculum-Making,
NSSE Twenty-sixth Yearbook (*Rugg, 1926d, pp. 13–25*)

It was partly that America had more pressing concerns than curriculum design. The Depression shook many people's faith in business and industry and inevitably cast doubt on the manufacturing model of edu-

cation espoused by such writers as Bobbitt. Economic stringency shrank
the resources available for education in general, and curriculum thought
became a dispensable luxury. The New Deal occupied the political attention of the public, to be followed by World War II. No sooner had the
shooting stopped than the Cold War began.

During this period the interests of many of those previously involved
in the curriculum movement changed focus. Bobbitt continued to write
on curriculum but had nothing new of importance to say. Other members
of the NSSE committee became politically active. George Counts became
heavily involved in the American Federation of Teachers and other ac-
tivist organizations and made visits to the Soviet Union—radical interests that he disavowed in the 1940s. Rugg's attention shifted almost
entirely to social studies. In the 1930s and 1940s he published a great
quantity of social studies materials, whose interest in labor history, cooperation, collectivism, and criticism of aspects of American life resulted
in attack by such groups as the American Legion. The materials were
eventually withdrawn from most school shelves, went out of publication,
and in at least one community were publicly burned. Like Counts and
Dewey, Rugg gained the distinction of an FBI file, which was opened in
1942 and continued almost until his death in 1960 (Nelson and Singleton,
1978).

The Progressive Education Association (PEA) was a major forum of
educational discussion during this period. Interminable and inconclusive
debates took place on the issues of individual versus social needs, child-
centered education versus preparation for adulthood, information versus
indoctrination, and needs versus interests. Discussion of the "project
method," of the "unit approach," and of curriculum integration indicated
concern with the method and content of curriculum rather than strategies of design. The PEA's major empirical work, the Eight-Year Study,
examined the effect on student achievement of programs differing in
content emphasis. Conservative educators, such as James Conant, Arthur
Bestor, and Robert Hutchins, were similarly interested primarily in content, urging a return to intellectual training and liberal studies. The interests of the educational community had, in fact, reverted almost entirely to the same kinds of issues that had exercised educators before
about 1920.

The Renaissance of Curriculum Design

Throughout the thirties and forties, serious thought about curriculum
design was largely restricted to a handful of professors in a few universities. Teachers College of Columbia University established a Depart-

ment of Curriculum and Teaching in 1938. Ralph Tyler taught a course in curriculum at Chicago and in 1949 published, as syllabus for the course, a disquisition entitled *Basic Principles of Curriculum and Instruction.* More than any other document, this book was responsible for a revival of interest in curriculum design. Its approach was summarized on the first page:

> Four fundamental questions . . . must be answered in developing any curriculum and plan of instruction. These are: (1) What educational purposes should the school seek to attain? (2) What educational experiences can be provided that are likely to attain these purposes? (3) How can these educational experiences be effectively organized? (4) How can we determine whether these purposes are being attained? (Tyler, 1949, p. 1)

Two things are surprising about Tyler's book. First, it closely paraphrased, restated, and elaborated the position taken by the NSSE committee twenty-four years previously. Second, Tyler did not acknowledge that fact: the book did not contain a bibliography or even a single reference.

But if Tyler's work was not an intellectual advance, it did serve to redirect the attention of educators who were now willing to examine questions of curriculum design. Major textbooks on curriculum appeared over the next decade. Those by Smith, Stanley, and Shores (1957) and Taba (1962) became classics; while saying little that was novel, they summarized the current state of the art comprehensively and thoughtfully.

Of long-term importance for the field of curriculum design was the increasing influence of experimental psychology, particularly learning theory, during the 1950s. One application of B. F. Skinner's thought resulted in the development of programmed instruction, and this was significant for three reasons. First, programmed instruction was the direct parent of computer-based instruction. Second, designers of programmed instruction found that in field testing and evaluating their programs it was essential to state clear criteria of pupil achievement. This, allied to an approach that was naturally behavioral in orientation, gave rise to the doctrine that objectives should be stated in terms of overt student behaviors. A book by Robert Mager, *Preparing Instructional Objectives* (1962), originally published as *Preparing Objectives for Programmed Instruction,* became a best seller. The debate initiated by the "behavioral objectives" movement tended to slow down curriculum advance by diverting attention into the somewhat stultifying controversy over how objectives should be stated. But it also stimulated curriculum thinkers to take an interest in measurement. The field of educational measurement had made steady progress since the 1930s, but its advances had had little impact on curriculum practice. With the emphasis on measurable outcomes, links between curriculum and measurement slowly began to be forged.

The third contribution of programmed instruction was that it provided a paradigm for the development of curricula. Anderson later described the process.

> As a first step, objectives were defined. . . . Next, a trial version of a portion of the program was prepared. This segment was tried with a series of individual high school students with one of the authors of the program monitoring each student's performance. After every few students, revisions were made. The remaining segments of the program were developed in the same fashion. Eventually the entire program was tested with small groups of students. Once again revisions were made. Throughout the development of the program, a lengthy criterion-referenced test . . . was used. . . . Generally, a segment of the program was judged satisfactory when all pilot subjects scored 90 percent or better on criterion test items keyed to that segment (Anderson, 1969, p. 9).

While these developments were taking place in the world of curriculum professionals, the public composure of education was shattered on October 4, 1957, when the Soviet Union successfully launched Sputnik I, the world's first artificial satellite. For the first time, the American people could not escape the conclusion that another country—and not just any country, but the U.S.S.R.—had achieved at least a temporary advantage in one area of technology. The public and political anxiety aroused soon found a target in the public schools. Public criticism was, to an extent, justified, and not only in the area of science teaching, which was undoubtedly mediocre in 1957. Had language programs been more extensively developed, American scientists might have read some of the technical articles on satellite research published over previous years in Russian scientific journals. And had social studies teaching been less insular and complacent, the American public might not have been laboring under the illusion that the Soviet Union in 1957 was still a pretechnological peasant society.

In any event, the Russians made a major contribution to education in the United States. The National Defense Education Act of 1958 authorized a billion dollars in federal aid to upgrade the teaching of science, mathematics, technology, and foreign languages. Spokesmen such as James Conant, president of Harvard, and Hyman Rickover, admiral and submarine expert, found a ready audience for their advocacy of academic rigor and selectivity in the schools. The National Academy of Sciences sponsored the Woods Hole Conference; its chairman, Jerome Bruner, in his report *The Process of Education* (1960), urged that students should be taught the "structure of the disciplines."

This was the background to a series of national curriculum committees, heavily funded by the National Science Foundation and other agencies. Staffed primarily by academic and research scientists, these committees rejected the teaching of factual information or technical application in favor of teaching the nature and structure of scientific inquiry (Bellack, 1969). Their underlying assumption was that of the 1890s: that curriculum design could best be carried out by experts in academic subjects. As a consequence, massive though these projects were, they added little to knowledge of curriculum design procedures. Cremin comments on the way in which rejection of "educational" principles led Zacharias and his colleagues on the Physical Sciences Study Committee full circle:

> Seeking to rid himself of the pedagogical preoccupations of the Progressive Era by avoiding the literature of education, Zacharias ended up accepting the paradigm of curriculum-making that had prevailed for three-quarters of a century. And in avoiding the literature, he and others like him inevitably impoverished the character of educational discussion. Insistently eschewing the past, the curriculum reformers of the fifties and sixties eventually became its captive (Cremin, 1971, p. 216).

The discipline-centered approach to curriculum inevitably produced a reaction in the 1960s. Bruner's thesis that children could at any age grasp the essence of intellectual concepts was clearly at variance with the evidence being produced by Piaget and other developmental psychologists. Educational psychologists were now able to reintroduce progressive ideals of child-centeredness with more light and less heat. Their critique of subject-centered curricula was echoed by a host of critics of the schools, ranging from distinguished scholars to romantic and apocalyptic crackpots of almost every hue. For some years many educators willingly fed the mouths that bit them. Ultimately, practitioners tired of the litany of destructive criticism, revolutionary rhetoric, and gut-level analysis. They were interested in what was to be done next Monday, not what should be done by the year 2000.

What both the subject specialists and the critics overlooked was the need for a comprehensive and coherent framework for curriculum design. The need was articulately stated by Goodlad in 1958:

> Nowhere in education is there greater need for a conceptual system to guide decision-making than in the field of curriculum. By a conceptual system, I mean a carefully engineered framework that performs the following functions: identifies the major questions to be answered in developing any instructional program; reveals separate elements that tie these questions together in a system and the elements that separate questions from one another; identifies subordinate questions and classifies them properly in relation to major questions; reveals the data-sources to be used in answering the questions posed by the system; and suggests the relevance of data extracted from these sources (Goodlad, 1958, pp. 391–392).

Despite advances on various curriculum fronts in the 1960s, notably objectives and instruction, the conceptual system Goodlad called for seemed to elude curriculum thinkers. Instead, the serious study of curriculum tended to withdraw into more arcane and abstract areas; the term "curriculum theory" began to gain currency. Curriculum thought appeared to be in danger of losing touch with practice, and it was this tendency that was attacked by Joseph Schwab in 1969.

Maturation of the Field

To describe the progress in the field of curriculum design since 1969 would require a book of its own. Many of the major advances are commented on elsewhere in this volume. It may be noted here, however, that much of the progress made in the 1970s was a witting or unwitting response to Schwab's censure of 1969:

> The field of curriculum is moribund. It is unable, by its present methods and principles, to continue its work and contribute significantly to the advancement of education. It requires new principles which will generate a new view of the character and variety of its problems. It requires new methods appropriate to the new budget of problems. . . . The curriculum field has reached this unhappy state by inveterate, unexamined, and mistaken reliance on theory (Schwab, 1969, p. 1).

Schwab's prescription for the ills of the curriculum field was the development of a practical and eclectic set of principles that would guide curriculum deliberation and aid decisions about goals and the actions necessary to achieve them. Progress would be by piecemeal improvement, not by monolithic revolution, and would start from a sophisticated understanding of existing practices and their effects. What Schwab was proposing, in essence, was that curriculum design develop in the direction of an applied science. And remarkable progress was made in this direction in the following decade.

Whatever the deficiencies of curriculum design by the end of the 1970s, they were not due to lack of effort. More people poured more energy into curriculum than ever before, even in the false dawn of the 1920s. Much of the progress that was made was due to a synthesis of education and psychology; the great majority of those who made significant contributions to curriculum in the 1970s were educational psychologists. This was not paralleled by a similar integration of philosophy and education, and questions regarding the ultimate and immediate ends of education still required attention.

New techniques of instruction during the period began to produce results previously beyond the grasp of the schools. This was partly because curriculum workers broke through narrow preoccupations with discrete elements of curriculum, such as objectives, teaching methods, and measurement, and began to see these components as parts of a system that called for a comprehensive strategy of design. One manifestation of this was the development of computer-based and computer-managed instruction. Perhaps the most important example was mastery learning.

Benjamin Bloom had suggested in 1968 that the partial learning typical of school programs was no longer appropriate in the light of current social needs and what was known of learning psychology. In 1976 he published *Human Characteristics and School Learning,* in which he reported extensive evidence that "what any person in the world can learn, almost all persons can learn *if* provided with appropriate prior and current conditions of learning" (Bloom, 1976, p. 7). For the first time, it was demonstrated that systematic planning of the variables in a learning situation could produce consistently high levels of learner achievement. It is not too much to say that Bloom's book signified the coming of age of curriculum design. A similar approach to instruction developed independently by the distinguished psychologist Fred Keller (Keller and Sherman, 1974) spread rapidly in universities in North and South America; for once, educational principles were influencing academia, rather than vice versa.

As the field matured, it expanded beyond the boundaries of a small community of specialists. Major corporations became involved in curriculum projects. Linkages were formed between curriculum in the schools and programs in business, industry, and the armed forces, where, away from the limelight, significant advances had been made in the design and delivery of training. The field also began to develop an international character. Individuals such as Torsten Husen in Sweden and Philip Taylor in England, and international institutions such as the Organization for Economic Cooperation and Development, stimulated and sustained the flow of curriculum ideas between the United States and Europe.

Increasing public pressure for a higher level of educational effectiveness, expressed both in civil lawsuits and in state legislation mandating "minimum competency," made it impossible to be complacent about existing curricula. Attempts early in the seventies at "bootstrap" curriculum development by untrained teachers showed the need for specialist training if curricula were to be designed with a minimum of cost and confusion. Such training became more widely available as universities and departments of education expanded their undergraduate, graduate, and inservice programs in curriculum.

By the end of the 1970s it was possible to say that curriculum design was at least on the threshold of emerging as an applied science. This was the goal sought by the National Society for the Study of Education in

1924, urged by Goodlad in 1958, and pointed to by Schwab in 1969. In the promotion of those aspects of human happiness that were within the domain of curriculum, much remained to be done. But, to borrow Winston Churchill's words from another context, if this was not the beginning of the end, it was, perhaps, the end of the beginning.

QUESTIONS

1. "Curriculum has been too traditionally minded and insufficiently historically minded." Discuss.

2. Early Greek education was characterized by the close personal relationship between teacher and pupil; later Greek education by training and technique. To what extent do modern schools of educational thought fit into these two camps?

3. What cultural and political factors account for the stranglehold that Greek and/or Latin (grammar, analysis, translation, and composition) held over the school curriculum from about 300 B.C. to about 1800 A.D. in most of the Western world?

4. The complaint that the younger generation cannot read and write as well as formerly goes back at least to ancient Egypt, where it has been found in hieroglyphic writing on tombs dating from 3000 B.C. What is the psychology of this phenomenon?

5. What are the main reasons that curriculum design emerged as a field of study in the United States, rather than in Europe?

6. Read Spencer's paper, "What Knowledge Is of Most Worth?" (1860); the Commission on the Reorganization of Secondary Education's *Cardinal Principles* (1918); and the Educational Policies Commission's "Ten Imperative Needs of Youth" (1944). What do the similarities and differences among the goals stated indicate about changes in society and in educational thought between 1860 and 1944?

Recommended Reading

Broudy, Harry S., and John R. Palmer. *Exemplars of teaching method.* Chicago: Rand McNally, 1965. An insight into the development of educational thought via the most accessible route: the teaching strategies proposed and followed by great teachers, from Socrates to the twentieth century.

Krug, Edward A. *The shaping of the American high school.* New York: Harper & Row, 1964. Detailed and scholarly account of the intellectual, social, and political currents within education and their effects on the high school from 1880 to 1920.

Marrou, H. I. *A history of education in antiquity.* New York: Sheed & Ward, 1956. An account of education in Greece and Rome, interestingly written, despite Marrou's enormous erudition.

Seguel, Mary Louise. *The curriculum field: Its formative years.* New York: Teachers College Press, 1966. The author, a pioneer in the history of curriculum thought, traces perceptively the ideas of Dewey, Bobbitt, Rugg, and other curriculum writers who shaped the development of the field.

Tanner, Daniel, and Laurel N. Tanner. *Curriculum development: Theory into practice.* New York: Macmillan, 1975. Within the framework of a general introduction to curriculum ideas, the authors present a detailed review of curriculum development in the United States in the 19th and 20th centuries.

References

Anderson, Richard C. The comparative field experiment: An illustration from high school biology. *Proceedings of the 1968 Conference on Testing Problems.* Princeton, N.J.: Educational Testing Service, 1969, pp. 3–30.

Bellack, Arno A. History of curriculum thought and practice. *Review of Educational Research,* 1969, 39, 283–292.

Binder, Frederick M. *Education in the history of Western civilization: Selected Readings.* New York: Macmillan, 1970.

Bloom, Benjamin S. *Human characteristics and school learning.* New York: McGraw-Hill, 1976.

Bobbitt, Franklin. *The curriculum.* Boston: Houghton Mifflin, 1918.

———. *How to make a curriculum.* Boston: Houghton Mifflin, 1924.

———. *Curriculum investigations.* Chicago: University of Chicago Press, 1926.

Bruner, Jerome S. *The process of education.* New York: Random House, 1960.

Callahan, Raymond E. *Education and the cult of efficiency.* Chicago: University of Chicago Press, 1962.

Commission on Reorganization of Secondary Education. *Cardinal principles of secondary education.* Washington, D.C.: U.S. Government Printing Office, 1918.

Cremin, Lawrence A. Curriculum-making in the United States. *Teachers College Record,* 1971, 73, 207–220.

Dewey, John. *The school and society.* Chicago: University of Chicago Press, 1899.

Educational Policies Commission. *Education for ALL American youth.* Washington, D.C.: National Education Association, 1944.

Goodlad, John I. Toward a conceptual system for curriculum problems. *School Review,* 1958, 66, 391–401.

Kazamias, Andreas M. "What knowledge is of most worth?" An historical conception and a modern sequel. *Harvard Educational Review,* 1960, 30, 307–330.

Keller, Fred S., and J. Gilmour Sherman. *The Keller Plan handbook.* Menlo Park, Cal.: W. A. Benjamin, 1974.

Kliebard, H. M. The Tyler rationale: A reassessment. *School Review,* 1970, 78, 259–272.

———. Curricular objectives and evaluation: A reassessment. In M. R. Kapfer (ed.), *Behavioral objectives in curriculum development.* Englewood Cliffs, N.J.: Educational Technology Publications, 1971, pp. 351–357.

Kneller, George F. *Educational anthropology.* New York: Wiley, 1965.

Krug, Edward A. *The shaping of the American high school.* New York: Harper & Row, 1964.

Leach, Arthur F. *Educational charters and documents 598 to 1909*. Cambridge: Cambridge University Press, 1911.

Mager, R. F. *Preparing instructional objectives*. Palo Alto, Cal.: Fearon, 1962.

Marrou, H. I. *A history of education in antiquity*. New York: Sheed & Ward, 1956.

Nelson, Murray R., and H. Wells Singleton. FBI surveillance of three progressive educators: Curricular aspects. Paper presented at the Annual Meeting of the American Educational Research Association, Toronto, March 1978.

Pounds, Ralph L. *The development of education in Western culture*. New York: Appleton-Century-Crofts, 1968.

Rugg, Harold. The school curriculum, 1825–1890. *Twenty-sixth yearbook of the National Society for the Study of Education: The foundations and technique of curriculum-construction*. Part 1: Curriculum-making: Past and present. Bloomington, Ill.: Public Schools Publishing Co., 1926a, pp. 17–32.

———. Three decades of mental discipline: Curriculum-making via national committees. *Twenty-sixth yearbook of the National Society for the Study of Education*. Part 1. 1926b, pp. 33–65.

———. Curriculum-making and the scientific study of education since 1910. *Twenty-sixth yearbook of the National Society for the Study of Education*. Part 1. 1926c, pp. 67–82.

———, et al. The foundations of curriculum-making. *Twenty-sixth yearbook of the National Society for the Study of Education*. Part 2: The foundations of curriculum-making. 1926d, pp. 11–28.

Schwab, Joseph J. The practical: A language for curriculum. *School Review*, 1969, 78, 1–23.

Seguel, Mary Louise. *The curriculum field: Its formative years*. New York: Teachers College Press, 1966.

Smith, B. Othanel, William O. Stanley, and J. Harlan Shores. *Fundamentals of curriculum development*. New York: Harcourt Brace Jovanovich, 1957.

Snow, C. P. *The two cultures and the scientific revolution*. (The Rede lecture, 1959). Cambridge: Cambridge University Press, 1962.

Spencer, Herbert. *Essays on education*. London: Dent, 1911.

Taba, Hilda. *Curriculum development: Theory and practice*. New York: Harcourt Brace Jovanovich, 1962.

Tanner, Daniel, and Laurel N. Tanner, *Curriculum development: Theory into practice*. New York: Macmillan, 1975.

Taylor, Frederick W. *The principles of scientific management*. (First published 1911). New York: Norton, 1967.

Tyler, Ralph W. *Basic principles of curriculum and instruction*. Chicago: University of Chicago Press, 1949.

Walker, Decker R. The curriculum field in formation: A review of the Twenty-sixth Yearbook of the NSSE. *Curriculum Theory Network*, 1975, 4, 263–280.

Wedgwood, C. V. *The king's peace*. London: Collins, 1954.

3

PRINCIPLES

- The most valuable resource used in education is the time of learners.

- The resources consumed by education require that curricula be justified.

- Many conventional justifications for existing curricula are inadequate.

- Ultimately a curriculum is legitimate only if it helps to meet a significant human need.

- Some basic human needs are: the need for self-actualization and for meaning, and aesthetic, social, and survival needs.

- Curricula designed today should aim to meet the needs of people in the future.

- Technological and manpower forecasting can help to predict future needs.

- Independent thought is a necessary but not a sufficient means for identifying significant human needs.

CONCEPTS

Need	Transfer
Interest	Intrinsic value
Client	Self-actualization

3

The Curriculum and Human Needs

Men know themselves to be unfinished; they are aware of their incompleteness. In this incompleteness and this awareness lie the very roots of education as an exclusively human manifestation.

—Paulo Freire (1970, p. 72)

Education and Human Resources

Pablo Casals, the Spanish cellist, conductor, and composer, once expressed what might be called the Educational Imperative:

> Each second we live in a new and unique moment of the universe, a moment that never was before and never will be again. And what do we teach our children in school? We teach them that two and two make four, and that Paris is the capital of France.

A society's most valuable resource is its people; education is a process by which society invests in the development of its people. Of the many resources committed to this investment, the most significant is time. Time is the one resource that is nonrenewable, noninterchangeable, finite. Anthropologists point to time as a distinctly Western preoccupation (Hall, 1959), but the Western world is not alone in the recognition that time is life itself. The Arabs have a proverb, "Time is the air we breathe." To the Chinese, "A moment of time is more precious than an eternity of jade."

By far the greatest amount of time that is used in schools is that of the young, time that is committed not by their own consent but by order of their elders. Children who are five years old today are likely to spend most of the best hours of the best days of their next twelve years in school. And each day they spend in school is subtracted not only from the limited total of their mortal span, but from the shorter, and most formative, period of their youth.

While time is the major and most valuable resource used in education, the financial cost of schooling is also a significant resource, partly because money often represents payment for people's time. The rapid escalation of education costs in the 1960s (Organization for Economic Cooperation and Development, 1974) meant that schools were consuming the product of more working days on the part of the labor force in 1970 than they had in 1960. In addition, expenditures on schools and colleges represent only a part of the picture. Vast sums are spent by business, industry, and government in training and retraining their employees. Major American firms spend collectively over two billion dollars a year in employee education (*University Affairs,* 1977). The textbooks produced by the United States Internal Revenue Service for their in-house employee training would fill twelve feet of bookshelf space. The armed forces, especially in peacetime, are heavily engaged in training their personnel in technical, vocational, and military skills. In fiscal year 1977

COUNTRY	PERCENT OF GNP
West Germany	4.5
Australia	4.6
New Zealand	5.4
United Kingdom	5.9
United States	6.7
Soviet Union	7.0
Sweden	7.9
Canada	8.5

Table 3–1 Public expenditure on education in 1971 relative to gross national product (UNESCO, 1974)

the Department of Defense provided a quarter-million person-years of training at a cost in excess of six billion dollars (McClelland and Wagner, 1978).

The total amount spent on education and training is impossible to ascertain, but it seems a safe estimate that in most of the industrialized world at least one-fifth of the gross national product is committed to education or training in one form or another.

These heavy commitments, human and material, by society to education, represent something more than the willingness of the old to sacrifice the young to ideals they pretend to believe in. The aspirations of many parents are still focused on the future of their children; the schools still enshrine the hope—albeit in the 1980s a somewhat jaded and cynical hope—of society for the future. Only such hope can justify the constraint of the young for so much of their youth.

Justifying Curriculum

How can an educator justify a curriculum? There have been fashions in this, as in other areas of education. It may not be true that Victorian pedagogues used to say, "It doesn't matter what you teach them, so long as they don't like it," but some other familiar arguments have about equal merit. Mathematics in the elementary school, for example, may be offered on the grounds that it prepares pupils for secondary-school mathematics; the upper grades of secondary school prepare students for university; the Master's degree prepares students for doctoral work. Similarly, physics assists students with chemistry, chemistry with biology, and so on. However far one follows such arguments, any ultimate justification for curriculum seems to remain out of reach.

Another kind of justification argues that curriculum considerations are secondary to the importance of students studying under dedicated and enthusiastic teachers. The argument has a certain seductive appeal; it is true that students will benefit more from studying hopscotch under an enthusiastic teacher than from studying literature under a bored and boring teacher. In neither case will they learn much of value, but in the first case at least the time will be enjoyably spent. But the argument has all the merit of the suggestion that surgeons should be encouraged to perform their favorite operations without reference to the actual condition of their patients. The task of the curriculum designer is first to determine the learnings that will be of greatest value to the students, and then to ensure that these learnings are brought about under the direction of competent and enthusiastic teachers.

Three other positions deserve closer attention, because each has exerted, and still exerts, considerable influence over the curriculum. These are the contentions (1) that knowledge has intrinsic value; (2) that learning trains the mind; and (3) that education enhances employability.

Knowledge for its own sake

The thesis is sometimes proposed that education, or knowledge, should be pursued "for its own sake." Thus a writer on higher education deplores the decline of

> the principles and practices according to which the university has operated since its emergence in the Middle Ages. The basic credo is that knowledge is important and must be pursued—knowledge per se, not *practical* or *relevant* knowledge (Harris, 1973, p. 8).

There is an immediate difficulty with this position. If knowledge is to be pursued as an end in itself, how can one decide *which* knowledge is worth pursuing? If all knowledge merits attention, simply because it is knowledge, there are no grounds for choosing to teach students an understanding of *Paradise Lost* rather than having them learn by heart the first ten pages of the Tokyo telephone directory.

Discussion of the "knowledge-centered" curriculum has been characteristic of British educational writing, as contrasted with the more "life-centered" emphasis of American curriculum thought. Justice cannot be done in a paragraph to the British school of thought represented by such thinkers as Dearden, Hirst, Peters, and White. Suffice it to say that these writers do not argue so much for the intrinsic value of knowledge as for the value of developing an understanding of the world, of modes of thought and of alternative ways of life: in sum, for the intrinsic value of an enhanced insight into the nature of human existence. The pursuit of knowledge in effect is usually an instrumental, not an intrinsic, activity; knowledge is sought with some ulterior goal in mind. Without some reference to the outcomes to which the acquisition of knowledge leads, arguments for the intrinsic value of knowledge tend merely to become weapons in the struggle among the purveyors of knowledge, that is, among teachers specialized in different academic disciplines. Treating knowledge as an end in itself deprives the curriculum decision-maker of any criteria for establishing curriculum priorities and reduces curriculum making to the status of a political exercise. This was the experience in England in the 1960s, when several attempts were made to broaden the highly specialized curriculum in the senior grades (sixth form) of secondary schools. Every effort was shipwrecked on the refusal of existing disciplinary interests to give up any share of time or resources to other and especially to newer areas of study.

This is not to suggest that learning cannot have intrinsic value. If the learner finds the process of learning interesting, satisfying, or enjoyable, the experience is valuable in itself. It is a curriculum ideal to manage all learning in such a way that this will be the case. But can one properly prescribe that the learner *should* find the pursuit of knowledge satisfying? One can argue that the learner should study biology rather than billiards on instrumental grounds, but to admonish that he or she should find it more intrinsically valuable is to engage in the fruitless task of legislating taste. The degree of student enthusiasm for knowledge does not relieve the curriculum planner of responsibility for ensuring the value to the learner of what is learned.

"Training the mind"

Another justification occasionally proposed is that the content of the curriculum is not of primary significance; the important thing is that study of any kind trains the mind. This belief takes various forms. One is that the mind can be improved like a muscle by specific exercise. More common is a belief in wide-ranging transfer of learning: that practicing memorization of irregular verbs will train the memory, or that studying mathematics will increase logical thinking, or that learning formal grammar will improve written expression, or that studying history will result in good citizenship. We are now approaching a century since experimental evidence began to cast doubt on such beliefs. In 1901 Thorndike and Woodworth (p. 250) summarized the results of numerous experiments by themselves and others: "Improvement in any single mental function rarely brings about equal improvement in any other function, no matter how similar."

It is disheartening evidence of the failure of educational research to affect the ideas and practices of teachers that the "mental discipline" myth is still alive in schools and is often used to prolong the death agonies of moribund curriculum subjects. Although subsequent researchers would be less emphatic than Thorndike, their work has generally supported his position. Transfer of training will not result automatically from any learning; but if learning situations are carefully designed to stress underlying principles, some transfer can be achieved (Cronbach, 1977; Ellis, 1965). The key appears to be careful design. Curricula developed by Professor de Bono at the Cognitive Research Trust in Cambridge and aimed specifically at improvement in "thinking skills" claim a success that has eluded generations of teachers of history, English, Latin, and mathematics, who have hoped that study of their subjects would enhance students' general intellectual ability (de Bono, 1974). The evidence appears to suggest that the curriculum content, far from being immaterial, is critical and must be designed and justified accordingly.

Thorndike on Transfer

Common observation should teach us that mental capacities are highly specialized. A man may be a tip-top musician but in other respects an imbecile: he may be a gifted poet, but an ignoramus in music: he may have a wonderful memory for figures and only a mediocre memory for localities, poetry, or human faces: school children may reason admirably in science and be below the average in grammar: those very good in drawing may be very poor in dancing. Careful measurements show that the specialization is even greater than ordinary observation leads one to suppose. For instance those individuals who are the highest ten out of a hundred in the power to judge differences in length accurately are by no means the highest ten in the ability to judge differences in weights accurately. . . . Many facts such as these prove that the mind is by no means a collection of a few general faculties, observation, attention, memory, reasoning, and the like, but is the sum total of countless particular capacities, each of which is to some extent independent of the others—each of which must to some extent be educated by itself. The task of teaching is not to develop a reasoning faculty, but many special powers of thought about different kinds of facts. . . .

Do not rely on any general mental improvements as a result of your teaching unless you have actual evidence of it. Teach nothing merely because of its disciplinary value, but teach everything so as to get what disciplinary value it does have. Consider in the case of every subject what ideas and habits of attitude and method the subject should develop that will be of general influence. After securing these ideas and habits in the special subject, give abundant practice in applying them to other fields. The price of acquisition of general power is eternal vigilance in the formation of particular habits.

—*Edward L. Thorndike (1906, pp. 238, 240, 248–249)*

Improving employability

A new way to justify curriculum developed in the 1960s. It held that what mattered was not the education, but the number of years of schooling that the young received. It was observed that university graduates tended to earn more than high-school graduates, who in turn earned more than adults who had not completed high school. This was interpreted as prima facie evidence that the longer a student stayed in school, the more he or she would earn later in life and in turn the more he or she would contribute to the national economy. In Canada this doctrine, fostered by the Economic Council of Canada (1965), produced a government publicity campaign in which billboards along major highways advertised the slogan "Every year you stay in school is worth $20,000 in lifetime earnings."

The naiveté of this expectation is now laughable, and the first people to laugh, albeit somewhat bitterly, are the unemployed school and college graduates, the M.A.'s, the Ph.D.'s, who were its victims. The actual relationship between education and employment was examined by Ivar Berg in a book sardonically entitled *Education and Jobs: The Great Training Robbery* (1971). In surveying the numerous studies in the area, he found little support for the hypothesis that years of education in themselves improved a person's job performance, productivity, or promotability. The higher incomes of the better educated appeared to be largely related to the role of educational institutions as licensing agencies, which excluded from lucrative careers individuals who had not met formal educational requirements (Berg, pp. 110, 188). Berg's conclusions do not attack the idea of manpower training; they do point to the fallacy of assuming that *any* education will enhance employability. A random increase across the board in years of education will simply result, in the long run, in upgrading the educational qualifications of the unemployed. This is exactly what has happened in much of the Western world over the past decade.

A moral issue is raised by curricula supported by false claims, even if these claims are made in good faith. The choice of educational programs, either by the student or by the school for the student, is a choice that has far-reaching personal consequences. The educator who makes a living by providing such programs, but who is ignorant of their effects or fails to advise students of their effects, is engaged in a kind of exploitation.

The extent to which employment considerations may influence the curriculum is discussed later in this chapter. At this point it is sufficient to suggest that while such considerations constitute an important criterion for curricula, they are not the only nor the most important criterion, nor will they apply to all parts of the school curriculum. If the manpower argument is used to justify existing programs, what is entailed is not automatic validation of all schooling, but precisely the reverse: rigorous design of the content of the curriculum to ensure that it leads to the promised employment results.

Each of these approaches to justifying curriculum turns out to be a bankrupt attempt to escape from justification. Each, on examination, points not to the irrelevance but the centrality of curriculum questions. For the professional educator there is no legitimate way to avoid the responsibility for justifying each curriculum in terms of its actual value for the learners whom it engages.

Let us now turn to the approach to the justification of curriculum that has been most widely addressed in American educational writing. Its basic axiom (with which, with some reservations, this text agrees) is: A curriculum is valid if it helps to meet a significant human need.

Meaning of Need

In the educational and psychological literature, "need" tends to be defined in terms of a deficit, as a discrepancy between an actual and an optimal state (Tyler, 1950, p. 5). The optimal state is a condition regarded as desirable for the individual, the actual state is his or her present condition. This adequately defines what we might call "discrepancy needs." But consider this fact: your body needs water *regardless* of whether you are thirsty at this moment. In this sense, needs are not discrepancies. "Basic" needs are those things or conditions without which the individual's state would be significantly less than satisfactory (Scriven and Roth, 1978).

At this point, we are primarily concerned with the first task of the curriculum planner, which is to identify basic needs. The curriculum designer determines the discrepancy needs at a subsequent stage. Basic needs are determined by prescription, discrepancy needs by description. If we decide that "everyone needs affection," then we can find out by empirical methods how far individuals are receiving, or think they are receiving, affection. But the basic need for affection cannot itself be determined empirically: it is an axiom that is prescribed by a process of valuing.

Needs, Wants, and Interests

Needs are distinct from both wants and interests, neither of which is an adequate basis for curriculum. A want or desire is always conscious, having to do with someone's state of mind. Needs are not necessarily perceived by the subject. Many early explorers of the Atlantic died of scurvy because they lacked vitamin C; they knew something was wrong, but not what basic need was unmet. While some needs may not be consciously wanted, it can also be debated whether all wants are needs. "Children who need dental care rarely want it, and patients who want Laetrile rarely need it" (Scriven and Roth, 1978, p. 2). It is legitimate to say, "I want a cigarette," but is it correct to say that I need one?

The needs approach to curriculum deliberately rejects children's interests as a starting point. Interest, in this sense, may be defined as "readiness to be concerned with or moved by an object or class of objects"

(Webster's, 1973). Children's interests may or may not be evidence of needs. The responsibility of the school is not discharged merely by reinforcing students' immediate interests; it is important to weigh their immediate interests against their immediate and long-term needs. It is a waste of time to try to teach people knowledge or skills they are not interested in; but this makes interest a constraint, not a starting point. Furthermore, it is a constraint that may be modifiable. If something is worth teaching, it is the job of the professional teacher to motivate the learners to want to learn it; if the students are simply not ready to learn, the wise teacher will wait until they are.

The critical question is not, Is the child interested in it? but Is it in the child's interest? If teachers of dramatic arts in North America had waited for student interest in the subject to express itself, there would still be very little drama taught in the schools. But like successful advertisers, they recognized the importance of creating interest rather than merely responding to it. By identifying certain basic needs—for physical self-expression, poise, and confidence, for example—a rationale was established for the widespread introduction of programs in theatre arts. This innovation in turn stimulated public interest in the development of repertory, experimental, and street theatre across the continent. Perhaps we could sum up the needs-versus-interests issue with a slogan: If it's in the child's interest, interest the child.

Merit of the Needs Approach

Clearly there are pitfalls present in basing curricula on needs. These have been cogently explored by such critics as Komisar (1961). Nevertheless, the merits of the approach appear to outweigh the difficulties, which can be largely overcome by a clear understanding of the concept. The principal advantage of making needs the starting point for curriculum is that this strategy immediately focuses attention on the learner. This is a valuable antidote to the inveterate tendency of educators to base curriculum on tradition, on the academic disciplines, or on their own intellectual

---

Three Approaches to Curriculum

Students should learn what they want to learn—Romantic
Students should learn what they need to learn—Programmatic
Students should learn what I want to teach—Idiotic

interests. As a starting point, "values" and "aims" lack this clear focus on the learner, allowing ambiguity as to who values the object in question. It is a further advantage that needs can be discussed in general and also in specific instances, such as in analysis of training needs in a given context. At the same time, the term lacks the narrow utilitarian implications of "usefulness" and "relevance." It is quite proper, for example, to talk of moral or aesthetic needs.

Whose Needs?

At first sight, the foregoing might appear to be a statement of the obvious. Where else would one begin designing curricula, if not with learner needs? But many curricula appear to be designed not to meet the needs of students, but to meet the needs of teachers. In most schools the programs offered reflect the areas of expertise and interest of teachers rather than an analysis of the needs of learners. A comparison of kindergartens and universities suggests that this tendency becomes more pronounced as one moves upwards through the educational system. Nor are schools unique in this respect. Investigation of training programs in business and industry indicates a proliferation of "human behavior" courses, apparently designed around the skills of the training staff rather than the training needs of employees (Howard and Gilmour, 1975). These phenomena attest to the prevalence of "goal displacement," an almost universal tendency of institutions and professions, once their mandate is secure, to cease to serve the needs of their clients and to begin to generate and serve their own purposes (Etzioni, 1961).

But it is inadequate to assert that the needs of the learner alone must determine the curriculum. On the other hand, exclusive emphasis on the needs of society can lead to a situation in which private needs must invariably be sacrificed to the good of the community or the state. In some countries this is national policy. The preamble to the 1961 Education Act in Hungary states:

1. The development of the educational system must be determined by the needs of a socialist society.
2. The system must be uniform both in its organization and its aims.
3. The responsibility for providing and maintaining the educational services belongs exclusively to the state (Richmond, 1971, p. 97).

The danger of conceiving society as a metaphysical entity with needs of its own, rather than simply as other people, is that the argument can easily become a smokescreen behind which the most powerful section of society, through control of education, arbitrarily converts its ideology or interests into curriculum policy. Arthur Foshay comments of American schools that the single-minded pursuit of social needs has led the schools to practice a social-class bias that has excluded millions of students from education at an early age. . . . When the schools do no more than reflect society's needs, they become enormous screening devices (Foshay, 1970, p. 3).

But it is unconvincing to argue, as Foshay does, that "what is good for the individual is good for the country" (1970, p. 4). Social needs are not always reducible to individual needs. There are instances in which one would want to restrain some individuals for the good of others. Income tax is an obvious example. Curricula designed only to promote the good of individuals would teach them how to read, but would not aim to restrain or change a student who always sought personal advantage regardless of the cost to others. More important, schools would not deliberately seek to develop in the student concern about, for example, starvation in the Third World. Altruism, by definition, is action in the interests of others, and who would want to exclude altruism from the curriculum?

Neither the demand of "personal relevance" nor that of "social relevance" can be sustained to the exclusion of the other. Consequently, when conflict occurs—and conflict is inevitable in curriculum decision making, if only over allocation of time—difficult decisions have to be made. A guiding principle in making such decisions might be to *identify the clients and develop the curriculum to meet their needs.* The burden of justification then rests with the educator who seeks to meet the needs of someone other than the clients.

Identifying the clients is not always straightforward. In elementary mathematics or in graduate business education, the clients will usually be the students who study the curriculum content. But the clients of prenatal classes are both parents and babies yet to be born. The ultimate clients of professional programs in the health sciences are not doctors and nurses but patients, and hence the needs of patients should be the starting point in developing health education curricula. In teacher education, the clients are not the trainee teachers but the pupils they will teach. Professionals do have needs that curricula can help to meet; but if the professions are to be something more than "conspiracies against the laity," these needs should take second place to the needs of the clients.

An agenda for reform must begin at the beginning, with people's real and immediate concerns; first build the school and then suggest the university; first repair the wooden footbridge and then suggest an asphalt road.

—*Regis Debray (1976)*

Significant Human Needs

Once human needs are accepted as the foundation for curriculum, the critical question is What are the significant human needs?

Anyone addressing this question does so in the shadow of the great American psychologist Abraham Maslow, who a generation ago attempted to place the study of needs on a scientific footing. Maslow (1954) identified five classes of human needs: physiological needs, need for safety, social needs, need for esteem, and need for self-actualization. His classification has much merit, although it could be argued that it contains some redundancy. The need for safety or security, for example, is not a discrete need, so much as the confidence that other needs will continue to be met in the future. The need for esteem contains elements both of social needs (esteem of others) and of self-actualization (self-esteem). There are also significant additional needs that cannot easily be contained within Maslow's categories.

Five fundamental types of human need, based largely on Maslow's taxonomy, may be suggested for the consideration of the curriculum designer. These are need for self-actualization, need for meaning, social needs, aesthetic needs, and survival needs.

Need for self-actualization

"The Greek definition of happiness," J. F. Kennedy used to say in discussing the presidency, "is the full use of your powers along the lines of excellence." The Greek ideal of pursuit of excellence by every man has unfortunately been captured all too often by those who believe that excellence is the exclusive property of a tiny minority of academically gifted people. This has produced twentieth-century schools in which, like Thomas Gray's eighteenth-century churchyard, are buried the unrealized talents of generations.

It would be both more realistic and more humane to begin with the assumption that every child can do at least one thing excellently and that most children can do many things well.

Every child in every classroom has the equivalent of a three-billion-dollar computer between his or her ears. This slightly alkaline three-pound electrochemical device runs on glucose at about 25 watts. It contains between ten and a hundred billion logical elements called neurons and operates on a scaling rhythm of about ten cycles per second. Each of its 10^{10} cells contains 10^5 macromolecules and receives 10^4 connections from other cells. In a lifetime, its data storage system can store up to 2.8×10^{20} bits of information, far more than any existing manufactured computer (Beer, 1974, p. 58). It is this brain that enables the child's vision to distinguish ten million different color surfaces, to detect light at five

Elegy

Beneath those rugged elms, that yew-tree's shade,
Where heaves the turf in many a mould'ring heap,
Each in his narrow cell for ever laid,
The rude forefathers of the hamlet sleep.
. . . .

Perhaps in this neglected spot is laid
Some heart once pregnant with celestial fire,
Hands that the rod of empire might have sway'd,
Or wak'd to ecstasy the living lyre.

But knowledge to their eyes her ample page
Rich with the spoils of time did ne'er unroll;
Chill penury repress'd their noble rage,
And froze the genial current of the soul.

Full many a gem of purest ray serene,
The dark unfathom'd caves of ocean bear;
Full many a flower is born to blush unseen,
And waste its sweetness on the desert air.

—*Thomas Gray, from "Elegy Written in a Country Church-Yard"*

thousand-billionths of an erg, to resolve objects at 0.0003 of a radian; it enables the nose to detect one part of vanillin in ten million parts of air, the sense of touch to detect a vibration with a movement of a fifty-thousandth of a millimetre. And yet many of the inheritors of this product of a hundred million years of evolution emerge from school with a profound belief in their total inability in many fields of endeavor and their low ability in all!

Self-actualization is a term coined by Maslow: "What a man *can* be, he *must* be. This need we may call self-actualization" (1954, p. 91). As used by Maslow it includes both realization of potential and absorption or engagement in activities that the individual finds directly fulfilling. The function of the school implied by the concept is to help learners discover those activities at which they can excel and those experiences that they find most intrinsically valuable. It is not enough to expect that the student will make these discoveries independently. Not every potential artist will be drawing masterpieces, like Rembrandt, at the age of eight. Much talent is hidden and requires the inspiration of gifted teaching to be discovered. How do you know that you don't have the potential to become a superlative woodcarver, discus-thrower, trumpet-player, gymnast, mountaineer, astronomer, poet, designer, dancer, or magician, if you never received enough instruction to liberate a latent gift? How many potentially talented actors, linguists, writers, athletes, and inventors work on assembly lines, stand in dole queues, or sit in prison? How many men and women die within a few months of retiring from work, a score of potential talents that should have enriched their working years as well as their retirment never explored?

Self-actualization is not limited to the development of particular skills and talents. It encompasses the whole area of evolving an identity: male or female, mental and physical, spatial and temporal. It means knowing who you are and liking what you know.

Need for meaning

The growth of self-consciousness is accompanied by a drive that is essentially philosophical: the need to find meaning, or (to use an existentialist term) authenticity, in one's existence. This drive has been a basic human characteristic throughout time and across cultures. It seems to become more pronounced once the necessities of life are satisfied and

---

All humans are born geniuses, but half of us are made idiots by the system of education.

—*J. P. Guilford, psychologist*

> By ignorant I mean, not those who do not know how to weave or how to make shoes, nor the people who cannot dance, but those who are ignorant of the things one must know if he is to be a good and noble man.
>
> —*Dio Chrysostom, Greek orator, c. 82* A.D.

when the attention of a society is not focused on some common emergency such as warfare. People are rarely satisfied merely by biological and material equilibrium. As Victor Frankl puts it, "What man actually needs is not a tension-less state, but rather the striving and struggling for some goal worthy of him" (1962, p. 107). The present-day interest in meditative practices, the proliferation of religious sects, and the appeal of political ideologies all attest to the contemporary search for philosophical commitment.

Who am I? What is the meaning of life? Can life have any purpose if it ends in death? Does any aspect of personality survive death? What is the good life? Are there any good brave causes left? Is the human species worth preserving? Those who are never perplexed by such questions are either (depending on one's point of view) fortunate or less than fully human; in the modern world they must also be a minority. It is not the role of the school to provide answers to these questions. What the school can do is to give youth the intellectual equipment to understand which questions are meaningful and which are meaningless. At the same time, it can introduce students to some of the answers that have been proposed by those who have thought most deeply about these issues.

All this clearly entails much greater attention to the place of philosophy in the school curriculum. The serious teaching of logic, epistemology, ethics, and the history of ideas is, in the schools of the English-speaking world (unlike those of France), conspicuous by its absence. Efforts to have teachers of English or health, who themselves back a minimal philosophical training, teach "critical thinking" or "values clarification," while well-intentioned, may be little more than the bland leading the blind.

It is difficult to achieve validity in curriculum planning while ignoring the need for meaning. For one thing, this need is a basic motivation for learning. Phenix, who makes meaning the cornerstone of his approach to curriculum, remarks that "without hope, there is no incentive for learning, for the impulse to learn presupposes confidence in the possibility of improving one's existence" (1971, p. 275). Second, the individual's undirected search for personal meaning may take him or her in some desperate directions. One of the saddest of social indicators of the 1970s was the increasing rate of suicide among the young. Materialism, withdrawal, neurosis, violence, delinquency, political extremism, drug addiction, and adherence to bizarre religious cults may also be seen as individual responses to the search for, or the failure to find, personal meaning. The educator who can ignore the import of such manifestations has forfeited any claim to responsibility.

Social needs

Homo sapiens is a social being. The extrovert needs many social contacts, the introvert a few intimate friends. The true isolate is rare, and likely to have chosen the existence of a recluse not so much by disposition as on account of some deep wound in his or her own personal relationships.

If we are to consider human happiness as the primary guide and criterion for education—and what better ideal is there?—then a high priority must be given to developing in the young the capacity for mutually enriching relationships. A disturbing feature of contemporary hedonism is the legitimation of life-styles that have room only for exploitive personal and social encounters. It is debatable whether the individual's social needs can be fulfilled if other people are regarded solely as competitors or sources of gratification.

In any classroom or playground the perceptive observer can discern children who lack social skill or confidence. Without intervention, the behavior pattern established in childhood—whether dominating and aggressive or shy and lonely—is likely to become a permanent aspect of character. The reserved child is considered aloof and rejected by his or her peers; rejection leads to more self-absorption and greater unpopularity. There is nothing foreordained about this kind of vicious circle. Proven strategies exist for reinforcing social interaction between shy children and their peers. Such intervention, which essentially consists of training the child in specific skills and habits, can have lifelong effects.

There is a wider dimension to social needs than that for friendship. From their earliest days, children in our society view human suffering displayed on the television screen. Thousands die in floods, earthquakes, and war: the camera is there. A child's body is pulled from a lake: the ubiquitous reporter thrusts a microphone into the stunned faces of the

It is the individual who is not interested in his fellow men who has the greatest difficulties in life and provides the greatest injury to others. It is from among such individuals that all human failures spring.

—*Alfred Adler (1958, p. 253)*

> No one, to the day of my graduation, had ever taught me to look understandingly at a painting, or a tree, or the facade of a building.
>
> —*George F. Kennan, U.S. diplomat*

parents. It is easy, perhaps inevitable, to become inured through such exposure to the suffering others. When we consider what the world rather than what the individual needs, one answer may be that it needs education or reeducation in compassion. However difficult such an endeavor may be, few educational goals deserve more determined effort.

Aesthetic needs

Aesthetic experience, the experience of beauty, is clearly necessary neither for survival nor for a satisfying social life. Such experience is intrinsically valuable and therefore does not depend for its justification on being instrumental to the fulfillment of any other kind of need. Lives that lack an aesthetic dimension are not damaged: they are merely impoverished.

A utilitarian approach to education that recognizes as valid in schools only instrumental activities while failing to enquire about the ultimate end of such activities will have little time for aesthetic education. But almost equally damaging is the "fallacy of perfect obviousness in aesthetic education" (Schiralli, 1978). This fallacy maintains that aesthetic appreciation is "merely" a matter of taste, of "gut feelings" that are instantaneous, innate, and outside the scope of education. The teacher whose only approach to teaching a poem is to read it to the students and ask, "How do you feel about it?" is often a representative of this fallacy.

Once it is recognized that perception of beauty can be developed by deliberate training in both abstract concepts and ways of seeing, it follows that the school has an obligation to provide learners with sufficient training in major aesthetic areas that they can begin to identify those art forms that are personally most rewarding.

The capacity of human beings to communicate through works of art across the barriers of time, language, and culture, is a miracle that all students should be allowed to share. But the experience of beauty is not limited to contemplation of the literary, visual, or performing arts. A mathematical proof, an elegant checkmate, or a skillful surgical incision may each have aesthetic beauty in the eyes of an educated observer. People's lives will be enriched to the extent that they experience beauty in all aspects of their environment. In developing the capacity for such experience, the school has a major role to play.

Survival needs

Survival needs include drives directed both at survival of the organism and at survival of the species. The logic that would give survival needs priority in the school curriculum is fairly compelling, for without life there can be no learning.

To ascertain what schools can do to meet survival needs, one must first identify the causes of premature death. In the United States, accidents are the major cause of death between the age of one and forty-four years, with motor vehicle accidents predominant (National Safety Council, 1975). While most of these deaths are in principle preventable, so are many of the causes of death that begin to predominate after the age of forty-five, such as certain kinds of heart disease, cancer, and emphysema, which are often linked to such voluntary activities as diet, smoking, and exercise.

Clearly education can make a contribution to the preservation or prolongation of life by teaching highway and home safety; information about tobacco, alcohol, and drugs; basic skills in driving, swimming, and first aid; and sound habits in the areas of nutrition and physical fitness. On the broader scale, there is now considerable evidence from both developed and developing countries that greater reductions in morbidity and mortality are achieved by education in literacy and health than by medical discoveries and improved medical services (Carr-Hill and Magnussen, 1973).

In view of the importance of self-preservation, resistance in schools to teaching knowledge and skills conducive to survival is intriguing. The first programs cut in times of economic constraint tend to be driver training and swimming. First aid is rarely the focus of systematic instruction, while physical fitness has so low a priority that one study found that children were at their fitness peak the day they entered school and deteriorated steadily thereafter (Dilling and Weiss, 1975). What is ironic about such policies is that, compared to the majority of traditional academic subjects, most survival skills can be taught relatively rapidly and cheaply. Water safety and drownproofing, home safety, much of first aid, fire emergency procedures, pedestrian safety, and defensive driving can each be learned in a few hours. The Heimlich maneuver, a simple procedure that, since its discovery a few years ago has saved the lives of thousands of choking victims, can be learned in thirty minutes.

The argument against the serious teaching of survival skills in schools is usually twofold: first, such teaching is the responsibility of the home; and, second, as these skills are recognized as important, people can be expected to acquire them without the help of the school. Why these arguments apply to swimming and not to reading or mathematics is not clear. The first part of the argument prompts the query What is

STATEMENT	PERCENT OF CHILDREN AGREEING
A person having a stomachache should usually take a laxative.	50
A good way to care for a bad burn is to put butter on it.	42
Children who cannot swim well should depend upon a tire innertube for safety.	42
When a boat you are in overturns, it is best to leave the boat and swim to shore.	38
Most accidents cannot be prevented.	29

Table 3–2   Safety concepts of sixth-graders (Dzenowagis, 1963)

the responsibility of the school to the children of irresponsible parents? The second part leads logically to the interesting conclusion that those learnings recognized as important will be learned outside the school, which leaves as the function of the school the teaching only of knowledge and skills whose significance is obscure.

It can be maintained that the more directly a learning is related to actual physical survival, the higher its priority should be. But knowledge in such areas as nutrition, in Western nations, is linked not so much to avoidance of starvation as to maintenance of an optimal physiological state. It has, in other words, as much to do with the quality as with the length of life. To some extent, the same is true of sexual needs. Obviously sex education is not necessary to the survival of the species. It is justified insofar as it contributes to the personally and socially functional expression of sexual drives, for the frustration of such drives interferes with the fulfillment of every other type of human need.

Each curriculum worker can devise his or her own hierarchy of human needs, in which both the categories and the priorities will vary with his or her value system. The five areas outlined above are neither exhaustive nor mutually exclusive: they are simply significant for the full development of personality.

Reflection on basic human needs quickly reveals how restrictive is an approach that makes conventional subject categories the starting point for curriculum development. The disciplines have a significant place in curriculum, and although, as Mauritz Johnson remarked (1979), it is better to begin with them than to end with them, to make the disciplines the starting point for curriculum is to bypass crucial value issues and to adopt uncritically assumptions that are open to question.

It is clear that the schools are not in fact teaching the kinds of learnings that equip a citizen for survival and social contribution. . . . The study of curriculum material . . . reveals that much of the reason for this is the absence of much critical, and the presence of much trivial content therein. The study of process, and of resource allocation and school management confirm the same conclusion. My assessment of the effects of schools is that they have spent far too much time and money on "new curricula" which are simply new versions of the old components in the curricula, and not indeed new curricula at all. There has been little significant payoff from these exercises, speaking in terms of the global needs. . . . We have the capability to teach what we ought to teach, and we have the resources. But we have simply not re-examined the needs that education should serve.

—*Michael Scriven (1974)*

The basic principle of curriculum development remains: *All valid curricula help people to meet their significant needs; all other curricula are a waste of time.*

Forecasting and Curriculum Design

If significant human needs are to become the foundation for curriculum, it is clearly insufficient to analyze the needs of people in the past. What makes curriculum planning especially problematic is that analysis of present needs is also inadequate. Curriculum design is essentially future-oriented, and it is the future needs of people that must be assessed.

Many of the world's best schools are doing an excellent job of preparing their students for life as it was in the 1960s and 1970s. But the students who are presently in school will embark on their careers in the 1980s and 1990s, will still be relatively young in the year 2000, and will reach early retirement age in the 2020s. The world for which students must be prepared is not the world of today, but the world of the next fifty years. Curriculum designers are nothing if they are not planners, and as planners they are useless unless they have the future in their bones. Constantinos Doxiadis puts it like this:

> Dealing merely with the present is unrealistic because by the time we have analyzed the situation, defined our problems, and planned how to meet them, the present has become the past; by the time we are ready to act and create new conditions, the present is the distant past. It is time that we learned to think about the present as a dynamically changing situation. If

we wish to ameliorate the conditions of our life, we have to think far ahead in order to understand where we are going and to define whether we like our destination or not. If we do not like it, we must decide how we can take a different road at some time in the future, which, when we act, will be the present. It is for these reasons that we must start thinking about life in the year 2000, life in the year 2050, life in the year 2100 (Doxiadis, 1967, p. 12).

This is not to say that curricula for the future should not include content from the past. To say that would be to repudiate the very concept of culture. If anything, it is to be hoped that the thought of Socrates, the painting of Turner, and the music of Beethoven will play a greater rather than a smaller part in the curricula of the future. Curriculum designers are planners, and the milieu of planners is history. One dimension of history is the past, and the other dimension is the future.

The schools, it is sometimes claimed, should not make a response until a demand has been expressed by society. Unfortunately, by the time the public has become aware of and aroused about an issue, the situation is often approaching catastrophe, and there is insufficient time for adequate planning. The result is that many of our public institutions that follow this "wait and see" philosophy—and they include governments as well as school systems—can only stagger from one crisis to the next, making every decision on the basis of expediency. This kind of decision making prevents institutions from taking initiatives, which the public has the right to expect them to take, and makes the decision-maker the hostage of particular interest groups. The educational system that attempts to make careful predictions is better placed to observe developing social trends and pressures, to influence public debate on emerging issues, and to make a reasoned response at the appropriate moment.

Prophecy in our age is regarded with suspicion, and the wild predictions of doom by some "futurologists," exaggerated in turn by sensationalist journalism, justify such suspicion. A misunderstanding of the nature of exponential growth and ignorance of systemic self-regulation has led to many forecasts of obvious absurdity: that there will eventually be "standing room only" on the earth or that we will all wake up one morning gasping for air as the world runs out of oxygen. The reputation of forecasting was not enhanced by one celebrated and superficially sophisticated prediction of calamity, *The Limits to Growth* (Meadows et al.), published in 1972, which had to be subsequently retracted by its spon-

Generals are always fighting the last war, and educators are always instructing the last generation.

—*John Wilkinson, educator*

sors, the Club of Rome, as mathematically incorrect (Hudson Institute Europe, 1974, p. 56).

But despite the excesses that have brought the field into disrepute, the striking feature of many predictions made in this century is their accuracy. The works of Jules Verne and H. G. Wells are well-known examples. Many of the technical developments of the 1970s, such as automated purchasing, ocean mining, the manned space laboratory, and synthetic body organs, were accurately predicted in the late 1950s. To describe the year 2050 is difficult; but to describe the year 1990 is less so, because what happens in 1990 is largely dependent on present events and on policies and decisions initiated now. Many of the factors that influence our lives today were apparent to the perceptive observer thirty years ago. They include atomic energy, jet propulsion, television, guerilla warfare, overpopulation in the Third World, national independence movements, the use of terrorism as an instrument of politics, and the emergence of the superstates.

Technical Developments

The educator who seeks to prepare students for life in the future must attempt to distinguish those present trends that will become increasingly significant in the future. These will include social, political, ideological, and technical trends, all of which are intimately related. By way of example, let us look at two technical trends.

The first of these is related to the rapid development of automatic storage and retrieval of information made possible by the computer. One aspect of this development is the multiplication of files of information on individual citizens. While this has some undoubted possibilities for good, let us examine some of the disquieting implications.

The day when there is an enormous and detailed file of information on every citizen, which can be accessed in seconds, is not in the future; it has already arrived. Government files contain details of citizens' health, income, debts, property, driving records, foreign travel, and political and charitable donations. Life insurance companies pool their data on the medical history, health risk, and life expectancy of all those who apply for life insurance. Banks and credit companies have a detailed picture of the individual's financial status, including his or her income, expenditures, debts, securities, and credit ratings. Employment agencies use investigators to find out about prospective employees' life-styles, friends and family, driving and drinking habits, and physical and mental health. Telephone companies, gasoline credit agencies, and airlines store in their data banks details of communications and travel by their customers. The police maintain huge data banks containing photographs,

BY 1990	
Alternative energy development	Extensive ocean farming
Automated libraries	Fuel cell automobile
Automated medicine	Magnetic suspension railways
Automated psychological counseling	Manned landing on Mars
Automatic language translation	Synthetic food from inorganic matter
Cheap pocket computers	Wide laser and maser application

BY 2020	
Artificial vision and hearing	Limb transplants
Communication with animals	Permanent moon base
Controlled nuclear fusion	Superperformance structural materials
Control of parapsychological healing	Three-dimensional television
Electronic communication with brain	Weather control
General immunization	Zero population growth

BY 2050	
Artificial enhancement of intelligence	Organ and limb regeneration
Brain transplants	Suspended animation
Control of ageing	Synthetic bodies
Gravity control	Three-dimensional telephone
Matter transmission	True artificial intelligence
Nuclear rocket propulsion	Wireless power transmission

Table 3–3   Possible technical developments in the next seventy years (Adapted from Toffler, 1970; Bell, 1973; Kahn, Brown, and Martel, 1976)

fingerprints, aliases, associates, and method of operation of criminals and other citizens in whom they may be interested. All this information can be retrieved in seconds from remote terminals connected to the central data banks by telephone line. Governments and private agencies share much of their information; information that is supposedly secret can be obtained for a price on a thriving information black market (Canada, Departments of Justice and Communications, 1972; National Computer Center, 1973).

We are probably only at the beginning of this development. A few people, working in government and business, have realized what the computer has made possible: that information is now the primary product and means to wealth and power in Western society. Information technology enables an investigator to compose quickly and cheaply a picture of you that is more accurate, objective, and complete than the picture you have of yourself; a skillful analyst can then predict your future behavior with phenomenal accuracy. Such predictions are of obvious value to those who are interested in lending you money, selling you goods, insuring your life, hiring you, winning your vote, or having you arrested. Institutions are learning more and more about individuals, but individuals know little about these institutions, about the files businesses and government agencies have on them, when and how often the files are used, by whom, and for what purposes.

As the number of computers in use is doubling at least every three years, it seems unlikely that information technology is going to be halted or slowed down. The curriculum designer must therefore come up with something more creative than indignation or resignation. The minimal requirement is that students learn something of the techniques and potential of information technology, the agencies that hold information about them, when and how to give and to withhold information, how to use what legal protection exists, and how to use the information industry to their own advantage. Information technology, like other technologies, has the potential for creating a two-class society, composed of those who use technology and of those who are used by it. It is one of the obligations of the curriculum planner to prevent as many students as possible from becoming the victims of technology.

Another example of technical change may be drawn from the fields of transplant surgery and synthesis of body parts. Surgical transplants were apparently attempted in the Middle Ages; it is not the concept, but its successful application that is modern. Freezing techniques and computer analysis of tissue compatibility have increased the scope of this kind of surgery, which is now well established for corneas, bone marrow, and kidneys, and less so for hearts. According to an American delegate at an international symposium on transplant surgery in 1972,

> Transplanting the brain, which until yesterday was the last frontier of experimental surgery, has today been overcome, even if all its problems have not been resolved. . . The tests we have tried with animals . . . show us that we are on the right road, and we will continue on it (Reuters, 1972).

Many successful brain transplants have already been performed on fishes, dogs, and apes. A successful human brain transplant is probably not far away. Our whole definition of life and death will be altered by the knowledge that the brain can be transplanted into a succession of bodies, each of which can be discarded as it wears out.

The process of developing artificial body parts has progressed in parallel with transplant technology. In recent years synthetic joints, larynxes, ureters, pacemakers, and heart valves have been implanted in humans, and synthetic hearts in animals. The union of transplantation and synthesis presents the possibility of transplanting a human brain into a body that is completely man-made. Such a body might be built to look and behave exactly like a natural human body, or it could be given superior capabilities: X-ray and infrared vision, superhuman speed or strength. It is theoretically possible to link the brain directly to an internal or external computer, enormously amplifying the speed and accuracy with which it could process information. Finally, research into artificial intelligence compels us to ask what kind of creature we would have if a synthetic body were equipped with an artificial brain, programmed with the memories, concepts, tastes, and abilities of a particular human being.

These issues are not raised to suggest that the curriculum planner should necessarily aim to produce scientists capable and willing to do such work. The wider questions concern the fact that our technology is constantly outrunning our ability to deal with the social, moral, and ethical issues it raises. This is illustrated by contemporary discussion of medical techniques that artificially extend the physical existence of terminally ill patients. This issue is relatively simple compared to the problems that will be raised by brain transplantation and synthesis and their implications for the extension and definition of human life.

Let us suppose that the first totally synthetic human body becomes available for installation with a human brain thirty years from now. The surgeons who will perform the operation, the nurses and technicians who will provide support, the journalists who will inform the public, the editorialists and preachers who will comment, the legislators who will enact the appropriate laws and the judges who will enforce them, and the general public who will look on: most of these people are now in school, and if they are to escape ethical and intellectual chaos, it is now that the appropriate intellectual and ethical foundations must be laid.

Manpower Forecasting

Earlier in this chapter, the assumption that increased years of schooling would lead to increased employability was rejected as fallacious. This is not to say that employment considerations should not influence the curriculum. A curriculum based entirely on vocational concerns would

---

Meanwhile, back in the social studies classroom, pupils are being readied for the crucial challenge via guided tours through the historical dustbin.

—*H. G. Vonk (1973, p. 514)*

One man's dustbin is another man's treasure house.

—*Mauritz Johnson (1979)*

overlook many human needs. But a curriculum that ignores a learner's future economic contribution to society leaves the graduate vulnerable in many areas.

Despite the talk about increased leisure and acceptance of alternatives to employment, there is little evidence that fewer people of working age are holding or seeking jobs, or that many employers are shortening the work day, or that society is prepared to accept unemployment as a legitimate way of life. It would be unwise for the schools to assume that there will in the near future be a radical change in the personal significance of employment.

The man or woman who works 7 hours a day, 5 days a week, 47 weeks for 40 years will spend 65,800 hours on the job: a tenth of all the hours in a 75-year life span, and five times the hours spent in school. Work will influence life-style, family, choice of friends, mobility, expectation of life, and happiness. If this pattern continues to be the norm, even in modified fashion, then it is a function of the school to prepare students for the kind of work that will suit them best. The school cannot discharge this responsibility simply by the award of a degree or diploma. Whatever other qualities they may have, college and school graduates who enter the job market without technical or professional training have "nothing to sell which it is worth anyone's money to buy" (Wiener, 1954, p. 154).

Although manpower forecasting is an inexact art, certain general predictions can be made. One is that in a world of economic and technical competition, a nation can maintain its living standards only by heavy investment in high-technology industries and hence in scientific and technical education. On the basis of this assumption, the *Hudson Report,* an uncompromising assessment of the future of Great Britain, declared

It is not enough simply to survey existing patterns of employment: it is the *future* pattern of manpower requirements that must guide today's educational decisions. The reason is that the "lead time" in producing qualified manpower is exceptionally long. . . . The educational planner must have in mind the prospective patterns of manpower requirements at least a decade or two in advance.

—*H. S. Parnes (1968, p. 263)*

bluntly that "Britain today educates too few people, and for the wrong subjects" and continued,

> It seems increasingly probable that the British graduate of the 1980s will find himself required to seek inappropriate work in such fields as supermarket management, factory floor supervision, or insurance sales because he has not received a formation that is relevant to the contemporary needs of the British economy (Hudson Insitute Europe, 1974, pp. 85, 90).

As an example of a missed opportunity by Britain to recognize the manpower implications of technical advance, the *Hudson Report* pointed to the development of the North Sea oil fields. It was evident from the 1960s that skilled manpower would be needed for this work. Yet it was not Britain, but Norway, which established a School of Navigation and Engineering for this purpose; by the peak drilling period of 1973–1974, over 60 percent of the drillers working the North Sea oil rigs were Norwegian (Hudson Institute Europe, 1974, p. 78).

In the same frame of mind, one might inquire in whose interest it is that in West Africa, a region desperately in need of civil engineers, agriculturalists, and health workers, significant numbers of students should be maintained at great cost in universities where they study Homer from the original Greek (Bowden, 1971).

A degree of sophistication is required to forecast exact technical skills that will be in demand a decade from now. It requires rather less expertise to guess what general capabilities will be needed. They will certainly include imagination, adaptability, and versatility, and even such old-fashioned qualities as accuracy, thoroughness, reliability, and "ability to read without lip-reading and without a glazing of the eyeballs whenever a word of more than two syllables comes along" (Rafferty, 1974, p. 173).

The combination of manpower forecasting (which is properly an aspect of planning, not of crystal gazing) with skilled vocational guidance and development of appropriate curricula should not be taken to imply constraint of students' freedom. That freedom can only be enhanced by enabling them to make intelligent career choices, by reducing the threat of unemployment, and by helping graduates assume the role in which they will achieve the greatest satisfaction. "The central function of the school," according to one writer, "is to provide legitimate grounds for self-respect" (Foshay, 1970, p. 21). There are few faster or surer routes to the loss of self-respect than unemployment. Educators who, in the name of "humanistic" education or any other slogan, refuse to entertain manpower considerations in educational planning should ponder whether anything is less humane than for their students to experience unemployment or demeaning, inappropriate employment after years of well-intentioned and hopeful endeavor under their tutelage.

Economic conditions in the Western world in the last part of this century suggest two main vocational responsibilities for the school. The first is to provide students with the qualities that will enable them to fill existing and emerging jobs effectively. The second is to develop in students entrepreneurial skills and attitudes enabling them to generate employment by the invention and marketing of valuable goods and services. These linked responsibilities will require curriculum planners to pay much greater attention to economic, social, technical, and manpower analysis than has been evident in the past.

At the same time, the educator should remember that other basic needs cannot be met by employment alone. An education that aims only at occupational competence is as much a distortion as schooling that views the entire question of employment with distaste.

The Limitations of "Armchair" Needs Assessment

So far, the question of determining the needs of learners has been discussed as if the curriculum designer were acting unilaterally. The curriculum designer, whether a specialist designing curriculum for a school system or a teacher designing a course for his or her classroom, is by definition the person charged with the task of deciding which needs a particular curriculum is intended to meet. As has been suggested, such decision making is to a great extent a valuing process, and the curriculum developed will reflect the designer's concept of the nature of humanity and aspirations for the future of society. In principle, a curriculum is not so much a policy as a proposal, which is subject to approval by the designer's superiors: school administrators or elected officials. But in practice, particularly at the classroom level, what the curriculum designer or teacher decides will usually determine the instruction that the students receive. These decisions are always made prior to the delivery of instruction; if they are not made deliberately and openly, they are made subconsciously and privately.

What has been proposed so far may suggest that a good deal can be achieved by hard and independent thought, and indeed this is an activity much undervalued by educators. But it is not enough. The curriculum designer is not omniscient, and a unilateral needs assessment may seriously misjudge the needs of the learners or may be a projection of the designer's own needs. One of Maslow's many contributions to the study of human needs was to point to the essential subjectivity of people's thinking on the subject:

> For our chronically and extremely hungry man, Utopia can be defined simply as a place where there is plenty of food. He tends to think that, if only

he is guaranteed food for the rest of his life, he will be perfectly happy and will never want anything more. Life itself tends to be defined in terms of eating. Anything else will be defined as unimportant (Maslow, 1954, p. 81).

While the hungry man is biased in his assessment of his needs, Maslow observed that the well-fed man is also biased in his assessment of his own and other people's need for food. This principle, that an individual cannot by himself accurately assess the needs of other people, is illuminating. It helps to explain why educators with lifetime tenure of comfortable positions undervalue students' needs for employment skills. A modicum of caution is required by those who venture to speak for other people. Much of the world's tribulation, according to some analysts, springs from the faulty definition of children's needs by their own parents.

The Brazilian educator, Paulo Freire, reached the same conclusion by a different route:

> In a long conversation with Malraux, Mao Tse-Tung declared, "You know I've proclaimed for a long time: we must teach the masses clearly what we have received from them confusedly." This affirmation contains an entire dialogical theory of how to construct the program content of education, which cannot be elaborated according to what the *educator* thinks is best for *his* students (Freire, 1970, p. 82).

One might not want to go quite so far. If the curriculum designer has and can acquire no special insight into human needs beyond that of the average citizen, then he or she is in the wrong field. What can be agreed is that the curriculum should not be developed *solely* according to what the educator thinks best. The next chapter discusses specific strategies for obtaining input from other sources into the assessment of human needs.

ACTIVITIES

1. Think of all the significant human needs you can. Group and rank them in order of priority. What changes does your analysis suggest in the existing school curriculum?

2. What significant needs should the school *not* attempt to meet? Do any general conclusions follow?

3. Write out a justification for a subject you teach or have taught. Challenge a colleague to justify his or her curriculum area.

4. Identify some instances in which the school subordinates the interests of the child or adolescent to the interests of others. In which instances is this justified?

5. Write down the dates 1990, 2000, 2010, 2020. Then write beside each the most significant event, discovery, invention, or change you think will have taken place by that date. What are the implications for curriculum?

6. What would be the implications for the curriculum if (a) more women were employed than men; (b) average length of marriages decreased to five years; (c) population decreased by 1 percent per annum; (d) scientists learned how to prevent ageing in humans; (e) half the population was over fifty years old; (f) full-scale pocket computers cost twenty dollars; (g) it became feasible to monitor people's thoughts without their knowledge?

QUESTIONS

1. All school programs consume time and other social resources. For this reason

   a.   authorities should permit the introduction only of inexpensive programs
   b.   educators should present a justification for proposed and existing curricula
   c.   the costs of schooling should be borne by the learners and/or their families
   d.   a curriculum should not be changed or discarded until it has been in operation at least five years

2. If the average student stays in school longer and follows a general academic curriculum, a probable economic effect will be an overall increase in

   a.   the educational level of the unemployed
   b.   the development or production of skilled manpower
   c.   the proportion of the population in the work force
   d.   economic productivity as reflected in the gross national product

3. The most important justification of a curriculum rests on evidence that it

   a.   will train the minds of the learners
   b.   meets a significant need of the learners
   c.   contains knowledge that has intrinsic value
   d.   will be taught by dedicated and enthusiastic teachers

4. Which of the following is one conventional definition of the term *need?*

   a.   something a person feels the lack of
   b.   a want that will be satisfied by a curriculum
   c.   a discrepancy between an actual and an optimal state
   d.   some quality, experience, or object considered to have value

5. Which of the following needs must normally be met before a person can attend to the other needs?

   a.   social needs
   b.   aesthetic needs
   c.   need for meaning
   d.   physiological needs

6. Which of the following is most clearly a "survival skill"?

   a. ability to ski
   b. ability to program a computer
   c. ability to correct a rear-wheel skid
   d. ability to read at least one foreign language

7. The major resource, in terms of value and quantity, used in education is

   a. teachers' time
   b. taxpayers' money
   c. administrative skill
   d. the time of learners

8. Which of the following curricula have the greatest potential for enhancing the future happiness of individuals?

   a. curricula in music and drama
   b. curricula in history and geography
   c. curricula in job selection and mate selection
   d. curricula in algebra, trigonometry, and geometry

9. In which of the following programs would the "clients" or "beneficiaries" be most likely to include people other than the students?

   a. prenatal classes
   b. fourth-grade mathematics
   c. an extracurricular course in music appreciation
   d. a Master of Business Administration program

10. Curricula have a reasonable likelihood of improving the employability of graduates provided that

   a. the curricula emphasize the basics
   b. students stay in school long enough
   c. students obtain some formal educational qualifications
   d. the curricula enable graduates to provide needed goods and services

Check your answers against the key in Appendix 2.
9 or 10 right: You understand the material presented.
8 or 7 right: Review the areas of uncertainty.
6 or less right: Reread the chapter.

Recommended Reading

Bell, Daniel. *The coming of post-industrial society*. New York: Basic Books, 1973. Bell's "essay in social forecasting" is distinguished by the great depth and breadth of its scholarship. Analyzing social, political, economic, and philosophical issues, Bell never strays far from his central question: What is the nature of the good life?

Frankl, Victor E. *Man's search for meaning: An introduction to logotherapy.* Boston: Beacon Press, 1962. An eloquent personal record of the development of an existentialist philosophy, by a psychiatrist who survived the Nazi concentration camps. Frankl makes a persuasive case that people do not need a reduction in tension so much as they need to discover meaning in life and to commit themselves to the pursuit of worthwhile goals.

Freire, Paulo. *Pedagogy of the oppressed.* New York: Herder and Herder, 1970. Freire's experiences in schooling in the Third World yield insights of profound significance for education everywhere. Freire's concern is to replace dominating education by liberating education, which "consists in acts of cognition, not transferrals of information."

Kahn, Herman, William Brown, and Leon Martel. *The next 200 years: A scenario for America and the world.* New York: Morrow, 1976. A serious but generally optimistic attempt to envision technical, political, and social change over the next two centuries, to map the uncertainties, and to identify the policy issues that will confront society.

Maslow, A. H. *Motivation and personality.* New York: Harper, 1954. Maslow's attempt to develop a taxonomy of human needs is still worth reading for its good sense on the question of needs and its commitment to humanistic values.

Scriven, Michael. Education for survival. In Kevin Ryan and James M. Cooper (eds.), *Kaleidoscope.* 2nd ed. Boston: Houghton Mifflin, 1975, pp. 128–150. A comprehensive discussion of basic needs that the school could meet. With characteristic incisiveness, Scriven argues that "the magnitude of the mismatch between our education and our needs has been grossly underestimated by even the 'extremist' critics."

White, J. P. *Towards a compulsory curriculum.* London: Routledge and Kegan Paul, 1973. White is an eloquent representative of the British school of educational philosophy, which tends to give pride of place in curriculum to the pursuit of knowledge. White analyzes the philosophical basis for selecting curriculum priorities and discusses the conditions under which it is justifiable to constrain the freedom of students to choose what they learn.

References

Adler, Alfred. *What life should mean to you.* New York: Capricorn Books, 1958.

Beer, Stafford. *Designing freedom.* CBC Massey Lectures, 1973. Toronto: Canadian Broadcasting Corporation Publications, 1974.

Bell, Daniel. *The coming of post-industrial society.* New York: Basic Books, 1973.

Berg, Ivar. *Education and jobs: The great training robbery.* Boston: Beacon Press, 1971.

Bowden, Lord. Dunning Trust Lecture. Kingston, Canada: Queen's University, October 5, 1971.

Canada, Departments of Justice and Communications. *Privacy and computers.* Ottawa: Queen's Printer, 1972.

Carr-Hill, Roy, and Olav Magnussen. *Indicators of performance of educational systems.* Paris: Organization for Economic Cooperation and Development, 1973.

Cronbach, Lee J. *Educational psychology*. 3rd ed. New York: Harcourt Brace Jovanovich, 1977.

De Bono, Edward. *Children solve problems*. New York: Harper & Row, 1974.

Debray, Regis. *Che's guerrilla war*. Harmondsworth, England: Penguin, 1976.

Dilling, H. J., and Debrah Weiss. *Fitness and our youth*. Scarborough, Canada: Scarborough Board of Education Research Department, 1975.

Doxiadis, Constantinos A. Life in the year 2000. *National Education Association Journal*, 1967, 56 (8), 12–14.

Dzenowagis, Joseph G. Prevalence of certain dangerous safety misconceptions among a group of sixth-grade children. *Journal of School Health*, 1963, 33, 26–32.

Economic Council of Canada. *Annual Report, 1965*. Ottawa: Queen's Printer, 1965.

Ellis, Henry C. *The transfer of learning*. New York: Macmillan, 1965.

Etzioni, A. *A comparative analysis of complex organizations*. New York: Free Press, 1961.

Foshay, Arthur W. *Curriculum for the 70s: An agenda for invention*. Washington, D.C.: National Education Association, 1970.

Frankl, Victor E. *Man's search for meaning: An introduction to logotherapy*. Boston: Beacon Press, 1962.

Freire, Paulo. *Pedagogy of the oppressed*. New York: Herder and Herder, 1970.

Hall, Edward T. *The silent language*. New York: Doubleday, 1959.

Harris, Robin. The plight of the academic dogma. *University Affairs*, 1973, 14, 8.

Howard, John H., and Clark Gilmour. Success and failure in management training. *Canadian Training Methods*, 1975, 7 (April), 12–15.

Hudson Institute Europe. *The United Kingdom in 1980: The Hudson Report*. London: Associated Business Programmes, 1974.

Johnson, Mauritz. Personal communication, February 1979.

Kahn, Herman, William Brown, and Leon Martel. *The next 200 years: A scenario for America and the world*. New York: Morrow, 1976.

Komisar, B. Paul. "Need" and the needs-curriculum. In B. Othanel Smith and Robert H. Ennis (eds.), *Language and concepts in education*. Chicago: Rand McNally, 1961, pp. 24–42.

Maslow, A. H. *Motivation and personality*. New York: Harper & Row, 1954.

McClelland, William A., and Harold Wagner. Quality control in technical military training programs. *New Directions for Program Evaluation*, 1978, 3, 27–36.

Meadows, Donella H., Dennis L. Meadows, Jørgen Randers, and William W. Behrens III. *The limits to growth*. New York: New American Library, 1972.

National Computer Center. *Privacy, computers, and you*. Rochelle Park, N.Y.: Hayden, 1973.

National Safety Council. *Accident facts*. Chicago, Ill.: N. A. C., 1975.

Organization for Economic Cooperation and Development. *The nature of the curriculum for the eighties and onwards*. Paris: OECD, Organization for Economic Cooperation and Development, Center for Educational Research and Innovation, 1972.

Parnes, H. S. Manpower analysis in educational planning. In M. Blaug (ed.), *Economics of education 1: Selected readings*. Harmondsworth, England: Penguin, 1968, pp. 263–273.

Phenix, Philip H. Transcendence and the curriculum. *Teachers College Record*, 1971, 73, 271–283.

Rafferty, Max. American education: 1975–2000. In Theodore W. Hepple (ed.), *The future of education, 1975–2000.* Pacific Palisades, Cal.: Goodyear Publishing Co., 1974, pp. 159–180.

Reuters, press report. July 7, 1972.

Richmond, W. Kenneth. *The school curriculum.* London: Methuen, 1971.

Schiralli, Martin G. The fallacy of perfect obviousness in aesthetic education. *McGill Journal of Education,* 1978, 12 (3), 80–90.

Scriven, Michael. Assessment of educational effects. Symposium at Annual Meeting of American Educational Research Association, Chicago, April 1974.

_____ , and Jane Roth. Needs assessment: Concept and practice. *New Directions for Program Evaluation,* 1978, 1, 1–11.

Thorndike, Edward L. *The principles of teaching based on psychology.* New York: A. G. Seiler, 1906.

_____ , and R. S. Woodworth. The influence of improvement in one mental function upon the efficiency of other functions. *Psychological Review,* 1901, 8, 247–261, 384–395, 553–568.

Toffler, Alvin. *Future shock.* New York: Random House, 1970.

Tyler, Ralph W. *Basic principles of curriculum and instruction.* Chicago: University of Chicago Press, 1950.

UNESCO. *Statistical yearbook 1973.* Paris: UNESCO, 1974.

University Affairs. News item. November 8, 1977, p. 16.

Vonk, H. G. Education and the 27-Year countdown. *Phi Delta Kappan,* 1973, 54, 514–517.

Webster's New Collegiate Dictionary. Springfield, Mass.: Merriam, 1973.

Wiener, Norbert. *The human use of human beings: Cybernetics and society.* Boston: Houghton Mifflin, 1954.

Part Two

PRELIMINARY STEPS IN A CURRICULUM PROJECT

4

PRINCIPLES

- The function of needs assessment is to identify and validate needs and to establish priorities.

- Needs assessment may examine the whole range of learner needs, or it may research one need in detail.

- The needs assessors should approach a wide range of people who have special knowledge, influence, or a right to be consulted.

- The most efficient way to conduct a needs assessment may often be to use a ready-made needs assessment package.

- Both subjective opinion and objective data should be collected.

- The limitations of public opinion make it necessary that needs assessment not be viewed as curriculum decision making by referendum.

- At the conclusion of needs assessment, the primary need to be addressed by the curriculum developers should be clearly stated.

CONCEPTS

Needs assessment   Social indicator
Problem   Brainstorming

4

Needs Assessment

*No single source of information is adequate to pro-
vide a basis for wise and comprehensive decisions about
the objectives of the school.*

—Ralph W. Tyler (1949, p. 4)

Needs Assessment in Curriculum

The term *needs assessment* refers to an array of procedures for identifying and validating needs and establishing priorities among them. Needs
assessment has been increasingly recognized as a necessary part of curriculum design since the United States Department of Health, Education,
and Welfare began to demand in the 1960s that school districts undertake
comprehensive studies to justify their requests for funds. In the past
decade declining school enrollments, economic stringency, and public
pressure have forced many school systems to reassess their goals; several
state legislatures have mandated needs assessment to meet demands for

educational accountability (Deleonibus, 1977). In the early 1970s an absence of detailed guidance on needs assessment often resulted in heavy reliance being placed on unsupported opinions gathered in surveys and a tendency to overlook distinctions between objective and subjective data, needs and goals, and causes and symptoms. These problems persist but cannot be blamed on a shortage of published research; since about 1975, publication on needs assessment has become a growth industry. At the same time, attention is switching to a new problem: that the results of district and state-wide needs assessment often have little impact on curriculum development at the school and classroom level (Witkin, 1976). This chapter outlines procedures that can be used on either a small or a large scale by curriculum workers who want to base their designs on a solid foundation of established client need.

General Needs Assessment

Curriculum development may begin either with a general assessment of needs or with a specific problem the curriculum designer attempts to resolve. The classroom teacher usually begins with a specific question, such as how the students' reading abilities can be improved. Or the teacher begins with a set of issues within narrow parameters; for example, what mathematical skills students need. But for a school or a school system embarking on a major consideration of its curriculum, it is preferable not to reduce the overall issue in the first instance to questions of what to teach within particular disciplines, but to consider the whole range of human needs and capabilities. General needs assessment will accordingly be discussed first, and assessment of specific needs subsequently.

The primary question in a general needs assessment is What human needs should the school endeavor to meet? The answer may pose a challenge to existing educational goals, laws, and codes. How far those who conduct and report a needs assessment are willing to live with that challenge will determine the scope of the needs assessment. This decision will have to be faced at the beginning of and throughout a needs assessment.

Needs assessment involves the collection of both opinion and factual data. One of the main innovations of the process is that it requires obtaining judgments from all the main constituents of the schools. The traditional "armchair needs assessment" relied primarily on educators to identify needs and risked institutionalizing and perpetuating the blind spots of this particular subculture in the school curriculum.

As the process is a public one and often (although not necessarily) expensive, official approval is needed before the work begins.

Blind Spot

Hold this page at arm's length. Close your right eye. Look steadily at the round dot with your left eye, and bring the page slowly towards you. At a certain point the square will seem to disappear.

This blind spot is always present in your vision. What about blind spots in our moral, ethical, social, aesthetic, and intellectual perception?

Sources of opinion

Three groups of people need to be consulted in a general needs assessment. They are: (1) people who have a right to be consulted; (2) people whom it is politically expedient to consult and (3) people who have special insight or expertise.

Parents and taxpayers are among those who have a right to be consulted. Their opinions will tend to spring from their own experience of schooling and its relation to their lives. However subjective their opinions, the aspirations they maintain for their children have an authenticity that demands respect.

Politically influential individuals and pressure groups should be identified at an early stage. These people may be in a position to affect the implementation of any curriculum that is subsequently developed. They may include committees within government offices of education and teacher organizations, members of school boards and parent-teacher associations, certain school administrators or teachers, religious or political groups with special interests in education, individual legislators, and commentators in the media. If such people are not consulted, they are more likely to oppose new curriculum designs on principle. The process of consultation will help the designer determine which curriculum possibilities can count on their immediate or eventual support and which others are politically unfeasible. Valuable cooperation can often be generated at this stage by treating the opinions received with respect. At the same time, the designers must avoid making commitments to partisan points of view.

Students might be included by right, since they or their successors

What a wise parent would desire for his own children, that a nation, insofar as it is wise, must desire for all children.

—*R. H. Tawney*

will be on the receiving end of the proposed curricula. In addition, they often have valuable insights into curriculum. "The school that I'd like," wrote a fifteen-year-old in a British survey, "would be one whose primary aim was to teach me how to live and make me a responsible member of society." Another student proposed that "the basic premise is that the teacher and the school have unlimited faith in the capabilities of the pupil." "I don't think I would get on very well in my ideal school," wrote a third, "because I am too used to being told what to do." (Blishen, 1969, pp. 66, 87, 64.) Even much younger children, in the writer's experience, have a keen appreciation of more and less worthwhile school activities.

Teachers by training, interest, and occupation should be expected to have special knowledge of the educational needs of students. They are well placed to observe the reaction of pupils to different instructional content. While too many curricula are based exclusively on the views of teachers, or even of a single teacher, attention should be paid to the opinion of the professionals as to what is feasible and desirable for the learners. Inclusion of teachers at this stage will also help to reduce teacher anxiety about impending curriculum changes. For political reasons, representatives from teacher organizations should also be invited to provide input.

Academic specialists have almost complete control of curricula in higher education. At the secondary level they have also had considerable influence through participation in curriculum development, or by assuming responsibility for setting college entrance requirements and other external examinations that have often dictated the content of secondary curricula (Young, 1971). King and Brownell (1966) claimed that the only people entitled to participate in curriculum planning were scholars qualified in the disciplines. This pursuit of the academic imperative has often resulted in secondary-school curricula that are watered-down university courses. One danger of relying too heavily on academic opinion in needs assessment is, as Eash suggested (1975, p. 5), the ultimate production of curricula that will provide students with theoretical knowledge "along the line acquired by hundreds of now unemployed Ph.D.'s, but with inadequate general knowledge of the skills commonly used by the layman." Academic specialists have an important contribution to make to curriculum development. They can also provide valuable judgments at the needs-assessment stage, but to do so they have to be asked the appropriate questions. Such a question is not Why do we need expert mathematicians or historians, and how do we develop them? but What basic human needs can your discipline help to meet? To this question, specialists who have a broad grasp of their discipline and its underlying philosophy are likely to provide the most reasoned and productive response.

Social experts, such as sociologists, psychologists, and anthropologists, can provide professional opinion on human needs.

Employers are commonly consulted in the design of vocational and technical courses. There is equal justification for consulting them in the design of such subjects as English and mathematics. A study at Laurentian University in Canada aimed to help mathematics teachers ensure that their students were adequately prepared in mathematical skills they would need in employment. More than 170 industries, businesses, and government agencies were visited to determine which mathematical procedures and applications were most commonly used and needed by employees. The results were the basis for production of "resource material from which teachers may draw practical illustrations of the use of various mathematical techniques" (Madgett, 1976). Unnecessary duplication of effort can be avoided by consulting studies of this kind before embarking on similar research.

Labor organizations can be consulted to complement the judgment of employers regarding the qualities needed for employment in the present and the future.

Recent graduates are a fruitful and frequently overlooked source for commentary on the curriculum. They are now finding out how their learnings apply to life. Graduates were a major source of data in the research leading to the Swedish curriculum reforms of the 1960s. In one study a comparison was made between the amount of time devoted in classrooms to various topics in social studies and the relative value of these topics as reported by adults who had left school within the previous ten years. An almost inverse relationship was found: those topics accorded the most time in class were found least valuable by the graduates, and vice versa (Bromsjo, 1965).

The educator can replicate these findings for himself by consulting recently qualified professionals. It is predictable that the physicians will complain that their training gave them no preparation to face such questions as how to set up a practice, utilize secretarial and paraprofessional help, or negotiate with government and corporate insurance plans. Teachers traditionally report that their training did not prepare them in classroom management, test design, or curriculum development.

Nongraduates or dropouts are at least as important a group as graduates. They can usually be counted on for a detailed critique of the programs from which they are refugees.

Community agencies handle numerous cases and inquiries from the public. Many of the issues with which they deal point to needs that are essentially educational or that have implications for education. Such agencies as alcohol referral centers, community volunteer bureaus, consumer associations, family counseling services, legal aid offices, senior citizens' councils, social planning councils, and youth bureaus can be asked to provide an analysis of inquiries received over a period of time. The officers of the organizations themselves should also be invited to give their perceptions of community educational needs, how well they are being met, and present and future priorities. Published research by and about such agencies may also be a useful source of information.

Frontier thinkers, those whose ideas depart from convention and tradition, should be asked for their views. They are not so much the educational propagandists whose opinions are well known, but the individuals who appear to have special insight into humanity and its future. It is always easy to spot these people once they are dead—Albert Einstein, Teilhard de Chardin, Saul Alinsky; the needs assessor's job is to identify and talk to them while they are alive!

Methods for Obtaining Data

Needs assessment packages

A needs assessment team may be able to save itself much labor by obtaining a needs assessment package "off the shelf." It would seem redundant to retread the path already taken by many other educational jurisdictions. Useful reviews of needs assessment models and instruments developed by various states, districts, publishers, and research agencies have been produced by the Rhode Island (n.d.) and Alameida County (1976) school systems. The Center for the Study of Evaluation at UCLA produces a Needs Assessment Kit complete with protocol materials (questionnaires, recording forms, etc.) for identifying goal preferences, obtaining baseline data on the status of goal achievement, and screening information to identify high-priority goals. If a suitable "canned" needs assessment package can be obtained, materials and personnel costs, as well as lead time, will be reduced substantially.

Questionnaires

Questionnaires have several merits for use in needs assessment. They can be reproduced and distributed simultaneously to many people relatively rapidly and inexpensively. They permit anonymity and can be answered in the respondent's own time. They aim to elicit judgments directly. The data is generally uniform and straightforward to tabulate.

The disadvantages of questionnaire research are in some respects related to its apparent simplicity; too often questionnaires have been designed by "well-meaning people who believe that anyone who can write plain English and has a modicum of common sense can produce a good questionnaire" (Oppenheim, 1966, p. vii). Designing questionnaires requires considerable expertise if the results are to be useful. Research has long shown that questionnaire responses regarding both attitudes (LaPierre, 1934) and biographical data (Haberman, 1966), even when anonymous, often have doubtful veracity. Even when the problem of frankness does not arise, it takes special skill to write questions that all the respondents will understand and to which they will be able to make valid responses. The questionnaire method, unlike such methods as observation, requires the cooperation of respondents. An overload of surveys, or the use of insensitively designed questionnaires, can quickly build community resistance.

For these reasons the nonexpert might consider the following guidelines:

1. Ask questions on which the subjects have some experience. "What degree of difficulty is your son/daughter having with spelling?" will produce more useful data than "How well is the school teaching English?" If necessary, give respondents details of the existing instruction before asking them to make a judgment about it (Witkin, 1979).

2. Refer to the general literature on measurement of attitudes (such as Henerson, Morris, and Fitz-Gibbon, 1978) or to the specific research on the design of needs assessment instruments (such as Witkin, 1977).

3. Purchase ready-made questionnaires for needs assessment, as mentioned earlier.

4. Use questionnaires as one of a number of data-gathering instruments, and cross-check the results with those of interviews, social indicators, etc.

Interviews

Interviews allow exploration of issues in depth in a face-to-face encounter. Because they require considerably more time than questionnaires, fewer subjects can be contacted for the same cost. It is therefore necessary to ensure that the degree to which the sample of people interviewed is unrepresentative of the community at large is taken into account in interpreting the data.

The value of interview data will depend largely on the skills of the interviewers. The development of such skills as establishing rapport, sequencing questions, and probing usually requires specialized training. Unlike the questionnaire, every interview is different. A structured format helps to reduce the variability among interviews and interviewers and to ensure that the necessary information is obtained in each case. The telephone provides a quick and efficient method of interviewing people—including the distant, the busy, and the famous—whom it is not feasible to interview in person.

Public hearings

A public hearing or community forum allows the collection of much data in a short time. Advance notification and a public invitation to attend should be given through the local media. Hearings should be informal to enable participants to explore and build on one another's ideas. The main limitations on hearings for gathering data is that the most influential and eloquent participants tend to dominate the proceedings; there is rarely time for everyone to speak; the impressionistic opinions expressed may have doubtful validity; and some people will not or cannot publicly express their needs (Bowers and Associates, 1976).

"Let's see now—your answers were: 37 'don't know', 42 'no opinion', and one 'education should commit itself to long-term affective development instead of concentrating instructional resources on low-level cognitive outcomes that satisfy conventional expectations'."

Analysis of social indicators

Much light can be thrown on people's needs by data that is already available. Statistics on employment, consumption, health, crime and delinquency, population, transiency, housing, voting patterns, and utilization of social services are normally obtainable inexpensively and already summarized and tabulated. These statistics are only indirect indicators of need. Against this can be set the advantage that, as the information is usually longitudinal, emerging trends may be discernible (Bell, Lin, and Warheit, 1977).

Observation

Observation of people's behavior may be used to make inferences about their needs. For instance, observing how adolescents spend their free time and money gives an indication of the needs to which they accord priority; this may be a useful addition to questionnaire or interview data. Since subjects may alter normal behavior patterns when they know they are being watched, unobtrusive observation provides more valid data. Unless an observer is provided with detailed and easily understood instruction for observing and recording behavior, special training or expertise will be necessary.

Reading

The literature on human needs, vast though it is, should at least be sampled. It is especially important to review the results of the needs assessment research. Enough assessments have now been conducted, at any rate within the United States, that a reasonably accurate general needs profile can be constructed. Only a small-scale empirical study may be necessary to identify the extent to which a particular community differs from the general pattern.

Thinking: brainstorming

Thinking about needs is justly disparaged as "armchair needs assessment" when it is used as the sole methodology. But the importance of independent and creative thought as an adjunct to other strategies should not be underestimated. Brainstorming is a form of free-flowing creative thought conducted in a group. A level of trust is necessary among members of the group; this is not the occasion to hear from those with vested interests. A relaxed atmosphere must be established, in which people feel free to speak what comes into their minds without self-censorship or fear of criticism. It is helpful to keep a visible record of the ideas submitted, so that people can build on one another's suggestions.

The process often helps to loosen up the thinking of curriculum planners and to make them conscious of needs that are commonly overlooked by more formal methods of inquiry.

Problems in Needs Assessment

Information overload

A full-scale needs assessment may produce so much data that the researchers become swamped by information. If this happens, they may lose sight of the central issues and begin to pay selective attention to data from particular sources, thus defeating the object of the exercise. This can best be avoided by marshalling the data to illuminate the specific questions that are the focus of the needs assessment.

Vocabulary

From the first conversations among the curriculum workers and between curriculum personnel and the public, it is essential that the terms used be understood by all parties. Semantic misunderstanding can invalidate the data collected and lead to unnecessary confusion. For this reason, it may be wise to write down and adhere to definitions of some of the critical terms such as *need, problem*, and *concern*.

Shifting public attitudes

Bowers and Associates (1976, p. 6) remark, apropos of needs assessment, that "in some instances programs have been installed based on considerable evidence of a need in one year, only to have a complete change in attitude the following year." The influence of the media, with their penchant for instant crises, can hardly be underestimated in this regard, but the media alone are not responsible for the quicksands of educational thought. The needs assessors and the curriculum developers must have the insight to see below surface problems to the underlying needs that have continuity.

Future orientation

The public tends to react to present or past needs. Curriculum designers must respond to future needs. However salient a present need, it can be made the basis of a curriculum only if it will be significant in the future. This obliges educators to seek input from those who have insight into future needs or to interpret data in light of their own perceptions of impending changes.

Retaining control of the curriculum

Curriculum developers cannot use needs assessment to delegate to the public their decision-making responsibilities. Needs assessment should not rely too heavily on unsupported opinion. The value of objective data in the form of social, economic, and demographic indices, and observed patterns of behavior, is that they are based on action rather than words. By illuminating, validating, or discrediting the opinions expressed by the public, they allow a more convincing determination of needs. Educators should also be careful not to lead the public into expecting that its opinions will determine curricula outcomes. Public opinion may or may not reflect significant needs; it invariably reflects political realities. These factors must be weighed by the needs assessment team, but the interpretation of the findings and the subsequent curriculum decision making must remain the functions of the people formally charged with those responsibilities.

Setting Priorities

The process of needs assessment will tend to identify a large number of needs. This is as it should be: if some important need is overlooked at this stage, it is unlikely to be considered later on. But a curriculum that attempts to meet too many different needs at once is unlikely to be effective. In order to decide which needs curriculum revision or development will address first, priorities must be established.

For this reason, when conducting needs-assessment surveys, it is desirable to ask respondents to indicate the priorities they would assign to the needs that they identify. To illustrate: In 1976 the Appalachia Educational Laboratory reported a needs-assessment survey designed to provide information for the development of a television series on effective parenthood. A representative sample of parents of young children from ten states was asked to indicate for each of sixty items relating to parenthood knowledge whether they needed "a lot more," "a little more," or "nothing more at all." The responses of 1,799 parents made it possible to rank the items in terms of the perceived need on the part of parents. Table 4–1 shows the seven items that headed the list. The findings suggested that the priorities of parents lay in the area of intellectual and personal development of children, rather than in such topics as clothing, nutrition, physical development, health, and medical care (Coan, 1976).

There are various specialized techniques for ranking items in order of priority, including the Delphi technique, card sort, and evaluation matrices of various kinds (Cyphert and Gant, 1971; Downey, 1960; Banghart and Trull, 1973). But it may be sufficient for a curriculum team to

ITEM	PERCENT OF PARENTS RESPONDING		
	"A lot more"	"A little more"	"Nothing more at all"
Help your child see and accept his or her own feelings.	54.6	37.0	8.3
How your child's personality is formed.	47.7	39.8	12.4
Talk with your child about his problems and answer his questions.	48.2	37.8	13.8
How the world looks and sounds to your child and how to help him learn about it.	45.1	43.7	11.0
What your child should be able to learn at his age, so as not to "push" your child too much.	43.7	43.7	12.5
Help your child to behave when he starts to fight.	45.6	39.9	14.4
What ways of teaching will work best with your child (the way you teach; use of books, TV).	39.0	48.8	12.1

Table 4–1   Perceived needs of parents for knowledge related to effective parenting (from Coan, 1976, p. 94)

identify needs as *critical, important,* or *desirable* for the present or future well-being of learners or society. The list of needs identified by consensus as critical is likely to provide a substantial agenda for curriculum developers. A further classification may be *immediacy.* Those needs that are critical to the student's well-being in the immediate future should be given priority. But needs critical in the long term should on no account be neglected. Left to their own devices, many people will react only to immediate needs, ignoring long-term needs until catastrophe is imminent. It is one of the functions of planning to counterbalance this human tendency.

Addressing a Specific Problem

General needs assessment is necessary if an educational system is to justify its consumption of social resources. But at the present, curriculum developers rarely enjoy the luxury of beginning their work with a general needs assessment. More frequently they identify or are presented with a specific problem to resolve, such as local underachievement in reading, rising juvenile delinquency, or complaints about the mathematics curriculum.

A problem may be defined as a specific obstacle to the satisfaction of a need. Problems may be visible or concealed. Visible problems are a source of conscious pain and therefore tend to receive prompt attention. But curriculum workers should also be alert for concealed problems, such as unrealized potential, which are more likely to be overlooked. When curriculum developers decide a problem exists, or are invited to respond to a specific problem, their obligation is to establish the nature of the problem and of the underlying need. But before embarking on the research, it is wise to assess the significance of the problem and its implications.

Problems referred to the curriculum designer from elsewhere in the school system will not have been arrived at by the rigorous process of needs assessment, and not all will deserve a curriculum response. No self-respecting educator will waste time thinking about a curriculum solution to pseudo problems such as boys wearing long hair or girls wearing short skirts. Other, more plausible problems may turn out on examination to be spurious. Is the rising delinquency rate a fact, or is it the last resort of the local newspaper's eagerness to find a story in an uneventful week? Is reading achievement declining, or is it a popular issue to win conservative votes in a school board election? The answers to such questions may be readily apparent or may require investigation.

Problems that have been brought to the attention of curriculum developers may or may not be curriculum problems; they may or may not have political implications. All curricula should meet human needs, but not all human needs can be met by curricula. The need for shelter is basic, but a shortage of housing in the community is unlikely to be directly affected by curriculum change. On the other hand, the fact that a need is being largely met by other agencies does not preclude the school from responsibility. Eighty percent of the students may learn to swim in the local pool, but the school may legitimately assume responsibility for the other 20 percent.

Political considerations must also be weighed. Some curriculum areas may be too politically sensitive for curriculum developers to handle without clear direction from their superiors. You may feel that a curriculum in "strategies and tactics in urban terrorism" meets an important contemporary need, but you are unlikely to get far in introducing it into a downtown high school.

The time perspective of the planner is an important consideration in assessing the political feasibility of new curricula. Short-term plans cannot conflict violently with contemporary values without risk to the plans or the planner. Longer-term projects may anticipate that current objections will disappear through cultural change or by educational or public relations efforts. If it is not feasible for political or other reasons to meet the identified need by means of a curriculum, then the developers must backtrack and begin work on the next need in order of priority on their agenda.

Researching a Specific Need

The groups consulted and the methods used to research a specific need will be similar to those mentioned in the discussion of general needs assessment. Sometimes a general needs assessment will itself provide most of the data required to illuminate specific needs, but this will usually occur only if the general needs assessment is a large-scale project with wide scope and substantial resources. Suppose that the specific need of concern were related to the level of physical fitness in children and adolescents. The data required would include empirical information about the fitness of the population; the relation of fitness to health; professional judgments of physiologists, exercise researchers, and recreation officers; and attitude data from parents, public, and students to gauge levels of awareness and potential support.

An indication of the quantity of research that can be undertaken into a specific need is provided by Bennett's investigation (1974) of the need for "death education." Interviews were conducted with specialists in the care of the terminally ill, with educators, and with elementary- and secondary-school students. Several courses and conferences on death and dying were attended. School children and graduate students in education were surveyed about their attitudes toward death. More than two hundred articles and books on the subject were read. The research threw interesting light on the nature of the need. It turned out that children had open and uninhibited attitudes towards death. It was rather the adults, and especially the professionals working in the area, who "were grossly undereducated regarding the complexity of death" (Bennett, 1974, p. 11). Thorough as this research was in most respects, it raises two questions. One is why the research did not solicit the views of the dying and the bereaved. The other, more basic question is what kind of general needs assessment or definition of priorities preceded the commitment of this amount of effort to this particular need.

Research into a specific need should clarify several issues. One is whether the need is real and significant. Another is the nature of the need that underlies a visible problem. It is common for problems to be mistaken for needs; policies directed at school vandalism often overlook the fact that vandalism is a classic symptom of alienation, and hence fail to address the underlying need. Needs research should also project the future status of the need, so that curricula are not developed to meet needs that are no longer significant. Finally, the research must identify the intended learners; it is often premature to do this in advance of the needs assessment.

This discussion of needs assessment has focused primarily on the identification of basic needs, those qualities that people need to lead satisfying and effective lives. It is common practice in needs assessment also to collect data on the "need discrepancies," the degree to which needs are met by existing programs. Surveys and interviews can obtain some data on this question; testing will often be the preferred method. The more specific the need being investigated, the more precisely the discrepancies can be studied and defined. More detailed discussion of the steps between identifying basic needs and determining whether new curricula are required is presented in the next chapter.

Researching a Specific Need: An Illustration

The example that follows illustrates some of the steps involved in researching a specific problem and identifying the underlying need. The hypothetical illustration constitutes a "narration simulation," a method for testing curriculum models developed by Silvern (1972). The basic model to which reference is made is shown in Figure 4–1.

Identifying a significant problem

In a general needs assessment conducted in a school district, almost all sectors of the community assigned high priority to health and expressed a need for high standards of health education. Specific research has been conducted into several areas of health education, and curriculum development is under way in some of these areas. One of the concerns expressed in the needs assessment was that young people in the community had poor nutritional habits and inadequate knowledge of nutrition and were in some cases in danger of malnutrition. The Health Education Consultant for the district and the Health Education Committee, with the support of the Board of Education, are now ready to embark on a specific study of this problem, which appears to be related to a need for nutrition education.

The first step is to assess the validity of the problem. A call to the local nutrition association leads the consultant to a number of recent national studies. These sources provide evidence of the seriousness of

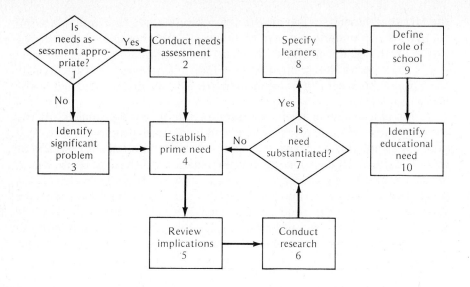

Figure 4–1   Model of needs assessment in curriculum design

the problem, not only among young people but across all groups. The major general deficiencies appear to be:

Iron, calcium, and vitamin D in young children;

Iron, calcium, vitamin D, vitamin A, thiamine, and riboflavin in adolescents and young adults;

Vitamin A, thiamine, and riboflavin in middle-aged men;

Protein, iron, calcium, vitamin A, thiamine, and riboflavin in middle-aged women and senior adults;

Iron, calcium, vitamin A, thiamine, and riboflavin in pregnant women.

These deficiencies, all of which entail medical risk, are found in more than a quarter of the total population. The problem is apparently a national one, but is it a local problem? The committee asks the local office of health for an opinion. The health officer reports that routine lab analysis on patients admitted to local hospitals over the past year indicates nutritional levels and deficiencies typical of those found nationally. The problem is therefore a significant one in the community.

Establishing prime need and implications

The committee concludes that the prime need is for the diets of members of the community to meet basic nutritional requirements. The reasons for deficiency have yet to be researched, but insofar as malnutrition may be a function of ignorance, misinformation, habit, or attitude, the need is one that has curriculum implications.

As the development of new curricula in nutrition is foreseen as a possible solution to the problem, the committee considers it judicious to consider the political implications of nutrition education. Nutrition education has implications for food purchasing, and a number of food retailers are active in local politics. A second political pressure group is parents, a number of whom tend to resist any attempt to include in the school curriculum subjects they consider the responsibility of the home.

The data from the general needs assessment did not indicate any public resistance to this branch of health education. However, as an additional check, members of the committee are detailed to seek the opinions of individual retailers and parents known to them. They report back that the idea of nutrition education met with approval or acquiescence in all cases.

Conducting the research

The Health Education Committee establishes a subcommittee consisting of the Health Education Consultant as chairman and two other members, a physician in family practice and a health teacher, to design and conduct the research into the need. The data the subcommittee decides that it requires and the sources and collection methods are shown in Table 4–2. In addition to gathering local data, the study will draw on existing scientific literature on nutritional needs. The research is intended to provide a first-hand picture of local levels of nutrition, dietary patterns, and knowledge of nutrition.

The three subcommittee members divide the review of a dozen main texts and reports on nutrition among themselves. General information on consumption patterns is obtained by telephoning managers of food stores and brokerages; this is amplified by official government data on food purchasing in the district. The telephone is also used to contact the chairman of the local horticultural society and a small sample of seed retailers and nurseries, pharmacists, dentists, social workers, school nurses, and general medical practitioners. A structured telephone interview is conducted with a sample of parents of school-age children regarding food preparation practices. One member of the subcommittee undertakes a content analysis of food advertisements in local newspapers over a one-month period, at the same time clipping any articles on nutrition. Another spends the lunch hour each day for two weeks visiting school cafeterias and short-order restaurants in the vicinity of schools and browses through the nutrition literature in school and public libraries and bookstores. The public health service provides a copy of its annual report on nutrition in the district, and the Red Cross blood donor service

DATA	SOURCES	METHODS
Nutrition and dietary standards	Texts, reports	Reading
Consumption patterns	Retailers and brokers, government reports	Telephone interview; Reading
Consumption by youth	School cafeterias, vending machines, short-order restaurants, bag lunches	Observation
Domestic food production	Horticultural society, seed retailers, nurseries	Telephone interview
Food preparation	Parents	Telephone interview
Malnutrition	Public health service, doctors, school nurses, blood donor service	Report, telephone interview
Diet supplements	Pharmacists	Telephone interview
Diet and dental health	Dentists	Telephone interview
Food advertising	Local newspapers	Content analysis
Social problems and diet	Social workers	Telephone interview
Knowledge of nutrition	General public	Questionnaire
Attitude to nutrition education	Parents	Questionnaire
Nutrition information	Libraries, newspapers	Spot-checking

Table 4–2   Researching a need: Data required, sources, and methods

provides a breakdown of numbers of would-be donors rejected for iron or other deficiencies. In the meantime, the consultant, who has some expertise in questionnaire design, draws up brief questionnaires on knowledge of nutrition and attitudes to nutrition education. These are tried out with staff at the board of education office and then mailed to a random sample of 100 parents and 100 members of the general public. The sample size is large enough to allow some general conclusions and small enough for the data to be processed by hand.

Two months after commencing its work, the subcommittee has collected the required data. In addition to a two-hour weekly meeting to review progress and make decisions, the consultant has had to commit about two hours a day to the research, and the other two members of the subcommittee about five hours a week. Typing, duplication, and mailing of questionnaires and tabulation of results absorbed some twelve hours of clerical staff time. Direct expenses were less than $100.

Substantiating the need

Much of the data obtained is impressionistic although often professional opinion. The opinions expressed tend to be consistent and to be confirmed by the textbooks and official reports on diet and nutrition. The subcommittee draws six general conclusions:

1. The general pattern is one of declining nutritional quality of diet over the past three decades throughout the country.
2. Little sound information on nutrition is readily available to the public in libraries or newspapers. The level of public knowledge of nutrition is generally low, with many fallacies accepted as fact.
3. The food available in school cafeterias and vending machines helps to establish poor dietary habits.
4. There is general agreement among the public that more nutrition should be taught in school; there is little or no feeling that school programs in nutrition usurp a family responsibility.
5. Food purchasing is heavily influenced by advertising, to the disadvantage of naive consumers.
6. Although the cost of fresh vegetables is high all year in retail outlets, only a small minority of people grow their own vegetables, particularly in urban areas.

Some of these findings represent symptoms rather than the basic problem, which appears to be threefold:

1. a lack of knowledge regarding nutrition,
2. a failure to establish healthy dietary habits, and hence
3. a tendency to consume by custom and whim, subject to such external influences as advertising.

The current situation defined, the subcommittee now attempts to forecast the relevant aspects of the problem in the future, utilizing information from the literature and from the experts consulted in the data collection. The members make the following predictions pertaining to the next few years:

1. Food prices will continue to rise more sharply than the overall cost of living.
2. A significant proportion of the population will suffer a decline in real income.

3. Many chemical additives and compounds in processed foods currently regarded as innocuous will come under suspicion as a result of independent scientific analysis.

4. Food technology will increase in scale and complexity; manufacturers will devote increased resources to the promotion of processed and convenience foods.

5. Government regulations concerning nutritional content of foods will require all processed foods to meet certain minimum standards, but will result in some processed foods being brought down to the minima as "surplus" nutrients are extracted during processing for conversion into diet supplements.

These developments suggest that nutrition education will increasingly need to emphasize

1. How to get the most food value for the money spent.
2. How to objectively assess advantages and disadvantages of processed foods.
3. How to obtain or produce, and to prepare, natural foods.

Specifying the learners

The subcommittee reports to the Health Education Committee that the need for nutrition education has been substantiated. The committee had originally perceived the school students as the probable clients of nutrition education, but the subcommittee report concludes that the entire public is in need of education in nutrition, especially the following groups:

1. Children and adolescents, who require good nutrition for tissue growth and need to establish sound dietary habits.
2. Pregnant women, whose nutrition will affect the health of the baby and its subsequent ability to absorb nutrients.
3. Parents, who are largely responsible for establishing dietary habits in their children.
4. Senior citizens, who of all groups have the most deficient diets.

The learners are therefore defined as "all children and adults in the community."

Defining the role of the school

The curriculum can deal only with part of the problem of malnutrition, and its contribution will be impaired if it operates in a vacuum.

Other agencies could help ameliorate the problem in their own spheres of operation. Accordingly, plans are made to take further steps:

1. Invite the district principals' association to develop guidelines regarding cafeteria menus and vending machines in schools.
2. Ask the media to give greater exposure to features on nutrition.
3. Request the National Nutrition Association to make its "Dial-A-Dietician" service available in the district.
4. Distribute a list of recommended books and periodicals to public and school libraries.
5. Urge the horticultural societies and municipal governments to cooperate in establishing and promoting free public plots for vegetable growing on unused land, particularly in urban areas.
6. Establish liaison with teachers and curriculum designers in consumer education to ensure that programs reinforce one another in teaching consumers how to spend their food dollars wisely.
7. Confer with the adult education office, the community colleges, and "Y" groups regarding the offering of courses for adults in nutrition, vegetable gardening, and related areas.
8. Attempt to persuade local nursing and medical faculties to give more instruction in nutrition counseling in their programs.
9. Urge local hospitals to include a dietician in their outpatient staff.
10. Establish liaison with health and social workers to arrange reciprocal referrals and sharing of concerns and resources.

Identifying the educational need

With the paraeducational responses to the need referred to the appropriate agencies, the curriculum area is left with the educational need, which is stated as: *To develop sound nutritional habits and to learn how to make wise decisions in the area of nutrition.*

The needs research is now complete. The curriculum developers can proceed confident that a significant need exists and has been accurately defined.

Conclusion

The simulation presented above is a detailed example of needs research in operation. Frequently such research can be conducted more rapidly than the example implies, but it should not be neglected. The cost of educational programs that fail to meet human needs cannot be counted merely in wasted time; it is to be calculated in the unfulfilled potential of individuals, in frustration of ambitions, in alienation and loss of self-esteem, in unnecessary or false dependencies, in bitterness and delinquency, and in loss and damage to society.

This is not to say that needs assessment is a panacea for these ills or a passport to Utopia; but it is to argue that whenever curricula are better designed to meet human needs, the benefits will be felt in subtle and varied ways throughout the whole community.

ACTIVITIES

1. Identify the three most significant needs you think can be met by the subject or one of the subjects you teach. What are the implications of these needs for the way the subject is taught?

2. List the ten specific human needs to which you think schools should give highest priority. Ask a cross section of people, including students, to do the same. Compare the responses.

3. Surveys based on questionnaire research are reported almost every day in the press. Read a summary of one. How much confidence can be placed in the results?

4. Conduct a small-scale survey of general educational needs in your community. Collect enough responses to be able to examine how opinions differ from one group to another and depending on the method (questionnaire, interview, etc.) used.

5. Talk or think through a narration simulation of the research that might be conducted to analyze the curriculum implications of one of the following events: (a) a proposal is being considered to build a nuclear power station close to your community; (b) the local newspaper reports an "epidemic increase" in juvenile alcoholism; (c) a leading authority on public health proposes that all high school students should receive basic paramedical training; (d) cloning and genetically engineered-to-order children become realistic options for the general public.

QUESTIONS

1. The major purpose of needs assessment is

    a. to determine the curriculum by democratic means
    b. to ensure that curricula are based on significant student need
    c. to find out how well existing curricula are meeting student needs
    d. to identify political problems that may face the curriculum designer

2. In many circumstances, the most cost-effective means of assessing community needs would be to

    a. not conduct any empirical research
    b. use only homemade questionnaires

c. conduct specific but not general needs assessment

d. obtain a needs assessment package "off the shelf"

3. You are designing a curriculum in personal finance. Which of the following groups could you safely omit from the needs assessment?

a. employees

b. bank managers

c. recent graduates

d. none of the above

4. An important reason for obtaining the opinions of parents is that

a. they have a right to be consulted

b. their views tend to be future-oriented

c. their opinions are not influenced by the media

d. they have special expertise in early childhood education

5. An advantage of using questionnaires to gather opinion data is

a. they are good predictors of actual behavior

b. they can be easily designed by the nonexpert

c. they can be administered relatively rapidly and cheaply

d. if they are anonymous, people will give truthful responses

6. You want to assess the reaction of drivers to highway speed limits. The most valid data is likely to come from

a. observing driving behavior on the roads

b. mailing a questionnaire to a sample of licensed drivers

c. talking with the highway patrol of the local police department

d. conducting telephone interviews with a cross section of the public

7. A *problem* is

a. a symptom of some underlying difficulty

b. a recognition that a need is not being met

c. a specific obstacle to the satisfaction of a need

d. a discrepancy between an actual and an optimal state

8. Insofar as absenteeism reflects student attitudes toward schooling, it could most appropriately be termed

a. a need

b. a concern

c. a problem

d. a symptom

9. Which of the following needs should be given highest priority?

a. a need that has been critical in the past

b. a need that will be critical in the immediate future

    c. a need that is important in both the short and the long term

    d. a need desirable in the past, the present, and the immediate and distant future

10. Unwanted pregnancy is identified as a major problem among adolescents in your community. What approach is likely to be most effective in meeting the underlying need?

    a. develop improved curricula in sex education

    b. refer the problem to the local medical services

    c. develop a cooperative approach between the school and health and social agencies

    d. avoid the problem because it is too politically sensitive for the school to handle

Check your answers against the key in Appendix 2.
9 or 10 right: You understand the material presented.
8 or 7 right: Review the areas of uncertainty.
6 or less right: Reread the chapter.

Recommended Reading

Public Opinion Quarterly. American Association for Public Opinion Research, Columbia University. Major periodical in the area of opinion research. Articles represent the leading edge of research findings and methodology in public attitudes.

Warwick, David P., and Charles A. Lininger. *The sample survey: Theory and practice.* New York: McGraw-Hill, 1975. Deals with theoretical and practical aspects of planning, conducting, and analyzing surveys. Outlines procedures for designing surveys, questionnaires, and interviews, for sampling, and for organizing and reporting results.

Warheit, G. J., R. A. Bell, and J. J. Schwab. *Planning for change: Needs assessment approaches.* 3rd ed. Washington, D.C.: U.S. Government Printing Office, 1977. Contains useful material on the principles and practice of needs assessment in various settings.

Witkin, B. R. *An analysis of needs assessment techniques at state, intermediate, and local levels.* Rev. ed. Washington, D.C.: National Institute of Education, 1977. Monograph by an acknowledged expert on educational needs assessment, which has become a standard guide to the subject.

References

Alameida County School Department and International Society of Educational Planners. *Educational needs assessment: Theme and variations. Abstracts of models presented.* Washington, D.C.: National Institute of Education, 1976.

Banghart, Frank W., and Albert Trull, Jr. *Educational planning.* New York: Macmillan, 1973.

Bell, Roger A., Elizabeth Lin, and George J. Warheit. Issues in need assessment data collection strategies. Paper presented at the Annual Meeting of the American Psychological Association, San Francisco, August 1977.

Bennett, Roger V. Death and the curriculum. Paper presented at the Annual Meeting of the American Educational Research Association, New Orleans, April 1974.

Blishen, Edward (ed.) *The school that I'd like*. Harmondsworth, England: Penguin, 1969.

Bowers and Associates, Reston, Va. *A guide to needs assessment in community education*. Washington, D.C.: U.S. Office of Education, 1976.

Bromsjo, B. *Smahällskunskap som skolamne*. Stockholm: Sgenska Bokforlaget, 1965.

Coan, Donald L. Television for effective parenthood. In *Parenthood education needs: A national assessment study*. Washington, D.C.: U.S. Office of Education, 1976.

Cyphert, Frederick R., and Walter L. Gant. The Delphi technique: A case study. *Phi Delta Kappan*, 1971, 52, 272–273.

Deleonibus, Nancy. Taking a new look at needs assessment. *The Practitioner*, 1977, 4(2), 1–12.

Downey, Lawrence W. *The task of public education*. Chicago: University of Chicago, Midwest Administration Center, 1960.

Eash, Maurice J. Systems design and the evaluation of educational programs. Paper presented at the Annual Meeting of the American Educational Research Association, Washington, D.C., March 1975.

Haberman, Paul W., and Jill Sheinberg. Education reported in interviews: An aspect of survey content error. *Public Opinion Quarterly*, 1966, 30, 295–301.

Henerson, Marlene E., Lynn Lyons Morris, and Carol Taylor Fitz-Gibbon. *How to measure attitudes*. Beverly Hills: Sage Publications, 1978.

King, Arthur R., Jr., and John A. Brownell. *The curriculum and the disciplines of knowledge*. New York: Wiley, 1966.

LaPierre, R. T. Attitudes versus actions. *Social Forces*, 1934, 13, 230–237.

Madgett, Alan C., Department of Mathematics, Laurentian University, Canada. Personal communication, February 1976.

Oppenheim, A. N. *Questionnaire design and attitude measurement*. New York: Basic Books, 1966.

Rhode Island Department of Education, Bureau of Technical Assistance. Needs assessment: Compendium of abstracts. Providence, R.I.: Rhode Island Department of Education, n.d.

Silvern, Leonard. *Systems engineering applied to training*. Houston, Texas: Gulf, 1972.

Tyler, Ralph W. *Basic principles of curriculum and instruction*. Chicago: University of Chicago Press, 1949, p. 4.

Witkin, Belle Ruth. Needs assessment models: A critical analysis. Paper presented at the Annual Meeting of the American Educational Research Association, San Francisco, April 1976.

——— . *An analysis of needs assessment techniques at state, intermediate, and local levels*. Rev. ed. Washington, D.C.: National Institute of Education, 1977.

——— . Personal communication, 1979.

Young, Michael. An approach to the study of curricula as socially organized knowledge. In Michael F. D. Young (ed.), *Knowledge and control: New directions for the sociology of education*. London: Collier-MacMillan, 1971, pp. 19–46.

5

PRINCIPLES

- A curriculum developer or development team can facilitate its work by careful planning of its role and activities.

- A design project should be undertaken only when a verified need is not being met.

- Alternative ways of meeting needs should be considered and a new curriculum designed only when it is a preferred alternative.

- The feasibility of a proposed course of action can be assessed by weighing constraints against resources.

- It is unwise to proceed with curriculum development until it is clear that minimal resources and support will be provided.

- For detailed planning and design, small groups are more efficient than large groups.

- A curriculum development team can generate high levels of motivation when the team is perceived as a temporary system and as a form of job enrichment.

- Before beginning to plan a curriculum, designers should endeavor to find out what related curriculum work has already been done elsewhere.

CONCEPTS

Front-end analysis	Feasibility	Consensus
Parameter	Impact analysis	Job enrichment
Constraint	Curriculum prospectus	Temporary system

5
Organizing for Curriculum Development

Individual commitment to a group effort—that is what makes a team work, a company work, a society work, a civilization work.

—Vince Lombardi, football coach

Front-end Analysis

Once an educational or training need has been identified for which it seems proper that the school should accept some formal responsibility, the designer has moved from the broad area of social analysis to the more deliberate domain of curriculum. The temptation at this point is to rush into the definition of objectives, or even more precipitately, development of instructional means. It is wise, before we set out on the arduous curriculum design journey, first to ensure that the journey is really necessary, and, if it is, to furnish ourselves with provisions and a map of the route. Some basic planning may reveal valuable short-cuts and will increase our chances of arrival at the destination.

This is the function of preliminary organization and planning. Harless coined the term *front-end analysis* to describe this phase of development and defined the term as "a series of analytical and decision-making steps that lead to plans for overcoming deficiencies in human performance" (Harless, 1973, p. 230). Datta defined front-end analysis as "the bridge between recognizing a need and deciding what to do about it" (Datta, 1978, p. 13). This process of analysis and decision-making is the focus of this chapter.

Is a New Curriculum Necessary?

Identification of a human need does not automatically establish the need for a new curriculum or for any other form of deliberate intervention. Needs assessment as outlined in the preceding chapter identifies significant human needs that have curriculum implications. Before curriculum development decisions are made, it is necessary to find out how well these needs are currently being met, either by existing school programs or by some agency or influence outside the school. This is best done by assessing students, rather than by investigating programs directly. Reading official courses of study and statements of policy may reveal what a school is attempting to do, but not whether it is achieving it.

At this point a dilemma sometimes occurs. Assessment of students is necessary before curriculum development begins; but until the curriculum has been developed, the tests and criteria for assessing students may not be available. Three possible solutions present themselves. (1) Use existing data. Many school systems will have enough data on students' achievement in conventional areas of instruction such as reading and mathematics to allow an estimate of overall competence in these areas to be made. (2) Use existing tests. Perusal of a source such as the *Mental Measurements Yearbook* (Buros, 1978) may suggest a number of published tests that assess areas of competence related to the identified need. (3) Use rudimentary homemade tests. A relatively brief and simple test of knowledge of first aid would almost certainly be adequate to reveal the general level of students' knowledge or ignorance of first aid procedures. A one-item questionnaire—"How far can you swim?"—would allow an estimate of how many people would drown if out of their depth for a few minutes.

"Failure" in any of these kinds of assessment would strongly support the need for new or revised curricula. On the other hand, "success" would have to be treated with more caution. Existing curricula might be unnecessarily wasteful or painful, and the success might be marginal.

The degree of certainty required depends on the significance of the need. We can tolerate a wider margin of error in assessing whether a new curriculum is required in art appreciation than in reading. If there is doubt regarding the adequacy of existing programs to meet critical needs, the designers should proceed with the development process; when specific objectives and performance criteria have been developed, the graduates of the present programs can be assessed again to ensure that further work is not redundant.

If it appears that the need identified is being met, then existing programs can be maintained. If the need is being largely met, existing programs require modification but not replacement. On the other hand, the fact that the need is not being met still does not necessarily mean that existing curricula are deficient. The music curriculum may, in itself, be excellent, but accorded too little time or used with the wrong age group; or the classes may include a range of pupils from child prodigies to the tone-deaf; or it may be attempting to work on a nonexistent budget; or it may be always scheduled for the last period on Friday afternoon. These deficiencies lie outside the curriculum itself; they should be reported to the appropriate administrative level, and assessment repeated after they have been corrected.

Only after these steps have been followed can the planners proceed with a degree of confidence that they are not engaged in an unnecessary exercise. This is the first set of decisions shown in Figure 5–1.

Curricular and Other Solutions

By this stage the planners have identified an unmet educational need. They still need to hold their eagerness to begin designing new curricula in check; a new curriculum is only one possible solution, and before it is chosen, other alternatives should be considered.

Let us suppose that the need identified is to reduce motor vehicle accidents by improving the attitudes and/or skills of young drivers and that there is no adequate driver-education curriculum in the school. One alternative is to develop and install a new driver-education curriculum. But other alternatives could also be considered:

1. Contract with a commercial driving school to operate driver-education courses in the school.
2. Persuade a commercial driving school to offer a substantial discount to students in return for advertising promotion in the school.
3. Offer high-school credit for the completion of a recognized driver-education course taken outside the school.

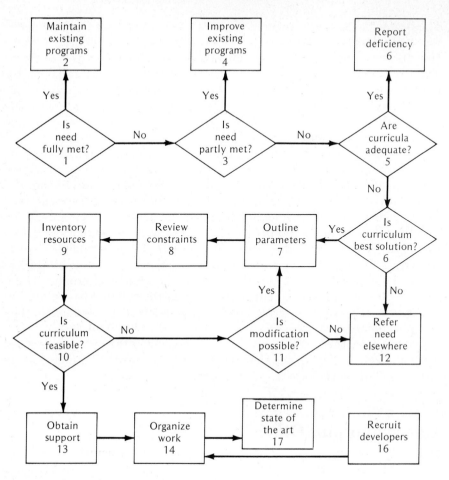

Figure 5–1   Main procedures in organizing for curriculum development

4. Run a safe driving campaign in the school encouraging the use of seat belts, discouraging impaired driving, etc.

5. Initiate an inter-school or inter-class competition for the lowest number of accidents or penalties.

6. Organize a series of addresses on the theme of safe driving by police, insurers, physicians, and lawyers.

7. Show films on driving and accidents in classes or school assemblies.

8. Use an extracurricular car rally club as a covert means for developing good driving habits.

The consequences of each of these alternatives is estimated; the expected benefits, notably predicted reduction in accidents, are assessed and balanced against the anticipated costs, such as financial cost, administrative or organizational effort, and potential opposition. The best alternative, or mix of alternatives, can then be selected.

Curriculum Parameters

The designers of the Anglo-French airliner Concorde decided before 1961 on a number of basic design characteristics for the plane. Concorde was to be a slim, delta-wing, medium-range aircraft. Conventional aluminum alloys would be used, and the plane would be powered by a modified Olympus engine available at that time. These design characteristics, or parameters, determined the nature of the aircraft that went into service fifteen years later (McKinlay, 1977).

Although the parameters of a curriculum are more flexible than those for an aircraft, the influence they exert on final design makes it important that they be determined with care. The main parameters to be considered at this stage in curriculum development are institutional context, target population, time, and cost. Specific questions arise regarding each of these parameters.

Institutional context

Where will the curriculum fit in the overall program and organization of the institution? Is it a core, optional, or extracurricular curriculum? What is its relationship with other curricula? Who will be responsible for its approval, development, implementation, maintenance, evaluation, and supervision?

It is unwise to develop curricula in a vacuum. Designers need to have a clear idea of the institutional, community, and social context within which the curriculum is to be implemented. The place of the curriculum in the overall program and organization of the institution and its relationship to other curricula must be determined. So must the question of who is to be responsible for its approval, development, implementation, maintenance, evaluation, and supervision. The impact the curriculum may have on other courses, programs, and teachers should be estimated. Consideration should be given to other parts of the institution and to other institutions that might be able to use or adapt the curriculum. At this early stage, it will not be possible to provide precise information in all of these areas. But full details should be worked out before the curriculum is complete; they will be included in the final document in a section on context.

The learners

Learner characteristics are described in detail later in the curriculum development process. At this stage it is necessary to ask Who are the students for whom the curriculum is being designed? What maximum and minimum numbers of students will be accommodated, in how many groups?

Time

What is the anticipated length of the course in clock hours and total elapsed time? How often will the course be offered? By what date will the course be ready for installation?

Cost

What is the minimum and maximum expected cost of offering the course, for the first time, and when repeated?

In order to answer these questions, it is necessary to audit the applicable constraints and resources. This will not produce exact answers, which will emerge only as the curriculum is developed in detail. But it will provide the basis for estimates that can support a request for the necessary development resources.

Reviewing Constraints

A constraint is a factor external to a system that limits the capability of the system. All terrestial engineering systems, for example, must operate within constraints imposed by gravity. Teachers and designers of curriculum face many kinds of constraints. These will vary with the institution and the kind of curriculum. The efficiency of the post office is not a constraint in most school curricula, but is an important constraint in the operation of correspondence courses. Some of the constraints that frequently influence the design of curricula are the learners, politics, policy, external examinations, financial and material limitations, staffing, time, and the physical environment.

The learners

In the minds of teachers the major constraints appear to emanate from the learners themselves: their ability, background, and motivation (Taylor, 1975). But these constraints need not be accepted fatalistically.

Inadequate background can often be remedied within a curriculum; motivation can be developed by providing learners with successful experiences with interesting and significant content; and there is mounting evidence that teachers generally underestimate the abilities of their pupils (Block, 1971). Many of these constraints can thus be overcome by skillful curriculum design and instruction and are therefore strictly not constraints at all.

Political constraints

The planner should not lose sight of the fact that curriculum design is about allocation of resources towards certain ends and is hence essentially a political process. Political constraints must therefore be taken into account. Within the school the attitude of administrators toward innovation in general or toward a particular curriculum innovation is critical. It is difficult to introduce new curricula in art or music in an environment that despises artists or in a school whose principal believes that the primary function of the music department is to stage a lavish musical once a year. In many subjects, notably languages, the attitude of parents will profoundly affect the motivation and achievement of their children (Burstall, 1974). The attitude of teachers will determine the extent to which the curriculum is implemented in the school. Increasing interest in curriculum questions by teachers' organizations should not be overlooked. The political ethos of the community or state also constrains the designer. It is sometimes thought that political constraints on the teaching of school biology ended with the Scopes trial in Tennessee in 1925; but in fact a high-school biology teacher was dismissed in the same state in 1967 for violating the law that made it illegal "to teach any theory that denies the story of divine creation of man as taught in the Bible and to teach instead that man has descended from a lower order of animals" (Beavan, 1967). The politics of implementation will be discussed in a later chapter. But the judicious planner thinks about implementation from the beginning and will therefore appraise the significance and intransigence of potential political opposition at this early stage in the design, rather than wait until the curriculum design is complete.

Policy constraints

Closely related to political constraints are policy constraints. State or local educational policy may dictate the curriculum to an extent that leaves little latitude for innovation. It used to be said (with some exaggeration) that the French Minister of Education could tell what every schoolchild in France was doing at a given moment by looking at his watch. Many jurisdictions place constraints on curriculum content by

---

Curriculum Constraints in Austria

The School Organization Law defines the subjects to be taught. It includes the number of hours per week to be devoted to each subject; the general aims of the type of school; the aims of instruction in each subject; the organization of subject-matter for each subject and grade. . . . For the planning of instruction and the development of materials by the individual classroom teacher, no facilities are provided at school level, neither in terms of space nor library or technical facilities. There are no institutional procedures to support cooperative planning, neither is there any support system whereby continued consultation and advice would be available. Nor are formal channels of communication to either colleges or universities open to the individual teacher, and there are few intrinsic (and no extrinsic) incentives motivating teachers to adopt a systematic approach to curriculum development. . . .

The individual school is not prepared to initiate and support curriculum development which at school level is at present the private affair of individual teachers. There are no local or regional institutions such as teachers' centers to support formal and informal development activities by teams or individuals. Pedagogical institutes are only concerned with isolated formal training courses, and no attention is paid to continuing informal teacher development. Curriculum development as an aspect of the teacher's role is neither explicit nor well-defined. Initiative on the part of teachers is not valued, and is incompatible with the operations of the centralized system. In addition, there are no established standards of quality for instruction, so there is little incentive for teachers to plan, evaluate, and improve their own teaching.

—*Organization for Economic Cooperation and Development*
(1975, pp. 138, 139, 147, 149.)

---

legislating the textbooks and other materials that may or may not be used in the classroom.

Policy constraints can sometimes be circumvented by human resourcefulness. A young teacher found herself teaching in an elementary school where it was policy that learning activities be decided daily by student vote in each classroom. This made planning impossible and led to ineffective teaching and student boredom and dissatisfaction. After a few days of experience with the policy, the teacher announced that voting would henceforth be by secret ballot. From then on, the announced results of the voting coincided with the lessons she had prepared in advance. It remained a mystery to her colleagues how her classes worked so smoothly and effectively.

External examinations

The policy constraint that outweighs all others, where it exists, is the external examination. Indeed, in many countries, such as England and Wales, it could be said that those who set the external examinations determine the school curriculum. (Who these people are, how they are selected, and how they operate, is itself a tragicomedy that cannot be examined here.) This constraint used to operate in caricature in countries of the British Commonwealth, especially in East and West Africa and the West Indies. Education was available only to a minority, and academic progress was controlled by highly competitive examinations. In many places, the examinations in the senior secondary grades were the General Certificates of Education, set by university-based examining boards in England. The examinations were the same as those taken by English students. Hence the history tests examined knowledge of English history, the geography tests the geography of the British Isles, while the test in botany would ask students, for example, to "describe four English trees in summer and winter." Enterprising teachers had to obtain specimens of pine needles and hawthorn leaves by mail from Britain. As far away as New Zealand, British examinations were taken by many students and sent back to Britain for marking, with disastrous results on one occasion during the war when submarines sank the ship carrying the examination papers.

Where the student's future depends on success in an examination, the conscientious teacher has no alternative but to prepare the learner as well as possible for the examination, no matter how irrelevant the actual learning required. This is not an argument against external examinations, but it is one reason why the validity of examinations is of critical significance in curriculum development.

Financial and material constraints

Financial and material constraints often loom large in the thinking of educators. The designers of such curricula as those in electronics, modern film, or gymnastics can foresee well in advance that expensive materials or equipment will be required. Specialized facilities may be needed, as for swimming or automotive mechanics. If a curriculum is to be successfully implemented, teachers must be provided with, or at least advised how they can obtain, any specialized materials or equipment that the curriculum requires.

Staffing

Staffing considerations are closely linked to finance. The planner must ask whether competent staff are available. A successful course in theatre arts, for example, requires a skillful dramatics teacher, not (as one of my colleagues likes to put it) a redundant English teacher who once saw a play. If suitable staff are not available, inservice training must be feasible. Staff will also be needed to develop the curriculum, and resource personnel may be required.

Time

Time is no more on your side in planning curriculum than in any other dimension of living. The amount of time available for developing, implementing and teaching a curriculum is a severe constraint. Detailed estimates of instructional time requirements are calculated much later in the design process. At this stage the designers must be reasonably confident that the man-hours needed to accomplish the task will be available.

Physical environment

Even the physical environment imposes constraints. Wilderness survival training is difficult to operate (in its conventional sense) in a downtown metropolitan school, just as urban education presents problems in a rural environment. The climate, especially in such subjects as physical education, will determine what activities are possible at certain times of year. Coupled with the absence of air conditioning in many North American schools, the climate is a major constraint on efforts to rationalize the organization of the school year.

Curriculum developers face two dangers related to constraints. One is ignoring them and developing curricula that are not feasible. The other is dwelling upon them and giving up in despair. A comprehensive list of constraints can be intimidating, but a more encouraging picture emerges when the designer comes to inventory the resources.

Resources

Most of the variables discussed above as constraints can also be regarded as resources. The political environment, for example, may be an asset if the proposed curriculum can be made to appear responsive to community feeling. Thorough needs assessment may go far to ensure that student attitude is a resource rather than a constraint.

The mistake most frequently made in assessing resources is to overlook those that lie outside the usual purview of the teacher. The financial

> It is no longer resources that limit decisions; it is the decision that makes the resources.
>
> —*U Thant, Secretary-General of
> The United Nations, 1961–71.*

resources available to a school that wants to develop a new curriculum are not limited to the total of the curriculum budget. Government agencies are often willing to support interesting curriculum projects; in the present economic context this applies particularly to projects that generate employment. Many philanthropic foundations also subsidize educational innovation and frequently fail to use all their available funds for want of sufficient qualified applications. In addition, private corporations are often prepared to support curriculum projects that have a clear public value.

There are, likewise, personnel resources beyond the existing instructional staff. The Southwest Regional Laboratory in the United States achieved significant results by training parents to tutor their children in beginning reading skills for a short period each evening (Southwest Regional Laboratory, 1972). There are in any school numerous tasks that community volunteers can perform with competence and enthusiasm, such as working with individuals or groups of children with special needs or interests. Consider how a history teacher could enliven a lesson on the invasion of Normandy in 1944, by inviting a veteran of the battle to address the class; few things please an old soldier more than the opportunity to refight his battles before a receptive audience.

The environment provides resources for almost every area of the curriculum, but these are often underutilized. Who is not familiar with the school on the edge of the wilderness that has no outdoor education program; the school whose physics students have never visited the local nuclear power station; or the school whose biology teachers have never considered utilizing the swamp that is two minutes' walk away?

Finally, the learners are themselves a resource. There is an eloquent scene in Ken Loach's remarkable film *Kes*, in which a deprived and awkward thirteen-year-old holds his classmates spellbound as he describes his passionate interest in training the young kestrel he has reared. Many children develop erudite interests and talents that are unsuspected by their teachers. In these and in more conventional areas students are capable of teaching themselves, teaching other students, and teaching teachers. It is unfortunate if insecurity and an outmoded concept of hierarchy prevent teachers from recognizing what their own students have to offer.

Is the Curriculum Feasible?

Once the constraints and resources have been reviewed, the parameters can be more clearly specified. The feasibility of the project can now be addressed. In the world of public policy, feasibility studies are often neglected or carried out in a slipshod manner. As a result, projects frequently outrun their budgets or are abandoned after the expenditure of millions of dollars. In curriculum design the operative question is whether a curriculum can meet the educational/training need within the specified parameters. If it cannot, the parameters may be adjusted; the course may be lengthened, the staff-student ratio reduced, etc. But as the parameters are largely governed by the constraints, unfeasibility is commonly due to the magnitude of the constraints. It may be necessary to ask whether any of the constraints can be changed. Perhaps decision-makers can be persuaded to release funds, or a longer time span considered during which public opinion may become more favorable. By definition, constraints cannot be changed from within the system; to change them it is necessary to leave the curriculum design system and become involved in the political or financial or some other system. If the constraints seem to be unyielding, then the role of the school must be reconsidered. It is pointless to proceed to develop a curriculum that is not feasible.

Impact Analysis

In addition to ensuring that the proposed curriculum is feasible, it is important to predict the effects that the change will have throughout the system. This is known as impact analysis. Major policies are often implemented without adequate impact analysis. The long-term effects of the introduction of slavery into the New World in the seventeenth century, and of the atmospheric testing of nuclear weapons in the twentieth, appear to have been overlooked by their proponents. Other examples are the effects of widespread use of synthetic herbicides and pesticides on water quality and marine life; the consequences for workers of manufacturing processes involving asbestos; and the results of national dependence on foreign supplies of oil.

Acting in the light of the consequences of one's actions is the essence of responsibility, and responsibility is at the heart of curriculum design. The designer should estimate both the direct and indirect effects a proposed curriculum will have on the students, on other programs, and on other people in and outside the institution. These effects must be taken into account in the design and made clear to decision-makers when the curriculum proposal is submitted.

Preparing a Curriculum Prospectus

Many teachers believe that all they need to design a curriculum is a pen and the back of an envelope. No doubt some good curricula are designed this way, and no more may be necessary in planning a minor course change that requires neither additional resources nor outside approval. But curricula that may be used over a period of time by many people usually require more substantial resources. A British institution with much experience in curriculum development, the Open University, was in the early 1970s spending $60,000 to $100,000 to produce each of its curricula (Swift, 1974).

In addition to the human skills required, which will be discussed shortly, three main kinds of support are needed for curriculum development: time, money, and approval. A commitment for this support should be obtained before development begins.

Time is the most significant resource consumed in curriculum development. As a rule of thumb, the planner should estimate that a minimum of one hour of development time is needed for each hour of instructional time. Thus a course to be taught 45 minutes a day for a school year of 180 days will require at least 135 hours of development time. Unfortunately the time is not greatly reduced by teamwork, although the quality of the curriculum may improve.

We are speaking here of the time required to develop the curriculum, not to plan the details of instruction, such as individual lessons, or to prepare instructional materials. The production of educational films or computer-based instruction may require hundreds of hours of development time for each hour of instruction.

Given the amount of time the task requires, it seems unreasonable for administrators to expect teachers to design curricula effectively in their spare time, especially in the evenings following long days in the classroom. Relieving a team of motivated teachers of classroom responsibility for a month for the purpose, on the other hand, or paying a modest stipend during the summer vacation to a curriculum development group, often produces impressive results.

Most development activity involves thinking, discussing, and writing. The major costs will be for the time of developers, secretarial staff, consultants, and other personnel involved. Money may also be needed for materials, travel, postage, and telephone. The development costs of producing the first draft or curriculum prototype are included, but not production costs, such as printing program materials for actual classroom use.

If the procedures by which curriculum developers and administrators reach agreement on what is to be done and how are haphazard and ill-defined, subsequent confusion and misunderstanding can be anticipated. The practice followed in engineering firms would appear to be a useful model for education. The project engineers draw up a prospectus outlining what is to be done and what resources will be needed to do it. The prospectus is a professional rather than a promotional document. If accepted, it forms a kind of contract between the management and the project team, giving both sides a clear outline of their commitments (Hall, 1962).

A curriculum prospectus should describe in general terms the curriculum envisaged; clearly it cannot go into detail, as the detail has yet to be developed. The process and results of the needs assessment should be fully described. The history of the problem and the inadequacy of present curricula to resolve it or to meet the need should be reported. The writers should show that constraints and resources have been taken into account. The prospectus is thus a summary of work done, conclusions reached up to this point, and a proposal for the task that lies ahead.

In addition to securing material resources, the proposal, if accepted, institutionalizes formal support for the curriculum project. Such recognition of legitimacy is essential to give the developers a sense of efficacy and to provide them with access to decision-makers during the development phase. Without the conviction that superiors regard their efforts as important, few curriculum planners can remain motivated for long.

Administrators who are concerned by the casual nature of much curriculum design (and in some schools by its apparent nonexistence) are likely to be impressed by a carefully researched and reasoned prospectus. They may, however, grant only a portion of the support requested.

The astute educator will not retire in dudgeon if offered only part of what is asked for. The estimate should provide enough latitude to tolerate some shortfall in resources. If the offer is significantly less than the request, this is evidence that the constraints were greater than estimated. It will be necessary to decide whether the need can still be met in the face of more severe constraints. Less than full support is not grounds for canceling the project. If resources are sufficient to complete large parts of the curriculum effectively, the planners may establish a base for obtaining the rest of the resources at a later date. Alternatively, a less expensive solution to the problem may be considered, or a lower standard of achievement accepted as preferable to aborting the project altogether.

If, however, none of the required resources are offered or the offer is grossly inadequate, there is no point in proceeding. Even if it were possible to make bricks without straw, such a response shows a lack of enthusiasm on the part of the administration and strongly suggests that the curriculum, even when completed, will never be implemented. The designers would do well to cut their losses and seek another project, or another employer.

Forming a Curriculum Team

One-person operations have a number of advantages. Problems of communication and consensus disappear. Decisions can be made and implemented rapidly. There is no division between control and consent. Some people are natural individualists and are simply more effective working on their own. Classroom teachers developing curricula for their own use are likely to work independently as a matter of course. Furthermore, it is a myth that two heads are necessarily better than one. Educators have a great belief that any problem can be solved by setting up a committee. But ten incompetents will not outperform one competent individual. Ten times zero is still zero.

One-person curriculum development, however, is rarely feasible

---

The fundamental fact of man's capacity to collaborate with his fellows in the face-to-face group will one day be recognized. Then, and only then, will management discover how seriously it has underestimated the true potential of its human resources.

—*Douglas McGregor (1960, p. 242)*

above the level of the individual classroom or school. For curricula developed at the district, state, or national level, the scale of the projects normally requires a team effort, and it becomes politically necessary to include on the team representatives from many constituencies, including the potential users of the curriculum. There are several advantages in a team operation. A more creative and broader interplay of ideas is possible than any member of the team could achieve autonomously. The task may not be completed faster, but for sociable people the time passes more agreeably.

A hybrid between the individual designer and the curriculum team is a committee that attempts to operate simply as the sum of its parts, by subdividing the work into individual units and collating the final results. Such committees usually combine the disadvantages of individual and group operation and reap the benefits of neither.

The curriculum design team may be set up at any stage prior to the beginning of the design work. The earlier the team is recruited and begins to work together, the higher the commitment to the project is likely to be.

Conditions of work

Certain conditions are necessary for effective team work. The need for time, funds, secretarial assistance, access to decision-makers, and political support has already been mentioned. These conditions should have been secured by management's acceptance of the prospectus. This document will also have established a specific task and a deadline, both of which are valuable assets to team effectiveness. An additional way in which management can support the curriculum project is to act as an interface between the team and the rest of the institution or the public. An administrator can be included on the team for this purpose, but it is often effective for the team to maintain liaison with an "outside person" who performs public-relations functions; this saves the team from spending undue time on political debate.

Team size

The size of a working group is important. The problems facing large teams can be demonstrated mathematically. Suppose that the probability of immediate agreement (on policy, procedure, or date of the next meeting) between any two members is 80 percent. We can expect a 41 percent probability of immediate unanimity among a team of five members. But with eight members the probability is only 21 percent, and with twelve members only 9 percent. The problems of division, deadlock, and dropout all appear to increase with the size of the committee. The cybernetician,

Stafford Beer, regards seven as the maximum size of a creative group (1975, p. 449), while Hare (1962, p. 245) suggests five as the optimum number for a small discussion group.

Clearly a committee working on a large-scale curriculum project could not operate with only five members. Much excellent curriculum work has in fact been done by committees containing several dozen people. Plenary sessions for deliberation or approval of policy may well be large. But the actual drafting of plans and documents is normally done by small subcommittees of five members or less.

Expertise required

The ideal curriculum team will include expertise in at least six areas. Three of them are critical: subject matter, pedagogy, and curriculum design. Three are important: measurement, organization, and writing skill.

Subject matter   It would be a rash committee that attempted to develop a curriculum in a discipline without including a scholar from the discipline among its members. The subject specialist must, however, have certain qualities. He or she must know not only the substance of the discipline, but its philosophy; not simply what it does, but what it aims to do; its scope, potential, and assumptions; its future as well as its past; in a word, the metadiscipline. Even more of a challenge, the subject specialist must recognize the limitations of the discipline, and his or her own limitations as a specialist. Joseph Schwab has written eloquently of the dangers that exist when curriculum development is dominated by scholars unaware of their own limitations. The history of curriculum in the past twenty years is evidence that such dangers are not illusory.

Pedagogy   Skilled and experienced teachers bring to a curriculum team essential practical knowledge of students, the school environment, and the teaching process. Respected representatives of the ultimate users of the curriculum add credibility to the work of the team. When the new curriculum is ready for implementation, they may also be the ideal people to demonstrate and promote the innovation among their peers.

Curriculum design   It is not redundant to mention the need for a curriculum team to include expertise in curriculum design. In the past this set of skills was absent more often than not, and that may be why many self-styled curriculum innovations consisted of nothing more than reorganized catalogs of items of content. The need is better filled today, as professional training in curriculum development, "instructional systems design," and related fields becomes more widely available. Expertise

Scholars and the Curriculum

Scholars, as such, are incompetent to translate scholarly material into curriculum. They possess one body of disciplines indispensable to the task. They lack four others, equally indispensable [knowledge about learners, about the school milieu, about teaching, and about curriculum making]. As scholars, they not only lack these other four, but also, as individuals, they are prone at best to ignore and at worst to sneer at them. Possessors of the other four necessary disciplines have an equal handicap; they do not possess the discipline of the scholar; they do not know the bodies of knowledge which his discipline has produced; they are often overawed by him. Yet, all five disciplines are necessary, and the curriculum work their possessors do must be done in collaboration.

—*Joseph J. Schwab (1973, p. 501)*

of this kind is ideally possessed by most or all of the team members. A team runs the risk of imbalance or collapse if only one member knows where the task is leading.

Measurement   Few curriculum teams can avoid the measurement issue. Although specialized techniques of educational measurement have been available longer than techniques of curriculum design, they are no more widely represented among teachers. In certain cases, curriculum teams can hire such expertise from outside as needed, but it is generally more satisfactory if the team includes a measurement person.

Organization   A curriculum team should organize its time, resources, and activities effectively. Organizational duties are often delegated to a committee chairman, but it is probably preferable if all team members have skills and share responsibilities in this area.

Writing skill   As the final product of the committee will be a written document, which must combine technical exactness with clarity and conviction, writing skill should not be underestimated.

It is no easy matter to include all these areas of expertise in a committee of five. By the same token, a consideration of the different skills needed illustrates the demands facing a one-person curriculum operation.

Personal qualities of curriculum teams

Numerous writers have described the characteristics of effective groups. The features commonly noted are closely interrelated. It is difficult to distinguish between necessary conditions for effectiveness and symptoms of effectiveness, because an effective group generates qualities that in turn facilitate greater effectiveness. Motivation is certainly a central factor and is itself multifaceted. But it may be supposed that the decisions that are critical to ensuring motivation will be those that have already been made: identification of a significant curriculum problem, provision of adequate working conditions, and selection of appropriate team members.

The atmosphere of an effective group is relaxed and informal, yet involvement is high. Every member engages in discussion on an equal basis. Members are socially and psychologically secure: they trust one another, express their feelings freely and openly, and show clear value commitments. Every idea is given a hearing; ideas may be challenged but are rarely attacked. Disagreement occurs without discord. Communication is multidirectional; members are self-conscious about the group process and take pains to make it work (McGregor, 1960).

Effective groups typically make decisions by consensus rather than by chairman's decision, majority rule, or unanimous vote. Consensus has been lucidly described by Schmuck:

> Group consensus is a decision-making method in which all participants contribute their thoughts and feelings and all share in the final decision. No decision becomes final which is not understood by nearly all members. But consensus does *not* mean that everyone agrees. Consensus means that (1) everyone can paraphrase the issue to show that he understands it; (2) everyone has a chance to describe his feelings about the issues; and (3) those who continue to disagree will nevertheless say publicly that they are willing to give the decision an experimental try for a prescribed time. In other words, consensus means that a sufficient number of participants are in favor of a decision to carry it out, while others understand the decision and will not obstruct its occurrence (Schmuck, 1972, p. 43).

Lest it should be assumed that a skillful leader is all that is necessary to achieve these conditions, McGregor comments on

> the mistaken idea that the effectiveness of the group depends solely upon the leader. As a matter of fact, the research evidence indicates quite clearly that *skillful and sensitive membership behavior is the real clue to effective group operation*. In a really competent and skilled group, the members can in fact carry on a highly effective operation with no designated leader whatever (McGregor, 1960, p. 239).

It is crucial that the members of a group be compatible. Extensive research suggests that similarity of attitudes is important in all human relationships, from marriage to judicial sentencing (Byrne, 1971). Against this must be balanced the need for diversity in a curriculum design team.

As a rule, such teams consist only of educators. This ensures that the assumptions, prejudices, shibboleths, taboos, and professional folklore of educators will pass unquestioned into the curriculum. Such a situation retards the development of valid and effective curricula. Thus every curriculum development team should include at least one member who is not an educator: perhaps a student, a parent, or an employer. It is not easy to find an outsider who has not only the confidence to challenge the assumptions of educators but also the tact and good will to generate growth rather than dissension; but the effort is worth making.

While the team as a whole should have breadth and diversity to match the curriculum problem, individual members should also have a broad rather than a narrow outlook. Each may have a particular specialization, but his or her interest should be in developing an effective curriculum as a whole rather than in promoting any single component. In contrast both to those technicians who know only how, and to those academics who know only why, the curriculum designer must be a true professional: one who knows both how and why.

People to avoid

Selecting the right people to serve on a curriculum design team is crucial; so is not selecting the wrong people. Those who should not be selected are, in general, the converse of those who should be. But in addition, some specific types need to be avoided.

Anxious, closed-minded, and dogmatic people have great difficulty participating as equals in free-flowing discussion, particularly on value-laden issues. Tense and humorless, they place excessive reliance on leadership from the chair and seek the guidance of authority in ascertaining the single right answer to any issue (Zagona and Zurcher, 1964). The extreme of this type is the fanatic (in Churchill's immortal definition, a man who can't change his mind and won't change the subject). Few people can frustrate a committee faster than the member impelled by a fanatical belief in or against open education, the communist conspiracy, or behavioral objectives.

People who will dominate the committee are poor choices. The experienced chairman and the political manipulator may thus be as unsuitable as the compulsive talker. According to Hare, "In newly formed leaderless groups without a formal structure, members tend to assume

> When we all think alike, no one thinks very much.
>
> —*Walter Lippman, journalist*

"You haven't been listening, Mr. Bradford. We already have readin', writin', and 'rithmetic."

the same positions which they had in other groups of long standing" (1962, p. 122). For this reason, it may be necessary to forgo appointing any member whose status is markedly greater than that of the other members. It is an exceptional person who can make a positive contribution to a committee of subordinates while putting them sufficiently at their ease to accept him or her as a peer. Fortunately such people do exist.

One way to guarantee the breakdown of a group is to include representatives from both sides of a feud. In such a situation, every issue, rather than being discussed on its merits, becomes a weapon in the dispute and makes consensus impossible.

Perfectionists, sometimes defined as individuals who take pains and give them to other people, present other problems. They fail to distinguish between excellence, which is a proper aspiration for curriculum designers, and perfection, which is unattainable. Perfectionists are usually obsessive arguers. They demand certainty before issues are resolved and can in this way successfully prevent or sabotage any decision. In fact doubt and uncertainty delight them, and education affords them a good supply of both. Perfectionists can be interesting people to talk to when you have the time, but in the pragmatic world of curriculum they have little to contribute.

Method of selection

There is no problem-free method for selecting a curriculum team. Election by their peers may identify the most politically visible and ambitious people, but the relationship between these qualities and skill in curriculum development is unknown. Calling for volunteers may produce an incompatible and inexpert team of compulsive joiners or people with an axe to grind. Appointment of the most promising people may overlook competent and motivated individuals and may cause resentment among those who have been omitted. Although local circumstances will determine the method of selection, three considerations should be kept in mind: (1) the team must be competent; (2) the team must be credible to the outside constituency; and (3) potential opponents may be included if their positive contribution will outweigh their negative contribution, or if it seems likely that they can be converted.

The Curriculum Team as a Temporary System

A love affair, a jury, a tennis match, a political demonstration, a party, a college class, an ocean cruise, and a theatrical production all share one common feature: they are temporary systems. In all of them, people act in concert for a limited period, disbanding once the task or activity is completed. Temporary systems take on a life of their own and generate a momentum uncharacteristic of routine activities. Most temporary systems have a unique appeal for their participants; they provide experiences to which much energy is committed and which are often highly valued at the time and in retrospect (Miles, 1964). In contemporary society the range of temporary systems appears to be increasing. Even the previously stable institution of marriage is coming to be viewed as a temporary system.

Business and industry capitalize on the productivity of temporary systems by extensive use of the task force for special projects. Many educational jurisdictions have institutionalized curriculum design and made it the responsibility of a permanent curriculum staff. But there appear to be major advantages in organizing curriculum design teams as temporary systems. Service on a curriculum team that is provided with a clear task and the necessary resources should be both productive and professionally enriching for the participants.

Curriculum design as job enrichment

The importance of motivation to the effectiveness of a curriculum development team has already been mentioned. While such incentives as salary and promotion may come to mind, there is substantial evidence that extrinsic incentives have less impact on teachers than intrinsic rewards related to the satisfaction teachers find in their work (Spuck, 1974; Kimball, 1974). Successful participation in curriculum design may itself be a means of motivating teachers.

Of the many strategies that have been attempted to motivate employees in various settings, one of the most consistently successful is job enrichment. The thesis of the originator of this concept, Frederick Herzberg, is that "the factors involved in producing job satisfaction and motivation are separate and distinct from the factors that lead to job dissatisfaction" (Herzberg, 1968, p. 53). Factors related to job dissatisfaction tend to be in the areas of company policy, supervision, and working conditions. Factors relating to job satisfaction have to do with achievement, recognition, responsibility, and personal growth. Herzberg identified a number of principles for job enrichment, including (1) removing some controls while retaining accountability; (2) increasing the accountability of individuals for their own work; (3) giving a person a complete natural unit of work; (4) granting additional authority to an employee in his activity; (5) introducing new and more difficult tasks not previously handled; and (6) assigning individuals specific or specialized tasks, enabling them to become experts. The positive effect on job satisfaction of applying these principles has been confirmed in studies in a number of different countries of several groups of employees, including nurses, accountants, engineers, and teachers (Paul, Robertson, and Herzberg, 1969).

Teacher participation in significant curriculum development appears to conform closely to Herzberg's principles of job enrichment. At present it is experienced by relatively few teachers (Reisman, Robinson, and Perenson, 1974). Moreover, when teachers do become involved in curriculum development, it is often without training or resources, and hence as likely to be a discouraging as an enriching experience.

The costs of effective curriculum design must not be minimized, but they can be regarded as an investment. The primary return is in the form of development of student potential. But more than a trivial spinoff is the enhanced motivation and professionality that results from successful participation by teachers.

Schedule and Budget

The curriculum team will have time at its disposal. It may also have funds. Unless it decides at an early stage how these resources are to be used, it will probably run out of both.

Figure 5–2 shows the master schedule for the 1969 Mariner Mars probe, developed by the California Institute of Technology Jet Propulsion

Figure 5-2 Mariner 1969 Project Master Schedule (Pickering, 1973, p. 141)

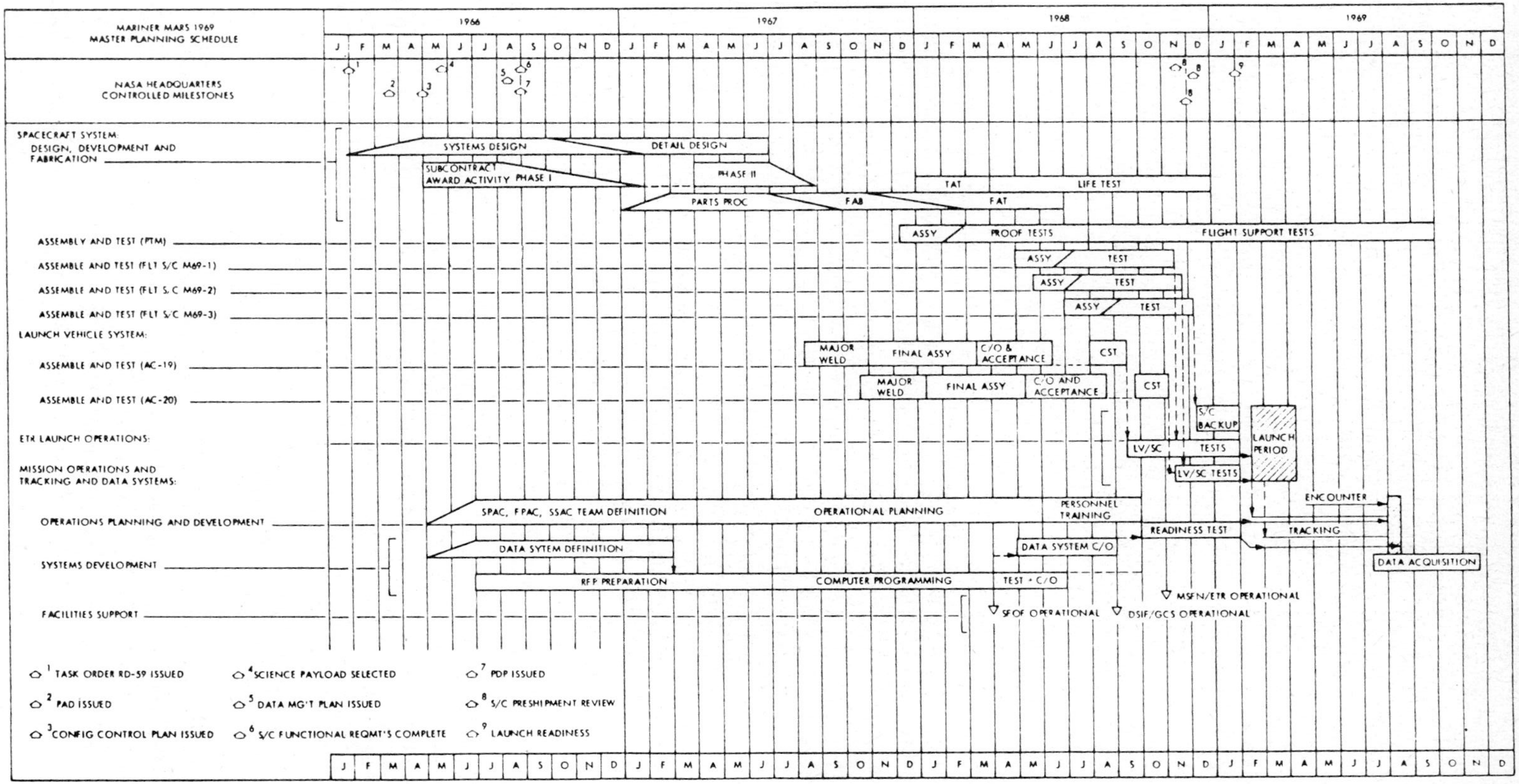

Laboratory. Such graphic schedules have strong visual impact but are time-consuming to prepare. Table 5–1 shows a simpler schedule, which indicates deadlines and responsibilities. The schedule could be extended back to include needs assessment, depending on the stage at which time planning is conducted and on the terms of reference of the team.

Similar care should be taken with the design budget. Salaries will be a major component if it is necessary to pay designers, their substitutes, or secretaries. Other costs may include visits to related institutions or programs, consultancy fees, reference materials or equipment, duplicating, stationery, telephone, and postage.

Determining the State of the Art

Although in the public mind intelligence work is synonymous with "procurement" of data by secret agents infiltrated into an alien country, the greater part of modern intelligence actually consists of "collection": the accumulation and analysis of data from overt sources such as newspapers, scientific journals, official government publications, yearbooks, news photographs, legislative debates, and broadcasts (Farago, 1962). Collection is prosaic work conducted by an officer safely seated at a desk at the home base. But it is work that is neglected at considerable cost. During the Second World War, British agents in France were captured by the Gestapo and executed for collecting information that was available in British public libraries.

There are analogies with contemporary curriculum design. All over the world, curriculum committees are busily engaged in largely redundant work. In an American school district, a committee of teachers develops language curricula, unaware that the Schools Council in Britain established a budget of £724,000 for a seven-year curriculum development project in modern languages that began in 1967 (Schools Council, 1968). Meanwhile, in an English county, the county curriculum consultant deploys a budget of £100 to develop a reading program, ignorant of the multimillion-dollar program in beginning reading developed by the Southwest Regional Laboratory (Niedermeyer, 1970).

This is not to suggest that curricula produced in one context can be applied without change in another. Sometimes this is the case. Carlton University in Ottawa and Stanford University in California are currently experimenting with a direct course exchange via satellite (*Canada Weekly*, 1976). But adopting a curriculum developed externally is often as uncomfortable as wearing another person's shoes. Nevertheless, it is folly to ignore relevant work that has been done elsewhere, and mere prejudice to assume that curricula "won't work here" simply because they are not locally developed. Many design problems may have already

MEMBERS: DESIGN TEAM A, B, C, D, E.			
Activity	Target completion date	Coordinator	Date completed
Design team established	Jan. 1, 1980		
Background			
review literature	Feb. 1, 1980	A	
visit programs	June 15, 1980	B	
Intents			
aim	Feb. 15, 1980	D	
rationale	Aug. 15, 1980	C	
objectives	March 15, 1980	D	
Entry characteristics			
description of learners	March 15, 1980	A	
prerequisites	April 1, 1980	C	
pretests	June 1, 1980	E	
Exit requirements			
performance criteria	April 15, 1980	E	
posttests	June 1, 1980	E	
grading and reporting	June 15, 1980	E	
Instruction			
subject matter	May 1, 1980	C	
teaching points	May 1, 1980	C	
methodology	May 15, 1980	A	
course schedule	May 15, 1980	B	
Monitoring			
formative tests	June 1, 1980	E	
remedial units	June 15, 1980	D	
enrichment units	June 15, 1980	A	
Logistics			
materials	July 15, 1980	B	
equipment	July 15, 1980	B	
facilities	July 15, 1980	B	
personnel	Aug. 1, 1980	E	
time	Aug. 1, 1980	A	
cost	Aug. 15, 1980	D	
Validation			
first draft	Sept. 1, 1980	A	
internal review	Oct. 1, 1980	D	
expert appraisal	Oct. 15, 1980	C	
pilot test	Jan. 1, 1981	B	
field test	July 1, 1981	E	
final revision	Aug. 1, 1981	B	

Table 5–1   Curriculum design master schedule

MEMBERS: DESIGN TEAM A, B, C, D, E.			
Activity	Target completion date	Coordinator	Date completed
Implementation			
information to users	July 1, 1980	B	
board approval	March 1, 1981	C	
presentation to schools	Oct. 1, 1981	A	
Design team dissolves	Dec. 31, 1981		

Table 5–1, continued

been solved; excellent materials may be cheaply available; new and effective teaching techniques may have been developed; entire curricula of proven effectiveness may be available off the shelf. Even an inferior curriculum may suggest pitfalls to avoid or components to improve.

Adequate national and international networks for the exchange of curricula have yet to be developed. In their absence, useful data on available curricula can be obtained from ERIC (Educational Resources Information Center, U.S. Office of Education) and from such organizations as the Association for Supervision and Curriculum Development in the United States, and the Schools Council in Britain.

Other means of tapping external resources are to engage consultants, visit innovating institutions, and attend relevant conferences. In some cases these approaches may provide useful shortcuts. In others they will consume time and money for no appreciable result. Many institutions on the visitors' circuit have earned a spurious reputation for innovation by providing antique curriculum content with a fresh coat of paint. Visitors sometimes find that the publicity releases have only a remote connection with what is actually happening in the school. Some amateur and professional consultants are worth their weight in gold; others are charlatans. And conferences may provide a rapid insight into the state of the art, or they may, as the philosopher R. G. Collingwood remarked, merely be occasions on which "one of the company reads a paper, and the rest discuss it with a fluency directly proportional to their ignorance" (1939, p. 54).

Curriculum designers must try to avoid either developing redundant or obsolete curricula, or engaging in so much reading, travel, and consultation that they have little time for original thought. The law of diminishing returns applies to any review of curriculum literature. The curriculum team must recognize the appropriate point at which to stop reading other people's works on curriculum and to begin developing their own.

ACTIVITIES

1. Think about the various ways in which the school could promote in students "responsible political participation." How does a formal curriculum approach compare with other methods in terms of expected costs and benefits?

2. Think of some project you would like to undertake in your professional or personal life. Write down the constraints, and identify them as (a) relatively easy to change; (b) relatively difficult to change; (c) virtually impossible to change. Then list the resources available. Estimate the feasibility of the project.

3. Impact analysis attempts to predict the short- and long-term consequences of a decision. Assess the consequences of one of the following: (a) school attendance laws are replaced by salaries for students over twelve, dependent on minimum learning achievement; (b) all school programs become optional, and teachers are paid on a per-student basis; (c) schools and colleges all operate on a year-round basis, with nine-week courses beginning every three weeks; (d) physical health and fitness is given overall priority as a goal of the educational system.

4. Write down the skills and qualities you have that would be valuable on a curriculum committee. Then write down those of your characteristics that would reduce the effectiveness of a curriculum team.

5. Draw up a directory of sources of information on curricula in your area of interest, at the local, regional, state/provincial, national, and international level.

QUESTIONS

1. Which of the following factors would a second-language curriculum development team probably find to be the most inflexible constraint?

   a. parental attitude
   b. teaching materials
   c. the objectives of the curriculum
   d. the availability of expert advice

2. A teacher decides that he needs $1500 and six weeks of release time to design a new curriculum. So he requests $2000 and eight weeks of release time. He is offered $500 and two weeks release time. This suggests that he made the error of

   a. underestimating the constraints
   b. incorrectly identifying the need
   c. failing to define his objectives
   d. overestimating the support required

3. You are considering developing a curriculum that will be taught one hour a day for 100 teaching days. You should allow a minimum of

   a. about ten hours of development time
   b. about fifty hours of development time

c. about one hundred hours of development time
d. about five hundred hours of development time

4. Effective curriculum development requires various kinds of support. When the curriculum designers have outlined the support they need, in order for design to proceed

a. all of what is requested must be provided
b. only the provision of adequate time is essential
c. at least part of what is requested should be provided
d. it is not essential that any of what is requested be provided

5. Which of the following resources are most necessary for a curriculum development team?

a. time, money, and support from the administration
b. public approval, official guidelines, and test materials
c. expert advice, physical facilities, and audiovisual equipment
d. achievement data, moral support of students, and reference material

6. An advantage of one-person curriculum development as against a team operation is with respect to

a. creativity
b. efficiency
c. sociability
d. division of labor

7. If a curriculum development team is to work effectively

a. it is not essential that any of the members of the team be expert in the subject matter of the curriculum
b. all members of the team should be experts in the subject matter
c. the majority of the members of the team should be experts in the subject matter
d. at least one team member should be an expert in the subject matter

8. A curriculum committee in English consists of a consultant who is an expert in curriculum design; a principal who is experienced in teaching English; a department head who has an M.A. in English; a teacher who is president of the local teacher organization; and another teacher with an M.Ed. in education measurement. The committee is defective mainly with respect to its

a. small size
b. limited power
c. lack of diversity
d. absence of expertise

9. In the long run, the most effective reward for participation by teachers in curriculum development is likely to be

a. improved salary and working conditions
b. a greater sense of satisfaction in their work

    c. sufficient release time to plan curriculum adequately

    d. promotion to a position commensurate with their expertise

10. If a curriculum development team has plenty of time but very little money, it should attempt to tap external resources primarily by

    a. attending conferences

    b. engaging consultants

    c. visiting related programs

    d. reviewing the literature

Check your answers against the key in Appendix 2.
9 or 10 right: You understand the material presented.
8 or 7 right: Review the areas of uncertainty.
6 or less right: Reread the chapter.

Recommended Reading

Hall, Arthur D. *A methodology for systems engineering.* New York: D. Van Nostrand, 1962. This monumental work, though now somewhat dated, makes many lucid and compelling points about project organization and planning that are directly applicable to education.

McGregor, Douglas. *The human side of enterprise.* New York: McGraw-Hill, 1960. Written with wisdom and common sense, this book outlines the conditions necessary for productive teamwork, based on the author's conviction that "an effective managerial group provides the best possible environment for individual development."

Harless, J. H. An analysis of front-end analysis. *Improving Human Performance*, 1973, 2, 229–244. Harless, a training and management consultant, outlines "all the smart questions that a manager, educator, trainer, and consultant should ask *before* deciding what specific solution to develop for a performance problem."

References

Beavan, K. A. Tennessee repeals monkey law. *Times Educational Supplement*, April 28, 1967, p. 1410.

Beer, Stafford. *Platform for change.* New York: Wiley, 1975.

Block, James H. *Mastery learning: Theory and practice.* New York: Holt, Rinehart & Winston, 1971.

Buros, Oscar. *Eighth mental measurements yearbook.* Highland Park, N.Y.: Gryphon Press, 1978.

Burstall, Clare. *Primary French in the balance.* London: National Foundation for Educational Research, 1974.

Byrne, Donn. *The attraction paradigm.* New York: Academic Press, 1971.

Canada Weekly, January 28, 1976. Ottawa: Information Division, Department of External Affairs.

Collingwood, R. G. *An autobiography.* Oxford: Clarendon Press, 1939.

Datta, Lois-Ellin. Front-end analysis: Pegasus or shank's mare? *New Directions for Program Evaluation,* 1978, 1 (Spring), 13–30.

Farago, Ladislas. *Spymaster.* New York: Warner, 1962.

Hall, Arthur D. *A methodology for systems engineering.* New York: D. Van Nostrand, 1962.

Hare, A. Paul. *Handbook of small group research.* New York: Free Press of Glencoe, 1962.

Harless, J. H. An analysis of front-end analysis. *Improving Human Performance,* 1973, 2, 229–244.

Herzberg, Frederick. One more time: How do you motivate employees? *Harvard Business Review,* 1968, 46, 53–62.

Kimball, R. B. A study of rewards and incentives for teachers. *Phi Delta Kappan,* 1974, 5, 637–638.

McGregor, Douglas. *The human side of enterprise.* New York: McGraw-Hill, 1960.

McKinlay, R. M. View from the top. *Aviation Engineering and Maintenance,* 1977, 1 (1), 13–18, 51.

Miles, Matthew B. On temporary systems. In M. B. Miles (ed.), *Innovation in education.* New York: Teachers College, 1964, pp. 437–490.

Niedermeyer, Fred C. Developing exportable teacher training for criterion-referenced instructional programs. Inglewood, Cal.: Southwest Regional Laboratory, 1970.

Organization for Economic Cooperation and Development. *Handbook on curriculum development.* Paris: OECD, 1975.

Paul, William J., Jr., Keith B. Robertson, and Frederick Herzberg. Job enrichment pays off. *Harvard Business Review,* 1969, 47, 61–78.

Pickering, William H. Systems engineering at the Jet Propulsion Laboratory. In Ralph F. Miles, Jr. (ed.), *Systems concepts.* New York: Wiley, 1973, pp. 125–149.

Reisman, S., L. D. Robinson, and E. Perenson. Curriculum guidelines: Implementation evaluation in Ontario. Paper presented at Annual Meeting of American Educational Research Association, New Orleans, March 1974.

Schools Council. *The first three years, 1964–1967.* London: Her Majesty's Stationery Office, 1968.

Schmuck, Richard. Developing collaborative decision-making: The importance of trusting, strong, and skillful leaders. *Educational Technology,* 1972, 12 (Oct.), 43–47.

Schwab, Joseph J. The practical: Translation into curriculum. *School Review,* 1973, 81, 501–522.

Southwest Regional Laboratory for Educational Research and Development. *PAL: Parent assisted learning. Parent guide.* Inglewood, Cal.: SWRL, 1972.

Spuck, D. W. Reward structures in the public school. *Educational Administration Quarterly,* 1974, 10 (1), 18–34.

Swift, Donald. Curriculum decision making in the Open University. In Allen T. Pearson (ed.), *Perspectives on curriculum.* Vol. 3. Edmonton, Alberta: University of Alberta, Faculty of Education, 1974, pp. 23–30.

Taylor, P. H. (ed.). *Aims, influence, and change in the primary school curriculum.* London: National Foundation for Educational Research, 1975.

Zagona, S. V., and L. A. Zurcher. Participation, interaction, and role behavior in groups selected from the extremes of the open-closed cognitive continuum. *Journal of Psychology,* 1964, 58, 255–264.

Part Three

SPECIFYING LEARNING OUTCOMES

6

PRINCIPLES

- Conscious pursuit of goals is characteristic of human life.

- Behavior has meaning only in relation to purpose.

- Clear definition of goals has been found to enhance human performance in many different contexts.

- In education, explicit goals generally seem to improve student learning.

- Curriculum goals are intended to guide and inform designers, teachers, students, evaluators, and the public.

- It is the goal that determines instruction, not instruction that determines the goal.

- Curriculum aims should express a significant intended change in the learner and should be concise, exact, complete, and acceptable.

- The overall intent of a curriculum can normally be expressed in a single statement.

- A curriculum rationale is an argument justifying the commitment of resources to pursuit of the aim.

CONCEPTS

Aim	Objective
Goal	Rationale

6

Purpose in the Curriculum

*Education must have an end in view, for it is not
an end in itself.*

—*Sybil Marshall, educator*

Aims in Education

Purpose in human life

A humane curriculum is one that enhances those qualities that are
of the essence of humanity. One such quality is intention, or purpose.

The significance of purpose in human life is indicated by the number
of terms that are used in relation to purpose: aim, ambition, end, goal,
intent, objective, target, and so on. In this book three main terms are
employed: aim, objective, and goal. *Aim* is used to refer to a statement
of the general change to be brought about in a learner. *Objective* is
defined as a statement of a specific change to be brought about in a

learner. And *goal* will be used as an umbrella term, including both general and specific purposes.

Inorganic matter does not have purposes. Its behavior is entirely in accordance with physical laws and can therefore be explained in mechanistic terms. A hammer, a torpedo, and a computer are not intrinsically goal-directed; nor is a book, a picture, or a symphony. They can act only as vehicles, instruments, or expressions of the purposes of human agents (Locke, 1969). Although it is common in everyday speech to use such phrases as "the purpose of life," strictly speaking abstract concepts such as life and education, and institutions such as schools, cannot have purposes of their own, apart from the purposes people seek in and through them.

Organic life is distinct from mere physical matter by its goal-directedness, which is apparent at every level, from the assimilation of food by an amoeba to the cognitive development of a child. Functional explanations are appropriate for organic life; and the position of an organism on the "scale of life" reflects the degree to which its behavior is goal-directed or functional (Sommerhoff, 1969).

Human life is set apart from most other organic life by consciousness of purpose, and human behavior is therefore subject to motivational explanation. People characteristically seek not only immediate purpose in their actions, but transcendent purpose, or meaning, in their lives. So embedded in human thinking is the concept of purpose, that it is difficult to speak rationally of behavior or to speak of rational behavior without recognition of intention. Actions can be described, but they cannot be explained or justified, and hence cannot be understood, without reference to purpose. In purposive explanations

> acts are given (or found to have) a meaning, and this meaning then enters as an essential constituent of the explanations offered for the resultant actions. . . . When an act is given a meaning it is interpreted as an action directed toward some end (though it may be an end realized in the action itself—as when an act is interpreted as being playful, for example). All act meaning, as I see it, is purposive. . . . Acts that are not in some sense goal directed are precisely those, it seems to me, that are designated as meaningless (Kaplan, 1964, p. 363).

Purpose in human institutions

In recent years definition of goals has come to be viewed as an important stage in planning in many areas of endeavor. Space exploration programs have always emphasized the importance of clear specification of ultimate goals, or "mission definition." President Kennedy's message to Congress in 1961, launching a new phase in the American space program, announced a commendably succinct and explicit aim:

> Without a clear and detached examination of means and ends, purposes and ideals, the nation becomes a slave of its prejudices, the victim of its gadgets, and a casualty of its passions.
>
> —*Irwin Edman*

> This nation should commit itself to achieving a goal, before this decade is out, of landing a man on the moon and returning him safely to the earth.

Until agreement is reached on an overall goal, competition is likely among subordinate goals. The French ministers and politicians engaged in planning the future of Paris in the early 1970s found consensus beyond their reach until an ultimate goal was established. Once the goal of making Paris a global rather than a national city was agreed upon, accord followed on such subordinate goals as to make Paris multilingual, which could not have been agreed upon if proposed in isolation. "Equipped with an explicit goal, however tentative," Ackoff remarks, "we can begin to invent efficient and effective ways of making it real" (Ackoff, 1974, p. 10).

As the current fashion of management by objectives shows, business and industry have found it valuable to devote resources to definition of goals. Robert Townsend described his experience at Avis:

> One of the important functions of a leader is to make the organization concentrate on its objectives. In the case of Avis, it took us six months to define one objective—which turned out to be: "We want to become the fastest-growing company with the highest profit margins in the business of renting and leasing vehicles without drivers." That objective was simple enough that we didn't have to write it down. We could put it in every speech and talk about it wherever we went. . . . It also included a definition of our business: "renting and leasing vehicles without drivers." This let us put the blinders on ourselves and stop considering the acquisition of related businesses like motels, hotels, airlines, and travel agencies (Townsend, 1971, p. 111).

Few social organizations achieve such clarity of purpose with respect either to ultimate or immediate goals. In mental hospitals, prisons, and schools, there is an apparent lack of agreement as to whether the object is to develop good citizens or good patients, prisoners, and pupils. In such institutions conflict over goals tends to be prevented by avoiding the subject. Teachers differ widely in the goals they pursue, and commonly are uncertain about goals themselves or claim to be pursuing goals that bear little relation to their actual instruction. Students are often conditioned "not to reason why." Still less are parents and the general public enlightened regarding the ends to which their children and their taxes are committed.

Empirical evidence

The mass of writing on educational aims and objectives has tended to be rhetorical. But as Eisner (1969) pointed out, the value of objectives for curriculum and instruction is to a degree an empirical question. As it happens, a considerable amount of empirical evidence has been gathered on the effects of goal setting on human performance.

A classic, although rudimentary, study was conducted in 1935 by Mace (Figure 6–1). He discovered that by giving a group of subjects working on computation problems a specific daily standard to surpass, he could elicit performance superior to that obtained simply by instructing subjects to "do their best to improve."

Thirty years later Mace's work was extended in a series of studies

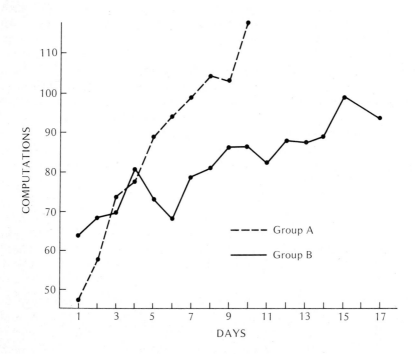

Group A: Instructed to surpass a specific standard prescribed for each day (ten subjects).

Group B: Instructed to do their best to improve and given no specific standard (ten subjects). (Mace, 1935, p. 21).

Figure 6–1   Performance under different instructions

> The time taken up by explaining, the time "lost" in treating the worker as a human being, will be caught up in the execution of the plan. People must know where they are going, and why.
>
> —*Frantz Fanon (1965, p. 154)*

by Locke and his colleagues. Their experiments showed that poorly motivated subjects who were given specific hard goals outperformed highly motivated subjects who were instructed to "do their best"; they also developed more interest in the task (Bryan and Locke, 1967a). Speed of performance could be affected by specifying in the objective the maximum time for task completion (Bryan and Locke, 1967b). Task satisfaction was found to be dependent on the extent to which goals were met (Locke, 1966; Locke, Cartledge, and Knerr 1970; Hamner, 1974). The studies as a whole led Locke to the conclusion that people's goals were their most significant motivator and mediated the effects of all other incentives (money, praise, knowledge of results, participation, and competition) on performance (Locke, 1968).

Locke's laboratory experiments were validated in an industrial setting by Latham and his colleagues, who successfully used goals as a means of increasing productivity in the American pulpwood industry. Goal setting was found to be more effective in increasing production than was supervision (Ronan, Latham, and Kinne, 1973). It was also effective in reducing absenteeism (Latham and Kinne, 1974). One company was able to save $250,000 on purchase of additional trucks alone, by setting and achieving high goals for logging teams in terms of utilization of logging truck capacities (Latham and Baldes, 1975). It was found that uneducated workers responded better when they participated in setting goals than when goals were merely assigned; for all workers, specific assigned or participative goals were more effective than instruction to "do their best" (Latham and Yukl, 1975). Steers and Porter (1974) reviewed the findings of some eighty empirical studies conducted in field and laboratory settings. They found that both specificity of goals and acceptance of goals were consistently and positively related to performance.

While such studies have done much to expand the influence of management by objectives in business and industry, educational writers have tended to overlook research conducted outside of school settings. The issue of the value of goals in instruction has been clouded by dispute over the form such goals should take: specifically, whether or not they should be stated in terms of pupil behavior. The questions "Do goals enhance learning?" and "Do goals improve instruction?" are unlikely to be answered conclusively by classical experiment, because it is extremely difficult to isolate use or nonuse of goals from other aspects of instruction. A feature of the intentional approach to instructional design is that it permeates every aspect of the curriculum.

Working within these limitations, Duchastel and Merrill, after surveying a number of educational studies, concluded that

> objectives sometimes help and are almost never harmful. Therefore, if the provision of objectives is relatively inexpensive, one might as well make them available to students (Duchastel and Merrill, 1973, p. 63).

More recently Melton (1978) identified fourteen experiments reporting positive effects of objectives on student learning and eight reporting no significant effect. He suggested that behavioral objectives would make little difference if students ignored them or if the objectives were too general, ambiguous, simple, or difficult. Specific studies suggest that the use of instructional objectives does not reduce the amount of incidental learning (that is, learning beyond that specified in the objectives) (Rothkopf and Kaplan, 1972) and that objectives are more likely to increase student learning when teachers are given extensive training in their use (Levine, 1972).

The latter finding may be critical. The definition and use of instructional objectives are not activities that are easily perfected by the uninitiated. On the contrary, to be performed adequately they usually require repeated practice under supervision. Business rarely attempts to introduce management by objectives by means of managerial fiat; yet many school districts have attempted to implement use of instructional objectives by administrative memorandum. Such mindless strategies go far toward convincing teachers that objectives are only the latest in the apparently endless train of educational bandwagons that have rolled through what passes for educational thought in our society.

Intention in the curriculum

The controversy over the place of intention in the design of curricula has produced hundreds of books and articles in the past decade. It is not the function of the present work either to summarize or to augment this body of literature. Interested readers may survey the main points of contention in numerous publications produced in the past twenty years (e.g., Mager, 1962; Eisner, 1967; MacMillan and McClellan, 1968; Popham, 1968; Broudy, 1970; Ebel, 1970; Finder, 1975). Elsewhere I have attempted to summarize the issues by suggesting that the opponents of the use of goals in curriculum have not succeeded in making their case that instructional goals are damaging or redundant. They have, however, helped to bring about a healthy reappraisal of the way in which goals are stated and the kinds of goals that are pursued (Pratt, 1976).

The functions of clear and exact educational goals may be summarized as follows:

1. *They guide the curriculum designer in developing an effective curriculum.* Failure of curriculum designers to agree on explicit goals and to recognize and resolve disagreement or uncertainty at an early stage often results in expensive backtracking at a later point or in the development of a curriculum that either lacks direction or seeks to move in several directions at once.

2. *They guide the teacher in creating appropriate learning experiences.* Teachers must seek to avoid two cardinal errors in instruction: omission and redundance. Omission of important material will tend to result in student failure; inclusion of irrelevant material wastes instructional time. The two best ways for the instructor to avoid both of these pitfalls are to maintain a focus on the goals and to tell the students what the goals are.

3. *They inform the students what they are expected to learn.* This provides a kind of "advance organizer," which in some circumstances appears to facilitate learning (Ausubel, 1978). As the empirical research summarized earlier suggests, commitment to an understood goal is a powerful, perhaps the most powerful, motivator. The probability of commitment is increased if the goal is based on a genuine need recognized by the learners.

4. *They provide a means to evaluate the success of a program.* Without an understanding of the purpose of an activity, it is impossible to evaluate its effectiveness or its efficiency—a situation that is all too attractive to some public servants. Educational programs without explicit goals tend to be evaluated in terms of their popularity with students and teachers and by means of ex post facto judgments ("These were the results: well, I guess that's pretty much what we were aiming at"). The formulation of general curriculum aims is the first step in a process leading to exact definition of operational criteria against which program success can be evaluated and necessary improvement identified.

5. *They inform the public exactly what the school intends to do with its resources and its children.* Political events in the United States

---

If only we knew what we were about, perhaps we could get about it better.

—*Abraham Lincoln*

in the 1970s gave rise to public assertion of a new civil right: the "right to know." At the same time, it became increasingly recognized that the ultimate price of secrecy or deception is usually too high. The principle of public access to government records was enshrined in the Freedom of Information Act. At the local educational level, the principle suggests that the public has a right to know what policies guide decisions in publicly funded schools. This knowledge is incomplete unless the public knows what goals the schools are pursuing.

Relationship of goals to instruction

Underlying this approach to curriculum is the conviction that *it is the goal that determines instruction, not the instruction that determines the goal.* Many teachers believe that *To teach mathematics* or *To study English* is a satisfactory curriculum goal. But the mathematics or English that is taught can only be selected and justified on the basis of the purposes it serves. Clear statements of the purposes of academic disciplines are sufficiently rare that teachers should not assume that simply because they are teaching a discipline they are pursuing clear and worthwhile goals. This insight has eluded not only many teachers, but also some national systems of education. In 1973 the representatives of the Ministry of Education for Cyprus reported to an international conference that in their country

> the curriculum does not state explicitly the fundamental goals and guidelines for each department because these general goals are accepted as emanating from the content of the subjects and the general frame of the syllabus and the materials fixing the periods allotted to each subject (Standing Conference of European Ministers of Education, 1973, p. 46).

A hypothetical Martian observer of our schooling system would no doubt wonder greatly how it happened that we so rarely, so sporadically, and so feebly consider what matters to address and what to emphasize in schools. Since our present knowledge indicates that this decision has as much influence on what students learn as any subsequent decision the school can make, this omission is indeed mysterious. Perhaps if as many people in schools, in government, and in foundations asked as insistently for evidence that schools were attempting to teach worthwhile and defensible things as ask whether the schools have taught what they set out to teach, we would have more and better research and maybe even better schools.

—*Decker F. Walker and Jon Schaffarzick (1974, p. 108)*

Writing the Curriculum Aim

Writing the curriculum aim is the first stage in the actual design of a curriculum. It is relatively straightforward, but its importance must not be underestimated. Just as the human body is a centralized system, with the brain as its leading part, so a curriculum's leading part is the aim. Any change or defect in the aim affects the entire curriculum.

Statement of the aim is facilitated when a prior needs assessment has identified an important educational or training need. The need "To develop sound nutritional habits and to learn how to make wise decisions in the area of nutrition" (p. 99) is easily rewritten as an aim: *Students will develop sound nutritional habits and will be able to make wise decisions in the area of nutrition.*

As a curriculum aim attempts to define the purpose of a curriculum in a single statement, it is necessarily phrased in fairly general terms. Just how general it is will depend on the scope of the curriculum. A four-year high-school physics curriculum can be expected to have a much more general aim than a one-week unit in gravity. But either aim could be contained in one sentence.

Six main criteria may be applied to curriculum aims. Aims should (1) specify an intention; (2) identify a significant intended change in the learner; (3) be concise; (4) be exact; (5) be complete; and (6) be acceptable.

Intention

An aim is distinct from an ideal or a hope. An ideal is "an outcome that can never be obtained but can be approached without limit" (Ackoff and Emery, 1972, p. 57). A hope is a wish for the future that lacks a strong element of intention. By contrast, an aim states something that the curriculum designer actually intends a program to bring about. The function of the aim is not to define perfection, but to identify a strategic goal. Such terms as "it is hoped" and "ideally" do not belong in an aim.

It is not uncommon to read such aims as *To provide the student with the opportunity to understand mathematical operations.* This is a subtle way of passing responsibility from the professionals to the clients. If the curriculum is intended to develop understanding of mathematical operations in students, it should say so without equivocation.

Significant change

The educator is in the business of changing people. A student who after instruction possesses a new skill, a new understanding, new insight, or new attitudes, is a changed person, not simply in an abstract sense, but in the literal sense of altered ganglionic connections in the brain.

The aim identifies the overall change that the curriculum is intended to bring about. The error to be avoided here is to write an aim that describes what will happen during instruction rather than as a result of it.

Consider the following aims: *To teach the geography of the Pacific; Students will study Renaissance art; The student will learn about statistical inference*. These are typical of aims found in many curricula. They all describe activities in which learners or teachers will engage during instruction. None, except by implication, defines what the learner will gain from the experience.

In the aim *Through a study of the aquarium, students will develop an understanding of a biological community*, the first phrase is inappropriate, although the remainder is well stated. By prejudging the method to be used, the curriculum developers close their minds to the multitude of other possible techniques that should be considered and from which the optimum approaches should be selected only after the learning outcomes have been specified.

The first thing the reader of a curriculum encounters is the aim. The immediate impact that the aim has will influence his or her attitude toward the whole curriculum. An aim such as *Students will know the causes of the American Civil War* provokes the response "So what?" As stated, the aim suggests nothing more than a further cramming of isolated information into the student's memory. The student and the teacher both need to know what purpose underlies the provision of such information. Further thought might reveal the purposes to be (for example) something like *The student will understand the historical background to regional political, social, and economic differences in the contemporary United States*. Unlike the previous version, this aim shows a clear link to the student's actual life.

Teachers of such subjects as history and English have special difficulties in writing curriculum aims, because their own training tends to be heavily content-oriented. The ambition of many newly graduated

---

It is quite plain, I think, that the task of improving the American schools is not simply one of technique—however comforting it would be to some professional educators to think so. What is at issue, rather, is a deeper problem, one that is more philosophical than psychological or technological in scope. Let me put it in all innocence. What do we conceive to be the end product of our educational effort? I cannot help but feel that this rather overly simplified question has become obscured in cant.

—*Jerome Bruner (1959, p. 191)*

teachers of English, as soon as they meet their high-school classes, is "to do a Shakespeare play." Leaving aside the problem of the cultural gap between the English adult of 1600 and the North American adolescent of 1980 and that "doing" the play usually means reading it, a mode of presentation for which the work itself was not intended, the teacher must first define what new or changed concepts, insights, or dispositions he or she wants to bring about.

Confusion sometimes arises between the aim, which is the change to be brought about in the learner, and the reason for pursuing the aim. *To better prepare students for the study of mathematics in the first year of college* might be a legitimate purpose behind a senior-secondary-school mathematics curriculum. As such, the statement belongs in the curriculum rationale (p. 152). The aim, rather than depending on some later learning experience, should state the actual effect the curriculum will have on students.

Timidity frequently weakens an aim and hence an entire curriculum. A curriculum team in health education might target the aim *Students will know the effects of exercise*. But in fact the intention is not merely that students will know the effects of exercise, but that they will internalize the knowledge and adapt their behavior and habits accordingly. Most people in our society know about the effects of exercise. Only a minority act on this knowledge. The belief that giving people knowledge is sufficient to produce changes in behavior is a major contributor to educational ineffectiveness. In this case, the actual aim is more likely to be *Students will develop a positive attitude towards exercise* or, simply, *Students will keep fit*. Diffidence prevents the designers from stating so explicit and ambitious an outcome. But if this outcome is not achieved, the curriculum itself will be a waste of time. And if it is not stated in the aim, it is unlikely to be achieved.

Conciseness

A curriculum aim has political as well as planning significance. The query "What is the purpose of this curriculum?" by an administrator, or "Why are we studying this?" by a student, should be answerable in a relatively short sentence. A five-hundred-word response is more likely than not evidence of vagueness or confusion on the part of the teacher. *To enable students to develop the feeling that they are better able to evaluate and respond to changes in technology* is an example of the verbosity that afflicts many educators when they attempt to set aims down on paper. *To enhance students' enjoyment of poetry* meets all the criteria of a good aim, although it is only six words. Economy, the soul of good curriculum writing, is nowhere more important than in the aim.

> Everything that can be thought can be thought clearly. Everything that can be put into words can be put clearly.
>
> —*Ludwig Wittgenstein (1961, p. 26)*

Exactness

Difficulties in drafting a concise curriculum aim are often an indication that the designers are working at too detailed a level. However, designers must beware of being so general that the aim ceases to communicate the intent of the curriculum. *To develop intellectual abilities* or *Students will be able to choose among different alternatives* are not helpful, as they could be the aims for almost any curriculum. On the other hand, *To develop in students ease and confidence in speech and movement* (Ontario Department of Education, 1970, p. 8) states a specific curriculum intent without becoming enmeshed in detail.

At this stage, it is best if the designer states aims in terms of ongoing capabilities rather than specific actions. *Students will understand the cell as the basic unit of life*, which expresses a basic understanding, is preferable to *Students will draw a diagram of cell meiosis*, which defines a single specific act. The latter statement identifies a means of assessing student learning rather than the learned concept or capability itself.

Completeness

The aim should encompass all the main intended outcomes. The specific objectives will be derived from the general aim; curriculum content and methodology will be developed to meet the specific objectives. A major omission in the aim will thus be repeated throughout the curriculum. Designers must frequently redraft the aim a number of times until they are satisfied that all major aspects of the intent have been included. The following drafts show a typical progression toward a complete statement of intent:

The student will be able to write.

The student will be able to write creatively.

The student will be able to communicate ideas creatively through writing.

> If a student cannot give a good answer to the question of why he is studying what he is studying, he probably should not be studying it.
>
> —*Arthur Foshay (1970, p. 34)*

The student will be able to express feelings and communicate ideas creatively and effectively through writing.

An aim must avoid becoming a catalog of specific intentions but may contain more than one focus. The two main purposes of first aid training are well stated in the *American Red Cross First Aid Instructor's Manual*:

> The purpose of First Aid training is to acquire knowledge and skills for the emergency care of the injured until a physician arrives and to create an active interest in the prevention of accidents through elimination of the causes (Markle, 1967, p. 2).

Acceptability

The political nature of the curriculum designer's work has already been mentioned. A question that can usefully be asked at many points during the development of a curriculum is What would be the public response if this part of the curriculum were published in the local newspaper? Its central place in the curriculum makes it particularly important that the aim be acceptable to teachers, to learners, and to the community.

Acceptability would in many social contexts be a problem with an aim for a family life curriculum such as *To increase the ability of students to select compatible life partners*. Critics would almost certainly hasten to point out that the aim does not mention marriage, does not specify that the partner be of the opposite sex, and is ambiguous as to whether the individual is choosing one partner, a series of partners, or a number of partners simultaneously. Given the volatile nature of such issues, the aim alone could jeopardize the entire curriculum.

A number of vocal citizens and self-appointed public spokespersons have made criticism of school curricula almost a full-time vocation. To attempt to anticipate at least some of the objections of these antagonists, several thoughtful evaluators should review the acceptability of every curriculum aim before its publication.

We are, in my view, faced with an entirely new situation in education where the goal of education, if we are to survive, is the *facilitation of change and learning*. The only man who is educated is the man who has learned how to learn; the man who has learned how to adapt and change. . . . Here then is a goal to which I can give myself whole-heartedly. I see *the facilitation of learning* as the *aim* of education, the way in which we might develop the learning man.

—*Carl R. Rogers (1969, p. 104)*

This is not to say that curricula must merely reflect existing cultural norms and mores. It is rather recognition that when official curriculum aims are seen as rejecting significant community values, the curriculum is likely to be killed before it is adopted. This renders the developers impotent to bring about any change. In this context, acceptability means simply political feasibility.

A justification of the curriculum aim can be presented in the curriculum rationale. The aim itself must be acceptable enough that the reader is prepared to examine the rationale that follows it.

The Curriculum Rationale

A curriculum rationale is an argument that seeks to justify the pursuit of an aim. Its logical position in a curriculum is immediately following the aim. However, it is often best written after the nature of the curriculum to be developed is more clearly defined in the minds of the designers.

The rationale should be eloquent and persuasive. Overblown rhetoric should be avoided, but the rationale can legitimately be written in a less austere style than is appropriate for other sections of the curriculum. Hoped-for effects, as well as intended outcomes of the program, may be outlined, and the general philosophy on which the curriculum is based can be discussed. The rationale provides the designers with the opportunity to convince those who will authorize, use, and learn from the curriculum that its merit justifies its introduction and the consumption of time and other resources it will require. This task will be facilitated if the aim is based on a thorough needs assessment, and in this case the methodology and results of the needs assessment should be described.

In writing the rationale, the designers need to bear in mind that their audience does not consist only of fellow teachers sharing their own background and philosophy. The rationale should be written with a view to convincing everyone who will read the curriculum, but especially those who have the power to prevent or intervene in its implementation. Some of these people will have no background in the subject or no experience with the learners in question. The rationale should be able to persuade an audience that includes, for example, a sceptical principal, an uncommitted student, a back-to-basics parent, a radical romantic teacher, and a school board member whose mandate is to reduce school taxes.

Arguments that the curriculum will benefit the learners, though necessary, may be insufficient to persuade all those who will read and evaluate the curriculum. It will often be an advantage to adduce "extrinsic" arguments as well: that the curriculum is responsive to community feeling, reflects official curriculum policy, will reduce alienation and with-

Rationale for Watercolor Painting:
A Unit in a High-school
General Art Course

Watercolor painting is one of the most versatile and expressive of artistic media. Its spontaneity and rapidity of execution, allowing the immediate expression of visual experiences; its freshness, delicacy, and personal quality; and its brilliant colors and transparent effects, make it one of the most attractive and satisfying forms of painting.

The fact that materials are inexpensive, and watercolors are relatively quickly and easily applied, make this an ideal medium with which to introduce the general art student to painting. However, the medium also requires certain technical skills and a high degree of concentration and precision; flaws in a watercolor cannot be overpainted. In the absence of appropriate instruction, many novices find it difficult and frustrating, and often give up after a few disappointing failures.

This unit will provide students with basic knowledge and skills in watercolor. Students will be exposed to the work of classical watercolorists such as Dufy, Sargent, and Turner, and to contemporary works and commercial applications. Students will work individually at their own pace. Watercolor is a medium in which any student can, with help, make impressive and satisfying progress. Exhibitions of students' watercolors invariably draw favorable comment from parents and general public, but the standard of primary importance is the students' own satisfaction with their work. By enhancing students' artistic appreciation, confidence, and discipline, and by providing rewarding aesthetic experiences, it is hoped that this unit will develop personal qualities of enduring value.

drawal among students, and will enhance the image of the institution.

In producing a clear and convincing rationale for a curriculum, the designers may find that they are the primary beneficiaries. The discipline of writing an argument to persuade others forces a clarity of thought and conciseness of expression that may well give a sharper focus to the designers' own rationale for developing the curriculum. Any such increase in self-consciousness and commitment is likely to benefit both the designers and their work.

ACTIVITIES

1. Identification of the basic purposes of the school, along with development of effective instruction, gives considerable power to the curriculum designer. Discuss the dangers this presents. What safeguards are desirable?

2. Try to write down in one sentence what you consider the overall purpose of education. If everyone agreed with your statement, how would schools and their programs change?

3. The philosopher Isaiah Berlin writes, "Where ends are agreed, the only questions left are those of means, and these are not political but technical, that is to say, capable of being settled by experts or machines, like arguments, between engineers or doctors." Discuss.

4. Despite the evidence in American business and industry that goal setting increases productivity, the Soviet experience with production quotas has been unimpressive. Why do you think this is so?

5. If you teach a suitable class, experiment with the effect of negotiating or prescribing a clear target for some aspect of performance and raising it slightly every day. Record results on a wall chart. What happens?

6. Determine your major personal life-goal for ten years from now, and write it down. What do you want to be doing? Where do you want to be? What do you want to have accomplished? Then repeat the procedure for five years and one year hence. What effect does this focus on goals have?

QUESTIONS

1. Which of the following is intrinsically goal-directed, but is not conscious of purpose?

   a. a child
   b. a curriculum
   c. a guided missile
   d. a duckbill platypus

2. Which of the following is most clearly a question about ends rather than means?

   a. whether college-bound students should learn how to type
   b. what proportion of an English budget should be spent on film rental
   c. whether a new elementary school should have traditional classrooms or open areas
   d. whether a historical research skills course should focus on the period 1867–1917 or 1940–1980

3. Which of the following aims could be described as life-enhancing rather than life-preserving?

   a. students will react calmly in the event of fire
   b. students will develop an increased capacity for friendship
   c. students will have a positive attitude toward home safety
   d. students will be able to dislodge an obstruction from the windpipe of a choking victim

4. Empirical evidence on the effects of specific goals on performance suggests that

    a. specific goals rarely have any effect in a learning situation
    b. money is generally a more powerful incentive than goal attainment
    c. setting and achieving specific goals can be a significant motivator to improved performance
    d. encouraging people to "do their best" is the most effective way of improving human performance

5. *Students will develop enjoyment of drama through acting a modern play.* This aim is defective because

    a. it is not exact
    b. it is not change-oriented
    c. it is not student-centered
    d. it includes instructional content

6. Which of the following is the best-stated curriculum aim?

    a. to enable students to make rational choices
    b. to provide every child with remediation as and when required
    c. to develop in students increased skill in freehand sketching
    d. students will demonstrate the ability to multiply one-digit numbers

7. Which of the following aims is stated best?

    a. students will know body language
    b. students will develop understanding and skill in the use of body language
    c. students will increase their body language skills through a program of improvisation
    d. students will study creative dance with a view to developing the skills and understanding of body language

8. Which would be the most logical order to address the following three elements in curriculum development?

    a. needs, aims, rationale
    b. aims, needs, rationale
    c. rationale, aims, needs
    d. aims, rationale, needs

9. The aim *Students' attendance and punctuality will improve* is defective because

    a. it is ambiguous
    b. it is too general
    c. it aims at a symptom, not a problem
    d. it does not indicate how students will be changed by the program

10. Which of the following should be included in a curriculum rationale?

    a. clear and precise statement of the curriculum objectives
    b. convincing argument that the curriculum meets a significant need

    c.   imaginative suggestions for teachers as to how the curriculum may be taught
    d.   detailed budget showing that the curriculum will not significantly increase educational costs

Check your answers against the key in Appendix 2.
9 or 10 right: You understand the material presented.
8 or 7 right: Review the areas of uncertainty.
6 or less right: Reread the chapter.

Recommended Reading

Ackoff, Russel L., and Fred E. Emery. *On purposeful systems.* New York: Aldine, 1972. Two leading scholars in the field of system theory argue for the central role of purpose in human consciousness and behavior as a unifying principle in philosophy and the sciences.

Beck, Clive. *Educational philosophy and theory: An introduction.* Boston: Little, Brown, 1974. This book, which reviews a wide range of philosophical issues bearing on curriculum, includes a singularly perceptive and lucid discussion of the debate on educational aims.

Bertalanffy, Ludwig von. *General system theory.* Rev. ed. New York: Braziller, 1968. The pioneer of general system theory, Bertalanffy was a biologist whose studies of organisms led him to develop the concept of a system as an organized structure characterized by wholeness, coherence, self-regulation, and goal-directedness. The reinstatement of purpose as a legitimate scientific concept provided an alternative to the mechanistic paradigm of classical science and is regarded by some scholars as a revolution in scientific thought.

Taylor, Charles. *The explanation of behavior.* London: Routledge and Kegan Paul, 1964. Taylor's principal interest in this philosophical treatise is in exposing the weaknesses in behavioral psychology's rejection of the notion of purpose. In so doing, he helps to establish the concept of purpose as central to the explanation of animate behavior.

References

Ackoff, Russell L. A management scientist looks at education and education looks back. Paper prepared for the American Association for the Advancement of Science, Symposium on Research on decision-making: Potential for education. San Francisco, Feb. 1974.
————, and Fred E. Emery. *On purposeful systems.* New York: Aldine, 1972.
Ausubel, David P. In defense of advance organizers: A reply to the critics. *Review of Educational Research,* 1978, 48, 251–257.
Broudy, Harry S. Can research escape the dogma of behavioral objectives? *School Review,* 1970, 79, 43–56.

Bruner, Jerome S. Learning and thinking. *Harvard Educational Review*, 1959, 29, 184–192.

Bryan, Judith F., and Edwin A. Locke. Goal setting as a means of increasing motivation. *Journal of Applied Psychology*, 1967a, 51, 274–277.

———. Parkinson's Law as a goal-setting phenomenon. *Organizational behavior and human performance*, 1967b, 2, 258–275.

Duchastel, Philippe C., and Paul F. Merrill. The effects of behavioral objectives on learning: A review of empirical studies. *Review of Educational Research*, 1973, 43, 53–68.

Ebel, Robert L. Behavioral objectives: A close look. *Phi Delta Kappan*, 1970, 52, 171–173.

Eisner, Elliot W. Educational objectives: Help or hindrance? *School Review*, 1967, 75, 251–282.

———. Instructional and expressive objectives: Their formulation and use in curriculum. In W. James Popham et al., *Instructional objectives*. American Educational Research Association Monograph Series on Curriculum Evaluation, no. 3. Chicago: Rand McNally, 1969, pp. 1–31.

Fanon, Frantz. *The wretched of the earth*. New York: Grove Press, 1965.

Finder, Morris. Rational solutions to curricular issues. Paper presented at the Annual Meeting of the American Educational Research Association, Washington, D.C., April 1975.

Foshay, Arthur W. *Curriculum for the 70s: An agenda for invention*. Washington, D.C.: National Education Association, Center for the Study of Instruction, 1970.

Hamner, W. Clay. Goal setting, performance, and satisfaction in an interdependent task. *Organizational behavior and human performance*, 1974, 12, 217–230.

Kaplan, Abraham. *The conduct of inquiry*. San Francisco: Chandler, 1964.

Latham, Gary P., and J. J. Baldes. The "practical significance" of Locke's theory of goal setting. *Journal of Applied Psychology*, 1975, 60, 122–124.

Latham, Gary P., and Sydney B. Kinne III. Improving job performance through training in goal setting. *Journal of Applied Psychology*, 1974, 59, 187–191.

Latham, Gary P., and Gary A. Yukl. Assigned versus participative goal setting with educated and uneducated woods workers. *Journal of Applied Psychology*, 1975, 60, 299–302.

Levine, Martin G. The effect on pupil achievement of a criterion-referenced instructional model used by student teachers. *Journal of Teacher Education*, 1972, 23, 477–481.

Locke, Edwin A. Relationship of task success to task liking: A replication. *Psychological Reports*, 1966, 18, 552–554.

———. Toward a theory of task motivation and incentives. *Organizational Behavior and Human Performance*. 1968, 3, 157–189.

———. Purpose without consciousness: A contradiction. *Psychological Reports*, 1969, 25, 991–1009.

———, Norman Cartledge, and Claramae S. Knerr. Studies of the relationships between satisfaction, goal setting, and performance. *Organizational Behavior and Human Performance*, 1970, 5, 135–158.

Mace, C. A. *Incentives: Some experimental studies*. London: Industrial Health Research Board, report no. 72, 1935.

MacMillan, C. J. B., and James E. McClellan. Can and should means-ends reasoning be used in teaching? In C. J. B. MacMillan and Thomas W. Nelson (eds.), *Concepts of teaching: Philosophical essays*. Chicago: Rand McNally, 1968, pp. 119–150.

Mager, R. F. *Preparing instructional objectives*. Palo Alto, Cal.: Fearon, 1962.

Markle, David G. Development of the Bell System First Aid and Personal Safety Course: An exercise in the application of empirical methods to instructional systems design. Final report. Palo Alto, Cal.: American Institutes for Research in the Behavioral Sciences, 1967.

Melton, Reginald F. Resolution of conflicting claims concerning the effects of behavioral objectives on student learning. *Review of Educational Research*, 1978, 48, 291–302.

Ontario Department of Education. *Dramatic Arts Curriculum Guideline*. Toronto: Ontario Department of Education, 1970.

Popham, W. James. Probing the validity of arguments against behavioral goals. Paper presented at the Annual Meeting of the American Educational Research Association, Chicago, Feb. 1968.

Pratt, David. Humanistic goals and behavioral objectives: Towards a synthesis. *Journal of Curriculum Studies*, 1976, 8, 15–26.

Rogers, Carl R. *Freedom to learn*. Columbus, Oh.: Charles E. Merrill, 1969.

Ronan, W. W., Gary P. Latham, and S. B. Kinne III. Effects of goal setting and supervision on worker behavior in an industrial situation. *Journal of Applied Psychology*, 1973, 58, 302–307.

Rothkopf, E. Z., and R. Kaplan. Exploration of the effect of density and specificity of instructional objectives on learning from text. *Journal of Educational Psychology*, 1972, 63, 295–302.

Somerhoff, G. The abstract characteristics of living systems. In F. E. Emery (ed.), *Systems thinking*. Harmondsworth, England: Penguin, 1969, pp. 147–202.

Standing Conference of European Ministers of Education. *The educational needs of the 16–19 age group: Country reports*. Strasbourg: Standing Conference of European Ministers of Education, 1973.

Steers, Richard M., and Lyman W. Porter. The role of task-goal attributes in employee performance. *Psychological Bulletin*, 1974, 81, 434–452.

Townsend, Robert. *Up the organization*. Greenwich, Conn.: Fawcett, 1971.

Walker, Decker F., and Jon Schaffarzick. Comparing curricula. *Review of Educational Research*, 1974, 44, 83–111.

Wittgenstein, Ludwig. *Tractatus logico-philosophicus*. Trans. D. F. Pears and B. F. McGuiness. London: Routledge & Kegan Paul, 1961.

7

PRINCIPLES

- Curriculum objectives are defined by breaking aims down into their component elements.

- Task analysis can be used to dissect and examine educational aims.

- Objectives may be classified as knowledge, skill, physical development, disposition, and experience.

- Objectives are intents to develop certain states in the learner.

- Objectives are distinct from performance criteria, which define actions required to assess the achievement of objectives.

- Major criteria for assessing objectives are outcome specification, consistency, precision, feasibility, functionality, significance, and appropriateness.

- It is sound practice to have objectives reviewed by teachers and by practitioners who will use the specified capabilities.

CONCEPTS

Task analysis   Intrinsic experience
Brain hemisphere   Behavioral objective
Disposition   Performance criterion
Instrumental activity

7
Curriculum Objectives

The success of the struggle presupposes clear objectives. . . . Neither stubborn courage nor fine slogans are enough.

—Frantz Fanon (1965, p. 108)

Aims and Objectives

The curriculum aim provides a basic orientation for the designer or user of a curriculum. But as a rule it is too general to guide specific instructional decisions. That is the function of the objectives. Writing a general aim is relatively straightforward. Writing specific objectives is difficult. According to Caswell,

> The fundamental problem facing curriculum specialists is to establish a consistent relationship between general goals, on the one hand, and specific objectives that guide teaching on the other (Caswell, 1966, p. 5).

The process of defining specific objectives is a process of analysis. This is the second of the seven main steps in specifying learning outcomes shown in Figure 7–1. The Greek verb *analyein* means to break down or break apart. Objectives are derived by breaking the aim down into its constituent parts, literally a process of *decomposition*. The elements of a general aim can almost invariably be separated in this way. Ebel maintains that this is the case with any general capability:

> I am persuaded that all useful learning begins with particular learnings, and that a general ability, like the physician's ability to diagnose a patient's ailment, consists entirely of a host of specific diagnostic abilities (Ebel, 1973, p. 9).

A good example of analysis of an aim into its components is provided by some of the curriculum work conducted at the Leeds University Central Language Laboratory in England on specification of realistic objectives for language teaching. A curriculum is planned for a class of adolescents or adults whose language aptitude is average or below average. The class time is limited, but the students have the common motivation of planning holidays in France. The aim of the curriculum is defined as *Students will be able to communicate in French at a basic level for purposes of tourism.* The aim entails a number of specific capabilities, such as rudimentary vocabulary, ability to read signs, ask questions, and understand directions. These capabilities could be explicitly defined in about a dozen objectives.

1. *The student will have a reading vocabulary of 300 common words and abbreviations.*
2. *The student will have a listening vocabulary of 300 common words plus numbers up to 100.*

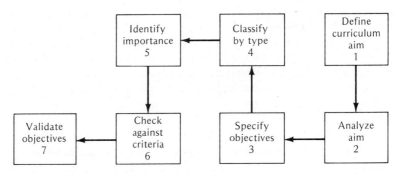

Figure 7–1 Specifying learning outcomes

3. *The student can understand written notices, signs, and menus.*
4. *The student can understand simple questions, statements, greetings, and directions.*
5. *The student can "get the gist of" a burst of spoken French.*
6. *The student can pick out unfamiliar passages from matter heard and repeat them approximately for clarification.*
7. *The student can use in speech 200 common words plus numbers up to 100 for time, quantity, and price.*
8. *The student can use about 30 useful phrases, questions, requests, greetings, statements, and responses.*
9. *The student can hold a bilingual conversation, speaking English slowly and clearly in simple words.*
10. *The student can use and understand appropriate gestures.*
11. *The student will have the confidence to initiate conversations in French, be unafraid of making mistakes, and attempt utterances outside his or her competence.*
12. *The student will be willing to learn from native speakers' correction of his or her errors.*
13. *The student will have a "success experience" of making himself or herself understood in, and understanding, a spoken foreign language.*

(Adapted from Harding and Page, 1974/75)

Like the aim, the objectives not only specify but also delimit the intent. The ability to write French, for example, is not included as an objective because it is not entailed in the aim. The objectives stated give clear guidance to the designer and the teacher regarding the instruction that will be required.

Analysis of aims is not a purely mechanical procedure; it involves professional judgment that pays regard to factors such as the age and interests of the students and the social environment. The question is not so much Given this aim, what objectives follow? as Given this aim, what objectives are most worth pursuing? Here are some objectives that might be considered appropriate for a first curriculum in map skills at about third-grade level, with the aim *Students will be able to read, understand, and use simple maps:*

1. *Students will know the meaning of the points of the compass.*
2. *Students will know the meaning of basic map symbols.*
3. *Students will be able to make accurate estimates of distances from maps.*

4. *Students will be able to plan efficient routes between points on simple maps.*

5. *Students will be able to locate places on different types of maps.*

6. *Students will be able to visualize topographical features from outline maps.*

7. *Students will be able to make social and economic inferences from regional maps.*

8. *Students will be able to draw simple maps.*

9. *Students will enjoy reading and drawing simple maps.*

(Adapted from Lawrence, 1978)

The skill of breaking down generalities into specifics is the key to defining curriculum objectives. Gagné emphasizes the value of this ability for educators:

> The ability to make analyses of the outcomes of learning has invariably turned out to be a highly valuable skill.... I have known some teachers who have learned to do this, and I wish all of them would.... I estimated that over a period of some five years of work in instructional improvement, no procedure proved to make a greater difference than properly conducted analyses of learning outcomes (Gagné, 1973, p. 142).

Curriculum Task Analysis

It is often useful to analyze aims in a more formal and detailed manner than that described above. The procedure known as task analysis has for many years been used for this purpose in the fields of technical and military training. Figure 7–2 illustrates a simple analysis of the ability to navigate terrain on foot (Branson et al., 1975, p. 21).

A larger-scale task analysis based on field data was conducted by Martin and Brodt (1973) in designing training for military hospital corpsmen. Hospital corpsmen were observed in operation and were interviewed about their work. These procedures yielded an inventory of over sixteen hundred tasks performed by the corpsmen. The task statements were then presented to over six hundred corpsmen who were asked to indicate whether they performed the task, and if so with what frequency, what the perceived difficulty of the task was, and the relative benefit of the training they had received for it. Emergency tasks (such as cardio-pulmonary resuscitation and control of hemorrhage) and tasks that were performed by at least 40 percent of the corpsmen were subsequently designated for the basic training program. All the tasks identified were then sorted into seven categories of patient need (for example, patient

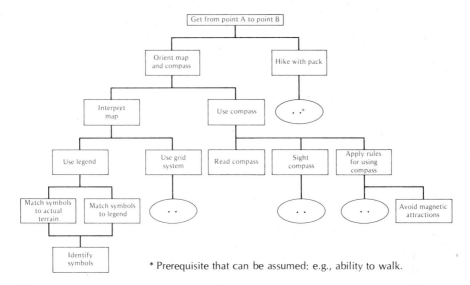

* Prerequisite that can be assumed: e.g., ability to walk.

Figure 7–2   Analysis of navigation of terrain on foot (Interservice Training Review Organization, 1975, p. 21)

skin care) based on an assessment of the needs of hospitalized and emergency patients. Martin and Brodt's work is an interesting combination of needs assessment and aim analysis.

Systematic analysis of job components helps to reduce the risk that significant elements will be overlooked in training. In designing a program for training history teachers, the author conducted a task analysis of history teaching. Most of the skills identified were conventional, for example, *can plan lessons efficiently; can organize a field trip; can bring about learning in pupils.* But the analysis also called attention to the somewhat obvious fact that to teach history successfully—or even at all—the teacher must first obtain a history teaching position. This led to identification of the tasks *Student can write an articulate letter of application* and *Student interviews well,* and development of appropriate training to meet these objectives (Pratt, 1975).

Table 7–1 shows a curriculum task analysis for a course in wilderness survival. It is to be assumed that a needs assessment has revealed that people who live close to or visit wilderness areas need special survival skills, both for emergency and safety reasons, and so that they can enjoy the wilderness with confidence and responsibility. The curriculum is limited to survival in wilderness (bush and forest) conditions. Survival in the arctic, on the tundra, in desert, or in mountainous terrain presents different sets of conditions that would call for different units of instruction. The curriculum aim is, simply, *Students will be able to survive in the wilderness.*

JURISDICTION: Minnesota		INSTITUTION: Hiawatha High School			
UNIT: Wilderness Survival					

OBJECTIVE	LEARNING CATEGORY	ENVIRONMENTAL CONDITIONS	EQUIPMENT	COMPLETION TIME	LEARNING TIME
1. Make fire	knowledge, skill	wind and rain	2 matches, knife, wire saw	40 minutes	4 hours
2. Build shelter	knowledge, skill	wind and rain	100m line, 2×3m polythene	1 hour	2 hours
3. Obtain food	knowledge, skill	winter	2 hooks, fish net, cooking pot		7 hours
4. Obtain water	knowledge, skill	no open water	polythene, cooking pot	24 hours	1 hour
5. Give first aid	knowledge, skill	any	200 gm emergency kit		10 hours
6. Find direction	knowledge, skill	cloudy sky, dense bush	compass	10 seconds	1 hour
7. Navigate on foot	knowledge, skill	broken terrain or bush		1 hour for 1 mile	2 hours
8. Signal	knowledge, skill	day and night	heliograph mirror		1 hour
9. Choose equipment	knowledge				1 hour
10. Maintain morale	disposition	alone and in group			whole course
11. Solo	experience	wilderness	all of above	24 hours	

Table 7–1   Curriculum task analysis

The first step in curriculum task analysis is to list the component tasks the student would need to be able to perform if the aim itself were to be attained. When the list appears to be complete, the designer asks: If the learner could perform all of these tasks, would the aim be achieved? If the answer is no, further tasks must be identified and the process repeated.

The task listing provides the designer with the objectives of the curriculum: *The student will be able to make a fire in the wilderness; the student will be able to build a shelter in the wilderness;* etc. The tasks are next analyzed on ten dimensions.

PROGRAM: Environmental Studies   COURSE: Outdoor Education

AIM: Students will be able to survive in the wilderness

PROBABILITY OF USE	CONSEQUENCES OF INADEQUATE MASTERY	IMPORTANCE	REACTION SPEED	PROFICIENCY	REMARKS
90%	serious	critical	5 minutes	high	to boil 1 liter water
60%	serious	critical	1 hour	moderate	1×2m lean-to to keep out rain
50%	significant	critical	24 hours	moderate	
90%	serious	critical	12 hours	moderate	1 liter in 24 hours
10%	disastrous	critical	2 minutes	high	
90%	serious	critical	5 minutes	high	
100%	serious	critical	1 hour	moderate	
5%	serious	critical	20 seconds	high	
100%	disastrous	critical	2 hours	perfect	
60%	serious	critical	5 minutes	high	
		important			
	Levels: disastrous serious significant negligible	Levels: critical important desirable		Levels: perfect high moderate	

Learning category

This dimension identifies the objective as knowledge, skill, physical development, disposition, or experience. It is important that each objective be correctly classified on this dimension. The rationale for and description of the five categories are discussed later in the chapter.

Environmental conditions

The environmental conditions under which students will learn should be as close as possible to the actual conditions experienced in real life. If the task must be performed under varying conditions, these should be itemized. If the conditions vary on a simple scale of difficulty, it is appropriate to indicate only the least favorable ones. Thus if learners can build a fire in rain and wind, it can be assumed that they can do so on a still, dry day.

Equipment provided

This dimension specifies the equipment on which the learner is taught to rely. It is essential therefore that this be both minimal and always available. If the learners are taught to rely on a compass for finding direction, the "choosing equipment" part of the course must drill them to carry a compass whenever venturing into the wilderness. In the same way, mathematics programs should allow reliance on calculators, and language programs on dictionaries, only if these resources will always be available and appropriate for performance of the tasks derived from the curriculum aims. In a wilderness survival unit, it would be a mistake to build reliance on, say, an axe, a rifle, and a tent, because no intelligent hunter or fisherman would stagger out into the wilderness laden down in that way.

Completion time

The time taken to complete a task is a primary indicator of degree of competence (Carroll, 1971; Crossman, 1959). A person who can speak correct Russian at 150 words per minute is fluent; the person who speaks Russian, however correctly, at 20 words per minute is not. A child who can give the product of any two one-digit numbers in half a second almost certainly knows his or her basic "multiplication facts," whereas the child who takes four seconds probably does not. Determining the maximum time allowed for a task is a useful exercise in quantification. In order to state the time allowed for building a fire, the question How much of a fire? must be answered. If it is ignored, the student could claim that the objective was achieved by striking a match. Heat output and duration would both have to be taken into account. "Enough fire to boil one liter of water" provides a firm and recognizable standard.

Learning time

This dimension relates to the difficulty of learning to perform the task. Its function is to guide the designer in the allocation of instructional time. The learning time includes time for both instruction and practice and must be sufficient to bring the typical learner to the level of proficiency identified.

Probability of use

The probability of use is based on how likely it is that the student will need to perform the task or skill within twelve months of completing the training. This dimension helps to establish priorities among objectives, but it does not follow that an objective with a low probability of use should be omitted or downgraded in a curriculum. Emergency skills, such as those involved in first aid, require rigorous training in part because they may not be used for years after the training is complete.

Consequences of inadequate mastery

This category is self-explanatory. The consequences entail not only the possibility of injury or death, but also of wasted supplies, damaged equipment, loss of time, harm to self-image or career prospects, and so on.

Importance

Teachers do not usually have enough time to develop all the abilities they would like to in a learner. When desires outrun resources, conflict can be resolved only by assigning priorities. Complex formulas exist for determining priority among goals (Banghart, 1973), but for most curriculum purposes it is adequate to classify objectives as *critical, important,* or *desirable.* These categories correspond to the familiar "must know," "should know," and "nice to know" classification.

An objective is critical if its omission or incompetent performance could, under any likely circumstances, jeopardize the overall aim. It follows that a student cannot properly be regarded as having completed or earned credit for a course, unless he or she has attained all the critical objectives.

Determining importance is essentially a subjective process of judgment. It is based mainly on the previous two categories, probability of use and consequences of inadequate mastery.

Reaction speed

Sometimes termed *task delay tolerance* (Mead, 1976), this category indicates how much time can be tolerated between the point at which the individual becomes aware of the need to perform the task and the time he or she commences the task. An activity such as "rotate automobile tires" allows sufficient delay for the person involved to consult a manual, seek guidance, or even be taught the task. "Correcting a front-wheel skid" has virtually zero delay tolerance. There are numerous sub-skills in such curriculum areas as reading, mathematics, languages, and music, which have little value to the learner until the reaction has become almost instantaneous. Identification of this aspect of an objective has significant implications for the design of instruction.

Proficiency

The degree of proficiency required will depend primarily on the importance and the reaction speed of the task. A critical task that requires an immediate reaction is likely to require perfect proficiency. Using a bicycle brake and arresting arterial hemorrhage would be examples. Notice that there is no level of proficiency lower than "moderate": life is too short to spend time training for trivialities.

Second-level analysis

Human activities can be decomposed indefinitely, and the designer must decide at what stage to stop breaking wholes down into parts. "First aid" is too large and diverse an area to be treated as a single objective. In a wilderness survival course, the design of instruction in first aid would require the identification of a number of specific procedures, including treatment of conventional injuries and conditions such as wounds, burns, fractures, shock, and poisoning, as well as those more specific to a wilderness environment, such as hypothermia, frostbite, and snowblindness. Each of these areas would lead to the specification of a separate objective. The activity of building a fire could be treated as a single objective. But it could also be broken down into seven component parts, as shown in Table 7–2. These components would constitute the main teaching

ACTION	COMPLETION TIME	LEARNING TIME
1. Choose site	5 minutes	20 minutes
2. Prepare site	3 minutes	40 minutes
3. Gather fuel	10 minutes	50 minutes
4. Construct fire	5 minutes	40 minutes
5. Light fire	10 seconds	10 minutes
6. Maintain fire	15 minutes	50 minutes
7. Extinguish fire	2 minutes	30 minutes
TOTAL	40 minutes, 10 seconds	4 hours

Table 7–2   Second-level analysis of the objective *Build a fire*

points. Analysis to this level allows a more precise estimation of time both for completion of the activity and for learning the skill. The effect of detailed analysis is usually encouraging: tasks that appear difficult when considered as wholes are often revealed as comprised of relatively simple components.

Curriculum task analysis has greatest value in the analysis of aims that are primarily oriented toward skills rather than knowledge or attitude. A thorough analysis of aims in the skills area provides invaluable data. In addition to definition of objectives, the procedure clarifies learning priorities, instructional time estimates, and needed supplies, and provides guidance for the design of instructional methodology and evaluation. By this point, a sound foundation has been established on which the rest of the curriculum can be constructed.

A Typology of Learning Outcomes

It is not always necessary to classify an objective on all ten dimensions of the task analysis described above; but it is always desirable to identify at least the dimensions of *importance* and *learning category*. Importance will determine the priority the objective receives in instruction and evaluation. Learning category must be determined because otherwise the teacher will lack a firm basis for choosing instructional procedures.

There are a number of well-known classifications of learning. The most familiar is that of Bloom and his colleagues (Bloom, 1956; Krathwohl, 1964), the taxonomy of educational objectives. It divides learning into three domains, cognitive, affective, and psychomotor, and attempts to establish a hierarchy of capabilities within each domain. Guilford's "structure of intellect" model (1959) classifies intellectual operations as figural, symbolic, and behavioral. Gagné (1974) proposes five "principal categories of learning outcomes": verbal information, or knowledge; intellectual skills (which enable the individual to deal with the environment symbolically); cognitive strategies (skills of self-management governing the processes of attending, learning, and thinking); attitudes; and motor skills.

Learning theorists are currently developing much more detailed taxonomies of human performance, which also have the merit of being based on empirical studies rather than on a priori considerations alone (Fleishman, 1975). Such research will have important implications for curriculum. But in the meantime, what is needed is a classification system specifically designed to guide teachers and curriculum developers by (1) distinguishing among those capabilities that require different means of instruction or evaluation and (2) including all the major areas of human development for which the school may legitimately assume responsibility. Existing taxonomies appear to be deficient particularly in the second of these functions. Our knowledge of human capabilities is constantly expanding and hence is in principle incomplete. But at least two basic areas are conspicuous by their absence from the classifications of Bloom, Guilford, and Gagné. These are physical development and experience. A minimally comprehensive typology of educational objectives would seem to require five main kinds of objective: knowledge, skill, physical development, disposition, and experience. Some comments need to be made about each type.

Knowledge

It would be reckless to attempt to present a thorough exposition of the nature of knowledge, an issue that has exercised philosophers for more than two millennia. However, it is worth reporting the judgment of several philosophers that minimal conditions for the statement "A knows that B" are (1) A has observed or thought about the fact that B; (2) A consciously or unconsciously believes that B; and (3) it is the case that B (Ayer, 1956; Barnes, 1963; Scheffler, 1965). The simplest criterion for classification is this: an objective that could properly begin "The student knows" (but not "knows how to") or "The student understands" may usually be classified as a knowledge objective.

Clearly knowledge objectives can include a wide range of states of awareness, from knowledge of individual facts to comprehension of complex concepts. Neuropsychological research conducted over the last two decades also suggests that there is more to human awareness than merely verbal or propositional knowledge.

The left and right hemispheres of the human brain are connected by a bundle of some two million nerve fibres, the *corpus callosum,* which transmits a continual stream of information between the two hemispheres. In certain surgical cases, the corpus callosum is severed, and from studies of such cases a picture has emerged of the specialized functions of the two hemispheres. According to a pioneer neurosurgeon, Roger Sperry,

> The surgically disconnected halves of the brain have their own private sensations, percepts, and learning experiences—all cut off from the awareness of its partner hemisphere. We also learned that each brain half stored its own separate chain of memories, which were inaccessible to the other hemisphere (Sperry, 1975).

The left hemisphere appears to control verbal and mathematical operations, writing, calculation, description, and propositional thought, using analytic, symbolic, and sequential logic. The right brain is essentially spatial-perceptual, controlling appreciation of visual patterns, nonverbal ideation, color, shapes, form, texture, appositional thought, and the melodic and harmonic aspects of music, but has some capability of understanding simple language and numbers. Ornstein refers to the two hemispheres as relative to "two major modes of consciousness," the rational and the intuitive (1972, p. 50).

The exact implications of this research for curriculum are still far from clear. But the criticisms by such specialists as Sperry and Bogen (see p. 174) of the rational-reductionism of much school curriculum seem to have some validity. If their thesis is correct, curriculum cannot properly be limited to the "body of public concepts . . . relevant knowledge and forms of reasoning" proposed by two eminent British writers, Hirst and Peters (1970, p. 62). It may be necessary to take another look at the "tacit dimension" of knowledge advocated by their compatriot, Michael Polanyi (1966). In any event, curriculum developers have some significant support for interpreting the knowledge category of objectives broadly enough to include the nonlinear, nonverbal perception characteristic of the arts and of metaphorical, poetic, and intuitive thought.

Knowledge objectives can use the verbs *know* and *understand* without becoming obscure; in some cases, *apprehend, recognize,* or *appreciate* (in its nonevaluative sense) may be more exact. At a subsequent stage in the development of a curriculum, the designer provides an

Education for the Right Hemisphere

Our education system and modern society generally (with its very heavy emphasis on communication and on early training in the three Rs) discriminate against one whole half of the brain. I refer, of course, to the non-verbal, non-mathematical minor hemisphere, which, we find, has its own perceptual, mechanical, and spatial mode of apprehension and reasoning. In our present school system, the attention given to the minor hemisphere of the brain is minimal compared with the training lavished on the left, or major hemisphere.

—*Roger Sperry (1975, p. 33)*

We are accustomed to hear, these days, of the "culturally disadvantaged," of those persons whose propositional potential has remained undeveloped for lack of proper schooling. There is likely a parallel lack of appositional development in persons whose only education consists of reading, writing, and arithmetic. . . . A better informed and foresighted community will strive toward a more harmonious development of the organism by assuring an appropriate training and a greater consideration for the other side of the brain.

—*Joseph Bogen and Glenda Bogen (1969, pp. 201–202)*

Only a romantic pedagogue would say that the main objective of schooling is to preserve the child's intuitive gift. And only a foolish one would say that the principal object is to get him beyond all access to intuition, to make a precise analytic machine of him.

—*Jerome S. Bruner (1974, p. 99)*

"operational definition" of the meaning of terms like know and understand by identifying specific actions or performance required of the learner. The definition of such performance criteria (which are roughly equivalent to the better-known behavioral objectives) is described in the next chapter. At this stage what is required is not identification of behaviors, but clear statement of the state or capability to be developed in the learner. Such terms as know and understand, although not "behavioral," do provide for relatively clear communication among educators. This is not true, however, of such terms as *be aware of* or *be familiar with,* which are a good deal vaguer and should be avoided in writing objectives.

Skills

Skills usually rest on a knowledge base, as is implied by popular (but in curriculum contexts confusing) use of the term *know how to* to refer to skills. But a skill involves much more than knowledge. In the performance of a skill, many different processes, actions, and subroutines are ordered and coordinated in temporal sequence (Welford, 1958). Such coordination can be developed only by practice; the necessity for practice to develop competent performance is the distinguishing mark of a skill (Roland, 1959; Smith, 1964).

Two main areas of skill may be distinguished. *Cognitive skills* include such abilities as recognition, discrimination, analysis, and problem solving. This category includes both rational/logical skills and creative/intuitive skills. *Motor skills* relate to control of physical movement primarily through muscular operation and range from the manipulative use of fingers to gross motor skills such as running or swimming.

It is often difficult and (from a curriculum point of view) sometimes unnecessary to separate the cognitive and motor aspects of a skill. Most motor skills require cognitive skills for their successful performance. Motor and cognitive abilities are closely integrated in many skills such as reading and speaking. The terms *mental skills* and *physical skills* are to be avoided, as all skills are mental skills. What is being trained in the development of motor skills is not the limbs or muscles, but those parts of the brain that control certain kinds of motor function.

In writing curriculum objectives, it is a useful practice to reserve the term *be able to* for skill objectives.

While it would be unnecessary and undesirable to rank the types of objective by importance, skills must be recognized as central in most educational endeavor. Knowledge without skills is inert; attitudes without skills are ineffectual. Providing students with a skill will not ensure that they use that skill: this will come about mainly through development of attitude. But a student who does not have a skill cannot use it. Skills training therefore increases the range of alternatives open to the student; and extension of choice might serve as a definition of education itself.

Physical development

The statement *Students will increase their level of physical fitness* is clearly an objective: it defines a legitimate and not uncommon intended outcome of certain school programs. But it is not a knowledge, skill, or attitude objective, although it might require the support of such objectives for its realization. The distinct characteristic of such an objective is that its focus is on the improvement of students' bodily state rather than their state of mind. The same is true of education in nutrition or dental health, the ultimate intent of which is development of physiological states that can be described in biochemical terms.

Most athletic training focuses on skill development, but many athletes also undertake programs of weight training, which aim to build muscle volume and strength. In physical education in schools, much can be done for the self-image of adolescents and young adults, concerned as they are about physical appearance, through programs of physical culture. The daily jogger is attempting (usually with success) to bring about diverse physiological changes in his or her cardiovascular system that will enable it to utilize oxygen more efficiently and hence sustain greater loads with less effort.

Objectives in physical development differ from those in knowledge and skill areas in that they are not learned capabilities. This in itself does not appear to justify their common exclusion from taxonomies of educational outcome. Such exclusion may explain why many physical education programs in schools emphasize almost everything—knowledge, skills, attitudes, enjoyment (all worthwhile objectives in themselves)—except physical development. Direct intervention in people's bodily concerns is widely regarded as being the role of medicine rather than of education. But medical intervention by drugs or surgery can sometimes be seen as consequential on the failure of preventive medicine, which is principally an educational function.

Although the "public" schools of nineteenth-century England were in many ways parodies of education, their motto *mens sana in corpore sano* (a healthy mind in a healthy body) recognized a truth that eluded the authors of Bloom's taxonomy of educational objectives. Education tends to focus exclusively on what occurs outside a person's skin; but to the individual, what happens inside is of basic importance. The relationship among fitness, state of health, and state of mind are now well enough known to justify the identification of objectives in this area as critical in every student's schooling.

Dispositions

The significance of dispositions in human life is reflected in the number of terms that are popularly used as approximate synonyms. They include attitude, affect, belief, character, conviction, emotion, feeling, interest, inclination, motivation, outlook, predeliction, predisposition, preference, proclivity, propensity, opinion, sentiment, taste, tendency, value, and view. *Attitude* is the term most commonly used in social psychology. Of the many definitions, probably the most succinct was coined sixty years ago by Thomas and Znaniecki (Allport, 1954): "a state of mind of the individual toward a value." The term *disposition* has the advantage of emphasizing the readiness or tendency to act in a certain way. "Dispositions," Ryle writes, "are latent properties, abstract sets, potentialites, habits, tendencies, or capacities" (1949, p. 116). For purposes of this discussion, we may define a disposition as a state of mind involving a qualititative, usually positive or negative, and often unconscious, judgment that influences an individual to act in a certain way toward a material or ideational object.

In considering dispositions as objectives in school curricula, two questions immediately arise: Are they legitimate? Are they feasible?

Legitimacy   Until the 1960s, educational rhetoric generally favored the deliberate teaching of attitudes. So long as the major interests of adolescents and college students were football, jitterbugging, swallowing goldfish, panty raids, and cramming large numbers of people into telephone booths, educators were vociferous about the need for young people to become more involved in the political process. These advocates fell suddenly silent when, in the 1960s, students actually began to take an active interest in political affairs.

Perhaps it was this experience that led to the attempt to develop "value-free" curricula. Stick to the facts, the argument went, and let the students draw their own conclusions: anything else would be indoctrination. The following passage from a Canadian curriculum proposal is typical of the internally contradictory thinking that resulted:

> No attempt should be made to develop specific attitudes in the minds of the students nor to arrive at predetermined conclusions . . . the program we are suggesting is value free. . . . Programs based on our concept . . . could help our young people to develop an intelligent, knowledgeable affection for their country and a critically responsible interest in it (Hodgetts, 1968, p. 121).

Value-free curricula are impossible in principle. The very existence of a curriculum implies a commitment to some kind of learning. As soon as learning is institutionalized in a school, many values inevitably begin to be modeled, and dispositions to develop: dispositions toward education, rationality, inquiry, freedom to work and speak freely, consideration for others, cooperation and competition, and so on. The way in which a school or classroom is organized, the way teachers treat each other and encourage students to behave toward one another: all these things influence the attitudes of learners in the school. Like the slogan that students should be taught not values but value clarification, the attempt to remove attitude commitments from the curriculum promotes not indifference to values, but merely a different set of values: the value of neutrality, fair-mindedness, objectivity. As an old Russian professor at Oxford used to say: "If we say we have no bias, we are immediately subject to the bias of bourgeois objectivism."

The question facing the educator is not whether the curriculum should be designed to develop certain dispositions. The pressing questions are rather Which dispositions should be developed? To what extent should the school support and to what extent counterbalance the influence of the family, peer group, and media? What is the importance of developing attitudes relative to developing knowledge and skill?

There are grounds for suggesting that dispositions are the most significant kind of objective. Without appropriate attitudes, skills will remain unutilized potential. All the training in logic in the world will not make a person behave logically unless that person has developed a positive disposition toward the use of logic in human thought and conduct. Young male drivers have better eyesight and faster reflexes than their elders. Little reduction could be expected in their horrendous fatality rate from better training in driving skills. But much could be expected from training that modified their attitudes related to driving. Dispositions are concerned not with what the learner *can* do, but with what he or she *does* do, not with ability but with will. A teacher who teaches mathematics or languages effectively but is unconcerned whether the learners like or detest the subject is not morally conscientious but unscrupulous.

The effect of the debate over dispositions as objectives has been to render many teachers ambivalent; they continue to aim at attitudinal outcomes but in a covert, hesitant, and half-hearted way. The responsibility is certainly a formidable one. Those who mold the dispositions of the young help determine the future of society. This is not a reason for abandoning such objectives; it is the reason why they should be clearly formulated and openly stated, so that they can be subjected to rigorous public scrutiny.

Feasibility   To what extent is it feasible to change or develop dispositions in schools? Certainly they are resistant to change; few deliberate efforts in this direction seem to have an appreciable effect. Nevertheless, attitudes are not innate but learned; and as such, it seems probable that some of them are learned in school. In fact, almost every adult can think of attitudes, both positive and negative, that were learned or modified in the classroom, even though they may not have been deliberately taught. The development of dispositions in students is difficult and demanding and requires wise and skillful teachers. The man in the street could teach a class of children the two times table, but teaching students to like mathematics, to develop a scientific attitude, or to have confidence in their own capacities calls for a professional.

Experiences

All the above kinds of objective are essentially instrumental. We develop knowledge and skills to control our environment and determine our lives; physical states to live longer or more vigorously; attitudes to achieve harmony with others and with ourselves. But an objective pursued for its own sake is the experiential objective.

Aristotle first formulated the distinction between instrumental activities and activities that are valuable in themselves. The one kind "always has an end other than itself." The other "is itself its end" (Aristotle, in Illich, 1971, p. 62). Driving to work, doing calisthenics, or disciplining children are not normally valuable in themselves, but they are believed to lead to conditions that are intrinsically valuable. On the other hand, painting a picture, seeing a play, riding a horse, lying in the sun, or wandering through the streets of Florence do not need an ulterior justification: they are their own ends.

Caution must be exercised in identifying experiential curriculum objectives. There is a great temptation for teachers who have run out of reasons for what they are teaching to assert that it is "worthwhile for its own sake." The best test of this argument springs from the recognition that whether an experience is intrinsically valuable is not a value judgment but an empirical question (Beck, 1968). An experience is intrinsically valuable if the subject actually finds it directly enjoyable, satisfying, or interesting. This question can usually be readily resolved in the classroom by asking or observing the learners.

Most people recognize this distinction between instrumental and intrinsic experiences. Misers are regarded as deviant because they treat a means (money) as if it were an end. But the Puritan ethic, which dominates educational thought in the English-speaking world, distrusts intrinsic experiences. Like the Englishman, who "never enjoys himself except for a noble purpose," schoolchildren may enjoy themselves only if their enjoyment can be justified in terms of developing their understanding, skill, or attitude. As one child says to another in a newspaper cartoon, "Don't touch the rabbit, or Teacher will make you write a report on it."

It is worth reflecting that education's purpose is to increase people's well-being. Ultimately, this means enhancing the quality or quantity of intrinsic experiences; the end is that the learners, or others through them, will experience more satisfaction, enjoyment, or interest in life. Thus to exclude from the curriculum those experiences that are themselves simply and directly satisfying or enjoyable is like saying: Living is something you will be able to do twenty years hence; the first twenty years of your life must be spent only in preparing to live.

Intrinsic experiences, which the educational puritans contemptuously dismiss as "frills," are, I suspect, at the heart of education as distinct from training. We can train people in knowledge, understanding, skills, attitudes, and physical states. But when someone says, "My education was three years in the infantry in the Pacific" or "I traveled round the world on a freighter when I was eighteen—it was an education," the person is not talking of the skills and knowledge acquired, but of the significance of the experience itself. If we could accept the distinction that training consists in developing new states in the learner, but education includes the provision of significant experiences, we could resolve

TYPE OF OBJECTIVE	EXAMPLE
Knowledge	The student will know the addition facts up to 10 + 10. The student will understand the Second Law of Thermodynamics.
Skill	The student will be able to translate written German into English. The student will be able to ride a bicycle.
Physical development	The student's percentage of body fat will be less than 20 percent if female and less than 16 percent if male.
Disposition	The student will develop an improved academic self-image.
Experience	The student will participate in a two-week cruise of the Greek Islands.

Table 7–3   Examples of types of objective

the sterile controversy whether the schools should concentrate on education or on training: clearly they are responsible for both. Obviously a balance must be struck: a school in which students did nothing but enjoy themselves would be as perverted as a school in which students never enjoyed themselves. The educational system that concentrates exclusively on training will produce a society of technocrats. On the other hand, the education that concentrates exclusively on intrinsic experiences will produce a society of lotus-eaters.

Table 7–3 shows examples of the types of objectives, and 7–4 indi-

TYPE OF OBJECTIVE	TARGET	PREFERRED METHOD OF INSTRUCTION	PRIMARY MEANS OF EVALUATION
Knowledge	mind	presentation	written or oral test
Skill	mind	practice	demonstration
Physical development	body	exercise, diet, etc.	objective physiological measurement
Disposition	mind (will)	engagement	unobtrusive observation
Experience	mind	provision of experience	check whether subject had experience

Table 7–4   Objectives, instruction, and evaluation

cates the reason for distinguishing among the five types of objectives. As the primary methods of instruction and evaluation vary with the type of objective, failure to distinguish among them poses the danger of designing ineffective instruction and invalid evaluation.

Behavioral Objectives

The function of education and training is to change the learner by altering one or more of the states that make up his or her identity: knowledge states, skill states, physical states, and so on. Most of these states are intended to be permanently changed; in the case of intrinsic experiences, the objective is to provide a particular kind of state limited in time. States are distinct from actions. But most educational objectives involve private states; states of mind that are not directly observable. Because knowledge, for example, is a private state, whether a person is knowledgeable can be ascertained only by inference from that person's actions. Similarly, a skill is neither a thing in the brain nor a performance, but a particular set of neuronal conditions that allow a certain kind of functioning. To summarize: All education and training aims to produce significant experiences that are transient, or mental or physical states that are lasting.

It follows that it is never the aim of education or training to produce a single behavior. The teacher is concerned not to have the child solve four out of five quadratic equations on one occasion, but to have the child acquire a lasting capability in this procedure. A first-aid instructor wants the trainee to demonstrate mouth-to-mouth resuscitation correctly on one occasion only to show that he or she has acquired a permanent skill.

The origin of the bizarre and widespread belief that single behaviors are adequate as statements of curriculum objectives springs from a simple confusion between the educational intent and the indicator of realization of the intent. This might be termed the "isomorphic fallacy"— the belief that the objective is the same thing as the measure of its achievement. Let us examine a simple example.

A physical education curriculum includes the following objective:

> *The student will run 2,000 meters in 10 minutes on level track or roadway on a still, sunny day, wearing appropriate running clothes, with pulse returning to normal ± 10 within 10 minutes of completing the run.*

The question one would want to ask of the curriculum designer is Why do you want the student to perform this action? The answer would probably be: By so doing, the student is demonstrating a basic level of physical fitness. In other words, the actual intent is for the student to be physically fit; running two thousand meters in ten minutes is merely the indicator that fitness has been achieved. There is, after all, little value in itself in being able to run two thousand meters in ten minutes; if we want to move rapidly from one point to another on the earth's surface, an automobile is faster and a bicycle more efficient. But there is obvious value in being physically fit. Running a certain distance in a certain time is only one of many possible indicators of fitness; one could equally well set a standard in terms of swimming, cycling, skipping, or the Harvard Step Test. None of these activities exhausts the meaning of physical fitness, but each provides a reasonably good partial criterion of such a condition in its normal sense of cardiovascular efficiency.

The "behavioral objectivist," however, when confronted with such an objective as *The student will be physically fit*, will assert that it is not an objective. One can only insist: This *is* the objective, this *is* what we are trying to achieve; running, swimming, or whatever is only the indicator. Lorin Anderson states the issue well:

> A well-written instructional objective specifies the desired learning outcome in *conceptual* terms. That is, it focuses on the *meaning* of the desired learning outcome. The test items, on the other hand, specify the desired learning outcome in *operational* terms. That is, they focus on *typical tasks* which are taken to be representative of the desired learning outcome (Anderson, 1978, p. 4).

To clarify the distinction between the intent and the indicator, the two terms *objective* and *performance criterion* will be used in this book. Thus the objective in our example would be *The student will achieve a basic level of physical fitness in terms of cardiovascular efficiency*. The performance criterion would be *The student will run 2,000 meters in 10 minutes . . .* etc.

It will be noted that the two kinds of statement call for different kinds of verb. Action words, such as *run, demonstrate, perform*, or *write down*, belong in performance criteria. The verbs in objectives should refer to states, and will thus be of the order of *know, understand, be, be able to, enjoy*, or *experience*, all of which are clear, although they are not behavioral. As mentioned earlier, vague terms, such as *be familiar with*, or *become acquainted with*, and ambiguous terms, such as *know how to*, should be avoided.

The behavioral-objectives position has had several effects on the curriculum field, not all of them negative. It has, for instance, forced designers to pay more attention to measures of student achievement. But it has also distracted attention from the crucial question of what objectives are worthwhile to the subordinate one of how objectives should be

> Care about what counts, not about what is merely countable.
>
> —*Herman Daly, economist*

written. To meet arbitrarily imposed criteria of measurability, teachers lacking measurement expertise have often felt compelled to trivialize their curriculum objectives. Confusion between objectives and performance criteria has tended to produce statements that are inferior both as expressions of intent and as indicators of performance. Objectives and performance criteria should be developed according to different sets of principles. The criteria to be applied to objectives should deal with the worth of the intent for the learners and will thus include significance, functionality, appropriateness, and feasibility. The standards to be applied to performance criteria will concern how well they measure the achievement of the objective and will thus include validity, reliability, and efficiency (Pratt, 1976).

Criteria for Curriculum Objectives

The processes of identifying the most pressing human needs, selecting those that are within the purview of the school, defining aims, and deriving objectives from those aims are intended to produce objectives of maximal significance and validity. At each of these stages, dependent as the designer is on human judgment, original intentions can become distorted. But the validity of the objectives ultimately selected for the curriculum is crucial. James Popham (1972) has suggested that one of the consoling things about contemporary education is that it is so ineffective that one doesn't have to worry about what objectives teachers are pursuing, as most of them will not be achieved. The purpose of systematic approaches to curriculum development, however, is to make instruction highly effective and efficient. Once it becomes possible to plan, predict, and bring about changes in the learner with a high degree of certainty, then the question of what objectives are being pursued becomes a matter of primary concern. For this reason, potential objectives should be carefully screened.

There are seven main criteria that curriculum objectives should meet. Three of them—outcome specification, consistency, and precision—have to do with the derivation and specification of objectives. Four—feasibility, functionality, significance, and appropriateness—relate to the value of objectives.

Objectives should identify a learning outcome

An objective is, by definition, an intended learning (or training) outcome of a curriculum. Objectives that begin, *The student will study . . .* or *The student will learn about . . .* usually refer to the student's activities during instruction, rather than to learning outcomes. Statements of single behaviors, such as *The student will write one page on . . .* or *The student will demonstrate . . .* refer not to outcomes but to performance criteria.

Experiential objectives constitute a partial exception to the rule that objectives should be defined in terms of outcomes rather than actions. In experiential objectives, the educational experience is an end in itself, and consequently objectives such as *The student will visit the Shenandoah caverns* or *The student will attend a live performance of a Shakespeare play* are legitimate to the extent that the experiences they specify are intrinsically valuable.

Managerial objectives should not be confused with curriculum objectives. *Students will submit their work on time* may be an intent, but it does not identify a learning outcome. A distinction should also be made between curriculum objectives and the reasons for offering a curriculum. *To prepare students for college-level science* may be the purpose of a curriculum, but as it does not identify a particular learning outcome, it does not qualify as a curriculum objective.

Objectives should be consistent with the curriculum aim

Objectives should conform with the aim from which they are derived. A survey of local health departments in the United States, conducted in 1970, showed that instruction regarding venereal disease was variously provided in such courses as home economics, driver education, humanities, and problems in democracy (*Consumer Reports*, 1970). In much the same way, "value clarification" and "critical thinking" tend to be promiscuously claimed as objectives by history, social studies, English, and health education courses. If an objective meets the other criteria but is not consonant with the curriculum aim, there are two paths of action open: change the aim, or include the objective in a more suitable curriculum.

Objectives should be precise

Objectives are useful only if they are sufficiently precise that different people obtain from them the same understanding of the intended learning outcome. *Students will observe intelligent health practices*, for example, is so vague and ambiguous that its usefulness is severely limited.

Precision is related to the scope of an objective, but it is not easy to say how much learning a single objective should include. Objectives identifying specific levels of achievement result in performances that are superior to those produced by vague injunctions such as "do your best" (Steers and Porter, 1974). But decomposition of knowledge and skills into minutiae can leave designers, teachers, and learners floundering in a morass of objectives. One authority suggests twenty-five objectives as an outside number for a single course, with twenty a more usual maximum (Popham, 1975). I would place the maximum slightly lower, at twelve or fifteen. What this means is that the precision of the objective will depend on the length and specificity of the curriculum. A one-year survey curriculum is likely to have rather general objectives. A one-week curriculum in a specific area will have very precise objectives. At the same time, it should be noted that remarkable success has been achieved in some programs using a large number of highly specific objectives. A case in point is the Oregon Direct Instruction Model (DISTAR) for compensatory education (Becker and Engelmann, 1977). The DISTAR Reading Level I curriculum contains forty-four objectives of the order of precision of: *When given a printed symbol, the student is able to recognize and produce the sound represented by the symbol*.

Statement of objectives must be situationally determined. A general principle governing level of precision might be: Write the objective precisely enough to provide clear guidance regarding the learning outcome to instructional designers, teachers, and evaluators of achievement.

Objectives should be feasible

Unfeasible objectives are relatively rare. Most curricula—probably more than 99 percent—are aiming at objectives that are known to have been achieved through other curricula, and are hence feasible in principle. In selecting objectives, designers tend to be unduly timid rather than the reverse, maintaining somewhat low expectations of what can be accomplished. For this reason, of the seven criteria this is the one least frequently violated.

As it relates to curriculum objectives, feasibility is a practical rather than an absolute standard. A perpetual motion machine is impossible in principle. On the other hand, producing fluency in ten languages in all children by the age of eight is not impossible; it is simply not viable in terms of the means and resources available. Consideration of the criterion of feasibility thus entails at least an implicit review of available means at the point of determination of ends.

Objectives should be functional

Objectives should be personally and socially functional. An objective is personally functional if its attainment is likely to benefit the learner at once or in the future. It is socially functional if it benefits people other than the learner. Teaching income tax evasion might be personally functional but would be socially dysfunctional. Teaching rigid conformity to social mores might (though it is doubtful) be socially functional but personally dysfunctional. Functionality transcends utility. Objectives may have little utilitarian value but have important aesthetic, emotional, or experiential value.

Objectives should be significant

It is not hard to make a case for the functionality of almost any objective. "Had we but world enough, and time . . ." all functional objectives could be pursued, and no one would object to years being spent on the intricacies of solitaire. But because life is finite, objectives must be selected according to criteria of relative value. The criterion of significance requires that every objective selected be of greater value than any alternative objective that could be, but is not being, pursued in the curriculum.

Trivial objectives are often the result of an overemphasis on detail. Use of the term *know that* usually indicates knowledge of a single fact or concept and hence a teaching point rather than an objective. *The student knows that Ouagadougou is the capital of Upper Volta* may be a necessary teaching point, but cannot itself be considered a significant objective.

Objectives should be appropriate

An objective may be functional and significant in principle and yet be inappropriate in a given curriculum. Appropriateness is primarily significance for particular learners. Significance is affected by such factors as the learner's background, interests, and developmental level. Objectives will be redundant if they specify capabilities acquired previously or elsewhere in or outside the school. Objectives having to do with preparation for retirement will be significant for anyone over forty, but inappropriate for elementary school children. Research suggests that many of the objectives of the Nuffield Chemistry Program were inappropriate because they demanded a level of abstract thinking beyond that usually achieved by the age group for which the program was intended (Ingle and Shayer, 1971). In this case, the inappropriateness was severe enough to limit the feasibility.

Examples of Deficient Objectives

COURSE: Consumer Economics

STUDENTS: Secondary school, age 15–18

AIM: *Students will be able to make wise decisions as consumers*

1. Not a learning outcome
   To give students the opportunity to learn about the consumer movement.
   To prepare students for advanced study in economics.
   Students will complete a consumer research project.
   Students will feel free to ask questions in class.

2. Not consistent with the aim
   Students will know the history of economics.
   Students will be able to design persuasive advertisements.

3. Not precise
   Students will exercise intelligent purchasing habits.
   Students will develop a more harmonious social identity.

4. Not feasible
   Students will develop immunity to the influence of advertising.
   Students will be able to calculate compound interest rates in their heads.

5. Not functional
   Students will avoid indebtedness at all costs.
   Students will be able to exploit loopholes in sales-tax regulations.

6. Not significant
   Students will know the exchange rate of ten major world currencies.
   Students will know the definition of the term "lien."

7. Not appropriate
   Students will be able to perform long division.
   Students will be able to minimize estate tax.

Validation of Objectives

Once the analysis and specification of objectives is complete, it is sound practice to validate the objectives immediately. This is best done by seeking the judgment of people in the work or training environment. The objectives for a curriculum in teacher education could be reviewed by practicing teachers and teacher educators. If a curriculum in automotive mechanics is being developed, the objectives should be reviewed by master mechanics and repair-shop managers as well as by teachers of the subject. Recent graduates might be an appropriate group to review objectives in languages or mathematics.

External validation of objectives may prevent revision at a later point and can serve to give the curriculum team an indication of probable professional reaction to the completed curriculum. The curriculum team itself may, however, be sufficiently representative of the work or training situation that external validation is unnecessary.

ACTIVITIES

1. Choose an activity with which you are familiar (producing a play, dissecting a frog, growing roses, etc.). Perform a complete task analysis of the activity. How does this illuminate the decisions that would be involved in teaching the activity?

2. Right- and left-handedness is related to dominance of right or left brain hemisphere. Although 92 percent of the general population are right-handed, only 60 percent of architects are. Austin (1975) reports that people's dominant hemisphere can be identified by asking them a difficult question, e.g., "14 × 23" and watching their eyes; if they look to the right, they are left-hemisphere dominant, and vice versa. Test this hypothesis on some acquaintances.

3. Talk to, or read something by, an advocate of "back to the basics." Which categories of objective are being emphasized, and which ignored?

4. Obtain a recent school or college examination. Analyze the kinds of performance the examination is evaluating, in terms of the typology of objectives. What does this indicate about the program?

5. Ask five educators to distinguish between "education" and "training." Compare the responses. In light of the consistency among them, what is the value of these terms in educational discussion?

QUESTIONS

1. A curriculum objective is a statement of

   a. the knowledge a student will acquire in the curriculum
   b. a specific change to be brought about in a learner by the curriculum
   c. the instruction that the teacher intends to deliver by means of the curriculum
   d. the behavior that a learner will be able to demonstrate on completion of the curriculum

2. In order to determine objectives, the curriculum designer

   a. decomposes the aim
   b. drafts the teaching points

    c. analyzes the curriculum content

    d. specifies the performance criteria

3. You are specifying objectives in a driver-education program. Which of the following should most clearly be classified as critical?

    a. *students will be able to parallel park*

    b. *students will know the function of the PCV valve*

    c. *students will have seat belts properly secured whenever the car is in motion*

    d. *students will be able to change smoothly from second to first gear with manual transmission*

4. Which two categories in curriculum task analysis determine the priority given to an objective?

    a. reaction speed and proficiency

    b. equipment and learning time

    c. learning category and environmental conditions

    d. probability of use and consequences of inadequate mastery

5. Which of the following terms is least ambiguous and hence most useful in stating a knowledge objective?

    a. *the student will understand*

    b. *the student will be aware of*

    c. *the student will be familiar with*

    d. *the student will become acquainted with*

6. The basic difference between knowledge and skill is that as a rule

    a. knowledge is voluntary, skills are involuntary

    b. skills are automatic, knowledge is deliberate

    c. knowledge involves attitude, skills do not

    d. skills require practice, knowledge does not

7. Which of the following objectives has to do with disposition?

    a. *the student will understand the nature of prejudice*

    b. *the student will achieve confidence in public speaking*

    c. *the student will undergo an intensive program of sensitivity training*

    d. *the student will be able to distinguish between statements of fact and statements of value*

8. *The trainee will make a parachute jump from an aircraft.* This statement

    a. could not be an objective

    b. could be a skill objective

    c. could be an experiential objective

    d. could be an attitudinal objective

9. The objective *Students will analyze a Shakespeare play* is deficient because

    a. it is not exact

    b. it is not concisely stated
    c. it does not identify an intention
    d. it does not identify a learning outcome

10. A slogan that would summarize this text's proposed approach to the specification of objectives is

    a. "back to the basics"
    b. "help stamp out nonbehavioral objectives"
    c. "if it's worth learning, it's worth learning well"
    d. "children should not be deprived of their childhood"

Check your answers against the key in Appendix 2.
9 or 10 right: You understand the material presented.
8 or 7 right: Review the areas of uncertainty.
6 or less right: Reread the chapter.

Recommended Reading

Gagné, Robert M. *The conditions of learning.* 3rd ed. New York: Holt, Rinehart & Winston, 1977. Deals with many aspects of learning. Particularly useful for its detailed examination of types of cognitive learnings.

Branson R. K., G. T. Rayner, W. H. Hannum, and J. L. Cox. *Interservice procedures for instructional systems development.* Ft. Monroe, Va.: U.S. Army Training and Doctrine Command, August 1975. Produced by a combined university and military team, this is the model for all training in the U.S. armed services. Contains much practical guidance on analysis of curriculum aims and objectives.

Ryle, Gilbert. *The concept of mind.* New York: Barnes & Noble, 1949. Classic text on the nature of intellect, still valuable for its vigorous treatment of such concepts as intelligence, emotion, and imagination.

Sagan, Carl. *The dragons of Eden.* New York: Random House, 1977. Fascinating exploration of the origins of human intelligence. Includes useful discussion of the nature of the right and left hemispheres of the brain.

Scheffler, Israel. *Reason and teaching.* London: Routledge and Kegan Paul, 1973. Thoughtful but understandable treatment of many issues of curriculum significance. Discussion of the different kinds of human capability will be of special interest to curriculum designers.

References

Allport, G. W. Attitudes in the history of social psychology. In G. W. Lindzey (ed.), *Handbook of social psychology.* Vol. 1. Reading, Mass.: Addison-Wesley, 1954, pp. 43–45.

Anderson, Lorin W. Mastery learning: One approach to the integration of instruction and measurement. Paper presented at the Annual Meeting of the American Educational Research Association, Toronto, March 1978.

Aristotle. Nichomachean ethics. Quoted in Ivan D. Illich, *Deschooling society*. London: Calder and Boyars, 1971, p. 62.

Austin, James H. Eyes left! Eyes right! *Saturday Review*, August 9, 1975, 32.

Ayer, A. J. *The problem of knowledge*. Harmondsworth, England: Penguin, 1956.

Banghart, Frank W., and Albert Trull, Jr. *Educational planning*. New York: Macmillan, 1973.

Barnes, W. H. F. Knowing. *Philosophical Review*, 1963, 72, 3–16.

Beck, Clive. Educational value statements. *The Monist*, 1968, 52, 70–86.

Becker, Wesley C., and Siegfried Engelmann. The Oregon Direct Instructional Model. Eugene, Oregon: University of Oregon, Follow Through Project, 1977.

Bloom, Benjamin S., et al. *Taxonomy of objectives: Cognitive domain*. New York: David McKay, 1956.

Bogen, Joseph E., and Glenda M. Bogen. The other side of the brain III: The corpus callosum and creativity. *Bulletin of the Los Angeles Neurological Societies*, 1969, 34 (4), 191–220.

Branson, R. K., G. T. Rayner, W. H. Hannum, and J. L. Cox. *Interservice procedures for instructional systems development: Phase II-design* (TRADOC Pam 350–30). Ft. Monroe, Va.: U.S. Army Training and Doctrine Command, August 1975. (NTIS No. ADA-019 487).

Bruner, Jerome S. *The relevance of education*. Harmondsworth, England: Penguin, 1974.

Carroll, John B. Problems of measurement related to the concept of learning for mastery. In James H. Block (ed.), *Mastery learning: Theory and practice*. New York: Holt, Rinehart & Winston, 1971, pp. 29–46.

Caswell, Hollis. Emergence of curriculum as a field of professional work and study. In Helen F. Robison (ed.), *Precedents and promises in the curriculum field*. New York: Teachers College, 1966, pp. 1–11.

Consumer Reports. Venereal disease. *Consumer Reports*, February 1970, 118–123.

Crossman, E. R. F. W. A theory of the acquisition of speed-skill. *Ergonomics*, 1959, 2, 153–166.

Ebel, Robert L. The future of measurements of abilities II. *Educational Researcher*, March 1973, 5–12.

Fanon, Frantz. *The wretched of the earth*. New York: Grove Press, 1965.

Fleishman, Edwin A. Toward a taxonomy of human performance. *American Psychologist*, 1975, 30, 1127–1149.

Gagné, Robert M. Characteristics of instructional technologists. *Improving Human Performance*, 1973, 3, 139–144.

——— . Educational technology and the learning process. *Educational Researcher*, 1974, 3 (1), 3–8.

Guilford, L. P. Three faces of intellect. *American Psychologist*, 1959, 14, 469–479.

Harding, Ann, and Brian Page. An alternative model for modern language examinations. *Audio-Visual Language Journal*, 1974/75, 12, 237–241.

Hirst, P. H., and R. S. Peters. *The logic of education*. London: Routledge and Kegan Paul, 1970.

Hodgetts, A. B. *What culture? What heritage? A study of civic education in Canada*. Toronto: Ontario Institute for Studies in Education, 1968.

Ingle, R. B., and M. Shayer. Conceptual demands in Nuffield 0-level chemistry. *Education in Chemistry*, 1971, 8, 182–183.

Krathwohl, David R., et al. *Taxonomy of educational objectives: Affective domain.* New York: David McKay, 1964.

Lawrence, Arnold. An introductory curriculum in map skills. Kingston, Canada: Queen's University Faculty of Education, 1978.

Martin, Mary Catherine, and Dagmar E. Brodt. Task analysis for training and curriculum design. *Improving Human Performance*, 1973, 2, 113–120.

Mead, Donald F. Determining training priorities for job tasks. Lackland AFB, Texas: Occupational and Manpower Research Division, Air Force Human Resources Laboratory, 1976.

Ornstein, Robert E. *The psychology of consciousness.* San Francisco: W. H. Freeman, 1972.

Polanyi, Michael. *The tacit dimension.* New York: Doubleday, 1966.

Popham, James. Accountability and teacher competence. Address to Presession of American Educational Research Association, Tempe, Arizona, March 1972.

———. Criterion-referenced testing. Seminar at Ontario Institute for Studies in Education, Toronto, 1975.

Pratt, David. A competency-based program for training teachers of history. *Teacher Education*, 1975, 8, 79–91.

———. Humanistic goals and behavioral objectives: Towards a synthesis. *Journal of Curriculum Studies*, 1976, 8, 15–26.

Roland, Jane. On "knowing how" and "knowing that." *Philosophical Review*, 1959, 67, 379–388.

Ryle, Gilbert. *The concept of mind.* New York: Barnes & Noble, 1949.

Scheffler, Israel. *Conditions of knowledge.* Glenview, Ill.: Scott, Foresman, 1965.

Smith, Robert G., Jr. *The development of training objectives.* Alexandria, Va.: George Washington University, Human Resources Research Office, 1964.

Sperry, Roger W. Left-brain, right-brain. *Saturday Review*, August 9, 1975, 30–33.

Steers, Richard M., and Lyman W. Porter. The role of task-goal attributes in employee performance. *Psychological Bulletin*, 1974, 81, 434–452.

Welford, A. T. *Ageing and human skill.* Oxford: Oxford University Press, 1958.

8

PRINCIPLES

- Evaluation of student achievement serves to inform, diagnose, predict, provide feedback, motivate, aid licensing, and promote educational equality.

- A performance criterion specifies actions from which realization of objectives can be inferred.

- The principal criterion for measures of learning achievement is validity.

- Congruence, completeness, objectivity, discreteness, and reliability are important aspects of validity.

- Different procedures are required in assessing achievement of knowledge, skills, physical development, dispositions, and experiences.

- Research evidence suggests that minimal required standards of achievement can and probably should be set higher than is traditionally the case.

- Defining standards of performance involves weighing several factors related to the learner's future use of the learning.

CONCEPTS

Performance criterion	Congruence	Domain exhausting
Validity	Discreteness	Domain sampling
Direct validity	Reliability	Mastery learning
Derived validity	Unobtrusive observation	

8

Criteria of Performance

Our experiences suggest that unless the school has translated the objectives into specific and operational definitions, little is likely to be done about the objectives. They remain pious hopes and platitudes.

—Benjamin S. Bloom (1961, p. 54)

The Functions of Evaluation

Evaluation practices in schools have been charged with a wide range of ill effects. It is claimed that evaluation contributes to racial discrimination and to trivial teaching. In North American schools it is said to encourage cramming and cheating, and in Britain and Japan it is blamed for student suicides. There has been more than a little truth in these accusations. In the 1960s they resulted in a movement away from testing in schools. But just as "No philosophy!" leads to bad philosophy, "No testing!" led to bad testing: testing that was subjective, biased, and erratic. One actually encountered experienced teachers in the 1960s who seriously claimed to award course credits on the basis of "the look in the student's eye."

Shifts in public opinion and economic trends in the late 1970s restored formal testing in almost all jurisdictions from which it was removed in the 1960s. Unfortunately such decisions were as often as not based once again on ideology rather than on an analysis of the needs of students, society, or the curriculum. It is a paradox that evaluation is the most sophisticated area of educational science, yet its application in schools is often governed by the most simplistic thinking.

One root of the problem is the assumption that evaluation serves only a single purpose: to help teachers make grading decisions. But evaluation has much wider functions, at least eight of which may be considered briefly at this point.

To inform learners of their attainment

"Knowledge of results" is one of the cornerstones of learning theory. Knowing whether one has attained a goal, or by how much it has been missed or exceeded, has been shown to be an important incentive in human performance, especially when knowledge of results quickly follows performance (Hilgard and Bower, 1966).

To diagnose areas of strength and weakness

It is not enough for evaluation merely to indicate that the student has "passed" or "failed." If remediation is to be effective in bringing the student up to the required standard, both the instructor and the student must know the areas of student weakness; if remediation is to be efficient, they must also know the areas in which the student is competent.

To guide decisions about the student's future

Adequate academic and career guidance must be based at least in part on sound data about the learner's aptitudes, interests, and attainments. At some point, decisions will be made to include some aspirants, and to exclude others, from certain courses, programs, institutions, and careers. Whether such decisions are made by educators, by students, or by others, if they are not based on valid assessment they will be open to question. Evaluative decisions in education and training are being subjected to judicial decision with increasing frequency (Warren, 1976). Assessment measures "of the highest possible technical quality" are essential to "eliminate charges of real or apparent discrimination" (Branson et al., 1975, p. 26).

To inform interested agencies of student competence

Parents have a right, and in fact a responsibility, to discover what their children have learned in school. Employers need to know what capabilities potential employees have acquired. Taxpayers are entitled to know what effects schools they are supporting are having on students. Universities, in order to design appropriate programs, need to know what attainments incoming students possess, just as secondary schools need data on the abilities and background of elementary-school graduates.

To provide feedback into the instructional system

An instructional system can achieve its potential only if the results of instruction are monitored and corrective action taken when necessary. Professional educators do not blame the students or themselves if objectives are not achieved. They first remedy the learner deficiency, then revise the instruction. Their professional life is a repetitive cycle of develop—try out—evaluate—revise.

To provide an operational target for the learner

Ideally students should be motivated most strongly by wanting to learn something that they believe worthwhile. Thus a group of students may be motivated by the objective *To learn to swim.* But in practice they will often tend to concentrate on the measure of assessment, for example, *To swim three lengths of the pool in five minutes on April 23;* and this operational target will act as the organizing principle behind their efforts to develop strength and skill in performance. Because this tendency to focus on the test is quickly learned by students and reinforced in most schools, teachers should remember that the function of instruction is to enable the learner to develop a capability, not to pass a test. They should avoid using examinations as a system of rewards and punishments.

To license candidates for a profession or occupation

The public expects that the competence of those who work in areas related to public health or safety will be formally assessed before being let loose on the community. Barbers and physicians, taxi drivers and airline pilots, must normally pass examinations to be allowed to practice. A number of American states require demonstration of minimal competence by teachers prior to certification. Many professions are adding to initial assessment the requirement for periodic reexamination to maintain professional status. To study the certification requirements for an occupation is to gain an insight into the politics and the self-image of the calling: compare the licensing regulations for lawyers, police officers, politicians, clergy, prostitutes, and academics.

To promote minimal educational equality

Differences in the quality of education will always persist between different regions, different schools, and different classrooms. In the absence of achievement data, the nature and extent of such differences will be obscured. Underachievement resulting not from student deficiency but from inadequate services may be unrecognized; neither the public nor the administrators will have the information required to make appropriate decisions. Objective data on the present level of achievement is therefore an important foundation for securing equality of educational opportunity.

The Limits of Evaluation

Considered collectively, the functions of evaluation render an educational program that has no assessment as useful a notion as a hospital where the thermometers and sphygmomanometers are discarded, the laboratory is closed down, and the status of patients is assessed by an occasional "How do you feel?"

But is every kind of learning outcome measurable? Or are there, as some educators claim, objectives that are untestable, unmeasurable, intangible?

It should be noted that one does not measure objects, but properties or attributes of objects: "One does not measure a table, but one may measure a table's length. . . . One does not measure a student, but one may measure his weight or his achievement in arithmetic" (Jones, 1971, p. 335). Some of these properties cannot be defined quantitatively: the student's name or hair color, for example. They can, however, be observed and recorded. Most mental qualities must be measured indirectly. We can obtain a direct measure of a student's height, but not of a learner's understanding of Shakespeare. Knowledge, skill, and attitude are private mental states, not amenable to direct public observation; their existence can only be inferred from the actions of the subject. Thus we would ask a student questions in French and assess the answers to examine his or her facility in the language, or give the child a bicycle to ride to obtain a measure of cycling skill.

As a rule, when teachers claim to be pursuing objectives that are unmeasurable, what they mean is that they do not know how to measure them. And indeed some human abilities, particularly in creative areas, are difficult to measure. Difficulty, however, is not the same as impossibility. Qualities considered "intangible" are frequently those that are inadequately defined. A student's commitment to freedom or to democracy cannot be evaluated until agreement has been reached on the definition of freedom and democracy. The beauty of a sunset cannot be directly measured because beauty is not an objective but an ascribed quality, related to a human reaction to a particular phenomenon. That reaction could be assessed in a number of ways, from asking a subject to rate a series of color slides to observing the dilation of the subject's pupils when looking at a sunset.

Many decisions we might regard as essentially nonrational are in fact arrived at through a largely subconscious process of weighing and comparing attributes. Choosing a meal in a restaurant, or the choice of a husband or wife, is neither random nor arbitrary, but at least in part a process of comparing existing possibilities along multiple dimensions with other real or ideal alternatives.

There appear to be no theoretical reasons for suggesting that some human attributes are unmeasurable in principle. The cost of evaluating attainment of some objectives may outweigh the benefits. But properly trained curriculum professionals could probably design effective and efficient assessment measures for 99 percent of the objectives identified in school programs.

Important as evaluation is, its emphasis in recent years has had some unfortunate consequences. The demand by administrators for publicly visible results has discouraged teachers from pursuing goals that are not readily measured. The evaluative expertise of teachers is often rudimentary, allowing confidence only in assessment of recall of information. As a result, they frequently neglect significant objectives in favor of trivial ones.

This is one good reason for keeping the definition of objectives separate from the identification of evaluative measures. When determining

---

A fifth myth in art education is that teachers should not attempt to evaluate work in art. . . . The fact is that evaluation—even for those who claim not to do it—is being done all the time. I would go even further and say that not to evaluate children's art, even if this were possible, is to be educationally irresponsible. As teachers we are concerned not simply with bringing about change, but with bringing about *desirable* change—improvement if you will. If a teacher does not evaluate what children do, how can he determine if what he is doing is contributing to or hampering their growth in art? . . . Children respect thoughtful evaluation and criticism because it testifies that their teachers are taking them and their work seriously.

—*Elliot W. Eisner (1974, pp. 96–97)*

the objective, the designer should not be unduly concerned about measurement. It is fallacious to argue that because a quality cannot be readily assessed, it is not worth pursuing. The objectives selected should simply be those that are most worthwhile. When such objectives are defined, the search can begin for the best means of evaluation.

Performance Criteria

Objectives identify desirable states in the learner, most of which are private and unobservable. The function of performance criteria is to specify actions on the part of the subject that will allow valid inferences that such states have come about.

The term *performance criterion* is related to the larger concept of what is known as *criterion-referenced measurement.* In a brief but significant article published in 1963, Glaser used the term *criterion standard* in making the distinction between criterion-referenced and *norm-referenced* measures. Criterion-referenced measures evaluate the student's achievement against a fixed standard of performance; norm-referenced measures evaluate the student's achievement relative to that of his or her peers. The concept of a performance criterion belongs within the criterion-referenced model; the educator who specifies a performance criterion is concerned with establishing a standard that the student is to meet, regardless of his or her rank relative to other students. The question is not How well did this student perform, as compared with other students? The question is Did the student achieve the objective? The concepts of norm-referenced and criterion-referenced measurement are explored more fully in the next chapter.

A performance criterion may range from a simple requirement such as nine out of ten correct answers on a true/false test for a knowledge objective, to a detailed description of actions for a skill objective, to a quasi-experimental design in evaluating an attitude. The performance criterion will usually provide exact specification of at least five important factors in performance: (1) the activity to be performed; (2) required speed; (3) standard of accuracy; (4) equipment and resources available; and (5) environmental conditions.

The student will be able to copy-type is a reasonably precise and explicit objective, but unless further detail were provided, the expectation of students or instructors could range from ten words per minute on an electric machine to one hundred words per minute on a manual model. An appropriate performance criterion could be stated quite briefly:

The student will copy-type five hundred words in ten minutes from randomly selected New York Times *editorials using an IBM Selectric II typewriter with a maximum of five errors or corrections under normal office conditions.*

This statement describes exactly what is required. Sufficient detail is provided to remove any ambiguity, but not to the point of absurdity. It would be redundant to specify the temperature, humidity, noise level, and crowdedness of the testing environment, because "under normal office conditions" specifies the conditions adequately.

The positive contribution made by the behavioral-objective school of thought is the recognition that a performance criterion does more than simply provide a measure of achievement of a goal; it also acts as an operational definition of the objective. That is, it amplifies and clarifies the basic goal statement by identifying an explicit behavior that will be required to assess its attainment. The student will often tend to focus on achieving the performance criterion: it is important that the teacher not lose sight of the objective. It is the *objectives*, not merely the *indicators*, that we want learners to achieve.

Complex skills call for extensive definition of required performance. Parallel parking is such a skill in driving. It is easy enough to state the objective: *The driver will be able to parallel park;* but when it comes to assessment, a great many questions arise. What kind of vehicle is to be parked? On which side of the road? On the level or on a gradient? How quickly and accurately? On the first attempt? A complete performance criterion would constitute a checklist of several factors:

The driver will park the automobile in which he or she expects to take the official driving test between two cars in a space 1½ times the length of the car driven. The driver will stop with the inside wheels within twenty centimeters of the curb, without the car touching any other car or the curb in the process. He or she will complete the task in not more than three manoevers, using correct signals and observing all traffic rules. This task will be performed once each on the left and the right side of the road, and on an uphill and a downhill gradient of between 2 and 10 percent. Front wheels will be turned away from/towards curb on upgrade/downgrade. The driver will meet all the above requirements on at least three of the four attempts and will not touch another car on any attempt.

Detailed specification of this kind benefits learners in several ways. Once they know what is required, they can practise the skill on their own and assess their own competence. Assessment is not an arbitrary or private judgment springing from a professional mystique, but a matter of meeting clear criteria open to public scrutiny. The anxiety students experience from "not knowing where they stand" disappears. Continuous assessment becomes a reality without the need for constant teacher intervention. Experimental research suggests that the provision of specific guidelines for self-evaluation improves both the accuracy of self-estimates and the performance of the learner (Carr, 1977).

Criteria for Measures of Achievement

Evaluation that is badly designed or executed brings the practice of testing into disrepute and is often worse than no evaluation. The value of assessment depends upon the extent to which it meets a number of criteria. Most of these criteria are comprehended by the single term *validity.*

Much has been written about test validity, and readers interested in a detailed discussion of the subject should refer to one of the many excellent texts available on educational evaluation (e.g., Bloom, Hastings, and Madaus, 1971; Ebel, 1972; Gronlund, 1977; Phi Delta Kappa, 1971; Sax, 1974; Thorndike, 1971; Tuckman, 1975). Writers have distinguished at least ten kinds of test validity: concurrent, construct, content, curricular, definitional, empirical, face, factorial, intrinsic, and predictive. Ebel classifies these into two basic kinds: *direct validity* and *derived validity.*

> *A test has direct, primary validity to the extent that the tasks included in it represent faithfully and in due proportion the kinds of tasks that provide an operational definition of the achievement or the trait in question. A test has derived, secondary validity to the extent that the scores it yields correlate with the criterion scores which possess direct, primary validity (Ebel, 1972, p. 381)*

The driving test could be said to have direct validity because (with some limitations) the tasks to be demonstrated are the same as those required in normal driving. On the other hand, suppose that it was discovered, after testing many thousands of drivers, that a person's height was a perfect predictor of driving skill: the taller the individual, the better the driver, without exception. In that case the traditional driving test could be abandoned: it would be necessary merely to measure the height of applicants. This would not be a driving test, but as a perfect predictor it would have complete derived validity.

While derived validity has its uses, the prudent curriculum designer will, where possible, aim for direct validity. To be able to say that a student has demonstrated certain knowledge or skills is at least to communicate something about the student that can be widely understood. But to say that someone has scored high or low on a test purported to be related to some other attribute takes the communication into more murky waters: the history of testing is strewn with the wreckage of supposedly predictive tests.

Validity has a number of aspects that need separate discussion. Six specific criteria for measures of achievements will be described: congruence, completeness, objectivity, discreteness, reliability, and efficiency. All but efficiency represent aspects of validity.

Congruence

Validity is usually defined as the extent to which a test measures what it is intended to measure. In curriculum terms, this can be rephrased as the extent to which a test measures achievement of the curriculum objectives. This will serve as a definition of congruence.

The most common violation of this criterion is the practice of testing knowledge of content rather than attainment of objectives. A history teacher may claim to be aiming at development of "good citizenship" but design tests measuring recall of specific bits of historical information. An English teacher's objectives may include "development of literary taste," but the examinations require memorization of the plot and characters of particular plays or novels studied in the course. An instructor in metallurgy may want graduates to be able to make sound decisions of the kind made by an industrial metallurgist, which would usually be team decisions made over a flexible time period; but the examinations call for reproduction of knowledge from memory, generated independently and under time constraints. Any test for which students can or do "cram" is likely to be invalid, for it will be testing short-term memory, which is hardly ever the target of instruction.

The significance of this criterion may be highlighted by a particularly stark example of invalid testing. I once worked in a government-sponsored program teaching English to recent immigrants to Canada. The federal government paid a living allowance to the learners, which enabled them to concentrate full-time on acquiring fluency in English. The five-month program aimed primarily at oral fluency, with secondary objectives concerning acculturation. Instruction was almost entirely oral and direct. Each one-month unit concluded with a test; failure resulted in repetition of the unit. A second failure at the same level meant termination from the program. The tests included such questions as "Read the following passage and punctuate it correctly" and "Convert the following paragraph from direct into indirect speech." Not surprisingly, the immigrant students, many of whom had limited formal education, were regularly failed out of the program. This could have disastrous personal consequences, including failure to develop fluency in English, to adjust to the English-speaking environment, to acquire a license in their trade or occupation, to obtain appropriate employment, or to support their families in accordance with the modest expectations that had motivated them to leave their home countries.

As one of the functions of testing is to guide decisions about the student's future, invalid testing is likely to result in misguidance. The consequences may be trivial or tragic. But wherever test results will have an effect on people's lives, the first criterion the test must meet is that it actually measures the attainment of intended outcomes.

Completeness

A good performance criterion should assess all the important aspects of the capability being evaluated in sufficient detail that sound generalizations can be made regarding the competence of the learner.

A distinction can be made between *domain-exhausting* and *domain-sampling* tests. In a domain-exhausting test every aspect of a capability is evaluated. Unitary skills, such as the ability to disassemble and reassemble an M-16 rifle, can be tested in their entirety. Similarly, the objective *The student knows the Greek alphabet* might be evaluated by requiring the learner to write the Greek alphabet in the correct sequence in upper and lower case, to write each letter when named in random order, and to name each letter when the instructor pointed to it. This would pretty well exhaust all aspects of the capability.

Most of the qualities curricula aim to bring about or enhance are not unitary but multiple, and the performance criteria must assess a sample of behaviors large enough to allow a judgment regarding total performance. The medical technician does not have to drain your body of blood to perform a blood test; a single drop of blood is adequate. Similarly, to test the ability to multiply together two sets of one- or two-digit numbers, it is not necessary to have the student solve all ten thousand possible problems. A sample of ten or twenty would serve equally well. To determine whether the student understands economic terminology, it would be inadequate to ask for the meaning of only three terms. But we would not need to ask the learner to define every term in a dictionary of economics. How large the sample should be is a matter of judgment that depends on the importance of the objective and the consequent level of reliability required.

Two more examples may serve to illustrate the criterion of completeness. Some police forces still train and test the marksmanship of their officers by means of timed shooting at a stationary target. But speed and accuracy in such circumstances by no means exhaust the significant dimensions of police marksmanship. A police officer must be able to shoot accurately at moving and intermittent targets, must know how to use a firearm when an assailant is shielded by a hostage, must be able to shoot in semi-darkness so as not to be temporarily blinded by the flash, and so on. These and other aspects of the skills would be revealed by a thorough analysis of "police use of side arms."

One objective in a curriculum in communication for the early grades

> If the measurement reported depends more on the person making the measurement than on the person being measured, it is unlikely to be very dependable or useful, and there would be little point in reporting it to anyone else.
>
> —*Robert L. Ebel (1972, p. 87)*

might be *The student will be able to use the telephone effectively*. When asked to write a performance criterion for this objective, teachers tend to produce something like this:

> *Given a domestic telephone, a local telephone directory, and the names of three people, the student will find the numbers in the directory and call each with a maximum of one dialing error.*

However, this is a very restricted use of the telephone. The performance criterion does not test the ability to use a pay phone or the Yellow Pages, to answer calls, to call the operator, to make long-distance or collect calls, to use the phone for emergencies, or to observe telephone etiquette. As it stands, it is clearly incomplete.

Objectivity

One generalization that holds true for the majority of people is that most of their judgments are subjective. Another generalization is that most people believe their judgments to be objective. Teachers are no exception. Subjectivity colors many of the judgments they regard as objective. Research suggests that assessment of student performance is affected by how closely the student's attitudes approximate those of the evaluator. (Smith, Meadow, and Sisk, 1970). Principals are apparently biased in hiring staff by attitude similarity or dissimilarity of applicants (Merritt, 1970). And instructors of education are influenced in assessing teacher performance by both the attitudes (Hamlish and Gaier, 1954) and the physical attractiveness of student teachers (Hore, 1971).

Complete objectivity is in many evaluative situations either unattainable or impractical. Carefully designed performance criteria can, however, keep subjectivity within narrow limits. Two principles are of particular importance. The first is to make the criteria of judgment explicit, and the second is to quantify the criteria whenever possible.

Consider the case of a teacher formulating a performance criterion for the objective *The student will be able to write creative and original description*. The first draft is:

> *The student will submit three hundred to seven hundred words of descriptive writing, written in his or her own time. This will be graded on a scale of A to E with respect to creativity and originality. A minimum grade of C is required.*

Stated in this way, the performance criterion does little to operationalize the objective. The student might arguably feel that the real criterion is whether or not the teacher likes his or her face. It is unlikely that a completely objective quantitative method for evaluating descriptive writing could be developed; the most erudite critics disagree violently over the literary merits of some writers' work. But the teacher can at least state the criterion of judgment more clearly. At the same time, the probability of injustice due to personal reaction to a single piece of work can be reduced by increasing the number of submissions and the number of judges.

> *The student will submit four pieces of descriptive writing, each three hundred to seven hundred words in length, written in his or her own time. These will be graded as follows:*
> *0: devoid of originality or creativity; trite, banal, or cliché-ridden.*
> *1: derivative or unimaginative in theme or treatment; tendency to use overworked expressions or images.*
> *2: competent, but lacking vivacity or inventiveness in style or content.*
> *3: imaginative choice of expression or subject; willingness to experiment, with some success.*
> *4: extremely original and creative; inventive use of themes, words, or images; interesting in substance and execution.*
> *Submissions will be evaluated by two judges and the grades averaged. A minimum grade of 2.5 is required on the best two of the four submissions.*

Lack of explicitness in a performance criterion invites the evaluator to improvise. Improvization is likely to be variable, and this introduces problems of bias and unreliability. This may be illustrated by an example from military training. At first sight, the following requirement appears to be highly explicit:

> *Must run one mile in ten minutes on straight, level, and smooth concrete roadway, with no wind blowing on a sunny day at 70°F., carrying a 30-pound load in addition to wearing 2 pounds of summer clothing and 2½ pounds of normal GI boots.*

But R. B. Miller comments:

> *A task analysis of load-carrying tasks would quickly reveal that the above statement is indeed lacking in a most critical factor: a description of the*

load. Will it be strapped to and supported on the back or carried in the arms? What is its bulk? Its contour and center of gravity? ... Clearly it is a different requirement to run with a bucket filled to the brim with 30 lb. of corrosive liquid acid than with the same 30 lb. composed of nuts and bolts in a padded knapsack on a shoulder harness (Miller, 1962, p. 197).

All evaluation of student achievement lies at some point on a continuum from judgment to measurement. Judgment is a "process of forming an opinion by discerning and comparing" (Webster's, 1967). Measurement is "the assignment of numerals to entities according to rules" (Stufflebeam, 1968, p. 6). A student's ability to paint in the abstract, or a nurse's ability to make a patient comfortable, are not directly quantifiable, although the impressionistic judgments of the evaluator may be transposed to a numerical scale. In such cases, reliance is placed on subjective assessment by an expert. But where measurement is possible, the decisions are accessible to the intelligent layman; they may not be simple, but in principle they can be performed mechanically or algorithmically and are hence open to public scrutiny. The skill of building a campfire, discussed in Chapter 7, was assessed by a simple yes/no question: Did the water boil in the time allowed? The quantification of the measure in that example allowed little scope for subjectivity.

Discreteness

A performance criterion should not only measure the quality it is intended to measure; it should measure *only* that quality. If a test is to determine whether a learner has mastered objective x, this evaluation should ideally be unaffected by factors y and z. In practice this is difficult to achieve. To succeed in any written test, the student must be able to read, whether or not reading is the skill being evaluated. But in most examinations, it is a legitimate working assumption that students are equal in reading ability. Writing skill is less evenly distributed. Essay tests give an advantage to the student who has the gifts of fluent self-expression under artificial conditions and of rapid and legible handwriting. If these are the qualities being assessed, validity is unaffected. But if the test is purportedly one of knowledge or understanding, these contaminating factors make it difficult to determine exactly what qualities are contributing to the judgment about the learner's performance.

The charge of cultural bias in intelligence tests is often essentially an accusation of lack of discreteness. The results of an intelligence test that required the subject to answer questions containing such terms as *accountant, air conditioning, freezer, golf, poodle,* or *swimming pool* would clearly be contaminated by the individual's social background and cultural experiences (Samuda, 1975).

Reliability

Reliability refers to the stability or consistency of the results produced by a test. Consider a bathroom scale that is in good working order. If your weight actually stays ~onstant, the scale will give the same reading whether it is Monday or Friday, morning or evening, whether you are elated or depressed, whether it is you on the scale or someone else of identical weight, and whether you read the scales in private or seek confirmation from another member of your family. We would say that the scale is perfectly reliable.

Now consider a typical classroom test. Two students whose ability is in fact equal may receive different grades. The same student may perform differently on equivalent tests given on different occasions, even though he or she has learned and forgotten nothing in the interim. Two teachers may give different scores to the same student's paper. The severity or liberality of a single teacher may vary substantially in the course of marking a large number of student papers. In all of these cases, we would say that the test was unreliable. Its inconsistency would also force us to conclude that it was less than completely valid.

Reliability is usually expressed as a correlation between plus 1.00 and minus 1.00 calculated between two sets of scores. The correlation may be between scores awarded to the same students by different evaluators (reader reliability), between scores achieved by the same students on equivalent forms (instrument stability), between scores achieved by the same students on two administrations of the same test (examinee reliability), or between scores achieved on two different parts of the same test (internal consistency).

There is a substantial interplay between objectivity and reliability. A test that lacks objectivity will allow scope for bias to affect the judgment. This will result in inconsistent, or unreliable, judgments to the degree that the biases of different judges are different in type or intensity.

Some technical aspects of reliability are discussed in the next chapter. At this point, three strategies may be mentioned that can be used to improve the reliability of performance criteria. First, allow the student an adequate number of trials. We would not test a student's spelling with a one-word test, nor marksmanship with a single bullet. Unreliability due to chance is reduced as the number of trials is increased. Second, test different abilities separately. One test designed to measure several distinct qualities is likely to be unreliable, and attempts to give it more internal reliability will be counterproductive. As Cronbach points out, there is no reason why a driver who correctly answers questions about the penalties for speeding should also be expected to answer correctly questions about legal speed limits (1971, p. 457). Third, where evaluation is subjective, provide more than one judge, and average the results; this strategy will reduce the unreliability due to individual subjective judgment.

Efficiency

The five criteria discussed above are "scientific" criteria and are of primary importance. Efficiency is a "prudential" criterion, which, though of secondary importance, should also be taken into account (Phi Delta Kappa, 1971).

Evaluation consumes resources, the chief of which is student time. The method of testing that meets the scientific criteria at a satisfactory level and consumes least time and cost should normally be selected. Choosing efficient tests is particularly important when the curriculum calls for evaluation of learner achievement of every objective, rather than for the conventional once-only test at the end of a course or semester.

The familiar assertion that "every test should be a learning experience" may be a threat to efficiency, as well as to some of the other criteria. A test may well be a learning experience, and if it is, so much the better. But the purpose of testing is evaluation, not instruction. To attempt to make a test serve two purposes may simply result in an inefficient test that is neither a good measuring instrument nor good instruction.

Evaluation of Different Types of Objective

One of the reasons for classifying objectives by type is that the different types of objective require differing strategies of evaluation.

Evaluating knowledge

Recall of information is easily assessed; it is more difficult to evaluate broader understanding. For this reason, many teachers develop tests that assess only recall.

Recall of information can often be efficiently and reliably evaluated by a short objective test. For example:

> Objective: *The student knows the flora and fauna that are abundant in the British Isles.*
> Performance criterion: *The student answers correctly at least eighteen out of twenty true/false questions, e.g., "The fallow deer is commonly found in the wild in the Southwest of England."*

Understanding may also be assessed by some kind of objective test. An objective of an art history course might be:

The student will understand the changes in style, technique, and theme that occurred in painting during the sixteenth century.

This understanding could be evaluated by showing a series of slides of paintings and asking such questions as:

—Which of these paintings was produced before 1520?
—Was this painting the work of the school of Florence, Venice, Antwerp, or Madrid?
—Which of these paintings shows most strongly the influence of Titian?
—The main innovation of such paintings as this was (a) perspective; (b) anatomical drawing; (c) virtuosity of execution; (d) dramatic style.

The paintings illustrated would not include any that had been studied in the course, as any test becomes a test of mere recall if the student has previously encountered the questions in some form.

The formal examinations most frequently encountered in schools and colleges are generally aimed primarily at the evaluation of knowledge. Special procedures for the development of such tests are described in the next chapter.

Evaluating skills

To determine an individual's skill, it is necessary to ask for demonstration of the skill. No one could expect to assess a person's ability to swim or ride a bicycle by having the novice write an essay or complete a ten-item quiz. Performance criteria would specify distance to be swum or ridden, maximum time allowed, and requirements regarding style and environmental conditions.

The following is an example of a performance criterion for a cognitive skill:

Objective: *The student will be able to use the Pythagorean theorem.* Performance criterion: *(1) Given drawings of five right-angled triangles with the length of two sides shown, the student will calculate correctly in each case the length of the third side. (2) Given the dimensions of five triangles, the student will correctly identify the three that are right-angled triangles. (3) Using pencil, ruler, unruled paper, and compasses only, the student will use the ratio 3:4:5 to construct three right-angled triangles. The right angles must be between 89° and 91°.*
In the above cases, all sides of the triangles will be in whole units. Total time allowed: ten minutes. Accuracy: maximum of one error.

It is sometimes impractical to test a student on a task as it would be performed in real life. Examples include emergency skills such as certain first aid techniques; professional abilities such as those required by a business executive or legal counsel; and dynamic decision-making skills such as those called for in psychiatric counseling, combat leadership, or classroom teaching (Root, et. al., 1978). In such cases, simulation can be used to evaluate a student's proficiency. Performance in computer-based business simulations is considered by some corporations a good predictor of executive potential (*Business Week*, 1967). Medical schools provide "patients" by means of computer programs, life-like models, and trained actors (McGuire, Solomon, and Bashook, 1976). The most advanced simulators are those used for flight training, which allow pilots to practice and be evaluated on everything from one-engine landings to defense against attacking missiles (Singer, 1977). The following performance criterion for a motor skill is a simulation, but only in the minor sense that the subject is uninjured:

> Objective: *The student will be able to tie a collar-and-cuff sling using a triangular bandage.*
> Performance criterion: *Using a triangular bandage approximately 100 cm. by 100 cm. by 140 cm., the student will tie a collar-and-cuff sling to support the wrist of a standing fellow student. The sling will be tied at the wrist in a clove hitch that is firm but not constricting; the bandage will be tied just above the collarbone in a reef knot. The extended fingers of the supported hand will touch the opposite shoulder. When this sling is judged satisfactory, the student will tie another sling for the opposite side. Each sling must be tied correctly but gently in one minute.*

Such a criterion provides clear enough guidance that a nonexpert could evaluate attainment of the skill. In some areas, such as ballet, painting, playing a musical instrument, or creative problem solving, it may not be possible to specify the criteria with the same precision, and more reliance must be placed on professional judgment. But the basic principle—that is, providing as clear a definition as possible of the skill to be assessed—applies to the evaluation of all skills, however complex.

Evaluating physical development

Sophisticated biometric apparatus exists for evaluating physical states in a clinical setting. However, assessment of such attributes as weight, strength, or fitness, which can be affected by training, can usually be simply assessed in an instructional situation. A test of cardiovascular fitness developed by the Canadian Department of Health and Welfare as part of a national fitness campaign, for example, calls for the timing of the subject's pulse after a two-minute period of stepping up and down two steps of set height to a piece of prerecorded music. The resulting score allows the subject to be classified into one of a number of categories of fitness (Canada, Department of Health and Welfare, 1976).

The following performance criterion evaluates an aspect of development that might be stressed in a general conditioning program.

> Objective: *The student will increase the endurance of the muscles of the trunk.*
>
> Performance criterion: *The student will perform situps with hands locked behind head and knees bent at about 90°. Feet are placed under a bar or held by another person. Elbows touch knees at maximum flexion. The number of situps performed in one minute is counted, and compared with pretest. Minimum increase required: 50 percent.*

This objective, like any other, could require either a common minimal standard all students are expected to attain, or could be expressed as an individual standard in terms of a specified degree of improvement from pretest to posttest.

Evaluating dispositions

Dispositions, or attitudes (the more common synonym), are notoriously difficult to evaluate. Like knowledge and skills, attitudes are private states that cannot be directly observed. But while knowledge and skills can be inferred from prescribed performance, "mental states [attitudes] which influence . . . choices of personal actions . . . are observed as *choices* on the part of the learner, rather than as specific performances" (Gagné, 1977, p. 28). The major problem here is ensuring that the choices made by the subject are sufficiently voluntary that a valid inference can be drawn regarding the individual's attitude.

Asking people about their attitudes—"Do you support the electoral system (or giving blood or racial integration)?"—may provide misleading information. Observation of whether people vote in elections or donate blood, or how they behave in racially mixed situations, provides information about actual choices. Such observation is ideally unobtrusive, so that subjects' behavior is not constrained or distorted by the knowledge that they are being watched. The literature on the evaluation of attitudes contains many examples of unobtrusive or "nonreactive" measures, such as counting empty liquor bottles in household garbage, measuring the diameter of a circle of children listening to a ghost story, and calculating the wear of tiles around certain exhibits in a museum (Webb, Campbell, Schwartz, and Sechrest, 1966). Recent research in visual perception has studied changes in pupil size as a measure of attitude. Figure 8–1 shows the effect on hungry and sated subjects of viewing color slides of various foods. Size of pupils has long been recognized as a sign of positive re-

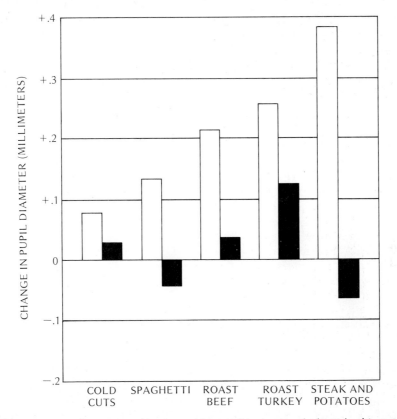

Differences in pupil response of hungry subjects (*white bars*) and of sated subjects (*black bars*) to color slides of various foods are shown. The subjects first viewed a control slide, then a slide of a food, and the change in pupil size was measured. The hungry subjects had not eaten at all for from five to eight hours. The sated subjects had eaten a meal two hours before. All the food slides produced dilation of the pupils in hungry subjects, whereas in two instances the slides produced a constriction of the pupils in the sated subjects. The results indicate the pupil response can be a valid measure of attitude change. From Eckhard H. Hess, The role of pupil size in communication. Copyright © 1975 by Scientific American, Inc. All rights reserved.

Figure 8–1   Change in pupil size as a measure of attitude

sponse or interest; recognizing this aspect of attractiveness, women in antiquity used extract of belladonna to dilate their pupils. This area of research appears to have potential for reasonably exact measurement of attitudinal response.

At the same time, asking subjects about their attitudes should not be dismissed out of hand. What people say has *some* significance, or they would not say it. The United States Air Force tried out many predictors of adjustment to duty in Alaska, including several personality and background tests. It was discovered that the best predictor was simply the answer personnel gave to the question "Do you like cold weather?" (Gottman and Clasen, 1972, p. 157).

Establishing performance criteria for attitudinal objectives requires the skills of imaginative experimental design. A team of teachers in a course I once taught developed a curriculum in outdoor education, which included a two-week canoe trip into the Canadian wilderness. The designers were concerned that the curriculum should not result in an increase in irresponsible use of the environment. Considerable debate took place before consensus was reached on the performance criterion for the attitudinal objective:

> Objective: *Students will have a positive attitude towards maintaining an unspoiled natural environment.*
> Performance criterion: *Toward the end of the canoe trip, a portage will be routed through a little-used picnic area, where students will be instructed in advance to prepare and eat lunch. The instructors will rendezvous with students at the end of the portage and will not be present during the lunch stop. The previous evening, one of the instructors will visit the picnic area, clear it of all litter, and note its condition. Unknown to the students, an instructor will visit the area after they leave. The required standard is met if all litter and rubbish has been properly disposed of, and there is no visible new damage to ground, plant life, or facilities.*

As this example indicates, students should not usually be apprised of the performance criteria for such objectives. For all other types of objectives, it is likely to benefit the student to know the means of evaluation. In the case of dispositions, such knowledge would invalidate the measure. This is one reason why attitude measures should not normally be used for grading purposes: awarding grades on the basis of "secret" criteria is ethically suspect. A second reason is that data from measures of dispositions should be grouped. Attitudinal evaluation is still relatively unreliable, and it is unwise to use it to draw conclusions about individuals. Attendance data, for example, may be a good measure of the attitude toward school when the average attendance for a school or a class is calculated, but it is a very uncertain measure for an individual student. Attitude data is valuable because it indicates the effectiveness of curricula; but the award of marks for "attitude," as commonly practised in innumerable classrooms, appears to be a fairly transparent abuse of the grading system for purposes of social control.

An exception to this guideline is presented by circumstances where the health, safety, or well-being of the student or other people is at risk. An attitude of care and caution when working with electricity would be an important objective in a course in house wiring leading to occupational certification. Certification could legitimately be withheld from trainee electricians who showed recklessness or carelessness in their work. The same principle applies to the student nurse who is callous toward patients, the law student who is unethical, or an education student who is psychologically damaging to children. To ignore evidence of such attitudes is irresponsible and guarantees a supply of injurious nurses, lawyers, teachers, and other professionals. On the other hand, a professional veto should be based on evidence strong enough to stand up in court, because that is where such a judgment may well be vindicated or overruled.

Evaluating experiences

There is little difficulty in evaluating attainment of experiential objectives. The relevant question is simply whether or not the student actually had the experience contained in the objective. Hence:

> Objective: *Students will visit the John F. Kennedy Space Center.*
> Performance criterion: *This objective will be met by all students who take part in the NASA tour of the JFK Space Center.*

Experiential objectives are the only ones for which it is legitimate, from a curriculum point of view, to require the physical presence of students. Knowledge, skills, dispositions, and physical development can be achieved outside the classroom, and if confirmed by evaluation should be graded accordingly. But a student is less likely to undergo independently the intrinsically valuable experiences provided by a curriculum.

Defining Standards of Achievement

In defining performance criteria, the designer specifies a minimum standard of achievement required of the learners. This is a crucial decision in curriculum development. The specific question of setting passing scores for conventional tests is dealt with in the next chapter. The issue of concern here is the general one of how high standards should be. This is an issue on which conventional practice is being challenged by a growing body of thought.

Conventional practice

Conventional practice calls for academic credit to be given if the student achieves an arbitrary mark, often 50 percent. Regardless of what a mark of 50 percent is intended to represent, the inference drawn by students is likely to be that success will reward the learning of half of the knowledge or skills assigned. If this were so, then half of the content or objectives would be unnecessary. In fact, students could be forgiven for reasoning that, as they are normally permitted to learn *any* half, then *none* of what is to be learned is essential, and hence why are they required to learn the subject in the first place?

It is likely that convention has established a passing grade of 50 percent not through a belief in half-learning, but because it considers that a higher standard would inevitably result in an unacceptable number of failures. This belief is related in turn to the conviction that only a small minority of students can achieve high levels of excellence (Block and Burns, 1976, p. 41). The assumption is that a normal curve with a mean of about 65-70 percent and a very few students scoring over 90 or under 50 properly represents the range of achievement to be expected from a typical group of learners. This conviction often persuades a teacher to adjust grades downwards if a class appears to have produced "too many" high grades.

Mastery learning

Conventional assumptions regarding the setting of standards have been challenged by the proponents of *mastery learning*. Their position is summarized by Bloom:

> What any person in the world can learn, almost all persons can learn if provided with appropriate prior and current conditions of learning (Bloom, 1976, p. 7).

The mastery school of thought maintains that curricula should be designed to produce high levels of success in almost all learners (in principle, all but the 5 percent or so with special learning difficulties). This position is supported by four main arguments.

The first argument notes that progressive selection of an educational elite by failing a majority of students might have had some justification when society was able to provide a prolonged education only for a minority of people. But failure of significant numbers of learners ceases to be functional when secondary and even postsecondary education is becoming nearly universal. In this situation, the role of education is not so much to select a talented minority, as to develop all of the human resources of society.

Second, many of the understandings and skills taught in schools have limited value if only a low level of proficiency is achieved. Schooling is a poor investment if it yields only a superficial or erratic understanding of history, science, or the arts. Half-developed skills in mathematics, communication, or athletics may serve only to give learners a sense of inferiority. Partial knowledge of chemistry or first aid may be more dangerous than ignorance. The product of four years of foreign-language learning that fails to enable the student to converse in the language may be little more than anger and regret for the wasted hours.

The third argument for mastery learning points out that students tend to respond to high or low expectations. A passing grade of 50 percent can be expected to produce a cluster of end-of-year scores around 51 percent. It is not unknown for a teacher to produce an equivalent cluster of scores around 71 percent simply by raising the passing grade to 70 percent. Studies of PSI (personalized system of instruction) programs, a mastery approach developed by Keller at the college level (Keller and Sherman, 1974), show that the higher the required achievement standards, the higher the student performance. The lowest performance occurs when no clear criteria are defined (Robin, 1976).

Finally, the most compelling reason for designing programs to produce consistent excellence of student performance is that academic failure tends to be cumulative. If a student does not learn something that is prerequisite to a later learning, subsequent failure is assured. Equally significant is the effect of failure on the student's self-concept, particularly regarding ability, which is a strong predictor of school achievement. (Brookover, Shailer, and Paterson, 1964) Figure 8–2 shows how consistent failure through the years of elementary schooling is associated with a progressive decline in the student's self-concept of ability. The costs of this process must be counted in pain as well as underachievement; as Erik Erikson declared, "The most deadly of all sins is the mutilation of a child's spirit."

Bloom proposed his thesis in the late 1960s. In the following decade a large number of experimental programs showed that high levels of achievement could be reached by most learners, provided that "the appropriate prior and current conditions of learning" were present: the learners must have the cognitive prerequisites; they must have an adequate level of motivation; and they must be given appropriate instruction. Block and Burns reviewed the research in 1976. By that time, mastery learning studies had been conducted with samples of from 1 to 179 classrooms with 29 to 12,500 students and class sizes of 20 to 70, covering subjects from algebra to moral education, courses from one week to nine months in duration, grade levels from Grade 1 to college, and schools in several different countries and cultures. The cumulated evidence pointed decisively to the feasibility of the principles of mastery learning. Out of 97 comparisons of mastery students with control groups, the mastery students learned better in 86 and significantly better in 59; their retention was better in all 97 and significantly better in 61 (Block and Burns, 1976, p. 19). Mastery learning was also associated with more positive attitudes toward the subject and the instruction and a higher academic self-concept. Two things seem to be clear: first, it is desirable to design curricula to produce high standards of student achievement,

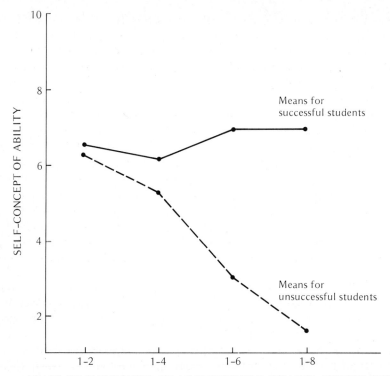

YEARS OF SUCCESSFUL OR UNSUCCESSFUL SCHOOL EXPERIENCES

NOTE: Successful students were in the upper fifth on teacher's grades, while unsuccessful students were in the lower fifth on the same criterion.

Figure 8–2   Self-concept of ability over years of schooling for successful and unsuccessful students. From *Human characteristics and school learning* by Benjamin S. Bloom. Copyright © 1976 by McGraw-Hill Book Company. Used with permission of McGraw-Hill Book Company.

and, second, it is feasible to do so. The question remains: How does the curriculum developer determine appropriate standards of achievement?

Factors to consider

Most proponents of mastery learning recommend that the minimum standard of achievement should be about the same as is conventionally expected of the top 10 or 20 percent of students: that is, a grade of A, or 80 percent. This recommendation does not seem entirely satisfactory. First, it is as arbitrary as the conventional 50 percent. Second, "80 percent" has little meaning in the absence of information about the difficulty of the tasks or questions on which the score is based. Third, raising the passing score is only one way of altering the performance standard.

Changes could just as well be made in the speed required of the learner, the standard of accuracy, the environmental conditions, the difficulty of test items or tasks, and the proportion of successful trials. The designer needs to consider several factors before deciding which variables to manipulate and in what way.

The number of factors to be weighed in defining minimum performance standards forces one to agree with Science Research Associates that "the establishment of standards of achievement . . . is exceedingly complex and subjective . . . a task not to be attempted lightly" (SRA, 1966, p. 16). One factor is time: the higher the standard, the longer students will take to reach it. Another is the present and future value that the learning has for the students: there is little point in requiring high standards in acquisition of knowledge and skills that have marginal value for the learners. The consequences of inadequate mastery must also be considered. Learnings that are prerequisite to later learnings need to be well learned; but one cannot agree with Millman's assertion that "tests of

---

Bloom on Mastery

The most wasteful and destructive aspect of our present educational system is the set of expectations about student learning each teacher brings to the beginning of a new course or term. The instructor expects a third of his pupils to learn well what is taught, a third to learn less well, and a third to fail or just "get by." These expectations are transmitted to the pupils through school grading policies and practices and through the methods and materials of instruction. Students quickly learn to act in accordance with them, and the final sorting through the grading process approximates the teacher's original expectations. A pernicious self-fulfilling prophecy has been created.

Such a system fixes the academic goals of teachers and students. It reduces teachers' aspirations and students' desire for further learning. Further, it systematically destroys the ego and self-concept of a sizeable proportion of students who are legally required to attend schools for ten to twelve years under conditions which are repeatedly frustrating and humiliating. The costs of such a system in reducing student opportunities for further learning and in alienating youth from both school and society are too great to be borne for long.

Most students (perhaps over 90 percent) *can* master what we teach. Our basic instructional task is to define what we mean by mastery of a subject and to discover methods and materials to help the largest proportion of our students reach it.

—*Benjamin S. Bloom (1971, p. 47)*

performances not viewed as prerequisite for future learning probably should not have passing scores" (1973, p. 209). Some learnings are prerequisite to life rather than to other learnings: the student in a terminal reading, electronics, or surgery course may still be encouraged or required to meet specific standards. Reaction time is also important: skills requiring immediate or very fast reaction require a higher level of competence than skills in which a slow response is acceptable.

Some of these factors involve tradeoffs. One can minimize either the probability of failing competent students or the probability of passing incompetent students; one cannot do both at once. Block (1972) reported an experiment in which students were randomly assigned to two instructional groups with different passing scores. A passing score of 95 percent enabled students to perform best in subsequent learning, but an 85 percent standard produced higher student motivation. As Millman puts it, "The question is, what passing score maximizes educational benefits?" (1973, p. 208).

The absence of an exact formula for establishing performance standards makes it necessary to depend on professional judgment. The following principles summarize the factors to be weighed in making such judgments.

1. Critical objectives will tend to require higher performance standards than noncritical objectives.

2. Objectives that are prerequisite to future learning will tend to require higher performance standards than objectives that are not prerequisite to future learning.

3. Learnings that have a high probability of being used by students will tend to require higher performance standards than learnings that have a low probability of being used by students.

4. Skills that require fast reactions will tend to require higher performance standards than skills that do not require fast reactions.

5. Designers who want to minimize the probability of an incompetent student passing will tend to require higher performance standards than designers who want to minimize the probability of a competent student failing.

6. Designers more interested in competence than in motivation will tend to require higher performance standards than designers more interested in motivation than in competence.

These factors collectively constitute a kind of risk equation, the values in which are situationally determined. As in the initial definition of curriculum aims, so it is in the setting of performance standards: the needs of the learners, and not arbitrary formulas, should determine curriculum decisions.

ACTIVITIES

1. Imagine that a student in a school you work in or are familiar with sues the school on the grounds that its testing procedures are invalid. Outline the case for the plaintiff and the case for the defense. What would the verdict be?

2. Write a performance criterion for one of the following skills:

    a. *The student will be able to administer mouth-to-mouth resuscitation.*
    b. *The student will be able to sketch a portrait likeness in pencil from a live model.*
    c. *The student will be able to predict weather without instruments.*
    d. *The student will be able to develop rapport in an interview.*

3. Discuss the pros and cons of awarding marks for attendance, "participation," and "general attitude."

4. Write a performance criterion for one of the following dispositions:

    a. *Students will enjoy reading.*
    b. *Students will take pride in their work.*
    c. *Students will develop responsibility in their use of energy resources.*
    d. *Students will value cooperation as a means of problem solving.*

5. In professional training programs, such as nursing, students fail sometimes on academic grounds and sometimes because they are judged by supervisors to lack an appropriate "professional attitude." Student appeals against academic failure are rarely upheld. But students are often successful in appeals against "attitude" judgments. Why do you think this is so?

6. What would be the effects of the schools beginning to graduate people whose competence was uniformly high? What social resistance would this policy encounter?

QUESTIONS

1. *Given three eggs, fifty grams of sharp cheese, salt, butter, and appropriate utensils, the student will produce an omelette in three minutes that, in the subjective judgment of the instructor, is satisfactory in taste, texture, and appearance.* This is

    a. an aim
    b. an objective
    c. a teaching point
    d. a performance criterion

2. What is wrong with the following performance criterion: *The student will correctly determine the density of at least four out of five roughly spherical objects between 2 cm and 8 cm in diameter correct to the nearest gm per cubic cm in fifty minutes?*

    a. it is vague
    b. too many variables are mentioned

    c. there is no indication what equipment is provided
    d. it does not take individual differences into account

3. *Given a topographic map showing contour lines with ten-meter intervals, the student will draw a transverse section of a given hill.* In which respect is this performance criterion most satisfactory?

    a. speed
    b. activity
    c. accuracy
    d. equipment

4. Which of the following performance criteria is least satisfactory to measure achievement of the objective *Students will develop safe driving habits?*

    a. *students will drive safely*
    b. *students will pass the official driving test*
    c. *students will drive accident-free for five years following the course*
    d. *students will not receive any moving violation citation for three years after completing the course*

5. *An experiential objective in a first-grade curriculum is: Students will visit the museum.* The most appropriate performance criterion would be:

    a. a check as to whether the students actually visit the museum
    b. a score of 8 out of 10 on a quiz, "What we saw at the museum"
    c. a grade of A or B on a two-minute oral report, "Visiting the museum"
    d. observation of whether children pay a second voluntary visit to the museum in the next twelve months

6. Only in special cases should students be graded on achievement of attitudinal objectives. In which of the following objectives would grading be legitimate?

    a. *the student will enjoy gymnastics*
    b. *the student will develop a liking for geometry*
    c. *the student will support antipollution campaigns*
    d. *the student will exercise strict precautions when using toxic chemicals*

7. Test validity refers to

    a. the administration of measurement with minimum time and cost
    b. the extent to which a test actually measures what it is intended to measure
    c. the extent to which the output of a curriculum corresponds to specified objectives
    d. the extent to which test scores are consistent for the same subject or identical subjects across different administrations

8. Which of the following criteria for educational measures is not essentially an aspect of validity?

    a. efficiency
    b. objectivity

c. discreteness
d. completeness

9. A curriculum objective is: *The student's cardiovascular efficiency will improve.* Which of the following is the most congruent performance criterion?

a. the student can run 3,000 meters in 15 minutes
b. the student's resting pulse rate decreases by 10 percent
c. an electrocardiogram shows that the student's cardiovascular system is healthy
d. the student scores in the top 5 percent of the population on the Harvard Step Test

10. Designers should set the minimum required standards of performance

a. at a level of 50 percent
b. at the 80 percent or honors level
c. according to a number of factors that are weighed judgmentally
d. high enough to guarantee that no student will pass who is not completely competent

Check your answers against the key in Appendix 2.
9 or 10 right: You understand the material presented.
8 or 7 right: Review the areas of uncertainty.
6 or less right: Reread the chapter.

Recommended Reading

Bloom, Benjamin S. *Human characteristics and school learning.* New York: McGraw-Hill, 1976. Perhaps the most important book on curriculum published in the 1970s. Explains the philosophy and research basis of mastery learning.

Henerson, Marlene E., Lynn Lyons Morris, and Carol Taylor Fitz-Gibbon. *How to measure attitudes.* Beverly Hills, Cal.: Sage, 1978. Provides concise and practical guidance on how to locate existing measures of attitude, and step-by-step instructions for developing measures, including questionnaires, interviews, and observation procedures.

Tuckman, Bruce W., *Measuring educational outcomes: Fundamentals of testing.* New York: Harcourt Brace Jovanovich, 1975. One of many excellent texts on educational measurement currently available, Tuckman's book is especially useful for its comprehensive discussion of measurement of different kinds of objectives and for its balanced and common-sense approach.

Webb, Eugene J., Donald T. Campbell, Richard D. Schwartz, and Lee Sechrest. *Unobtrusive measures: Nonreactive research in the social sciences.* Chicago: Rand McNally, 1966. Interesting and authoritative review of methods, ranging from the orthodox to the ingenious, for investigating the voluntary behavior of individuals and groups.

References

Block, James H. Student learning and the setting of mastery performance standards. *Educational Horizons,* 1972, 50, 183–190.

——— , and Robert B. Burns. Mastery learning. In Lee S. Shulman (ed.), *Review of research in education 4.* Itasca, Ill.: Peacock and American Educational Research Association, 1976, pp. 3–49.

Bloom, Benjamin S. Quality control in education. In *Tomorrow's teaching.* Oklahoma City: Frontiers of Science Foundation, 1961.

——— . *Human characteristics and school learning.* New York: McGraw-Hill, 1976.

——— , J. Thomas Hastings, and George F. Madaus. *Handbook on formative and summative evaluation of student learning.* New York: McGraw-Hill, 1971.

——— . Mastery learning. In James H. Block (ed)., *Mastery learning: Theory and practice.* New York: Holt, Rinehart & Winston, 1971, pp. 47–63.

Branson, R. K., G. T. Rayner, W. H. Hannum, and J. L. Cox. *Interservice procedures for instructional systems development: Executive summary and model.* Ft. Monroe, Va.: US Army Training and Doctrine Command, August 1975.

Brookover, Wilbur B., Thomas Shailer, and Ann Paterson. Self-concept of ability and school achievement. *Sociology of Education,* 1964, 37, 271–278.

Business Week. Profits set score at B-school tournament. *Business Week,* March 18, 1967, pp. 156–158.

Canada. Department of Health and Welfare. *Canada Home Fitness Test.* Ottawa: Department of Health and Welfare, 1976.

Carr, Rey A. The effects of specific guidelines on the accuracy of student self-evaluation. *Canadian Journal of Education,* 1977, 2 (4), 65–77.

Cronbach, Lee J. Test validation. In Robert L. Thorndike (ed.), *Educational measurement.* 2nd ed. Washington, D.C.: American Council on Education, 1971, pp. 443–507.

Ebel, Robert L. *Essentials of educational measurement.* Englewood Cliffs, N.J.: Prentice-Hall, 1972.

Eisner, Eliot W. The mythology of art education. *Curriculum Theory Network,* 1974, 4, 89–100.

Gagné, Robert M. *The conditions of learning.* 3rd ed. New York: Holt, Rinehart & Winston, 1977.

Glaser, Robert. Instructional technology and the measurement of learning outcomes: Some questions. *American Psychologist,* 1963, 18, 519–521.

Gottman, John Mordechai, and Robert Earl Clasen. *Evaluation in education: A practitioner's guide.* Itasca, Ill.: Peacock, 1972.

Gronlund, Norman E. *Constructing achievement tests.* 2nd ed. Englewood Cliffs, N.J.: Prentice-Hall, 1977.

Hamlish, Erna, and Eugene L. Gaier. Teacher-student personality and marks. *School Review,* 1954, 62, 265–273.

Hess, Eckhard H. The role of pupil size in communication. *Scientific American,* 1975, 233 (Nov.), 110–119.

Hilgard, Ernest R., and Gordon J. Bower. *Theories of learning.* 3rd ed. New York: Appleton-Century-Crofts, 1966.

Hore, T. Assessment of teaching practice: An "attractive" hypothesis. *British Journal of Educational Psychology,* 1971, 41, 327–328.

Jones, Lyle V. The nature of measurement. In Robert L. Thorndike (ed.), *Educational measurement*. 2nd ed. Washington, D.C.: American Council on Education, 1971, pp. 335–355.

Keller, Fred S., and J. Gilmour Sherman. *The Keller Plan handbook*. Menlo Park, Cal.: W. A. Benjamin, 1974.

McGuire, C. H., L. M. Solomon, and P. G. Bashook. *Construction and use of written simulations*. New York: Psychological Corp., 1976.

Merritt, D. L. The relationships between qualifications and attitudes in a teacher selection situation. Unpublished doctoral dissertation, Syracuse University, 1970.

Miller, R. B. Task description and analysis. In R. M. Gagné (ed.), *Psychological principles in system development*. New York: Holt, Rinehart & Winston, 1962, pp. 186–228.

Millman, Jason. Passing scores and test lengths for domain-referenced measures. *Review of Educational Research*, 1973, 43, 205–216.

Phi Delta Kappa National Study Committee on Evaluation. *Educational evaluation and decision making*. Itasca, Ill.: Peacock, 1971.

Robin, Arthur L. Behavioral instruction in the college classroom. *Review of Educational Research*, 1976, 46, 313–354.

Root, Robert T., Claramae S. Knerr, Angelo A. Severino, and Larry E. Word. Tactical engagement simulation training: A method for learning the realities of combat. Paper presented at the Annual Meeting of the American Educational Research Association, Toronto, March 1978.

Samuda, Ronald J. *Psychological testing of American minorities*. New York: Dodd, Mead, 1975.

Sax, Gilbert. *Principles of educational measurement*. Belmont, Cal.: Wadsworth, 1974.

Singer Aerospace and Marine Systems. *The multidimensional world of simulation*. Binghamton, N.Y.: Singer Company, Link Division, 1977.

Smith, R. E., B. L. Meadow, and T. K. Sisk. Attitude similarity, interpersonal attraction, and evaluative social perception. *Psychonomic Science*, 1970, 18, 226–227.

SRA. *ITED: The Iowa tests of educational development: Manual for the school administrator*. Chicago: SRA, 1966.

Stufflebeam, Daniel L. Toward a science of educational evaluation. *Educational Technology*, 1968, 8, 5–12.

Thorndike, Robert L. (ed.). *Educational measurement*. 2nd ed. Washington, D.C.: American Council on Education, 1971.

Tuckman, Bruce W. *Measuring educational outcomes: Fundamentals of testing*. New York: Harcourt Brace Jovanovich, 1975.

Warren, Jim. The Supreme Court looks at testing for employment. *Educational Researcher*, 1976, 5 (June), 8–9.

Webb, Eugene J., Donald T. Campbell, Richard D. Schwartz, and Lee Sechrest. *Unobtrusive measures: Nonreactive research in the social sciences*. Chicago: Rand McNally, 1966.

Webster's seventh new collegiate dictionary. Springfield, Mass.: G. & C. Merriam, 1967.

9

PRINCIPLES

- Before designing a formal test, it is often wise to determine what published tests are available.

- Formative evaluation, which monitors progress, may be distinguished from summative evaluation, which assesses final achievement.

- As summative evaluation, the essay test presents serious difficulties.

- Construction of a table of specifications can help to provide balance in a test.

- Selected-response tests can be improved by avoidance of a number of common errors in item design.

- Norm-referenced measurement ranks students on a continuum of achievement; criterion-referenced measurement evaluates students against specific standards.

- Item analysis provides information that can help the educator improve both instruction and testing.

CONCEPTS

Formative evaluation	Table of specifications	Item analysis
Summative evaluation	Guessing correction	Difficulty
Selected-response tests	Norm-referenced measurement	index
Constructed-response tests	Criterion-referenced measurement	Discrimination index
		Grading

9

Designing Formal Tests

> *Examinations are formidable even to the best pre-*
> *pared, for the greatest fool may ask more than the wisest*
> *man can answer.*
>
> —*Charles Colton*

The Function of Formal Tests

Tests and examinations have been associated with education in almost every culture that has developed a system of formal schooling. In the public mind, examinations conjure up Dantesque pictures of legions of agonized students intensely scribbling responses to a sequence of elegantly phrased conundrums. The conventional examination is indeed a kind of Purgatory, through which the student is forced to pass to attain either the Paradise of success or the Inferno of failure.

This chapter deals with the special considerations that relate to the design of tests in which the student responds, usually in verbal form, to a series of predetermined questions. The function of such tests is normally to assess knowledge and cognitive skills. Excessive reliance on formal tests can result in either neglect or invalid assessment of other kinds of curriculum objective, such as motor skills and dispositions. These attributes are generally better assessed by means of the kind of performance criteria described in the previous chapter.

A body of fairly sophisticated expertise has grown up over the past fifty years concerning the design of formal tests. The professionalization of testing has been one of the reasons for the growth of central testing agencies. In many schools much of the formal testing is now carried out by standardized tests, leaving the teacher little responsibility for test design. This situation may change as a result of a reaction against standardized testing, which is occurring within parts of the educational community (National School Boards Association, 1977; Quinto and McKenna, 1977). But even if standardized tests remain the norm, it is valuable for the professional teacher to have a basic understanding of the main procedures and criteria for test construction.

At the same time, the educator who is responsible for test design might be wise to ascertain what published tests are available, before embarking independently on the task of test construction. Most available tests are listed in *Tests in Print* (Buros, 1974), and many are described with critiques in the *Mental Measurements Yearbook* (Buros, 1978). A review of these sources is an important early step in the process of designing evaluation, the main stages in which are shown in flow-chart form in Figure 9–1.

Much of the testing that takes place in classroom will be *formative* rather than *summative*. Michael Scriven (1967) first applied these terms to the evaluation of curriculum, but they have come to be used to refer to evaluation of student achievement as well. Formative evaluation is conducted in the course of instruction and consists of "the observation of student progress and difficulty in learning followed by adjustment in instructional procedures to improve that progress" (Ebel, 1973, p. 7). Summative evaluation is conducted after instruction is completed, to make judgments about the effectiveness of the learning, the instruction, or the curriculum. We might say that the purpose of summative evaluation is to prove achievement, and the purpose of formative evaluation is to improve achievement. The principles of good test design apply to both formative and summative tests.

Types of Test

Within the area of formal testing with which this chapter is concerned, three types of test, or more exactly, test question, may be distinguished:

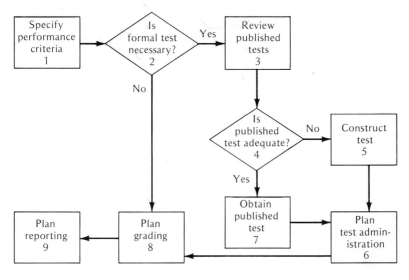

Figure 9–1   Main stages in designing evaluation

the oral test; the essay, or constructed-response, test; and the "objective," or selected-response, test.

Oral tests

Oral examinations were universal in medieval universities and have maintained a traditional place in final evaluation for higher degrees, admission to graduate and professional programs, and selection for employment. A survey of universities in several countries showed that in the early 1970s a third of them were using oral examinations at the undergraduate level and considerably more at the graduate level (Bligh, 1975, p. 48). The interview may have some value in assessing interpersonal skills and career commitment (Ulrich and Trumbo, 1965). In a longitudinal study of teachers, I found that the interview conducted prior to admission to training was the best available predictor of subsequent survival in the teaching profession (Pratt, 1977). But the bulk of the research evidence on oral tests is not encouraging. In medical training and licensing, once a stronghold of oral testing, such tests have been largely abandoned in recent years as a result of evidence that they tended to demand recall of isolated fragments of information, that agreement among judges was low (Menges, 1975), and that standards tended to soften as a day or week of oral tests wore on (Colton and Peterson, 1967).

Because each oral examination is unique, every student is treated differently, and this variation presents intractable problems of validity and reliability. The conclusion that seems to follow from the accumulated evidence of some fifty years of research is that, so far as educational contexts are concerned, almost any knowledge or skill that can be assessed by an oral test can be evaluated more validly, more reliably, and more efficiently by some other kind of test.

Essay tests

The term *essay test* will be used to refer to any test in which the student generates a response to a question and writes it in his or her own words. The answer may be one sentence or several thousand words. Essay tests have an established position in most educational jurisdictions. In many parts of the world they are the dominant and unquestioned form of academic examination. Among their merits are the ease with which they are constructed, and their potential for evaluating a learner's ability to select, organize, synthesize, and report information and argument. Their deficiencies relate to the difficulties that essay tests have shown in meeting four of the basic criteria for educational measures: reliability, discreteness, efficiency, and congruence.

Reliability   Unreliability of marking is the most serious weakness of essay tests. This problem has been known for many years. In a series of articles published in 1912 and 1913, Starch and Elliott showed that in English, mathematics, and history, different teachers would assign widely differing grades to essays written by the same students. Agreement among individual essay markers typically ranges from about .25 to .40 (Godshalk, Swineford, and Coffman, 1966), indicating that differences among grades are due to differences among the markers rather than to differences in quality of essays. In practice this means that while evaluators may be able to distinguish reliably between very good and very bad essays, they will tend to assign to many students grades that do not accurately reflect their performance.

There are certain strategies that can help to increase the reliability

---

To control the matriculation examinations of a country is to control its educational system; to develop tests that are widely used for selection and prediction purposes is to determine which human qualities are prized and which are neglected; to develop instruments that are frequently used to classify and describe human beings is to alter human relations and affect a person's view of himself.

—*Benjamin S. Bloom (1970, p. 25)*

of essay tests. Drawing up an itemized marking scheme is not one of them. The evidence shows that marking with such schemes is not consistently more reliable than impressionistic marking (Coffman, 1971). Increasing the length of essay tests and the number of markers can improve reliability but presents problems of practicality. Godshalk and his colleagues estimated that score reliabilities of .92 could be achieved by a test including five different topics, each read by five different readers (Godshalk, Swineford, and Coffman, 1966). The designers of the Advanced Placement Examination in American History calculated that a score reliability of .90 could be obtained with an eleven-hour essay test containing fifteen questions, each marked by a different rater (Coffman, 1971).

Reliability of marking essays can be achieved, then, but only by an investment of time in marking that is beyond the will or the resources of most schools. This constraint raises questions about both the usefulness and the ethics of judging student competence on the basis of essay tests.

Discreteness   Essay tests are usually intended to assess a student's understanding of a subject as well as his or her ability to organize and articulate ideas. But several other factors may influence the student's grade, including the ability to predict which questions will be asked; test anxiety; writing speed, fluency, and glibness; handwriting, spelling, and grammar; and the examiner's acquaintance with and opinion of the learner (Marshall and Powers, 1969). Scannel and Marshall (1966) showed that essay grades will be adversely affected by errors of punctuation, spelling, or grammar, even when markers are specifically instructed to disregard such errors. Research on the effect of handwriting on essay scores spans fifty years and shows similarly that, despite instructions to the contrary, markers are influenced by this factor (James, 1927; Markham, 1976). If rapid writing is an advantage in essay tests, then such tests may be sexually biased, as women apparently write faster than men (Gust and Schumacher, 1969). With all of these variables influencing the results, it is difficult indeed to know exactly what is being assessed by an essay test.

Efficiency   Writing essays is time-consuming, and consequently only a few topics can be addressed per hour of examination time. Marking essays also absorbs substantial human resources; and although procedures have been developed for computer scoring of essays, these are expensive and require a considerable amount of programming time (Bhushan and Ginther, 1968). For an acceptable level of reliability to be achieved, the investment of student and marker time would need to be even greater than is conventionally the case.

Congruence   The problems described above are all interrelated. The contaminating variables introduce the possibility of marker bias, which can affect the reliability of marking. Reliability can also be reduced by the inefficiency of essay tests: it is difficult to maintain consistent standards over a marking period of several days. Some practices, such as allowing students a choice of essays on a test, may further interfere with the value of the results, as the abler students may penalize themselves by attempting the more difficult questions. All these factors bear on the issue of validity, or congruence.

In assessing the congruence of a test, it is necessary to ask what it is that the instrument measures, simulates, or predicts. The essay test typically assesses the ability of a student to express understanding of a subject in writing within a limited time. This is a valuable skill for a future journalist or diplomat, but for the majority of students it is a skill they will seldom need in real life.

Further disappointment is in store for the proponents of essay tests as measures of complex understandings and the ability to organize concepts and arguments. Extensive analysis of university examinations in Britain, where final qualifications depend heavily on essay tests, showed that the great majority of questions required simple recognition and

---

An Exceptional Case

Cleverness in written expression and bluffing tend to inflate the scores assigned to essay answers. Even the student who says nothing, but expresses it well, is apt to receive some credit. An exaggerated example of this was reported in the literature some years ago. A college test bureau selected a student with special writing skills and sent him into a midsemester examination in place of a regular student, to determine how well he could do on an essay test without preparation. The main question called for a critical evaluation of a novel which the student had not read. His answer started out somewhat as follows: "This is not the best novel I have ever read, but neither is it the worst. It has some real strengths, such as the detailed attention given to the development of the main characters. On the other hand, some of the minor characters have not been as fully developed as they might be . . ." His evaluation continued along this same vein. The paper was returned at the next class meeting with the professor's comment: "This is the best evaluation of this novel I have ever read." Although extreme, such experiences illustrate the great difficulty encountered in obtaining an uncontaminated measure of achievement with the essay test.

—*Norman E. Gronlund (1978, p. 76).*

memory of facts, with some ability to apply factual information in fairly routine ways (Black, 1968; Beard and Pole, 1971).

Value of the essay   None of the foregoing impugns the value of student essays in instruction. The essay, research paper, or passage of creative writing, produced in the student's own time, when the writer can draft and redraft, read aloud and correct, refer to sources, and work in a preferred environment, has considerable merit. It provides the teacher with a unique insight into the learner's understanding of concepts, prose style, self-expression, and ability to organize thoughts and evaluate ideas. It is a useful diagnostic device, and oral or written comments by the instructor can aid and encourage improvement in the learner. This seems to be the proper place for a student essay: as a learning process and a diagnostic tool. But when students are required to produce essays under the artificial and stressful conditions of a formal examination, when grades are unilaterally assigned to essays by a single marker, and when these grades are used to make decisions about the learner's future, a potentially valuable activity becomes open to serious question.

Selected-response tests

Selected-response questions come in various forms, including true/false, multiple-choice, and matching items. "Fill in the blanks" and sentence-completion questions fall between the selected and the constructed response; alternative choices are not provided and in theory are almost infinite in number. But in practice the student tends to select from a relatively limited range of possibilities that come to mind.

In the ensuing discussion, the multiple-choice question containing four responses will be used for purposes of illustration. It is probably true, as Ebel assets, that "true/false tests can do about the same job that multiple-choice tests can do, about as well, and sometimes more conveniently" (Ebel, 1973, p. 12), but it is likely that good true/false items are even more difficult to write than good multiple-choice questions. The four choices limit the probability of blindly guessing the correct answer to 25 percent; this probability is only marginally reduced by the difficult process of generating more than three plausible wrong answers (distracters).

Although selected-response tests are widely accepted and used in North American schools and colleges, a good many teachers, especially in European schools, question their value. One reason may be that the defects of a badly designed multiple-choice test are more obvious than those of a badly designed essay test. The marker of an essay test can adjust for weaknesses in the questions: no such flexibility is possible in marking selected-response tests. The major advantage of selected-response questions is that the marking is reliable and can be done very rapidly by a machine or an inexperienced marker. But if the questions themselves are badly conceived, this strength becomes a fatal weakness. Many multiple-choice and true/false tests taken by students in schools and colleges are devised by teachers who lack training in item writing and are ignorant of the powerful techniques available for test improvement. The frustration that poor tests generate in students tends to justify the suspicion of such tests among other teachers and administrators.

A related reason for teacher resistance to selected-response tests is the belief that they can test only trivial knowledge and low-level cognitive skills. Many tests do in fact evaluate only simple learnings, but this is a limitation of the test designer's expertise, not of the type of test. The example on page 235 from a humanities course at the University of Chicago suggests that the multiple-choice format can be effectively used in an interesting and challenging way to evaluate complex intellectual skills.

Writing good multiple-choice items requires knowledge of subject matter, technical skill, and creative ability. According to Wesman (1971, p. 81), "experienced professional item writers regard an output of 5 to 15 good achievement test items a day as a satisfactory performance." Adequate lead time must be allowed for the writing of a selected-response test; only bad items and essay questions can be produced at the last minute. If items cannot be pretested, enough time should be allowed for them to be reviewed by a knowledgeable colleague before the test is printed. Procrastination is the enemy of good selected-response testing, as it is the undoing of all good design.

Achieving Balance in a Test

Suppose that a mathematics instructor spends six weeks of a twelve-week semester teaching differential calculus. The examination at the end of the semester contains twenty questions, only two of which are on differential calculus. Unless the instructor has so informed the students, they have a right to feel that they were misled as to what would be examined. To guard against a lack of balance in a test, it is a good practice to draw up a table of specifications.

Table 9–1 shows a table of specifications for a one-semester course in nineteenth-century European history. The chief emphasis of the course is on social history, with economic and political history, international relations, and historical interpretation playing subordinate roles. This emphasis reflects the priority among the objectives and/or the time distribution in instruction; or the instructor has directly advised students of the themes that are regarded as having major significance. The distribution of questions is identical with the proportionate emphasis in the

This test section requires the student to recognize the values, points of view, and assumptions made by four critics of Hemingway's *Farewell to Arms*. Only one of the book review extracts and the relevant questions are reproduced here. (From Bloom, Hastings, and Madaus, 1971, p. 213)

In its depiction of war, the novel bears comparison with its best predecessors. But it is in the hero's perhaps unethical quitting of the battle line to be with the woman he has gotten with 5 child that it achieves its greatest significance. Love is more maligned in literature than any other emotion, by romantic distortion on the one hand, by carnal diminution on the other. But 10 Author Hemingway knows it at its best to be a blend of desire, serenity, and wordless sympathy. His man and woman stand incoherently together against a shattered, dissolving world. 15 They express their feeling by such superficially trivial things as a joke, a gesture in the night, an endearment as trite as "darling." And as they make their escape from Italy in a rowboat, survey 20 the Alps from their hillside lodgings, move on to Lausanne where there are hospitals, gaze at each other in torment by the deathbed of Catherine, their tiny shapes on the vast landscape are ex- 25 pressive of the pity, beauty, and doom of mankind.

1. Critic I finds the "significance" of the novel to lie especially in
   a. its account of the psychology of a deserter
   b. its evocation of pity and fear
   c. its representation of the true nature of love
   d. its combination of realistic fatalism and symbolic beauty

2. In support of this view, Critic I directs attention to certain details in the novel. When he describes the characters' methods of expressing their feelings as "superficially trivial," one understands that he must mean that
   a. these "things" are trivial only on the surface
   b. the characters are mediocre and lacking in depth
   c. the novelist has been deficient in invention
   d. there is a clear, but unimportant, weakness in the diction of the novel

3. The last sentence of the passage implies that
   a. the human figures are distorted by the romantic setting of the action
   b. the emotions of the characters, being the common experience of all men, are shared by the reader
   c. the particulars of the novel stand for universal propositions about life
   d. the inevitable consequence of errors in conduct is symbolized in the outcome of this action

4. Consequently, it is apparent that Critic I is judging the novel primarily as
   a. an imitation of life
   b. an interpretation of life
   c. a means to the end of good conduct
   d. an extension of the reader's experience

course. At the same time, the instructor is concerned that students can recall basic information, more importantly that they understand what they know, but above all that they can apply what they have learned. This balance is reflected in the distribution of questions on the total test

TOPIC	EMPHASIS IN COURSE	TOTAL QUESTIONS	QUESTIONS ON KNOWLEDGE (20%)	QUESTIONS ON UNDERSTANDING (30%)	QUESTIONS ON APPLICATION (50%)
Political history	10%	5	1	1	3
Social history	40%	20	4	6	10
Economic history	20%	10	2	3	5
International relations	10%	5	1	2	2
Historical interpretation	20%	10	2	3	5
Totals	100%	50	10	15	25

Table 9–1   Table of specifications for a course in European history

and within each theme. It is of particular importance to set a "quota" of questions testing understanding, problem solving, or application as appropriate. Otherwise, recall questions, being by far the easiest to draw up, are apt to constitute an unduly high proportion of the test.

Common Errors in Selected-response Questions

There is no easy recipe for producing good test items, but a number of known pitfalls can be avoided. By steering clear of them, the evaluator can remove the basis for many of the common criticisms directed at selected-response tests.

Internal clues

Over forty years ago some researchers examined a large number of true/false tests produced and used by classroom teachers. Their analysis of the questions revealed that more than 75 percent of the statements containing "only," "all," "none," and "always" were false (Hawkes, Lindquist, and Mann, 1936). One cannot say whether the same phenomenon would be found today, but it is clear that the existence of any such pattern in test questions serves to measure the astuteness rather than the knowledge of examinees.

The following item contains an obvious grammatical clue:

A polygon of eight sides and eight angles is called an
★*a.. octagon*
b. pentagon
c. hexahedron
d. cube

This can be easily corrected by writing the question:

> *A polygon of eight sides and eight angles is called*
> ★*a.   an octagon*
> *b.   a pentagon*
> *c.   a hexahedron*
> *d.   a cube*

Another clue sometimes inadvertently given is the consistent provision of greater detail or length in the correct answer:

> *If you hear an ambulance or fire engine siren behind you when driving along the highway, you should*
> *a.   speed up*
> *b.   slow down*
> *c.   sound horn*
> ★*d.   draw over to the edge of the road and stop until the ambulance or fire engine has passed*

Overlapping answers

All of the choices provided should be mutually exclusive.

> *Which of the following groups is most likely to support protectionist policies?*
> *a.   businessmen*
> *b.   consumers*
> *c.   foreign industrialists*
> ★*d.   manufacturers.*

As *a* and *d* overlap, either could be correct, and the student whose answer was *a* would be unfairly penalized.

BLONDIE   **By Dean Young and Jim Raymond**

Confusing questions

Questions should always be written for maximum clarity.

> *Considered from an economic viewpoint, which of these proposals to maintain world peace derives the least support from the military potentialities of atomic energy?*
> *a.   an international police force should be established*
> *b.   permanent programs of universal military training should be adopted*
> *★c.   sizes of standing military forces should be increased*
> *d.   the remaining democratic nations of the world should enter into a military alliance (Ebel, 1972, p. 199)*

It becomes a triumph of logic to work out the meaning of this question, with its negative stem and complex wording. Questions should be written and arranged for maximum readability and comprehension:

> *The present number of native Indians in Canada is about*
> *a.   5,000,000*
> *★b.   500,000*
> *c.   1,000,000*
> *d.   50,000*

This question would be improved by arranging the numbers in ascending or descending order.

"All of the above" and "none of the above"

"All of the above" and "none of the above" are sometimes used as the last choice in a question.

> *Which of the following factors must the curriculum designer recognize as a constraint?*
> *a.   student ability*
> *b.   school policy*
> *c.   available facilities*
> *★d.   all of the above*

One weakness of this kind of question is that where "all of the above" is the correct answer, the student who chooses *a, b,* or *c,* is penalized although the answer is technically correct. The test-wise student, on the other hand, need only recognize that two of the alternatives are correct to realize that "all of the above" is the answer required.

"All of the above" and "none of the above" tend to be most appropriate for questions that have absolutely right or wrong answers, as in mathematics tests. These alternatives are less appropriate in tests where the student is instructed to choose the most plausible or probable response. In addition, the fact that "all of the above" and "none of the above" must be the last choice makes for inflexibility in constructing the test.

Trick questions

The test designer, like the instructor, should avoid cleverness at the expense of the student.

> *During the last thirty years of her reign, Queen Victoria*
> *a. frequently consulted Albert on various state affairs*
> *b. consulted Albert only on state affairs relative to Germany*
> *c. consulted Albert only on Royal Family business*
> ⋆*d. did not consult Albert on state affairs*

The question appears to be asking the student to work out the most plausible response; actually the answer depends on knowing that Albert died in 1861. The function of distracters is not to trap the unwary, but to identify flaws in knowledge or understanding. To this end the instructor should base distracters on common misconceptions that arise in class discussion or in students' written work; it is useful to maintain a log of such errors for this purpose.

Trivial items

The following question appeared in the examination at the conclusion of a graduate course in one of America's most distinguished universities:

> *A German philosopher and theologian who was influenced by neo-Kantian ideas and in turn influenced modern Protestant thought was*
> *a. Ernest Troeltisch*
> *b. Ernst von Troelshe*
> *c. Eric Troiszche*
> ⋆*d. Ernst Troeltsch*

It is easy to write trivial items. Sometimes teachers are actually teaching trivial information. More commonly, asking petty questions is the result of failing to identify the important outcomes of instruction and to develop tests to assess attainment of these outcomes. One way to reduce triviality is to avoid questions beginning with Who, What, and Where, and to try to develop questions beginning How, Why, and If.

Items based on opinion

Students feel justifiably aggrieved if the response chosen depends primarily on values on which agreement is not substantial.

Which of the following is the greatest threat to schools as transmitters of culture?
a. *progressive education*
b. *behaviorism*
*c. *the demand for relevance*
d. *student militancy*

Incorrect items

The item writer must be knowledgeable and up to date in his or her field. Consider the following item:

A major social difference between the U.S.A. and Europe is that
a. *family mobility is lower in the U.S.*
b. *higher education is more widely available in Europe*
c. *women have more economic opportunity in Europe*
★d. *people have a higher standard of living in the U.S.*

A student could make a case against *d* in terms of the distribution of wealth in several European states, and in favor of *c*, on account of the greater proportion of women in Europe in professional and managerial positions. It is no defense to argue either that the major textbooks (written ten years ago) support *d* and oppose *c*; or that the best students (reared on those textbooks) all choose *d* rather than *c*. The information in the question must be currently correct.

Alternatives to Conventional Items

The selected-response question is not limited to a verbal format. Visuals, such as maps, graphs, drawings, or photographs, may be shown, and questions asked about them. Questions may be asked about a piece of music, a speech, or birdsong, a defective automobile engine, or a counseling interview, a tape of which is available to students during the test. Even the sense of smell can be used:

In the kit of materials provided with your test, you will find a small yellow capsule containing a ground herb. Sniff it lightly to identify it by smell. The herb is
*a. *dill*
b. *mint*
c. *basil*
d. *thyme*

Or taste:

> *Take one of the cubes of apple pie from the table and taste it. The ingredient that has been omitted in cooking is*
> a. *salt*
> *b. *sugar*
> c. *shortening*
> d. *baking soda*

The possibilities are limited not so much by the nature of the selected-response item as by the creativity and imagination of the test designer.

Test Administration

In most systems of individualized instruction, tests are available on request: students take the tests whenever they feel ready for them. This is in many ways an ideal situation, but in most programs tests have to be administered to groups and hence administrative arrangements have to be planned with care.

As far as is practicable, the test conditions should allow students to perform at their best. The room should be quiet and have good illumination, with adequate space for each student. Evidence shows that students perform better using desks than if seated only in chairs with desk arms (Traxler and Hilkert, 1942).

Students should be explicitly advised in the test instructions of the time available and the scoring system, so that they can organize their time appropriately. Enough time should be allowed for almost all students to answer all the questions comfortably. Time pressure does not appear to depress achievement or reliability, but it does increase examinee frustration and anxiety (Ebel, 1972). Instructions should be clear as to how the student is to indicate answers and make corrections, especially if the test is to be machine scored. Like human markers, marking machines penalize untidiness and ambiguous responses.

Test administrators should take note of two practices that can seriously weaken test validity: cramming and cheating. Both have become deeply ingrained in the culture of schools, are resistant to easy solutions, and are often treated by educators with an apathy that borders on acquiescence.

Cramming involves storing information in the memory for long enough to regurgitate it on an examination, after which it is promptly forgotten. Such a practice bears little relation to any desirable learning outcome. Giving students insufficient notice of an impending test may encourage cramming, but early warning may not prevent it. Unannounced spot tests and delayed posttests may serve to reveal the incidence of cramming. A radical approach to solving the problem is to reexamine the objectives of instruction and ask why they have so little intrinsic interest or perceived value to students that they are not integrated into long-term memory.

Cheating is sufficiently widespread that upwards of 40 percent of American students questioned in surveys admit to cheating on examinations (Bushway and Nash, 1977). Cheating is not an exclusively modern phenomenon. According to Brickman (1961), cheating took place on the civil service examinations in ancient China despite strict precautions and regulations, including provision of the death penalty both for guilty students and for their examiners.

Students seem likely to cheat when motivation is low but anxiety is high. Hence cheating will be more likely if students are not clear about the expected outcomes of instruction, or are not committed to them, and feel that they are not prepared for the examination. At the same time, students expect adequate supervision of tests as a right; cheating causes resentment that is often projected onto the examiner, even by those students who engage in it.

A number of strategies may be considered to reduce cheating. A review of course objectives, as mentioned earlier, may be in order. As formal tests are rarely appropriate to assess achievement of objectives other than knowledge or cognitive skills, the instructor should consider whether the weight given to the examination properly reflects the major intended outcomes of the program. Having students cooperate in the design of the test may help to reduce anxiety and build commitment. Allowing students to use reference books in an examination may in fact be a better test of the behavior needed for real life than forcing total reliance on memory. On formative tests it is often an advantage for students to share answers and to complete a test cooperatively in small groups: a great deal of informal peer tutoring often takes place in such contexts.

If none of these approaches is suitable, recourse may be necessary to the conventional procedures of security and supervision. Recently, sophisticated statistical techniques have been developed that appear able to identify cheaters on selected-response tests with great accuracy (Frary and Tideman, 1976). Prevention, however, is always preferable to detection.

Both cramming and cheating appear to be related to test anxiety, which is also a factor in psychological illness among students (Still, 1963). Thorough preparation in the material to be tested can reduce student anxiety. Teachers might also consider the merits of training students in "test-taking competencies." Giving students some basic instruction in following directions, form-filling, managing time, guessing, and

"I got an 'A' in ethics—but I cheated."

using question-answering strategies does seem to raise student test scores (Callenbach, 1973). It may also be worthwhile to give students the opportunity to express their feelings about tests, and to learn how to reduce tension and increase concentration and self-confidence (Young et al., 1978). These techniques should not be seen as giving a student an unfair advantage. They are "life skills" that reduce the influence of extraneous factors on the student's test performance and help to increase the accuracy with which a test measures his or her true competence.

Scoring Tests

Standardized tests are usually scored by the testing agency. The teacher-designed test can be rapidly scored by use of a template made from an answer sheet with holes punched to correspond with the key. Automatic scoring machines are commercially available from about $1,000. They will mark response sheets at the rate of at least one a second, indicating the wrong answers and printing the student's score on the response sheet. While it is not common to write comments on returned objective examinations, there is strong evidence that doing so improves subsequent student performance (Page, 1958).

The question whether a guessing correction should be applied must be decided, and students advised accordingly, before they answer the questions. The assumption behind a guessing correction is that the student's wrong answers are due to guessing wrong; if the student guessed and guessed wrong on some answers, then he or she must have guessed and guessed right on some others. On this basis, examiners have sometimes deducted marks from a student's raw score, according to an estimate of the number of "correct guesses."

Current feeling among measurement experts is generally against the use of guessing corrections. The usual effect is simply to lower all but perfect scores proportionately. According to R. L. Thorndike (1971, p. 60), "Corrected and uncorrected scores arrange people in identically the same order, and correlate perfectly with one another." Porter (1978) suggests that a guessing correction is in fact a misnomer for imposing an additional penalty for wrong answers. Some evidence also suggests that guessing corrections may penalize those students "characterized by introversion, rumination, anxiety, low self-esteem, and undue concern with the impression they make on others" (Sherman, 1976, p. 4). These characteristics are irrelevant to the qualities achievement tests are normally intended to measure. There is therefore much to justify students' intuitive objections to being awarded corrected scores lower than their raw scores on a test.

The solution to the guessing problem—insofar as it is a problem at all—lies in deciding on an appropriate passing score. Clearly 50 percent would be an absurd cutoff score on a true/false test. But even on such tests, the probability of a student scoring 60 out of 100 by blind guessing is less than 2 percent, of 65 less than 1 in 1,000, and of 70 less than 1 in 50,000. The decision facing the curriculum designer is one of setting a cutoff score that is appropriate and realistic in the light of the nature of the test and of the objective: more on this in due course.

Norm-referenced and Criterion-referenced Tests

Norm-referenced measurement and criterion-referenced measurement were mentioned briefly in the previous chapter. They need to be described more fully at this stage because they bear directly on the procedures and decisions that follow the administration and scoring of tests.

Classical test design was based on the assumption that a major purpose of testing was to rank students in terms of their knowledge or skill. Students' final standing on tests depended on their score relative to the "norm" represented by the scores of other students. The more a test "spread students out," the more reliable the ranking would be. Hence such tests tried to increase the variance of student scores by choosing questions that the best students would consistently answer correctly and the weakest students would consistently get wrong. The model for these norm-referenced test was a competitive one, like a 100-meter race or a political election: what generally mattered was the final position in the competition, not the actual speed or number of votes obtained.

In the last decade increasing attention has been paid to criterion-referenced measurement. Criterion-referenced tests aim not to distribute students along a continuum, but simply "to yield measurements that are directly interpretable in terms of specified performance standards" (Glaser and Nitko, 1971, p. 653). The designer of a criterion-referenced test is less interested in whether test items separate the most knowledgeable from the least knowledgeable students than in whether the items accurately reflect the knowledge or skills identified in the objectives of a particular curriculum domain. The terms *domain-referenced tests* and *curriculum-embedded tests* are sometimes used to emphasize this goal of criterion-referenced testing. Mastery learning, with its emphasis on high achievement of clear objectives, naturally finds criterion-referenced testing the more congenial model.

The value of criterion-referenced measurement has been vigorously espoused by such writers as Popham (1975, 1978). While the relative merits of norm-referenced and criterion-referenced testing are controversial and problematic, the earnestness of the debate may have exaggerated the differences between the two kinds of test. As Glaser and Nitko have pointed out, "The distinction between a norm-referenced and a criterion-referenced test cannot be made by simple inspection of a particular instrument" (1971, p. 654). The same test might be used for either purpose: to display student ability on a continuum or to separate students above and below a cutoff score. The decision whether to judge students by comparison with one another or with a criterion has at least as much to do with grading as with testing, as the discussion of grading later in this chapter indicates.

The advent of the concept of criterion-referenced testing has stimulated a reexamination of the standard procedures of test analysis developed since the 1930s. In the outline of these procedures that follows, the reader needs to bear in mind that they were originally developed within the context of the norm-referenced model of evaluation. At specific points, attention is drawn to the implications the procedures pose for criterion-referenced measurement.

Norm-referenced testing: An early insight

The essential fault of the older schemes for school grades or marks was that the "86" or "B−" did not mean any objectively defined amount of knowledge or power or skill—that, for example, John's attainment of 91 in second-year German did not inform him (or anyone else) about how difficult a passage he could translate, how many words he knew the English equivalents of and how accurately he could pronounce, or about any other fact save that he was supposed to be slightly more competent than someone else marked 89 was, or than he would have been if he had been so marked. . . .

School marks functioned as measures of superiority and inferiority amongst pupils, and of little else. A pupil who made excellence an aim of his school work was encouraged by every feature of the school's measurements of his work to think of excellence as excelling others—relative achievement—outdoing someone else.

—*Edward L. Thorndike (1919, p. 287)*

Item Analysis

It is a major advantage of selected-response tests that well-established procedures exist for determining the merit of each item from the data provided by student responses. Many universities and school systems have computer programs for this purpose, and this procedure is likely to be the most thorough one, especially if the test is taken by large numbers of students. Such programs usually show the pattern of student responses to each distracter as well as to the correct response, which is valuable in revising items. But for small numbers of students, basic item analysis can be conducted quite quickly by hand. The practice of routinely performing an item analysis on test data is a reasonably valid touchstone to separate the professional evaluator from the amateur. The main steps are as follows:

Step 1: On the basis of the students' total scores on the test, identify a "high group" and a "low group." Ideally, each group should be 27 percent of the total: if the class contains between thirty-four and forty students, ten in each group is a convenient approximation. If the item analysis is being conducted in the classroom, by show of hands (Diederich, 1960), dividing the class into the top half and the bottom half has the advantage of including all or all but one of the students in the procedure.

Step 2: For each question, identify the number of students in the high group and the number in the low group who answered the question correctly. Record these figures; an item analysis sheet such as that shown in Table 9–2 is convenient.

Step 3: Sum the two totals just calculated to produce the total number of students in the two groups who answered the question correctly, and divide by the number of students in both groups. Enter the resulting statistic in the "difficulty" column.

Step 4: Subtract the number in the "low" column from the number in the "high" column and divide by half the total number of students. Enter the statistic in the "discrimination" column.

When the data for all questions has been recorded, the difficulty and discrimination indices can be examined. The difficulty index (which logically should be called the facility index) indicates the proportion of the examinees who answered the question correctly. Conventional norm-referenced test design prefers a difficulty of .50, which allows a theoretical discrimination as high as 1.00 (item 3 in Table 9–2).

The discrimination index indicates the extent to which each item distinguishes between those students who scored highest and those who scored lowest on the test as a whole. The higher the average item discrimination, the higher the reliability (i.e., the internal consistency) of the test itself. Conventional test design aims for as high a discrimination as possible, with .30 often being regarded as a minimal level. Items that all students get right (number 4) or wrong (number 5) yield nil discrimination. A negative discrimination (number 6) indicates that the question penalizes the more knowledgeable students and needs to be revised or rejected.

COURSE: 132 Jurisprudence MEAN SCORE: 42.5 NO. OF ITEMS: 50			TEST: Final STANDARD DEVIATION: 4.5 NO. OF STUDENTS: 37			TEST DATE: Dec. 15, 78 RELIABILITY: .685 NO. IN HIGH/LOW GROUP: 10	
ITEM	HIGH	LOW	HIGH +LOW	DIFFI-CULTY	HIGH -LOW	DISCRIM-INATION	REMARKS
1.	8	4	12	.60	4	40	Acceptable (N-R model)
2.	10	9	19	.95	1	.10	Check for redundance
3.	10	0	10	.50	10	1.00	Acceptable (N-R model)
4.	10	10	20	1.00	0	.00	Check for redundance
5.	0	0	0	.00	0	.00	Revise item or instruction
6.	5	8	13	.65	−3	−.30	Check key. Revise or reject
7.	10	7	17	.85	3	.30	Acceptable (C-R model)

Table 9–2 Item analysis

In the item discrimination described above, a feature that is sometimes overlooked is that as it is a measure of the match of the item to
the total test, it provides useful information only if the test is intended
to be homogeneous. For example, ten items testing knowledge of Greek
would show low discrimination if the other ninety items on the test
assumed knowledge of Latin. As Cronbach points out, "When the test
constructor routinely discards the item whose correlation with the total
score for the item pool is low, he risks making the test less representative
of the defined universe" (1971, p. 458). This is an argument in favor of
"domain-referenced" tests or subtests, which assess a single objective or
closely related objectives.

Item analysis of criterion-referenced tests

In conventional item analysis, a high discrimination index can be
achieved only if about half of the examinees answer the items incorrectly. Teachers attempting to implement mastery learning would not
be satisfied with such an outcome, and evaluators adopting the criterion-
referenced model want to evaluate attainment of performance standards,
not to discriminate between high and low scorers. Hence, while items
1 and 3 in Table 9–2 would be acceptable in a norm-referenced model,
they would indicate to a mastery teacher that the items were unreason-
ably difficult, or that the related instruction was inadequate, or that the
skill or concept tested was beyond the grasp of some students. Mastery
teachers would be likely to welcome the data for item 7 and possibly for
item 4, which all students got right and hence had zero discrimination.

While the criterion-referenced evaluator is mainly interested in the
difficulty index for its value as a measure of instructional effectiveness,
the discrimination index can also provide valuable information for test
improvement. A number of authorities (Glaser, 1963; Haladyna, 1974;
Gronlund, 1976) have suggested an item-analysis strategy for criterion-
referenced tests. Instead of comparing item scores within a group of students after instruction, compare pretest and posttest scores for the same
or for equivalent groups of students. The discrimination index will then
reveal the item scores to which instruction made a difference. A test
composed of items with high discrimination would be a test that consistently discriminated between students who had received instruction
and students who had not.

Building an item bank

Item analysis should yield cumulative benefits. Over the course of
several test administrations, a file of highly discriminating items of appropriate difficulty can be built up. The bigger the pool, the more of the

items can be used in each test, thus reducing the labor involved in writing new items and ensuring a certain level of test reliability.

Many institutions in which testing is an integral part of the program design have developed item banks of up to fifty thousand items, from which the questions for formal examinations are drawn (Sivertson, Hanson, and Schoenberger, 1973). The eight medical schools in Australia are cooperating on construction of such an item bank (Bligh, 1975, p. 44). These items are recorded in a data bank and can be accessed from a typewriter terminal at any time by students for purposes of review and self-testing. The computer can be programmed to record all responses to every item, maintain an ongoing item analysis, try out several different distracters for each question, and drop inadequate choices and items. The item banks are too large for students to memorize questions in the expectation that they will encounter the same items again in formal examinations.

Improving Test Reliability

Because the scoring key is completely determined in advance, the marking of selected-response tests is normally perfectly reliable. The question

---

A teacher decides that he needs $1500 and six weeks of release time to design a new curriculum. So he requests $2000 and eight weeks release time. He is offered $500 and two weeks release time. This suggests that he

  ★a. underestimated the constraints
    b. incorrectly identified the need
    c. failed to define the learners
    d. overestimated the support needed

DATE OF TEST	COURSE	NO. OF STUDENTS	FUNCTION	DIFFICULTY	DISCRIMINATION
3.15.78	05.310	63	posttest	.86	.20
7.1.78	15.310	60	pretest	.42	.32
5.3.79	15.310	123	posttest	.89	.18
12.15.79	25.310	18	posttest	.93	.10
2.7.80	15.310	58	mid-term	.72	.26
7.5.80	25.310	76	pre + post	.74	.51

Table 9–3   Item analysis record

of reliability of such tests tends to focus on their internal reliability—the extent to which all parts of the test consistently measure the same attributes.

An estimate of the reliability of a test may be calculated from the following formula (Gronlund, 1977, p. 141):

$$\text{Reliability} = 1 - \frac{M(k - M)}{ks^2}$$

where k = the number of items on the test

M = the mean of the test scores

s = the standard deviation of the test scores.

The standard deviation may be estimated by subtracting the sum of the bottom sixth of the scores of the group from the sum of the top sixth and dividing by half the number of students (Gronlund, 1977, p. 123):

$$s = \frac{\text{high sixth} - \text{low sixth}}{N \div 2}$$

The reliability coefficient is a statistic between 0.00 and 1.00. A reliability of 1.00 means that all the differences among students' scores are accounted for by differences in performance on the main qualities measured by the test. A reliability of 0.00 means that none of the differences between scores are explained by differences in performance: they must all be due to extraneous factors such as chance, erratic marking, or abilities unrelated to those primarily evaluated by the test. If the reliability were .90, 81 percent ($.90^2$) of the score variance would be accounted for by differences in performance. But if the reliability were .50, only 25 percent of the variance would be due to this factor.

Professional evaluators usually insist on a reliability of at least .90 for any test that is to be used to make decisions about people (Menges, 1975, p. 184). But the reliability of tests set by teachers in most schools and colleges probably rarely exceeds .50. What does this mean in practice? With a test reliability of .99, all but 5 percent of the students in a typical class graded on an A to F scale will receive the correct grade. If the reliability is .90, 23 percent of the students will be graded too high or too low, and if the test reliability is only .50, 50 percent of the students will be erroneously graded (Ebel, 1972, p. 426).

There are three main strategies by which test reliability can be improved:

1. *Increase the number of items on the test.* For the benefit of the statistically-minded reader, the effect of this may be described as follows. Assuming that the items added have the same properties as those already

in the test, lengthening the test will increase the reliability as a function of the Spearman-Brown formula (Ebel, 1972, p. 413):

$$r_n = \frac{nr_s}{(n - 1r_s + 1)}$$

where r_n is reliability of new test

r_s is reliability of original test

n is length of new test ÷ length of original test

Hence doubling the length of a 20-item test whose reliability is .50 would increase the reliability to .67. The test would have to be nine times as long, or 180 items, to attain a reliability of .90. By the same token, in an essay test, asking the students to write several short essays rather than one or two long ones, is likely to increase the reliability. For tests that are marked subjectively, increasing the number of judges will have an equivalent effect on reliability to that produced by increasing the number of questions.

2. *Increase the discrimination of the test items.* It is unlikely that an acceptable test reliability (above .90) can be achieved unless the average discrimination of items exceeds .30.

3. *Increase the homogeneity of the test.* A test that measures only student vocabulary will be more reliable than an equivalent test that attempts to measure vocabulary, spelling, punctuation, and creative writing. This underlines the importance of precise definition of objectives, attainment of each of which is separately assessed.

Estimating reliability of criterion-referenced tests

In the formulas and procedures described above, test reliability is a function of the score variance in a test. These procedures are therefore suitable for norm-referenced tests that aim to produce a high variance, but not for criterion-referenced, or mastery, tests, in which it is expected that all students will make high scores and the variance will therefore be small.

The basis of reliability is consistency. Reliability formulas for norm-referenced tests indicate how consistently a test discriminates between more and less competent students. In criterion-referenced tests, the evaluator is interested in how consistently the test indicates which students have reached the criterion and which have not. One approach is to artificially increase the score variance by including pretest and posttest scores (Haladyna, 1974), as described earlier (p. 248), and then use conventional reliability measures. Millman (1974) developed a specific procedure for examining the reliability of criterion-referenced tests. As elaborated by Martuza (1977), the steps are as follows:

1. Administer a test of appropriate length, i.e., at least twenty items, which measures attainment in a single domain.
2. Divide the test randomly into two parts, e.g., odd- and even-numbered questions.
3. Compute each examinee's total score on each part and express it as a percentage.
4. Calculate the absolute difference between the two scores.
5. Compute the average of these differences: this is the reliability index. The lower the statistic, the more consistent the result of the test.

Example:

STUDENT SCORES (PERCENT)

	Test 1 (odd items)	Test 2 (even items)	Absolute difference
Student #1	90	81	9
Student #2	75	70	5
Student #3	98	94	4
Student #4	86	92	6
Student #5	73	85	12

Sum of differences 36
Mean difference 7.2

An even simpler approach is to calculate the agreement between two parts of a test in terms of the criterion decision (Millman, 1974, p. 357). Suppose that in the previous example the cutoff score for a "pass" were set at 80 percent. The procedure would be as follows:

CRITERION DECISION

	Test 1 (odd items)	Test 2 (even items)	Agreement
Student #1	pass	pass	yes
Student #2	fail	fail	yes
Student #3	pass	pass	yes
Student #4	pass	pass	yes
Student #5	fail	pass	no

Agreement: 80%

This statistic indicates directly the consistency with which the test determines which students have reached the criterion.

Grading

Although evaluation and grading are often integrated in practice, in principle they are separate and sequential processes. Evaluation appraises, and grading provides a label. There is a rough analogy to judicial processes: first the accused is judged, then sentenced.

It is at the grading stage that the characteristics of norm-referenced decisions show up most clearly. Figure 9–2 shows the results of a hypothetical course taught to classes in two consecutive semesters. The first-semester class was relatively unsuccessful: achievement in the final examination ranged from about 5 percent to 60 percent. According to his usual practice, the instructor divided the class into six groups of equal size and awarded grades of A to F. The course was repeated in the next semester with better results. This time terminal performance ranged from 40 to almost 100 percent. Again the top sixth of the students received As and the bottom sixth Fs. Although this example is extreme, it highlights the relativity of judgments in norm-referenced grading. A student who received an F in the second semester, had he or she achieved the same level in the first semester, would have received an A, and vice versa. In neither class do the grades awarded give any indication of actual learning acquired by the students.

In the United States, recognition of these limitations of norm-referenced judgment has contributed to the development of programs of individualized instruction, especially at the elementary-school level, in which evaluation is almost entirely criterion-referenced. Nevertheless, norm-referenced thinking is still endemic in most Western education. Implicit or explicit quotas are set for the number of high and low grades to be awarded. Within any institution these quotas tend to remain fixed even if actual student achievement goes up or down (Baird and Feister, 1972). If an instructor violates the convention and awards "too many" high grades, administrators may order some or all grades to be reduced.

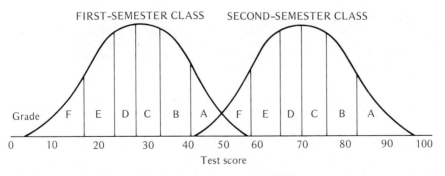

Figure 9–2   Norm-referenced grading

The belief that high grades are to be reserved for a small and more or less fixed minority of students is a basic tenet of elitist educational philosophy and is the antithesis of the mastery approach. It is an interesting reflection on the world of education that administrators should respect courses in which few students earn high grades and despise those in which many students earn high grades. It is an even sadder fact that they are often right. But it is because grades are linked to institutional expectation rather than to observed performance that it is felt necessary to control fluctuations. In recent years there appears to have been a general inflation in academic grades: the proportion of high grades has significantly increased without any apparent increase in student achievement (Balderson, 1976).

Students quickly recognize the competitive nature of norm-referenced grading and tend to respond accordingly. There is a well-known story of a college that had a policy of failing the bottom 10 percent of students in every class; one class of eighteen students hired two other students to take the course and deliberately fail it to safeguard passing grades for themselves. Grading policies that express final grades in fine gradations, such as percentages or letters A to F, emphasize competition more than those in which the categories are limited to complete/incomplete or honors/credit/fail. By 1971 the majority of medical schools in North America were using pass/fail grading (Abrams and Byrd, 1971). The rationale sometimes offered was that contemporary medical practice re-

Norm-referenced Grading in Action

It was with some fascination that I entered the examination board. The secretary, who is head examiner . . . had invited me to an award meeting, at which he and the chief examiner for one of the history exams were to discuss what marks to set as the minimum for each grade. This meeting would seal the fate of all those 18,050 children waiting anxiously out there to hear their results. . . .

The chief examiner suggested 61 percent and upwards should be awarded a grade one. The secretary then looked at a graph he had drawn up from the marked papers and said, "But if we fixed the minimum at 61 percent only 6 percent of the candidates would get grade one, and that's very few."

He paused and examined his graph again. "If we fixed it at 60 percent that would still mean that only 9 percent of the candidates would get a grade one. Yet you say you feel there should be a few more grade ones this year?"

The chief examiner said, "The paper this year was of exactly the same standard as last year, and I do feel there should be just a few more grade ones. What about 58 percent as the minimum for grade one?"

The secretary checked his graph. "A 58 percent minimum would mean that 12 percent of the candidates would be grade one. That sounds about right to me."

—Polly Toynbee, reporting a visit to a Certificate of Secondary Education Board, England, 1977.

quired teamwork and competition that were inconsistent with the interpersonal comparison often associated with traditional forms of academic grading. Other institutions often prefer three categories, such as honors/credit/incomplete, to recognize outstanding achievement. The number and names of categories, however, are less significant than the emphasis on actual rather than relative learner achievement.

Setting the cutoff score

Some of the problems associated with arbitrary cutoff scores of 50 percent were discussed in the previous chapter. The question mainly affects summative testing: cutoff scores are less important in formative tests, whose function is primarily diagnostic.

While the traditional 50 percent is arbitrary, a score of 90 percent also means little in the absence of information about the difficulty of the items on the test (Crambert, 1976). An experienced test designer can develop tests that will predictably produce class means of 40 percent or 90 percent simply by deliberate choice of difficult or easy items. The cutoff score chosen is therefore going to depend on the difficulty of the items on the test, as well as on several other factors. Some factors noted in the previous chapter are the nature and importance of the objective, the type of misclassification of students the instructor wishes to avoid, and the trade-off between motivation and competence. An additional factor is the number of retests allowed. Quirk comments on

> the ludicrous situation in which the student is retested on the same or an alternate form of the test until some coincidence of regression toward the mean, practice effect, the standard error of measurement, and random error combine to produce the magical cutoff score on a single occasion (Quirk, 1974, p. 317).

Other things being equal, the more retests allowed, the higher the criterion score should be set.

It is worth reemphasizing that the test designer is on strongest ground if test items are based on considerations of importance and relevance. The question to be asked about every item on the test is not so much how difficult it is, but whether it tests knowledge or skill that is important in relation to the aim of the curriculum. Importance, it will be recalled, is related to the probability of use and the consequences of inadequate mastery. The cutoff score will be a function of potential costs: how many items can safely be missed? On tests of mechanical skills and knowledge a higher cutoff would be set for aircraft mechanics than for automobile mechanics (Meskauskas, 1976). Likewise, higher standards of performance would be required of pilots than of car drivers, of heart surgeons than of teachers, of police officers than of salesclerks.

A word of caution is necessary at this point. Because every test contains a "standard error," one cannot say that a score of 9 out of 10 indicates that the student is 90 percent competent or that it is 90 percent probable that the student is competent. The score only indicates that we can be confident within certain limits that the student's competence falls within certain limits. Table 9–4 illustrates the relationship between cutoff scores and probability of correct classification of examinees. Many teachers would feel that 4 out of 5 on a test was a reasonably high standard: the table shows that it yields only a 36 percent probability that the student's true competency level is at least 80 percent. Hence in determining cutoff scores, it is necessary to take into account the degree of certainty required in making the judgment of competence. As the table shows, such certainty increases with the number of items on the test. Gronlund (1976, p. 123) recommends a minimum of ten items for most mastery-nonmastery decisions.

TEST LENGTH	STUDENT'S SCORE	PROBABILITY OF CORRECT CLASSIFICATION AS	
		"competent at .80 level"	"competent at .90 level"
5 items	5	.7539	.5006
	4	.3558	.1235
	3	.0940	.0174
12 items	12	.9524	.7784
	11	.7790	.4021
	10	.5173	.1493
	9	.2660	.0398
20 items	20	.9939	.9135
	19	.9479	.6618
	18	.8359	.3818
	17	.6501	.1720
	16	.4364	.0619

Table 9–4   Probabilities of correct classification of students for selected levels of competence, obtained scores, and test lengths (from Davis and Diamond, 1974, p. 135)

This discussion of grading may be concluded by identifying five basic principles.

1. Grades should be based on an appropriate number of observations, using instruments of adequate reliability.

2. The grading system should reflect the relative importance of the objectives. Critical objectives should carry more weight than important objectives (for example, by accounting for a relatively greater number of test items); important objectives should carry more weight than desirable objectives.

3. Credit for a course should not be granted until a student has at least mastered the critical objectives. To award credit to a student who has not achieved a critical objective is simply to say that the objective is not critical.

4. So far as possible, any significant achievement by students should be acknowledged. Outstanding achievement can be recognized by an Honors category. A simple pass/fail system may unnecessarily depress the achievement of highly motivated students.

5. It should be possible to achieve the maximum grade, be it Honors, A+, or 100 percent. Such grades should not indicate perfection, but rather that the student has achieved all objectives at the highest standard identified.

Reporting Student Achievement

The reporting of student achievement needs to be conducted with care. Recent court cases indicate that unduly critical reports can result in accusations of defamation, while euphemistic reporting may lead to charges of misrepresentation.

While few lay people have ever heard of "criterion-referenced measurement," the practice of reporting actual attainments seems to be gaining acceptance, as witness the growing use of checklists in school reports. A prospective employer is likely to recognize the advantage of a statement like "can type 40 wpm" as against "stood third in typing class" or "received a B+ in typing." Many parents, however, while not uninterested in actual achievement, also want information about their childrens' standing relative to their peers.

This demand can be accommodated by providing in reports both individual achievement data and normative information. For example, a third-grade report might provide a checklist of such skills as addition with whole numbers, linear measurement in metric units, etc., and show both the student's attainment or nonattainment of each skill *and* the average age at which children normally master the skill. The larger the group providing this "average" the better. Comparison only with other children in the same class invites invidious personal comparisons and can at the same time be misleading if the class as a whole is achieving significantly above or below the average.

Reporting student achievement presents valuable opportunities for communication between the school and the community. School reports should therefore be designed to meet the needs of all the users of reports; there is some merit in inviting parents, teachers, and other users to cooperate in designing the reporting system (Gronlund, 1974, p. 49). One group of users is the students. Many schools allow students to write their own self-appraisal as a formal part of their school reports. This encourages students to reflect on their own learning and constitutes a valuable source of student comment on school programs.

Went to hear Mrs. Turner's daughter play on the harpsichon; but Lord! it was enough to make any man sick to hear her; yet was I forced to commend her highly.

—*Samuel Pepys (Diary, May 1, 1663)*

Self-appraisal

Language arts

    I have great trouble writing stories if I am given a limited amount of time to complete them. I would rather take my time. I plan to be a writer when I am older.

Mathematics

    I have worked very hard in math but I have not made any progress in division. I have learned a lot of problems with decimals.

Environmental studies

    I have really enjoyed doing projects. Everytime I do one I learn something new. They are an enjoyable learning experience.

Music

    I don't like singing but I like playing the recorder. But I don't think it's a good idea to put music right after gym.

Art

    I enjoy the art that is chosen for us. But sometimes I want to do whatever I want.

—Fifth-grade child, 1978

The Professional Standpoint

Evaluation, grading, and reporting link the teacher to the larger contexts of the school administration and the community. Decisions made at this stage are highly visible and often have significant consequences for learners. Hence it is a sensitive area, one in which the teacher can feel uncomfortably exposed and can be subject to powerful pressure to make decisions that are in conflict with the educator's professional judgment.

    In this situation, the principles of systematic curriculum design stand the practitioner in good stead. The instructor who develops clear and worthwhile objectives, valid and reliable measures of performance, and a sound and relevant grading system; who commits these design variables to paper and has them formally approved; and who can show that the design has been adhered to in arriving at the evaluative decisions made: such an educator is in a position that is both professionally and politically secure.

ACTIVITIES

1. Talk to a number of educators at different levels about evaluation of student achievement. How do attitudes vary according to the subject and age group taught and according to the age, rank, personality, and background of the teacher?

2. Consult *Tests in Print* and the *Mental Measurements Yearbook* to identify published tests in your teaching area. If possible, obtain sample copies of the tests. List the advantages and disadvantages of using a published test as against developing your own.

3. Obtain a short student essay. Give some colleagues a handwritten copy and others a typed version. Ask them to grade the essay. Compare the results within and between the two groups.

4. If you teach an appropriate class, on the next occasion that a formal test is in order, include both constructed-response and selected-response items. After scoring, describe the scoring methods and conduct an item analysis with the class. Invite general discussion. What student attitudes are expressed?

5. Suppose that you are planning a course that has five critical objectives and five important objectives. School policy requires that a student earning 50 percent in a course be awarded credit. Design a feasible grading system that conforms with school policy but ensures that all students receiving credit have mastered all critical objectives.

6. Review the evaluation procedures used in a college, faculty, or university department familiar to you. Obtain a general picture of (1) the types of evaluation used; (2) the validity and reliability of the measures; (3) the probable extent of plagiarism; and (4) the degree to which the evaluation practices have been influenced by research in educational measurement. Account for the situation your review discloses.

QUESTIONS

1. The conventional type of formal written test is generally most appropriate to assess achievement of

   a. motor skills
   b. dispositional objectives
   c. knowledge and cognitive skills
   d. physiological and experiential objectives

2. A teacher returns a test to students with marginal notes on each test. Those who pass the test advance to the next unit; those who do not pass must take another test in a week's time. The first test therefore serves as

   a. formative but not summative evaluation
   b. summative but not formative evaluation
   c. both formative and summative evaluation
   d. neither formative nor summative evaluation

3. A major problem with use of the traditional essay test for evaluating learning is that

   a. agreement among markers tends to be low
   b. essays can test only low-level knowledge and skills
   c. the marker cannot make allowances for badly phrased questions
   d. the essay has little value for diagnosis or formative evaluation

4. The most effective way to increase the reliability of scoring essay tests is to

   a. use an itemized marking scheme
   b. mark essays impressionistically
   c. allow students a wide range of essay topics
   d. increase the number of essays required and the number of judges

5. This question contains a

   a. opinion bias
   b. grammatical clue
   c. overlapping answer
   d. informational error in the stem

6. Applying a "guessing correction" to scores on a selected-response test will tend to increase

   a. student resentment
   b. validity of the test
   c. reliability of the test
   d. student scores on the test

7. Which of the following item analysis statistics most clearly identifies a question that needs revision?

   a. difficulty .50, discrimination 1.00
   b. difficulty .60, discrimination .30
   c. difficulty .70, discrimination −.30
   d. difficulty .80, discrimination .20

8. In instructional programs, grading is the process of

   a. marking students' work
   b. measuring student achievement
   c. judging student achievement against criteria
   d. classifying students on the basis of data from evaluation

9. Norm-referenced grading is unlikely to develop

   a. test anxiety in students
   b. cooperation among students
   c. competition among students
   d. extrinsic motivation on the part of students

10. Which of the following distinctions is conferred primarily on a criterion-referenced basis?

    a. an Oscar award
    b. an Olympic gold medal
    c. election as a U.S. Senator
    d. the Congressional Medal of Honor

Check your answers against the key in Appendix 2.
9 or 10 right: You understand the material presented.
8 or 7 right: Review the areas of uncertainty.
6 or less right: Reread the chapter.

Recommended Reading

Bloom, Benjamin S., J. Thomas Hastings, and George F. Madaus. *Handbook of formative and summative evaluation of student learning.* New York: McGraw-Hill, 1971. Contains much sound and practical information on strategies for different kinds of evaluation in various subject areas.

Ebel, Robert L. *Essentials of educational measurement.* Englewood Cliffs, N.J.: Prentice-Hall, 1972. A standard textbook by one of America's leading authorities on evaluation; particularly useful on the design of formal and norm-referenced tests.

Gronlund, Norman. *Constructing achievement tests.* 2nd ed. Englewood Cliffs, N.J.: Prentice-Hall, 1977. A brief but thorough treatment of test construction, written with the classroom practitioner in mind.

——— . *Improving marking and reporting in classroom instruction.* New York: Macmillan, 1974. Concise and excellent guide to grading in norm-referenced and criterion-referenced contexts, designing reporting procedures, and planning and conducting parent-teacher conferences.

Popham, W. J. *Criterion-referenced measurement.* Englewood Cliffs, N.J.: Prentice-Hall, 1978. A wise and witty review of the subject by one of its foremost proponents.

References

Abrams, H. K., and A. R. Byrd. Survey of grading procedures of American and Associated Medical Colleges. *Journal of Medical Education,* 1971, 46, 316–339.

Baird, Leonard L., and William J. Feister. Grading standards: The relation of changes in average student ability to the average grades awarded. *American Educational Research Journal,* 1972, 9, 431–442.

Balderson, James H. Academic inflation or better schools? Questions for research. *Canadian Society for the Study of Education News,* 1976, 3 (1), 10.

Beard, R. M., and K. Pole. Content and purpose of biochemistry examinations. *British Journal of Medical Education,* 1971, 5, 13–21.

Bhushan, Vidya, and John R. Ginther. Discriminating between a good and a poor essay. *Behavioral Science*, 1968, 13, 417–420.

Black, P. J. University examinations. *Physics Education*, 1968, 3 (2), 93–99.

Bligh, Donald, G. J. Ebrahim, David Jaques, and D. Warren Piper. *Teaching students*. Exeter, England: Exeter University Teaching Services, 1975.

Bloom, Benjamin S. Toward a theory of testing which includes measurement-evaluation-assessment. In M. C. Wittrock and David E. Wiley (eds.), *The evaluation of instruction: Issues and problems*. New York: Holt, Rinehart & Winston, 1970, pp. 25–50.

———, J. Thomas Hastings, and George F. Madaus. *Handbook of formative and summative evaluation of student learning*. New York: McGraw-Hill, 1971.

Brickman, W. W. Ethics, examinations, and education. *School and Society*, 1961, 89, 412–415.

Buros, Oscar Krisen. *Ninth mental measurements yearbook*. Highland Park, N.J.: Gryphon Press, 1978.

———. *Tests in print II*. Highland Park, N.J.: Gryphon Press, 1974.

Bushway, Ann, and William R. Nash. School cheating behavior. *Review of Educational Research*, 1977, 47, 623–632.

Callenbach, Carl. The effects of instruction and practice in content-independent test-taking techniques upon the standardized reading test scores of selected second-grade students. *Journal of Educational Measurement*, 1973, 10, 25–29.

Coffman, William E. Essay examinations. In Robert L. Thorndike (ed.), *Educational measurement*. 2nd ed. Washington, D.C.: American Council on Education, 1971, pp. 271–302.

Colton, T., and O. L. Peterson. An assay of medical students' abilities by oral examination. *Journal of Medical Education*, 1967, 42, 1005.

Crambert, Albert C. Use of mastery cutoff scores in criterion-referenced measurement. Paper prepared for the Annual Meeting of the American Educational Research Association, San Francisco, April 1976.

Cronbach, Lee J. Test validation. In Robert L. Thorndike (ed.), *Educational measurement*. 2nd ed. Washington, D.C.: American Council on Education, 1971, pp. 443–507.

Davis, Frederick B., and James J. Diamond. The preparation of criterion-referenced tests. In Chester W. Harris, Marvin C. Alkin, and W. James Popham (eds.), *Problems in criterion-referenced measurement*. Los Angeles: UCLA Center for Study of Evaluation, 1974, pp. 116–138.

Diederich, Paul B. *Short-cut statistics for teacher-made tests*. Princeton, N.J.: Educational Testing Service, 1960.

Ebel, Robert L. *Essentials of educational measurement*. Englewood Cliffs, N.J.: Prentice-Hall, 1972.

———. The future of measurement of abilities II. *Educational Researcher*, 1973, 2, (March), 5–12.

Frary, Robert B., and T. Nicolaus Tideman. Evaluation of statistics for detection of cheating on multiple-choice tests. Paper prepared for the Annual Meeting of the American Educational Research Association, San Francisco, April 1976.

Glaser, Robert. Instructional technology and the measurement of learning outcomes. *American Psychologist*, 1963, 18, 519–521.

Glaser, Robert, and Anthony J. Nitko. Measurement in learning and instruction. In Robert L. Thorndike (ed.), *Educational measurement*. 2nd ed. Washington, D.C.:

American Council on Education, 1971, pp. 625–670.

Godshalk, Fred I., Frances Swineford, and William E. Coffman. *Measurement of writing ability*. New York: College Entrance Examination Board, 1966.

Gronlund, Norman E. *Improving marking and reporting in classroom instruction*. New York: Macmillan, 1974.

———— . *Measurement and evaluation in teaching*. New York: Macmillan, 1976.

———— . *Constructing achievement tests*. 2nd ed. Englewood Cliffs, N.J.: Prentice-Hall, 1977.

———— . *Stating objectives for classroom instruction*. 2nd ed. New York: Macmillan, 1978.

Gust, T., and D. Schumacher. Handwriting speed of college students. *Journal of Educational Research*, 1969, 62, 198–200.

Haladyna, T. M. Effects of different samples on item and test characteristics of criterion-referenced tests. *Journal of Educational Measurement*, 1974, 11, 93–99.

Hawkes, Herbert E., E. F. Lindquist, and C. R. Mann. *The construction and use of achievement examinations*. New York: Houghton Mifflin, 1936.

James, A. W. The effect of handwriting on grading. *English Journal*, 1927, 16, 180–205.

Markham, Lynda R. Influences of handwriting quality on teacher evaluation of written work. *American Educational Research Journal*, 1976, 13, 277–283.

Marshall, Jon C., and Jerry M. Powers. Writing neatness, composition errors, and essay grades. *Journal of Educational Measurement*, 1969, 6, 97–101.

Martuza, Victor R. *Applying norm-referenced and criterion-referenced measurement in education*. Boston: Allyn & Bacon, 1977.

Menges, Robert J. Assessing readiness for professional practice. *Review of Educational Research*, 1975, 45, 173–207.

Meskauskas, John A. Evaluation models for criterion-referenced testing: Views regarding mastery and standard-setting. *Review of Educational Research*, 1976, 46, 133–158.

Millman, Jason. Passing scores and test lengths for domain-referenced measures. *Review of Educational Research*, 1973, 43, 205–216.

———— . Criterion-referenced measurement. In W. James Popham (ed.), *Evaluation in education: Current applications*. Berkeley, Cal.: McCutchan, 1974, pp. 309–397.

National School Boards Association. *Standardized achievement testing*. Washington, D.C.: NSBA, 1977.

Page, E. B. Teacher comments and student performance: A seventy-four classroom experiment in school motivation. *Journal of Educational Psychology*, 1958, 49, 173–181.

Popham, W. James. *Educational evaluation*. Englewood Cliffs, N.J.: Prentice-Hall, 1975.

———— . *Criterion-referenced measurement*. Englewood Cliffs, N.J.: Prentice-Hall, 1978.

Porter, Richard D. Guessing on standardized achievement tests: Implications of current practice. Paper presented at the Annual Meeting of the American Educational Research Association, Toronto, March 1978.

Pratt, David. Predicting teacher survival. *Journal of Educational Research*, 1977, 71, 12–18.

Quinto, Frances, and Bernard McKenna. *Alternatives to standardized testing*. Washington, D.C.: National Education Association, 1977.

Quirk, Thomas J. Some measurement issues in competency-based teacher education. *Phi Delta Kappan*, 1974, 55, 316–319.

Scannel, D. P., and J. C. Marshall. The effect of selected composition errors on grades assigned to essay examinations. *American Educational Research Journal*, 1966, 3, 125–130.

Scriven, Michael. The methodology of evaluation. In Ralph Tyler, Robert Gagné, and Michael Scriven, *Perspectives of curriculum evaluation*. Chicago: Rand McNally, 1967, pp. 39–83.

Sherman, Susan W. Multiple-choice test bias uncovered by use of an "I don't know" alternative. Paper prepared for the Annual Meeting of the American Educational Research Association, San Francisco, April 1976.

Sivertson, Sigurd E., Richard H. Hanson, and Adeline O. Schoenberger. Computerized test bank for clinical medicine. *Educational Technology*, 1973, 13 (March), 38–39.

Starch, Daniel, and E. C. Elliott. Reliability of grading high school work in English. *School Review*, 1912, 20, 442–457.

——— . Reliability of grading work in mathematics. *School Review*, 1913, 21, 254– 259.

——— . Reliability of grading work in history. *School Review*, 1913, 21, 676–681.

Still, R. J. Psychological illness among students in the examination period. Mimeo. Leeds, UK: University of Leeds Department of Student Health, 1963.

Thorndike, Edward L. *Educational psychology*, vol. 1. New York: Teachers College, Columbia University, 1919.

Thorndike, Robert L. (ed.). *Educational measurement*. 2nd ed. Washington, D.C.: American Council on Education, 1971.

Toynbee, Polly. How to pass exams. *Manchester Guardian Weekly*, July 10, 1977, p. 19.

Traxler, A. E., and R. N. Hilkert. Effect of type of desk on results of machine-scored tests. *School and Society*, 1942, 56, 277–279.

Ulrich, Lynn, and Don Trumbo. The selection interview since 1949. *Psychological Bulletin*, 1965, 63, 100–116.

Wesman, A. G. Writing the test item. In Robert L. Thorndike (ed.), *Educational measurement*. 2nd ed. Washington, D.C.: American Council on Education, 1971, pp. 81–129.

Young, Patricia, Roger J. Fishman, James E. Ayrer, William E. Loue III, Wendy Gollub, and Mark Levin. The effects of teaching test-taking competencies on students' achievement. Paper presented at the Annual Meeting of the American Educational Research Association, Toronto, March 1978.

Part Four

DESIGNING INSTRUCTION

10

PRINCIPLES

- To design appropriate instruction, curriculum developers need to define and describe the learners for whom the curriculum is intended.

- Many cognitive, personality, and background characteristics influence people's learning.

- The concepts that can be taught successfully are limited by the level of intellectual development of the learners.

- Personality factors affect student preferences for subject matter and learning strategies.

- Ideally, prerequisites aim to identify those factors that are necessary if learners are to benefit from the instruction.

- Elitist and egalitarian ideologies do not necessarily produce optimum definition of prerequisites.

- Pretests ascertain the status of learners prior to instruction and help to identify those who are unlikely to benefit from the instruction.

CONCEPTS

Intellectual development   Elitism
Stereopathy   Egalitarianism
Field dependence   Prerequisite

10

Entry Characteristics of Learners

If I had to reduce all of educational psychology to just one principle I would say this: The most important single factor influencing learning is what the learner already knows. Ascertain this and teach him accordingly.

—David P. Ausubel (1968, p. vi)

Describing the Learners

From an early stage in their deliberations, the curriculum designers will have a general impression of the kind of learners for whom the curriculum is intended. The development of a complete curriculum requires that this inexact concept be clarified in as exact a description of the expected learners as is feasible. The identification of learners helps designers select appropriate instructional content and methods. It also provides valuable information to other educators who may subsequently review the curriculum for their own use.

Many background variables affect the design or the effectiveness of

269

a curriculum. They include intellectual, emotional, and social development; educational progress, motivation, and attitude; background and
aptitude in the subject; special interests and talents; anxiety level, personality, and preferred learning style; age and health status; aspirations,
career plans and probabilities; parental expectations, home and family
conditions; and nature of the community and the peer culture. Ethnicity,
social class, and political or religious beliefs should be described only
where clearly relevant, and then with caution on account of the danger
of promoting stereotyping and prejudice.

Teachers who become familiar with the background characteristics
of their students have a considerable advantage in planning their teaching. Just as the investment of time in coming to know students as individuals reaps a generous return in the classroom, so time invested in
ascertaining the expected characteristics of a learner population will benefit the curriculum designer.

Such factors as parental expectations and aspirations for their children may be profoundly important but not readily apparent. The attitude
of parents toward the study of a foreign language by their children appears
to affect student motivation significantly (Burstall, 1974). Student motivation itself must be ascertained in advance in order to design appropriate instruction. The student who finds the subject interesting or useful
is ready to receive the most relevant and efficient instruction. For less-
motivated students, it will be necessary, especially in the early stages,
to use subject matter that is less directly related to the objectives but
highly motivational, and methodologies that are less rapid but more interesting to the learner.

The designer attempts to discover or predict the probable range of
such student characteristics and describe them. The same must be done
concerning the general educational background of the learners. But in
respect to the learner's background in the subject, prior learnings may be
of such significance (e.g., addition in the case of a unit in multiplication)
that prescription is more appropriate than description. Such cases belong
in a later discussion of prerequisites.

Two student characteristics merit more detailed attention: level of
intellectual development and personality.

Intellectual development

The notion of stages of intellectual development is associated primarily with the work of Jean Piaget. While Piaget's concept of intellectual development does not exhaust our understanding of this subject, his
description of the main stages of development (see box, p. 272) provides
educators with guidelines that have direct application in teaching and in
curriculum development. To neglect the constraints that maturational
level presents is to risk developing unfeasible curricula.

As a case in point, Bereiter comments:

> In my experience social science is a dead loss for twelve-year-olds. The concern for people outside their immediate experience, which psychologists since G. Stanley Hall have noted as an outstanding development in adolescence, has not yet taken hold. It appears that without this broadened social identity, most of what interests social scientists is seen as pointless and boring—at best of purely "academic" interest (Bereiter, 1976, pp. 313–314).

Clearly any curriculum in which formal reasoning is necessary must grapple with the fact that this capacity rarely develops before the age of twelve, and apparently *never* develops in a substantial minority of adults (Kohlberg, 1973).

Accurate appraisal of the intellectual level of prospective students will guide the designer in selecting appropriate subject matter and methodologies; it may also reveal objectives that are unfeasible or redundant. Intellectual development, however, is a challenge as well as a constraint, and curricula should not be developed at such low developmental levels that they fail to stimulate the learners or to provide opportunities for intellectual growth.

Personality

Much remains to be discovered regarding the effect of personality on learning. But parts of the picture are beginning to emerge, particularly with respect to student response to the structure of the learning situation. Studies have found that active, assertive people learn less well from films and better from live instruction than do submissive individuals (Snow, Tiffin, and Seibert, 1965). Introverts, given a choice, spend more time learning from self-instructional materials, while extroverts spend more time interacting with the instructor (Johnson, 1974).

Numerous studies have compared learning styles with various measures of "authoritarianism" or "dogmatism." In a typical study, Zagona and Zurcher (1964) used Rokeach's "dogmatism scale" to select the "most open-minded" and the "most closed-minded" 30 students from among 517 undergraduates and unobtrusively observed their behavior in seminar discussions. The open-minded students had little difficulty in organizing their group, discussed sensitive issues candidly, and tended to debate questions at length among themselves and with the chairman and the instructor. The closed-minded students had great difficulty in choosing a chairman, but having done so allowed him to direct the discussion; their discussion of personal issues was tense and anxious, and they accepted the chairman's report and the instructor's criticisms without challenge.

Stages of Intellectual Development

Jean Piaget, the dean of developmental psychologists, identified four main stages in intellectual development (1962). The sequence of these stages is inviolable; although an average age for each stage can be stated, the age at which each stage is reached will vary with the social and cultural environment of the child: that is, intellectual development can be accelerated or retarded by environmental enrichment or impoverishment.

Sensorimotor stage (birth to two years)

Actions are at first random and reflex, with gradual development of coordination and sense of space. The child reacts at first only to perceptual signs: if a toy is removed from sight, the child is not sure that it still exists. Increasingly the child is able to apply actions to new situations and to experiment with new means to desired ends: for example, by pulling a blanket on which a toy rests. By age one and a half to two, the beginning of memory and planning is evident, as the child invents new means by mental combination; symbolic thought becomes apparent in representational play.

Preoperational stage (two to seven)

The development of language gives great flexibility to intelligence. At first, children center their attention on only one aspect of an object or situation; later they can perceive relationships among parts. At this stage they reason from what they see, not from abstractions. Classification is undeveloped; if shown a bunch of flowers, half of which are daisies, they cannot say whether there are more flowers than daisies. They begin to use space and time and to observe rules of social behavior by age seven, but cannot explain them. From two to four the child's social view is entirely egocentric; from four to seven this gives way to socially directed thought and action.

Stage of concrete operations (seven to twelve)

Ability to classify and serialize, to arrange objects by size, and the concept of reversability develop between about seven and eight. The child's social competence is increased with development of language and an understanding of the relativity of viewpoints. The child is concerned with the actual and characteristically solves problems in terms of direct experiences.

Stage of formal operations (twelve to sixteen)

Preadolescents begin to solve purely verbal problems, to understand the concepts of proportion and reciprocity. They are able to integrate their new intellectual capacities for explanatory purposes. They can manipulate abstract ideas, and they become concerned with the possible rather than the actual. They are idealistic and tend to believe in the omnipotence of thought. The ability to distinguish between what is conceptually possible and what is attainable in fact comes after adolescence as a result of experience in the real world.

A number of studies have used Stern's "inventory of beliefs" to rank students on a "stereopathy scale." Some of the differing preferences between stereopaths and nonstereopaths are shown in Table 10–1, drawn from studies by Stern, Stein, and Bloom (1956) and Gladstein (1960). It is interesting to note that the differences between the two classes of students are also reflected in the differing philosophies of "traditional" and "progressive" education. The characteristics of stereopathic or closed-minded students imply that they suffer from crippling anxiety that limits their capacity for self-fulfilment. This finding suggests that such learners might benefit from school experiences that sought to build up their confidence and make them more autonomous and self-directing.

Considerable recent research has been conducted into an aspect of personality or cognitive style known as *field dependence.* People who are field-dependent tend to perceive and judge objects in relation to their field, or context, whereas field-independent people tend to judge objects on their independent merits. Field-dependent people are relatively more influenced by others' opinion, more affected by criticism; they like to be with people more and like to be physically closer to people. They are

---

STEREOPATHS

Keeping out of trouble at all costs.
Finishing something begun even if no longer enjoyable.
Being given specific rather than general instructions.
Studying science or mathematics.
Attending in class to the instructor rather than to other students.
Recopying notes or memoranda to make them neat.
Memorizing main points from instructor or textbook for final exam.
Being confused when class discussion becomes theoretical.

NONSTEREOPATHS

Disregarding unfair rules and regulations.
Organizing a protest meeting.
Arguing with the instructor or supervisor.
Writing about political and social issues.
Engaging in abstract and theoretical thought and discussion.
Sketching, painting, reading, studying art and music.
Rereading favorite books.
Taking care of youngsters.

Table 10–1   Habits and preferences of stereopaths and nonstereopaths

more popular and better known and are perceived as more warm, considerate, outgoing, and affectionate. They are more likely to study arts, languages, humanities, education, and subjects with human and social content. They prefer discussion as a teaching and learning technique and are more student-oriented. Field-independent people are more impersonal and individualistic and less sensitive to social undercurrents. They are more likely to study math, science, engineering, and architecture. If they become managers, they will work in production rather than personnel; if they enter nursing, they will be successful as surgical rather than as psychiatric nurses. In education they are standard-oriented and prefer lecture and discovery methods. Students perceive field-independent teachers as teaching the application of principles, whereas field-dependent teachers are more likely to be perceived as teaching facts (Witkin et al., 1977).

While some of the implications of the research into cognitive development are relatively straightforward, it is far from clear how instruction should be adapted to match the personality characteristics of learners. A large body of research has been conducted over the past decade in the subject of aptitude-treatment interaction (ATI) and trait-treatment interaction (TTI). After reviewing this research in 1976, Snow commented that "while some ATI findings are plausible and some are replicable, few are well understood and none are yet applicable to instructional practice" (1976, p. 50). Certainly until group instruction ceases to be the norm (and it shows little sign of doing so), the implications of this research seem to be remote. What can be said, however, is this: Almost any group of learners will contain a wide variety of cognitive and personality attributes. Therefore a wide variety of instructional strategies will need to be employed. This idea is explored more fully in the next chapter.

Prerequisites

The specification of prerequisites is problematic. The right to include or exclude students in or from learning experiences can give designers a seductive sense of power and result in decisions that are arbitrary, paternalistic, or ideologically motivated. While there is a wide range of opinion on the place of prerequisites in schooling, it is instructive to look at the two ideological poles of elitism and egalitarianism.

Elitist ideology

Elitist educational institutions set high prerequisites to exclude as many people as possible. The overt intent is to minimize the probability

Classroom in Alaska, 1902

Whenever I enter a school and see a multitude of children, ragged, thin, and dirty but with their clear eyes and sometimes angelic expressions, I am seized with restlessness and terror, as though I saw people drowning.

—*Leo Tolstoy*

that anyone who is admitted will subsequently fail. This is the practice in some West European states where a university education is seen as the privilege of a tiny minority. Selection begins early in a student's career. A series of barriers, mostly in the form of examinations, must be negotiated, ultimately allowing one British or West German student in fifteen or so to enter a university. Not surprisingly, these procedures have the effect of excluding from higher education most students who are not of middle- or upper-class origin. Despite significant expansion of the British university system in the 1950s, the proportion of working-class undergraduates in British universities was no higher in the 1960s than it had been in the 1930s (Robbins, 1965).

> Some college departments feel that by failing a large proportion of their students, they maintain their standards. The reverse is the case. By failing so many, they demonstrate their own incompetence in the selection of students, their incapacity to teach, the invalidity of their methods of assessment, or some combination of these three.
>
> —*Donald Bligh (1975, p. 52)*

The extreme example of elitist educational philosophy in the modern world is found in Japan. The limited number of places in universities has resulted in intense academic pressure all the way down to the age of two, when the Japanese child takes an entrance examination to nursery school. Japanese students in the twelve-to-fifteen age group spend almost nine hours a day after school doing homework and attending the *juku*, a cramming school that drills students for exams. Drucker reports,

> To get into the "right" school requires larger and larger "voluntary contributions." The most expensive school to get into is medical school. A candidate, even if his father is a physician, will have to pay about $100,000 in

Notes Towards the Definition of Elitism

It is now the opinion of some of the most advanced minds that some qualitative differences between individuals must still be recognized, that the superior individuals must be formed into suitable groups, endowed with appropriate powers, and perhaps with varied emoluments and honors. . . . These groups are what we call elites. . . .

It follows from what has been said . . . about classes and elites, that education should help to preserve the class and select the elite. It is right that the exceptional individual should have the opportunity to elevate himself in the social scale and attain a position in which he can exercise his talents to the greatest benefit of himself and of society. But the ideal of an educational system which could automatically sort out everyone according to his native capacities is unattainable in practice; and if we made it our chief aim, would disorganize society, by substituting for classes, elites of brains, or perhaps only of sharp wits. . . . Furthermore, the ideal of a uniform system such that no one capable of receiving higher education could fail to get it, leads imperceptibly to the education of too many people, and consequently to the lowering of standards to whatever this swollen number of candidates is able to reach.

—*T. S. Eliot (1949, pp. 103–104)*

If one accepts the idea that colleges exist in order to *educate*, then the model of selective admissions based on test scores makes little sense. If an institution exists to educate students, then its mission is to produce certain desirable changes in students, or, more simply, to make a difference in the student's life. This kind of "value added" approach to the goals of higher education suggests that admission procedures should be designed to select students who are likely to be *influenced* by the educational process, regardless of the student's entering level of performance. Instead admissions officers in selective institutions function more like race track handicappers: they try merely to pick winners. By looking over the various candidates and evaluating their respective talents, those who are likely to perform well are selected. Handicappers, it should be stressed, are interested only in *predicting* the horse's performance, not in helping it to run better and faster. The problem here is that an educational institution should function not like a handicapper, but like a jockey or trainer: it has the responsibility of improving the performance of the student, not just identifying those with the greatest potential.

—*Alexander W. Astin (1975, p. 17)*

"voluntary gifts" and "voluntary presents" to the faculty members on the admissions committee to have his application even considered (Drucker, 1978)

These circumstances make the high suicide rate among Japanese teenagers all too understandable.

Elitist ideology has deep political, social, philosophical, and emotional roots. It is gratifying to be associated with an academic institution that admits only *la crème de la crème*. The slogan "more means worse" can be used to justify exclusive admissions policies in the interests of "maintaining academic standards." But the logic is basically flawed. The academic standards of an institution are, surely, reflected in the qualities of students as they leave, not as they enter a program. The "best" institutions, Astin suggests (see box), are not those that admit the brightest students and leave them unchanged, but those that add the most to their students' initial qualities.

The ideology of unrestricted access

Egalitarian institutions tend to set low prerequisites to include as many people as possible; the intention is to minimize the probability of excluding any student who might subsequently succeed. In one particularly naive and romantic form, this philosophy leads to the doctrine of unrestricted access to all educational programs.

The effects of this doctrine in operation can be seen in the Italian universities. In 1969 a government edict made all students who completed five years of secondary school eligible to enter any university faculty. A massive increase in enrollments ensued. Contact with professors, which was not an academic requirement, was further reduced by overcrowding; it is estimated that only 10 percent of university students attend lectures. On completion of the degree, the student faces competition with up to one million unemployed university graduates (Moorman, 1978). Prestigious faculties such as medicine have been most affected by swollen enrollments. Training in anatomy is usually confined to noncompulsory demonstrations by television; laboratory experience is a rarity. The medical degree is obtained by passing twenty-seven separate examinations, which if failed may be repeated without limit. Italy currently has proportionately twice as many physicians as the United States, but, as a medical professor at the University of Rome put it, "If I ever get a serious disease, I won't seek treatment in Italy" (Greenberg, 1977).

Just as elitists concentrate on quality of input rather than quality of output, so the extreme egalitarians concentrate on equality of input rather than equality of output. By failing to recognize the need of many students for guidance and remediation, they guarantee subsequent failure and disappointment for many students. The facile abandonment of prerequisites thus defeats its own intent by producing ultimate inequality.

A Rational Principle

Neither elitist nor egalitarian ideology appears to serve the best interests of learners. What is needed is a rational principle governing curriculum prerequisites. As the function of prerequisites is essentially to ensure that the learner can benefit from a program, such a principle may be stated as follows: A prerequisite is valid if it identifies a quality that is necessary for a student either to achieve the objectives of a curriculum or to apply the learning effectively.

To achieve the objectives of the curriculum

A teacher planning a course aimed at fostering appreciation of medieval English verse would be completely justified in requiring applicants to have at least a fifth-grade reading level. The student who could not read at that level would have difficulty in reading a daily newspaper, let alone the work of Chaucer or Langland. The responsible decision is to counsel such a student to enroll in a remedial reading program, on successful completion of which he or she can reapply for the course desired.

No Formal Instruction

An official of St. John's School of Ontario said Wednesday that the 12 St. John's students who drowned on Lake Timiskaming earlier this week received no formal instruction from the school in swimming, life-saving or first aid.

Michael Maunder, the school's assistant headmaster, said in an interview that St. John's does not require students or supervisors to have formal certification in such skills.

The tragedy occurred Sunday when a violent storm on the north-western Quebec lake overturned three of four canoes. A 21-year-old instructor, Mark Denny of Queen's University, also died in the accident.

Maunder said some instructors do have first aid certificates, but they are not a requirement.

Instructors have a demonstrated skill in first aid, assessed by the school to be satisfactory, he added.

Maunder said he was sure that three instructors on the trip were trained in artificial respiration but was not certain about the fourth instructor.

"It's mandatory that there be a man on the trip that knows it," he said.

—Canadian Press Report, June 14, 1978

The safety of the student must also be considered. A color-blind student may run a risk in a course on electrical circuit wiring. It is certainly hazardous to encourage a nonswimmer to participate in a course in sailing or canoeing.

A student who has already attained the objectives of a course will not benefit from taking it. Hence prerequisites may identify maximum as well as minimum prior achievement.

To apply the learning effectively

The long-term effect of a curriculum will depend on a student's experience after, as well as within, a course. A student may achieve the objectives of a program but be unable to apply them in real life and hence realize little benefit. A life insurance company might legitimately make initiative a prerequisite for a sales training program, not because initiative is necessary to succeed in the program, but because it would be necessary to make a successful career in insurance sales.

Effective application of training may require the graduate to have certain human qualities, the absence of which will present a threat to other people. The law student who is unethical, the nurse who is incapable of empathy, the applicant for teacher training who does not like children: unless these characteristics can be changed by training, the admission and professional certification of such people presages unhappiness for others at some later time.

The chief difficulty in identifying personality variables as prerequisites is the problem of valid testing. Psychological tests have been found inadequate in this regard by researchers (Guion, 1967) and by courts in the United States, which have ruled that unless a psychological test has been empirically related to job performance, it cannot be used in employment decisions (Warren, 1976). "Will it stand up in court?" is a necessary criterion for prerequisites, as for many other educational decisions. At the same time, lest educators should conclude that prerequisites are too inflammatory to deal with, they need to remember that a hands-off, laissez-faire policy will probably not stand up in court either.

Types of Prerequisite

Cognitive prerequisites

A cognitive prerequisite identifies some competence, in terms of a knowledge, skill, or other capability, that the applicant must possess. It is essentially an objective to be achieved before rather than during the program. *Ability to read at least the sixth-grade level, Knowledge of basic algebra,* and *Understanding of modern political ideologies* might be general statements of the kind of cognitive prerequisites required for courses in literature, calculus, and Cold War diplomacy, respectively. Curricula can be adapted to the needs of a particular group of learners by reclassifying prerequisites as objectives or vice versa.

The role of cognitive prerequisites in curriculum planning may be expressed by means of a simple formula:

$$a = b - c$$

where

a is what the student is to learn in the program;

b is the capabilities of the learner on completion of the program;

c is the student's capabilities on entry to the program.

COMPETENCE TO BE ACHIEVED

Before training begins   *Before training ends*

prerequisite   objective

Stated in this way, it becomes clear that the student's entering knowledge, ability, and so forth *must* be ascertained if the content and objectives of the curriculum are to be correctly identified. To the degree that there is uncertainty about entering capabilities, the danger will exist of omitting relevant instruction and including redundant material. Bloom reports that "cognitive entry behaviors" are more important than any other factor in determining "the extent to which a specific learning task *can* be learned," accounting for approximately 50 percent of the variation in school achievement (1976, p. 169). Most teachers would agree; they have witnessed the significant effect that basic reading and calculation skills have on almost all school achievement.

Biographical prerequisites

Biographical prerequisites include age, height, and state of health. Age criteria are most commonly a reflection of the conventional but questionable practice of grouping learners by age. Such prerequisites as height probably have more to do with the public image of the police officer or the guardsman than competence to perform the job.

Health criteria may be intended to protect the student or the institution. Programs requiring rigorous physical exertion may require a medical certificate of health or at least a waiver from the parents or the learner. It is some reassurance to know that the mountaineer above you on the rope is not an incipient heart attack victim. Normal vision, hearing, or mobility may be required for the attainment or application of certain objectives. The United States Congress passed the Education for All Handicapped Children Act in 1975, committing substantial resources to the accurate detection of handicaps that interfere with learning, as well as to special educational provision for the handicapped. Particular care needs to be exercised in regard to these students to ensure that any prerequisites imposed are in the interests of the learners and those with whom they interact, and not based on outmoded assumptions or prejudices.

Academic prerequisites

A third kind of prerequisite is academic or programmatic. It identifies a course or program that the applicant must have completed, often with a stipulated level of achievement. The kind of statement commonly found in school and college calendars is: *Sociology 202: Prerequisite, Sociology 102 with at least a B standing.* This prerequisite is valid if both of the following conditions obtain: (1) all those students who have completed Sociology 102 with at least a B standing will be able to master the objectives of Sociology 202; and (2) only those who have completed Sociology 102 with at least a B standing will be able to master the objectives of Sociology 202. Since it is rare that both of these conditions do obtain, the prerequisite often reads: *Sociology 202: Prerequisite, Sociology 102 with at least a B standing, or approval of the instructor.*

The point that needs to be made here is this: if one program teaches learnings that are prerequisite to another program, it is in principle better to identify and require those learnings than merely to name the course. For example, most employers, when seeking a competent typist, prefer to administer a typing test to applicants rather than place sole reliance on grades earned in secretarial courses completed by the applicants. This is not to say that a course can never be assumed to be a satisfactory surrogate for a cognitive prerequisite, only that considerable caution is needed in making this assumption.

Further light is thrown on academic prerequisites by research comparing such attainments with subsequent professional achievement. In many areas, including medicine (Bartlett, 1967), teaching (Crocker, 1974),

---

On the Predictive Value of Academic Prerequisites

Sir Richard Burton, foremost Arabist of his day, who learned forty languages, was expelled from Oxford University.

Charles Darwin, naturalist, dropped out of both medical and theological school.

Thomas Edison, inventor of the electric light and holder of over one thousand patents, had a total of three months of formal schooling.

Albert Einstein, physicist, failed in his first attempt to gain admission to the Zurich Polytechnic.

A. E. Housman, poet and professor of Latin at Cambridge, failed his final examinations in Classics at Oxford University.

Christopher Isherwood, writer and professor of English, failed his final examinations in English at Oxford.

Gregor Mendel, the founder of modern genetics, twice failed the examination in Vienna to qualify as a teacher.

Auguste Rodin, sculptor, failed three times to gain admission to art school in Paris.

W. M. Thackeray, novelist, left Cambridge University without a degree.

Leo Tolstoy, novelist, dropped out of the University of Kazan.

Werner von Braun, rocket scientist, failed high-school mathematics and physics.

W. B. Yeats, poet and leading figure in Irish cultural life, failed to gain admission to Trinity College, Dublin.

Emile Zola, novelist, scored zero in literature at his lycée in Paris.

science (Hudson, 1960) and engineering (Pym, 1969), academic attainments have proved extremely weak predictors of professional and career success. The prediction is even less reliable (and therefore implicitly discriminatory) in the case of ethnic minorities (Haney, Michael, and Martois, 1976). Summarizing the research in 1965, Hoyt concluded that "the present evidence strongly suggests that college grades show little or no relationship to any measures of adult accomplishments."

An alternative to the conventional courses and grades as admissions criteria is "documented accomplishments" (Baird, 1978). As art schools generally recognize, a portfolio of drawings provides more useful evidence to the admissions committee than grades in high-school art courses. Documentary evidence of experiences in working with children is likely to be more valuable than undergraduate grade-point average in the selection of candidates for graduate teacher training. These examples are more straightforward than the questions confronting the educator planning a course in philosophy or social science who regards "ability to grapple with abstract concepts" as a prerequisite to success in the course. No single measure would be likely to provide a valid index of this ability, but it is possible that a combination of previous achievement in related areas, submission of writing on abstract issues, and a structured interview could provide sufficient evidence to make a judgment.

Competitive Admission

A complex problem arises when the number of applicants who meet the minimum prerequisites for a course or program exceeds the available places. One solution is to introduce additional criteria. A typical case was that of civil pilot training in the 1960s. Prior to about 1964, United States Air Force pilots could expect little difficulty, on return to civilian life, in being accepted for pilot training by civil airlines. As the Vietnam War began to produce increasing numbers of pilots, the airlines were able first to restrict admissions to bomber pilots, and later to bomber pilots who possessed degrees in engineering. Even then, they had many more applications than they could accept.

In such situations, institutions adopt various practices. They may increase the number of places to accommodate all qualified applicants. In vocationally oriented programs, however, unless the number of job opportunities also increases, increasing places merely postpones selection to the hiring stage and means that many graduates, after the effort and expense of training, are unable to find suitable employment. Or the institution may choose some random method of selection such as lottery or date of application, which has the appearance of impartiality, although not of rationality. Or increasing reliance may be placed on recommendations and letters of reference, which effectively passes responsibility to people outside the institution and gives a competitive advantage to those applicants most successful in eliciting effusive praise from prestigious people. Or the institution may raise requirements on the irrelevant but politically safe criterion of academic scores.

Most controversial is the use of criteria recognized as irrelevant to subsequent success, but considered to have social utility on other grounds. An example is giving preference to applicants from minority groups or deprived backgrounds. The arguments that this issue raises are too intricate and numerous to be recited here. Suffice it to say that in the cases of *Defunis* and *Bakke,* the United States Supreme Court itself had considerable difficulty in arriving at a clear and unanimous statement of principle.

Insofar as the issue of competitive admission can be simplified at all, it may be viewed as a problem of balancing benefits among individuals, social groups, and the community at large. As with any issue involving the allocation of scarce resources, the best policies seem to be those that can be justified on the basis of solid evidence.

The Onus of Proof

A school cannot discharge its responsibility by ignoring or abandoning prerequisites, by declaring the curriculum open to all, and by failing to advise students of the probable consequences of their curriculum choices. On the other hand, all proposed prerequisites must be subject to close scrutiny. The long and still unfinished history of discrimination against women aspiring to enter the professions—to take a single example— shows how powerful are prerequisites that have no justification beyond tradition and prejudice.

In a society that values equality of opportunity, it is the exclusive rather than the inclusive decision that requires special justification. The onus of proof therefore rests with the instructor or designer who specifies a prerequisite. A prerequisite unsupported by sound logical argument or empirical evidence should be regarded as suspect. Even a justified prerequisite is better seen as a basis for advising students rather than pro-

---

All the errors which a man is likely to commit against advice and warning are far outweighed by the evil of allowing others to constrain him to what they deem is good.

—Isaiah Berlin, political philosopher

hibiting them from a particular course. There is merit in allowing highly motivated and persistent students to enter programs for which they lack the prerequisites. Their subsequent degree of success will provide useful evidence on the validity of the prerequisites.

Pretests

Not all curricula require prerequisites, nor do all curricula require pretests. Where pretests are appropriate, their design constitutes the third main function in the identification of the entry characteristics of learners (Figure 10–1).

Figure 10–1   Defining entry characteristics of learners

Pretests are used to ascertain the status of students prior to instruction. They may perform one or more of five specific functions: (1) to identify students who lack prerequisites; (2) to identify students who have already attained the objectives; (3) to provide a baseline with which ultimate performance may be compared; (4) to indicate the students' present level of attainment; and (5) to provide the student with an overview of the course.

Identifying students who lack prerequisites

If this is one function of a pretest, the test must be administered soon enough for the student to make alternative choices or to remediate deficiencies in time to enter the course. This part of the pretest must meet all the requirements of a sound test discussed previously.

The pretest may reveal that all or most of the applicants lack the prerequisites, with the result that there are too few qualified students to constitute a class. If applicants are deficient in learned capabilities, one of the following courses of action may be taken:

1. Convert the prerequisites into objectives and omit some of the planned objectives of the course; i.e., lower the overall level of the course.

2. Offer a remedial program prior to commencement of the course.

3. Postpone the course, directing students in the meantime into preparatory courses.

4. Readvertise the course and rerun the pretest in the hope of obtaining a sufficient number of qualified applicants.

5. Change the prerequisites to corequisites, to be attained by fixed points before the end of the course.

6. Cancel the course.

Identifying students who have already attained the objectives

If there is a possibility that students who have mastered the objectives will apply for the course, the pretest should contain a sampling of items like those used in posttests. A student who performs well on these items can be invited to take the full posttest. Some universities have adopted this approach, sometimes known as "challenge for credit" (*University Affairs,* 1976) or "curriculum of attainments" (Harris, 1975). A student may request assessment of his or her competence before embarking on a course. If successful, the student is excused from further requirements and granted credit for the course in question.

Credit tends to be the crucial question. Luis Gonzaga, fourteen years old, arrives from Mexico. He has had eight years of schooling, but in terms of demonstrated proficiency in Spanish, he is ready for the twelfth-grade level. He might well be encouraged to embark on twelfth-grade Spanish, but will he be given credit for ninth- , tenth- , and eleventh-

"What with the primary mental ability test and the differential aptitude tests and the reading readiness test and the basic skills test and the I.Q. test and the sequential tests of educational progress and the mental maturity test, we haven't been learning anything at school."

Pretests

Dr. DeMere was an unusual figure in Memphis. A wiry, energetic man in his fifties, he had been medical aide to General Patton in World War II. He was a plastic surgeon with an international reputation, a professor of law at Memphis State University Law School, medical director of the Shelby County Sheriff's department, a trained police officer, and a redoubtable long-distance runner. For a number of years Sheriff Morris had required all candidates for the Sheriff's Reserves to run the mile against Dr. DeMere and accepted only those who outran him.

—Gerold Frank (1972, p. 225)

"They were Sherif Ali ibn el Hussein of Modhig, and his cousin, Sherif Mohsin, Lords of the Harith. . . . Ali is a devil. . . . He was with our Lord Feisal from the first day's battle in Medina, and led the Ateiba in the plains round Aar and Bir Derwish. It was all camel fighting; and Ali would have no man with him who could not do as he did, run beside his camel, and leap with one hand into the saddle, carrying his rifle. The children of Harith are children of battle."

—T. E. Lawrence (1940, p. 83)

grade Spanish, which he never took? The answer will depend on whether the school operates on a competency model or a residence model. The competency model awards qualifications on the basis of demonstrated accomplishments. The residence model awards qualifications on the basis of physical location over a period of time. Drivers' licenses, music diplomas, and life-saving medals are certificates of competence. Many school graduation diplomas and university degrees remain essentially certificates of residence.

Valid pretesting might provide an antidote to the local and national chauvinism that so often works to the disadvantage of students and professionals who emigrate across jurisdictional boundaries. The dentists who fled to North America from Hungary in 1956 were obliged in a number of jurisdictions to repeat their entire professional training to be licensed to practice. Such requirements suggest either a lack of confidence in existing examinations to assess professional competence, or undue weight being given to considerations other than those of proficiency.

Providing a baseline

Instructors are usually satisfied if the average achievement of their students at the end of a course is above 70 or 80 percent. But the attempt to measure the initial level of achievement is rarely made, and there is therefore no evidence of improvement. Pretesting provides a basis for comparison.

When pretests are used for this purpose, the items used for comparison must be equivalent to the posttest items. In the case of objective tests of knowledge and cognitive skills, it is best to design both pretests and posttests before the course begins and ensure equivalence by parallel development or random selection of items. On the other hand, the items on the two tests must be sufficiently different that the posttest does not become simply a measure of the students' ability to remember the answers to items on the pretest.

Indicating the students' present level

It is helpful for a teacher to be aware of the level of knowledge and skill in a class. A pretest may give more exact information than will emerge incidentally in the course of instruction. Teaching either above or below the students' level will be inefficient and unpopular. In some subjects it is occasionally safe to assume a complete lack of knowledge on the part of students. An experienced teacher can often predict fairly exactly the initial level of a class, but the amount of redundancy in school instruction suggests that pretesting could be usefully increased for this purpose.

It is also valuable for the students to know their level of knowledge or skill in the subject to be taught. The process of pretesting itself apprises students of the instructor's concern to meet their learning needs as closely as possible.

Providing an overview

The cliché that is anecdotally used to describe effective preaching—"First you tell them what you're going to tell them. Then you tell them. Then you tell them what you've told them"—has more than a little application to effective teaching.

Ausubel found in a number of experiments that providing students with an "advance organizer" of what was to be learned facilitated the learning by enabling students to relate new material to already established ideas (1962). A recent survey of thirty-two studies indicated that in twelve cases advance organizers helped learning and in twenty cases made little or no difference (Barnes and Clawson, 1975). A conservative conclusion is that advance organizers rarely do harm and sometimes do good.

To function as advance organizers, pretest questions should relate, at a general level, content to be learned to the student's existing knowledge. In practice most pretests are, in Ausubel's terms, overviews rather than advance organizers (Ausubel, 1978). However, research evidence indicates that, as overviews, "conceptual prequestions" share with advance organizers the potential to increase subsequent learning and recall (Rickards, 1976). In a pretest the overview is presented in the same form as the posttest, and hence focuses sharply on the expected terminal competence. The value of the exercise can be enhanced by providing students with detailed "knowledge of results" after they have completed the pretest (Hartley and Davies, 1976).

Formal Knowledge and Personal Acquaintance

Rather formal processes of establishing the background characteristics of learners have been discussed in this chapter. But this is only part of a more holistic approach. Learn about your students: this is the essential message for both instructors and curriculum designers. I share with many teachers the experience of having confident assessments of student abilities turn out to be false upon personal acquaintance. The teenager whose progress is halting in class turns out to be handling a 5 A.M. paper route to augment a small family income. The child who appears to be making little effort is doing five hours of homework each evening. The student whose spelling is erratic speaks three languages fluently. Both parents of the adolescent who is silent in class are patients in the local psychiatric hospital.

Effective instruction requires an understanding of the learners: a knowledge of their homes, their families, their places of part-time employment, their social groups, their previous classrooms. Teachers need to appreciate students' experiences, attitudes, hopes and fears, prejudices and ideals, and to build bridges between these dimensions of their lives and the content of instruction. Knowing students formally is a necessary part of this appreciation; knowing them personally not only enlarges this insight, but contributes to a rewarding professional life.

ACTIVITIES

1. Study a class of students with whom you work. Write a description of them in sufficient detail to guide a teacher who will shortly be taking the class over from you.

2. Analyze the concepts and themes dealt with in a curriculum or textbook designed for students from ten to thirteen. How suitable is it for students who will mostly be at the stage of concrete operations?

3. Specify the prerequisites you would consider most appropriate for the following: (a) admission to kindergarten; (b) admission to a training program for preschool teachers; (c) employment as a police officer; (d) licensing as a hunting guide; (e) nomination to elected political office at the national level.

4. Consider the following facts: (a) Several medical schools that have admitted experimental groups of students who lack the usual academic prerequisites but have strong personal qualities and motivation have found no significant differences between their achievement and that of regular students in or after medical school; (b) In a number of developing countries, paramedics are being trained in a few months to perform almost all the procedures normally conducted by fully trained physicians; (c) Frank Demara, the "Great Imposter," practiced successfully as a naval surgeon during the Korean War, although he had only a tenth-grade education. What implications, if any, do these facts have for the prerequisites for admission to medical school and to the practice of medicine?

5. A city characterized by high unemployment, especially among unskilled and minority workers, and low educational achievement in downtown schools, advertises a work-training program for 500 people who will be paid a salary while they train as teacher aides. Five thousand people apply, including downtown and suburban residents, from all educational, social, and income levels, and from both majority and minority racial groups. How would you select the 500 for the program?

6. Think back to your secondary-school and college education. If it had been possible for you to "pretest out" of courses and programs, (a) in which programs, if any, would you have done so? (b) why? (or why not?); and (c) how would you have used the time saved?

QUESTIONS

1. Which kind of information is least likely to be appropriate in a description of learners?

   a. native language
   b. racial or ethnic origin
   c. background in the subject
   d. aptitude in the field of learning

2. A literature course is designed that will follow the theme of fate versus free will from Sophocles to Thomas Hardy. To be able to handle the intellectual content of the course, students will need to have reached

   a. the sensorimotor stage
   b. the preoperational stage
   c. the stage of formal operations
   d. the stage of concrete operations

3. We could anticipate that students classified as stereopaths or as closed-minded would have greatest preference for

a. student-led seminars
b. open-ended discussion
c. self-directed learning
d. the lecture method of instruction

4. A prerequisite for admission to a job or professional training program is legitimate if

a. it predicts success in training or on the job
b. it is based on valid and reliable test results
c. it is accepted by the professional organization
d. it does not include racial, ethnic, or religious qualifications

5. If it is critical that workers in a profession have certain attitudes, and if these attitudes cannot be reliably developed in training or in professional practice, then it would be best to

a. abandon the attitude criteria
b. apply the criteria at the licensing stage
c. make the attitudes prerequisite to training
d. exclude people from the profession who do not develop these attitudes within five years of commencing practice

6. A program in advanced conversational French is designed. Which of the following is a *cognitive* prerequisite?

a. students must have spent at least three weeks in France
b. students must have completed introductory conversational French
c. students must have a speaking vocabulary of at least 500 words
d. students must have maintained at least a B average in French for at least two years

7. A training course for prospective tour guides in Europe is being developed. Which of the following is the most valid prerequisite?

a. born and brought up in Europe
b. no physical or medical disabilities
c. a university degree in history, geography, or languages
d. near fluency in at least two European languages in addition to English

8. Which of the following is in principle the most appropriate prerequisite for admission to nursing training?

a. the applicant likes people
b. the applicant has a strong background in psychology
c. the applicant has a good knowledge of human anatomy
d. the applicant has an 85 percent minimum in twelfth-grade biology and chemistry

9. Pretesting for prior achievement will be most likely to benefit students if

a. there are adequate remedial programs
b. students are grouped on the basis of age

    c.   there is strict adherence to academic prerequisites

    d.   there is provision to adapt instruction to the entry characteristics of learners

10. Which of the following objectives commits the designer or instructor to pretesting?

    a.   the student will be able to swim under water

    b.   the student will improve his or her golf handicap

    c.   the student will know the rules and etiquette of squash

    d.   the student will master the basic technique of the forehand smash

Check your answers against the key in Appendix 2.
9 or 10 right: You understand the material presented.
8 or 7 right: Review the areas of uncertainty
6 or less right: Reread the chapter.

Recommended Reading

Ausubel, David P. *Educational psychology: A cognitive view*. New York: Holt, Rinehart, & Winston, 1968. In this major work, Ausubel discusses many factors affecting learning. Particularly valuable for its treatment of the significance of background variables.

Cronbach, Lee J., and R. E. Snow. *Aptitudes and instructional methods*. New York: Irvington, 1977. A comprehensive report on the state of the art of aptitude-treatment interaction research and its educational implications.

Hunt, David E., and Edmund V. Sullivan. *Between psychology and education*. New York: Holt, Rinehart, & Winston, 1974. A useful review of the theories of major psychologists and their application to education. Contains a concise summary of theories of cognitive development and of Hunt's model of conceptual level.

References

Astin, Alexander W. The myth of equal access in public higher education. Paper presented at the Conference on Equality of Access in Post Secondary Education, Atlanta, Georgia, July 1975.

Ausubel, D. P. Organizer, general background, and antecedent learning variables in sequential verbal learning. *Journal of Educational Psychology*, 1962, 53, 243–249.

――――. *Educational psychology: A cognitive view*. New York: Holt, Rinehart & Winston, 1968.

――――. In defence of advance organizers: A reply to the critics. *Review of Educational Research*, 1978, 48, 251–257.

Baird, Leonard L. Using data on documented accomplishments as an alternative to tests. Paper presented at the Annual Meeting of the American Educational Research Association, Toronto, March 1978.

Barnes, Buckley, R., and E. U. Clawson. Do advance organizers facilitate learning?

Recommendations for further research based on an analysis of 32 studies. *Review of Educational Research*, 1975, 45, 637–659.

Bartlett, J. W. Medical school and career performances of medical school students with low Medical College Admission Tests scores. *Journal of Medical Education*, 1967, 42, 231–237.

Bereiter, Carl E. SMPY in social perspective. In Daniel P. Keating (ed.), *Intellectual talent: Research and development*. Baltimore: Johns Hopkins University Press, 1976, pp. 308–315.

Bligh, Donald, G. J. Ebrahim, David Jaques, and D. Warren Piper. *Teaching students*. Exeter, England: Exeter University Teaching Services, 1975.

Bloom, Benjamin S. *Human characteristics and school learning*. New York: McGraw-Hill, 1976.

Burstall, Clare. *Primary French in the balance*. London: National Foundation for Educational Research, 1974.

Crocker, A. C. *Predicting teaching success*. London: National Foundation for Educational Research, 1974.

Drucker, Peter F. Japan: The dilemma of over-education. *Manchester Guardian Weekly*, June 4, 1978, p. 9.

Eliot, T. S. *Notes towards the definition of culture*. New York: Harcourt Brace, 1949.

Frank, Gerold. *An American death*. New York: Doubleday, 1972.

Gladstein, G. A. Study behavior of gifted stereotyped and nonstereotyped college students. *Personnel Guidance Journal*, 1960, 38, 470–474.

Greenberg, David S. The ruinous plight of Italy's universities. *Canadian Association of University Teachers Bulletin*, 1977, 25 (1), 3.

Guion, R. M. Personnel selection. *Annual Review of Psychology*, 1967, 18, 191–216.

Haney, Russell, William B. Michael, and John Martois. The prediction of success of three ethnic groups in the academic components of a nursing training program at a large metropolitan hospital. *Educational and Psychological Measurement*, 1976, 36, 421–431.

Harris, John. Reasons for the curriculum of attainments. Paper presented at the Annual Meeting of the American Educational Research Association, Washington, D.C., April 1975.

Hartley, James S., and Ivor K. Davies. Preinstructional strategies: Role of pretests, behavioral objectives, overviews and advance organizers. *Review of Educational Research*, 1976, 46, 239–265.

Hoyt, D. P. *The relationship between college grades and adult achievement*. Iowa: American College Testing Program, 1965.

Hudson, Liam. Degree class and attainment in scientific research. *British Journal of Psychology*, 1960, 51, 67–73.

Johnson, James R. Development and implementation of a competency-based teacher education module. Paper presented at the Annual Meeting of the American Educational Research Association, Chicago, April 1974.

Kohlberg, Lawrence (ed.). *Collected papers on moral development and moral education*. Cambridge, Mass.: Harvard University Press, 1973.

Lawrence, T. E. *Seven pillars of wisdom*. London: Cape, 1940.

Moorman, Paul. In Italy universities are one centre of ideological conflict. *University Affairs*, 1978, 19 (5), 32.

Piaget, Jean. The stages of the intellectual development of the child. *Bulletin of the Menninger Clinic*, 1962, 26, 120–128.

Pym, D. Education and the employment opportunities of engineers. *British Journal of Industrial Relations*, 1969, 7, 42–51.

Rickards, John P. Interaction of position and conceptual level of adjunct questions on immediate and delayed retention of text. *Journal of Educational Psychology*, 1976, 68, 210–217.

Robbins, Lord (chairman). Committee on Higher Education. *Report*. London: Her Majesty's Stationery Office, 1965.

Snow, R. E., J. Tiffin, and W. F. Seibert. Individual differences and instructional effects. *Journal of Educational Psychology*, 1965, 56, 315–326.

Snow, R. E. Research on aptitude for learning: A progress report. In Lee S. Shulman (ed.), *Review of research in education 4*. Itasca, Ill.: Peacock and American Educational Research Association, 1976, pp. 50–105.

Stern, G. G., M. I. Stein, and B. S. Bloom. *Methods in personality assessment*. Glencoe, Ill.: Free Press, 1956.

University Affairs, October 1976, p. 12. Carleton adopts "Challenge for credit."

Warren, Jim. The Supreme Court looks at testing for employment. *Educational Research*, 1976, 5 (5), 8–9.

Witkin, H. A., C. A. Moore, D. R. Goodenough, and P. W. Cox. Field-dependent and field-independent cognitive styles and their educational implications. *Review of Educational Research*, 1977, 47, 1–64.

Zagona, S. V., and L. A. Zurcher. Participation, interaction, and role behavior in groups selected from the extremes of the open-closed cognitive continuum. *Journal of Educational Psychology*, 1964, 58, 255–264.

11

PRINCIPLES

- The selection of instructional strategies is the area of curriculum requiring least prescription from the curriculum designer.

- In the selection of appropriate instructional strategies, a wide variety of alternatives should be considered.

- General principles for instruction indicate the importance of motivation, prerequisites, directed attention, presentation, and practice.

- Knowledge is taught primarily by presentation; retention can be enhanced by variety of questions and examples.

- The three stages of skill development—cognition, fixation, and automation—require strategies of presentation, practice, and overtraining.

- Exercise, environment, and acquisition of habit can aid physical development.

- Dispositions can be developed by information, reinforcement, modeling, and involvement.

- Experiences may be provided at direct, simulated, and vicarious levels.

CONCEPTS

Computer-based instruction (CBI)	Team competition	Overtraining
	Guided practice	Modeling
Intrinsic motivation	Drill	Reinforcement
Extrinsic motivation	Rote learning	Simulation

11

Selecting Instructional Strategies

Teaching is not a lost art, but the regard for it is a lost tradition.

—*Jacques Barzun, historian*

The Role of the Teacher

The relationship between the curriculum developer and the teacher is a partnership. In many phases of curriculum design, the initiative rests with the curriculum developer. But when it comes to selecting instructional strategies, the teacher is the primary decision-maker. There are two main reasons for this.

First, teachers traditionally regard decisions about the ways in which they interact with their students as being their prerogative. This is the aspect of their work with which they tend to feel most competent and comfortable, and they are usually prepared to accept responsibility for the decisions they make in this area. Teacher autonomy over the nature of classroom interaction, the selection of learning activities, and the pacing of instruction is generally recognized. It would seem to follow that the attempt to prescribe specific teaching strategies in a curriculum developed outside the classroom would at best be futile, and at worst be rejected as a trespass on professional territory.

Second, decades of research have produced few general principles governing the choice of instructional strategies. To a significant degree, issues of teaching method can be usefully decided only at the classroom level, where one can be sure that they are appropriate for the particular learners and particular objectives. Curriculum developers might therefore be wise to capitalize on the advantageous position of teachers and allow them to control instructional strategy. At the same time, teachers may welcome nonprescriptive approaches to instruction that are especially creative or effective.

Harnischfeger and Wiley (1976) define the role of the teacher relative to the curriculum and to the learner in the diagram shown in Figure 11–1. The diagram indicates that pupil pursuits, not teacher activities, most directly affect learning:

> All influences on pupil achievement must be mediated through a pupil's pursuits. No one can gain knowledge or take up new ways of thinking, believing, acting, or feeling except through seeing, looking and watching, hearing and listening, feeling and touching. These control what and how one learns. Less proximal influences, whether as general as the district curriculum and policy and the school organization or as idiosyncratic as a given teacher's education, personality, planning, and activities, directly control and condition these pursuits, and not the student's ultimate achievement (Harnischfeger and Wiley, 1976, p. 11).

This model serves as a useful reminder of the many factors that intervene between the curriculum and pupils' learning.

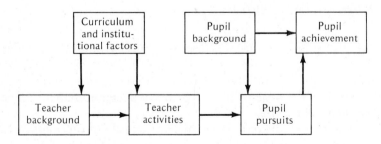

Figure 11–1   Determinants of pupil achievement (Adapted from Harnischfeger and Wiley, 1976, p. 11)

Individual and Group Instruction

Research on human learning has found that learning is highly idiosyn-cratic. Different people learn best in different ways; an instructional strategy that helps one student may have little value for another. While this may seem to be stating the obvious, what is known of classroom practice over the past three thousand years suggests that the principle had little effect on teaching styles before the twentieth century. "Individualized instruction" became a major theme of educational in-novation in the 1960s. Some notable advances were made, particularly in individualized programs in such areas as reading in the early grades. But, in general, group instruction remained the norm. It has persisted for many reasons, three of which may be noted.

Some proponents of individualized instruction tended to exaggerate the distinction between teaching groups and teaching individuals. The typical classroom teacher is not an automaton. In a group situation, teachers adapt their instruction in response to students with great fre-quency—according to Hunt (1976), an average of a hundred times per hour. The skillful teacher directs and monitors the learning of individuals and can respond to different learning problems and preferred learning styles even when a group of students are all apparently engaged in the same activity. As teachers develop such skills, they have less need to establish formally individualized, or tutorial, modes.

A second inhibition to the development of individualized instruction is theoretical. The knowledge we now possess about the ways of teaching that are most suitable for individual learners with differing characteris-tics is rudimentary. Snow, as we saw in the previous chapter, went so far as to say of the aptitude-treatment interaction findings that "few are well understood and none are yet applicable to instructional practice" (1976, p. 50). Although much of the research is promising, there is not yet sufficient field-tested evidence to allow educators to assign individual learners to specialized instructional treatments with a great deal of con-fidence.

The third and probably the decisive reason why individualized in-struction is unlikely to become the norm within the foreseeable future is the amount of resources it requires. Almost any system of individual-ization calls for a substantial expansion of teaching resources that, al-though it may increase effectiveness, shows up as a net increment in educational costs. Under existing economic circumstances, such in-creased expenditures are unlikely.

At present, therefore, curriculum developers can realistically assume that group instruction will continue to be the normal pattern of teaching. One important exception that bears mentioning is computer-assisted, or computer-based, instruction.

Computer-based instruction

Computer-based instruction (CBI) is a lineal descendant of programmed learning but more flexible than many of the early programmed learning materials. CBI is capable of great variety and considerable adaptation to the individual learner. It is not an alternative to human instruction, but a type of human instruction; the student working at a CBI terminal is not interacting with a machine any more than a student reading a book is interacting with paper. He or she is interacting, via the computer, with the expert teachers, subject specialists, and programmers who designed the program. And in fact users can communicate directly through some systems with the program authors and with other students using the system in different parts of the world.

Current CBI programs can operate in modes of presentation, practice and drill, tutorial, inquiry, dialogue, simulation, and problem solving. They can use writing, speech, and audio communication; graphics, slides, animation, and film. The computer can continuously scan the learner's record to determine the appropriate content. It addresses the student by name, has endless patience, and continually reinforces the student's progress by confirmation of responses, verbal praise, or even the sound of applause or a peal of bells. CBI programs can operate twenty-four hours

Children working at CBI terminals

a day, over great distances, teaching several hundred students at once with a response time of less than a second and maintaining complete records on every student. When used with large numbers, the software is inexpensive; and the hardware is becoming so cheap that within a few years the ordinary home will be able to afford its own system. CBI is being used successfully to help teach subjects from reading to Swahili, from genetics to music. Although it is not yet entirely clear how far personality type predisposes certain students to learn from CBI more effectively than others, the overall effects are encouraging; on average, students appear to learn faster from CBI than from most other kinds of instruction (Edwards et al., 1975). Not least important, it is enthusiastically received by learners (Hess and Tenezakis, 1973).

CBI is not a single method, but a system that utilizes many different strategies. It is not a panacea; it is not appropriate for all kinds of learning; and it is not a potential replacement for the classroom teacher. What CBI makes possible is individual instruction for particular learners and parts of the curriculum for which it is a useful alternative or adjunct to group instruction. By assuming some instructional and management tasks such as providing drill and practice, CBI can free the teacher to concentrate on those activities in which direct human contact is more appropriate. In thinking about instructional strategies, then, computer-based instruction is one possibility that cannot properly be ignored.

The Value of Variety

In making instructional decisions, teachers tend to rely heavily on their past experience (Leithwood et al., 1978). The style of beginning teachers is strongly influenced by the way in which they themselves were taught in school. In some cases a role model in the person of an experienced colleague working at the same level is also a powerful influence (Newberry, 1979). After their first year, teachers tend to rely on their experience the previous year. Subject matter may be largely determined by the official course of study, by the content of external tests, or by authorized textbooks. In a study of several hundred social-studies classrooms in Canada, Hodgetts (1968) discovered that the main teaching method of the great majority of teachers was to recite or ask questions from the text. A survey of three hundred teachers of economics in Britain found that the teachers viewed economics textbooks both as their major source of content and as one of the main influences on their teaching methods (Taylor, Holley, and Sretzer, 1974). Major American studies (Hughes, 1959; Goodlad and Klein, 1970) have similarly found that a large proportion of teaching time in schools is consumed by a small number of traditional techniques, including heavy reliance on textbooks, teacher narration, and questioning.

This restrictiveness is not due to a paucity of possible teaching styles. Joyce has identified "more than eighty distinct models of teaching, each grounded in a rationale or theory and clearly enough defined to be of practical use" (1978, p. 4). One is bound to conclude that the methods teachers use are chosen on the basis of familiarity rather than as a result of review of the possibilities. But such review is central to the concept of planning, defined by Novick of Rand Corporation as "the production of a range of meaningful potentials for selection of courses of action through a systematic consideration of alternatives" (1968, p. 269).

At a more mundane level than Joyce's models of teaching, Table 11–1 lists more than 150 teaching methods and resources. Many of these items are materials or devices, but in each case they imply a particular range of instructional approaches. This by no means exhausts the possibilities. Within the item "community," for example, Wurman (1972) lists an entire Yellow Pages of resources, from airport to cemetery to junk yard to zoo. Twenty minutes of brainstorming by a group of teachers will produce a hundred or more ways of using almost any item in the list. Consider the humble newspaper, often available to schools in quantity at half price, and the curriculum areas it can serve: students can write captions for untitled pictures; list the figures of speech on the editorial page; plan a cruise based on the travel section; write foreign-language headlines for news items; roll newspapers into tubes and build abstract sculptures; graph population trends from the birth and death announcements; calculate the depreciation rate on automobiles; try out published recipes; and estimate the number of trees needed to produce one edition.

A teacher planning a lesson could do worse than to work through the list looking for ways to achieve a specific objective. What strategies, for example, might be appropriate to teach pupils *To understand the place of insects in the biological environment?* An aquarium . . . collection . . . diagram . . . exhibit . . . field research . . . microscope . . . motion picture . . . museum . . . and so on. From this wide range of possibilities a short list can be selected that will surely have greater potential than the standard half-dozen techniques normally used.

Why, it may be asked, is it better to use a variety of instructional strategies than to concentrate on the few best methods? The answer is that there is no "best" method. The research conducted until now does not justify dogmatic advocacy of particular strategies. When the overall effect of different instructional techniques (excepting CBI) is compared, the rule of "no significant differences" almost invariably applies (Walker and Schaffarzick, 1974). At most we have particular strategies that are better than others for particular students and types of learning. Until such time as specific instructional approaches can be provided to specific students on the basis of accurate diagnosis of their optimal learning styles, most teachers will be faced with a great variety of learners. Teachers who select only those methods they find congenial may unwittingly

album	drama	mock trial	research paper
anecdote	drawing	model	role playing
apprenticeship	drill	modeling	sandtable
aquarium	electric map	montage	scrapbook
artifact	essay	motion picture	sculpture
audio record	exercise	movie photography	seminar
book	exhibit	mural	silkscreen
brainstorming	experiment	museum	simulation
bulletin board	facsimile	music	sketch
card game	feel bag	newspaper	slide transparency
cartoon	feltboard	notebook	song
case study	field research		source material
chalkboard	field trip	opaque projection	sports
charade	filmstrip	outdoors	stamps and coins
chart	flashcards	overhead transparency	sticker book
chip talk	flow chart	painting	story
club	game	pamphlet	student lecture
collage	globe	panel	survey
collection	group project	pantomime	tachistoscope
coloring book	guest	parents	task cards
comic book	hand calculator	participant	teacher
community	holograph	observation	teacher aide
competition	imitation	pegboard	team competition
computer	improvisation	photography	team teaching
computer-based	interview	play	telephone
instruction	jigsaw	poem	telescope
cooking	kit	poster	television
correspondence	laboratory	printing press	terrarium
crossword	language master	problem	test
cutout	lecture	programmed	textbook
dance	library	instruction	time-lapse
data sheet	magazine	project	photography
debate	magnetic board	psychodrama	toy
demonstration	map	puppets	treasure hunt
design	microfilm	puzzle	tutorial
diagram	microfragrance	questionnaire	typewriter
dial-a-lecture	microscope	quiz	videotape
dialogue	mnemonic	quotation	vivarium
diary	mobile	radio	word game
diorama		real-life experience	workbook
discussion		replica	

Table 11–1 Some learning resources and teaching methods

discriminate against students whose personalities or cognitive attributes differ from their own. The appropriate response to learner variety is instructional variety. This dictum does not imply a random selection of methods, but choice of a wide range of strategies, guided by the nature of the objectives and by the few basic principles that research supports.

"Actually this is a very experimental college. We have no curriculum and no classes. How it works, essentially, is if you want to learn something, you go someplace and you learn it."

General Principles

A few instructional principles seem to apply almost universally. The International Study of Educational Achievement suggested that characteristics of effective teaching that applied across situations and cultures included structuring and organization (as against disorganization) of teaching; clarity of communication; and flexibility and variety of materials and activities (Rosenshine, 1971).

At a more detailed level than these apparently common-sense findings, some guidance can be given regarding the necessary elements in an instructional sequence. The following sequence of "instructional events," based largely upon Gagné (1974), applies to the planning of either a single lesson or a longer unit of instruction.

1. *A preliminary step is to verify or activate student motivation.* Motivation is discussed more fully later in this chapter. Some factors that contribute to motivation are the intrinsic interest or meaning of the learning, the recognition that the learning leads to valued ends, and experiences of success with the learning. If some learners enter the unit

unmotivated, then motivation should receive first priority. To give one example: a required course in modern American history might begin with an examination of some of the controversial questions concerning the assassination of President Kennedy or Martin Luther King, Jr.

2. *At an early stage it is also necessary to ensure that the learners have the cognitive prerequisites for the course.* If a lesson is part of a series, prerequisites may often be taken for granted or checked with a few quick questions. The prerequisites may be knowledge of facts or terminology, understanding of concepts, or possession of skills. Immediate remediation may be given in the event of minor deficiencies; more serious shortcomings may require individual remedial work out of class.

3. *The instructor should ensure that the learners understand the objective or objectives of the learning.* This is important both for motivation and for focusing attention.

4. *The attention of the learner should be focused on the learning.* Prequestions, stimulated recall, and advance organizers are some techniques available. Prequestions direct attention to specifics and appear to diminish "incidental learning"—the learning of material unrelated to the objectives. Stimulated recall of related material learned previously may help to focus the student's attention. Advance organizers, "introductory material at a higher level of abstraction, generality, and inclusiveness than the learning passage itself," help to relate the learning at hand "to presumed ideational content in the learner's current cognitive structure" (Ausubel, 1978, p. 252).

5. *New material is next presented to the learner for acquisition and retention.* The material—information, rules, concepts, examples, etc.— should be presented with clarity and in logical sequence. As much guidance, repetition, exposition, and prompting should be given as is necessary to ensure that what is to be learned is properly understood by the students.

6. *To help students retain and retrieve the learning, ample application, rehearsal, review of knowledge, and practice of skills should be provided.* Spaced reviews at subsequent points can further enhance retention.

7. *Transfer and generalization can be helped by requiring the student to apply the learning to a variety of examples or in a variety of contexts.* This appears to enhance understanding and transfer by increasing the number of relevant memory structures and the mutually supporting links among them (Gagné and White, 1978).

Sequencing instruction

The sequence of instructional events described above is based as much on conventional wisdom as on experimental evidence. In fact few verified principles govern the sequencing of instruction. Much human learning is like a jigsaw puzzle; different people will put the pieces together in different order, but if all the pieces are provided, the picture will eventually be completed.

The internal logic of a subject will sometimes suggest a certain order in which concepts or skills must be acquired. Addition is taught before multiplication, velocity before acceleration, swimming before diving, Gagné's model of levels of complexity in intellectual skills (Figure 11–2) suggests a logical pattern for presenting cognitive material. An experiment by Partin (1976) showed that students could learn complex intellectual skills as effectively using a random sequence but required significantly less time if the learning was presented in some logical hierarchy.

The essence of most principles proposed for sequencing instruction is that the easy should precede the difficult, the familiar the unfamiliar. It makes sense to begin a study of poetry with the lyrics of contemporary pop songs rather than with the *Cantos* of Ezra Pound. Similarly, the study of geography might best begin with the geography of the students' own country or locality, the study of history with the present century. A course on environmental pollution could begin with the effects of pollution of which students are already aware, deal next with causes of pollution, and finally analyze solutions (Posner and Strike, 1976).

While such sequences seem likely to enhance motivation and learning, they are not inviolate. Human learning is not a linear process, and "the claim that a designer wishes to improve learning in a total course by establishing a novel or optimal order should probably be viewed skeptically, until evidence indicates otherwise" (Gagné, 1973, p. 26).

PROBLEM SOLVING

(HIGHER-ORDER RULES)
|
requires as prerequisites
|
RULES

(including DEFINED CONCEPTS)
|
which require as prerequisites
|
CONCRETE CONCEPTS
|
which require as prerequisites
|
DISCRIMINATIONS

Figure 11–2   Levels of complexity in intellectual skills
(Gagné and Briggs, 1979, p. 62; derived from Gagné, 1977).

> Knowing the contents of a few works of literature is a trivial achieve-
> ment. Being inclined to go on reading is a great achievement.
>
> —*B. F. Skinner, psychologist*

Motivation

Student motivation is of central concern in curriculum development, for three main reasons. (1) A minimum level of motivation is necessary for short-term, and especially for long-term, learning. (2) The higher the level of motivation, the greater the proportion of time the learner will spend "on task," and the more efficient the learning will be. (3) Curricula that stimulate high student motivation are attractive to teachers and hence better implemented. The principles of motivation that deserve the attention of curriculum developers are related to intrinsic motivation, competition, and success.

Intrinsic and extrinsic motivation   The difficulty of learning or teaching something that is devoid of intrinsic interest or meaning has been clearly shown by numerous experiments (Ausubel, 1967). But meaningful material is also difficult to teach if the student can see no application for it, that is, if the material lacks meaning for the particular learner. Australian teachers comment on the difficulty of teaching French in Australia. Munitions instructors in the air force find it difficult to develop and maintain high standards of performance among their men in loading bombs, which unlike engine maintenance has no urgency in peacetime, and unlike electronics no payoff on return to civilian life.

Intrinsic motivation can best be assured by developing aims and objectives from verified student needs. Indeed, lack of interest among students is almost prima facie evidence that the designers and instructors have failed either to select appropriate learnings or to persuade the learners of their value. But even interested students can be turned off by unimaginative choice of content. Why select boring material when interesting subject matter is available? Many objectives of history teaching can be achieved as effectively by studying the development of espionage in the Second World War as by studying the incredibly dull Hundred Years' War. The student is more likely to develop enjoyment of reading by exposure to the novels of Kurt Vonnegut, Jr. or James Baldwin than to those of Rudyard Kipling or Sir Walter Scott.

Not least among intrinsic motivators, although usually beyond the control of the curriculum designer, is the direct influence of an enthusiastic and inspiring teacher.

Extrinsic incentives are unrelated to the learning itself; achievement is recognized by some external reward. One of the problems of extrinsic motivators is that if the learners work for such rewards as money, prizes, free time, or praise, will they lose interest once the reward is obtained? One study strongly suggested that they would: children who performed a task for an extrinsic reward spent less time performing the activity in a later free-choice situation than did those who received either no reward or an unexpected reward (Lepper, Greene, and Nisbett, 1973). Although further research is needed in this area, a tentative conclusion is that extrinsic rewards may be productive in the short run but not over the long term.

Just as money has become the motivational currency of society, grades are the dominating extrinsic reward in many schools. Many children internalize the grading system at an early age; getting good grades, rather than learning something worthwhile, becomes the major purpose of studying, learning, and going to school. Institutional practices often encourage an emphasis on the token rather than the substance of learning. The whole apparatus of honor rolls, dean's lists, degree classes, and academic prizes and scholarships reinforces the importance of grades as an incentive. This can be interpreted either as a useful reward system or as an admission of failure to develop curricula that have intrinsic value or meaning for the learners.

Competition and cooperation   Both competitive and cooperative structures are evident in contemporary schools. The main characteristic of competitive structures is that one student's receipt of a reward reduces the probability that other students will be rewarded. The complementary feature of cooperation is that one student's achievement increases the likelihood of another student being rewarded.

Competitiveness pervades Western society. Evidence from the fields of sport, business, and warfare suggests that competition can stimulate superlative achievement. Evidence from the classroom suggests that there are costs as well as benefits. A survey of experiments in classroom settings indicated that individual competition produced higher achievement than individual rewards, group rewards, or group competition (Michaelis, 1977). Other surveys indicate that cooperative structures are more effective in increasing group productivity, especially in problem-solving tasks (Johnson and Johnson, 1974), and in enhancing the social atmosphere of a classroom (Slavin, 1977). Apparently cooperative learning is preferred by most children, especially rural children, younger children, and American children from non-European backgrounds (Madsen, 1971). Individual competitive grading appears to reduce continuing motivation and the interest students have in a task once it is completed (Salili et al., 1976).

In view of the evidence on each side of the cooperation-competition debate, educators might consider the merits of team competition in class-

---

Two Worlds of Motivation

U.S.S.R

It is now Larissa's turn. She walks primly to the front of the room, starts off bravely and finishes two stanzas. Suddenly, silence. Larissa has forgotten. There is no prompting, either from teacher or from friends. The silence continues.

Then the teacher speaks, softly but firmly, "Larissa, you have disappointed your mother, you have disappointed your father, and above all, you have disappointed your comrades who are sitting here before you. Go back to your place. They do not wish to hear anything more from you today."

With head down, Larissa silently returns to her seat, a teardrop flowing down each cheek.

—*Urie Bronfenbrenner (1970, pp. 63–64)*

China

Everywhere children appeared well-fed, well-clothed, and well-cared for. In all of the time of our tour I never saw a child scolded, reprimanded, or even spoken harshly to. Responsible children often attended our seminars and responded to our questions. The attitude teachers, as professionals, expressed toward the children was loving, kind and understanding. Once in a performance of a playlet a child forgot her lines. The teachers waited patiently and smiled and the child proceeded.

—*Alfred L. Karlson (1977, pp. 392–393)*

---

room learning. It has the advantage of using the incentives of both cooperation within teams and competition among teams, without the possible harmful effects of individual rivalry. As compared with individual competition, team competition has been found to produce more insight into problems, less anxiety, higher self-esteem, more peer cooperation, and better human relations (Julian and Perry, 1967; Devries and Edwards, 1973).

Success as an incentive   In Chapter 6 evidence was reviewed that suggested that people are motivated by goals more than by all other such incentives, including money, praise, competition, and even intrinsic interest (pp. 142–143). Research studies show consistently that success stimulates more success, failure breeds failure, and the effects of success and failure are cumulative over years of schooling (Bloom, 1976). High levels of motivation can therefore be expected in programs designed so that genuine success in significant and challenging learnings is achieved and recognized by all learners.

Matching Instruction and Objectives

The principles discussed above are summarized in barest outline in Figure 11–3. More specific principles guide the design of instruction for particular kinds of objective. One of the functions of classifying objectives into the five main types described in Chapter 7—knowledge, skills, physical development, dispositions, and experience—is to distinguish types of learning that require distinct instructional treatments.

Knowledge

In almost any educational or training context, a body of information, concepts, terminology, and understandings must be acquired. Unlike skills and other learnings, knowledge can be imparted, directly communicated from one person to another. Such communication, usually by the spoken or written word, is the basis of human culture.

For knowledge to be acquired, retained, and integrated, it must be meaningful. The learner must understand what is being communicated, be able to relate it to a wider network of concepts, and recognize its psychological meaning or significance. As Bruner puts it, "Perhaps the most basic thing that we can say about human memory, after a century of intensive research, is that unless detail is placed into a structured pattern, it is rapidly forgotten" (1960, p. 24). Illustrating concepts or information by a wide variety of examples or instances of application develops "combinations of memory structures" (Gagné and White, 1978) and helps to deepen understanding and improve retention.

The method by which knowledge is presented affects both the effectiveness and the efficiency of learning. Students rarely seem to learn more than half of the information presented in an academic lecture, and much of what they learn is forgotten within a few days (McLeish, 1968). It is apparent that expressive speech, clarity, good organization, enthusiasm, humor, use of gestures, and use of students' names all make lectures more popular with students (Murray, 1977); organization and clarity of presentation are highly correlated with student achievement (Frey,

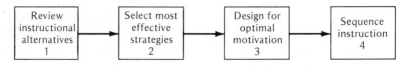

Figure 11–3   Main steps in selecting instructional strategies

Leonard, and Beatty, 1975). The way in which students take and use notes makes a difference to their learning (Faw and Walker, 1976), which suggests that early training in note-taking and study skills would yield benefits throughout a student's schooling.

Teachers who present information orally face the difficulty of maintaining student attention. They are often urged to intersperse presentation with questions, but a weakness of most classroom questioning is that only one student may be actively involved at a time. A number of devices can help overcome this limitation. For example, a teacher may prepare a number of multiple-choice questions on overhead transparencies, which are introduced at appropriate points. Students respond by means of a cardboard cube with different-colored sides or by pressing the appropriate button on a console on their desk. Special signals can be prearranged indicating "slow down," "repeat," "understood," or "don't understand." Such techniques allow students even in a large class to communicate unobtrusively with the instructor and enable the teacher to monitor learner understanding almost continuously. They also appear to be enthusiastically received by students (Littauer, 1972).

Unlike the live presentation, written material can be studied independently by the learner, at a time, place, and speed of his or her choice; the reader can backtrack, skim, review, and interrupt the reading at will. Lectures are likely to be more effective if accompanied by text material. As in oral presentations, overviews and thematic subheadings orient the learner to the information that follows. Questions inserted in a text and feedback on the answers help to maintain the attention of the reader and improve recall, especially if they require reflection and interpretation of generalizations rather than mere memory of facts (Rickards and Di Vesta, 1974). Prequestions appear to "activate search, selection and coding strategies that encourage the retention of highly specific facts, whereas postquestions encourage more general learning of the material" (Gagné, 1973, p. 16).

While live lectures and books tend to be the prevailing media in schools for presenting information, other vehicles are being increasingly employed. The Open University in Britain is one of several institutions providing college courses in part through radio and television. The University of California offers course credit for mastery of material that is published in more than a hundred daily newspapers across the United States. Busy physicians can keep up with medical developments by means of audio cassettes that they can listen to while driving or between appointments. "Dial-a-lecture" may become a common method of learning in the future. Ideally knowledge is presented in a variety of ways appropriate to students' different learning styles and preferences.

Not all knowledge is verbal or communicable in verbal form. Polanyi gives an example of what he calls "tacit knowledge":

We know a person's face, and can recognize it among a thousand, indeed among a million. Yet we usually cannot tell how we recognize a face we know. So most of this knowledge cannot be put into words (Polanyi, 1966, p. 4).

Knowledge involving spatial perception, characteristic of the visual arts but entailed in many other subjects, must be presented in visual or iconographic form. Similarly, musical knowledge requires listening, knowledge of a gymnastic routine requires observation of a demonstration, and knowledge in a plastic art like pottery requires development of a "feel" for the material, which can be achieved only by direct experience.

Skills

Almost every skill has a knowledge base and will usually be learned most efficiently if the learner masters relevant knowledge before beginning to practice the skill (Smith, 1966). But knowledge, while necessary, is not sufficient for skill learning. When learning to ride a bicycle, you need to know the location of the brake before mounting the vehicle. But no one ever learned how to ride by memorizing the rule for maintaining balance on a bicycle: "Turn the handlebars away from the direction of unbalance so as to force the bicycle into a curve whose radius is proportional to the square of the bicycle's velocity over the angle of imbalance" (Polanyi, 1958, p. 49). This particular piece of knowledge is unnecessary for performance of the skill. The twin pitfalls of skills training are (1) neglect of relevant knowledge and (2) overreliance on it.

Three main stages in skills learning are cognition, fixation, and automation. Practice is not essential at the first stage, when the learner gains a cognitive understanding of the skill. Practice is necessary at the second stage, when variable and awkward performance gradually becomes consistent, accurate, and precise. At the third stage a high degree of speed and coordination are achieved, and control of the skill shifts to lower brain centers, where it is largely automatic and does not require conscious thought (Fitts, 1962). To reach the stage of automation requires a great deal of repetitive practice, or drill. A reaction against rote learning, which we might define as learning meaningless material by drill, has sometimes led to a suspicion of practice and drill in general. The result is, in Ausubel's words, that "there is still considerable reliance on drill in actual classroom practice, but the drill is half-hearted, apologetic, and performed in ways which detract from its effectiveness" (1967, p. 245).

In the learning of a skill, guided practice is superior to trial and error or discovery. In a typical experiment, one college class practiced archery by trial and error, while another class was given specific instruction in stance, holding the bow, and releasing the arrow. After eighteen periods the trial-and-error students were hitting the target on average with 45 percent of shots, and the other class with 65 percent of shots (Davies, 1945). Guided practice normally includes demonstration, provision of relevant cues, specific practice, feedback, and progress from the simple to the complex.

Demonstration provides learners with a mental image of the whole or part of a skill. The learner watching a skill being demonstrated is not entirely passive: physiological monitoring shows that some "mental practice" occurs when people watch performance of a motor skill (Jacobson, 1932). If the attention of learners is directed toward relevant cues, they will be better able to evaluate and correct their own performance. The instructor also needs to monitor the student closely and provide feedback so that correct responses are reinforced and errors are extinguished before they become ingrained: for example, once the student has written the word leisure as "liesure" several times, it will be very difficult to eradicate the error. Skilled performance can be built up by practicing and combining subroutines, by gradually increasing the difficulty of the tasks to be executed, and by increasing the variety of contexts in which the skill is performed (Oxendine, 1968).

Several of the above examples are of motor skills; guided practice is also an appropriate strategy for developing cognitive skills. The educational writing on "lateral thinking," "divergent thinking," and "creative problem-solving" suggests that the ability to generate multiple imaginative solutions to problems can be improved with practice. Many of the teaching techniques claiming success utilize extensive practice of such problems as How would you weigh an elephant? Prevent a cat and dog fighting? Improve a mailman's bicycle? (De Bono, 1972). What name would you give to a greaseless sunburn lotion that is delicious on hamburgers? What would happen if you had invisible teeth? (Shackel, 1976).

Teachers of creative writing also report success with similar techniques. Creative writing, especially poetry writing, depends on the development of intuition; for while it is a verbal form, it requires the use of appositional, or metaphorical, thinking, which is known to be a function of the right (primarily nonverbal) hemisphere of the brain (Bogen, 1969). Teachers of creative writing have found it valuable to have their students write down as rapidly as possible responses to such questions as the following: If you had a choice, where would you like to be right now, and why? If only three items could be saved in a time capsule from our civilization, what would you select and why? You are to be executed in three minutes; what are your last thoughts? Or the teacher may bring objects such as an old wine jug, a large key, or a broken clock into class; students are asked to answer certain questions as the framework for a story: how old is it, where was it found, by whom, to whom did it belong, what was it used for, who gave it to the original owner and why? Or, to develop use of nonvisual cues, students write a formula poem suggested by listening to an unusual piece of music or sound effect, or feeling some object they cannot see (Schleich, 1977).

At its highest level of development, a skill becomes automatic, and this level is associated with what is known as *overtraining:* taking the learner beyond the point at which proficiency is achieved by conscious effort. There are two main reasons for overtraining. The first is that the value of many skills is severely limited until they can be performed automatically. The speaker of a foreign language who has to mentally translate every word or phrase before speaking is at a serious disadvantage. The student who has to work through a computation in order to establish the product of two one-digit numbers will find mathematics slow and stressful. Many skills in such areas as reading, music, sports, and driving must be automatic before they are fully functional.

The second reason for overtraining is that most skills will begin to decay as soon as practice stops. Once children have learned how to speak their native language or to read, little decay will be experienced, because practice is continuous. But skills in typing or in speaking a foreign language will decay following instruction in the absence of further practice. Many skills may not be used for years after they are learned. Consequently, in teaching a subject like first aid, it is insufficient to teach merely to the point of competence. Successful students must be super-competent, so that they will still be proficient when an emergency arises perhaps twenty years later, despite forgetting, fatigue, distraction, or the emotional stress of the moment.

The drill required for overtraining can but need not be tedious. Many imaginative teachers of reading, mathematics, and languages turn classroom drills into a game or competition and use varied content and contexts so that the learners are not wearied by monotonous repetition. In teaching modern languages, for example, such games as Simon Says, Bingo, I Spy, What's My Line, Twenty Questions, Concentration, Hangman, Treasure Hunt, and Tic-tac-toe can be adapted to appeal both to child and adult learners. Teachers welcome imaginative suggestions of this kind in the curriculum. It does not require much expertise to provide students with repetitive practice. It does require the finesse and creativity of the expert to do this in a way that will motivate students rather than demoralize them.

Physical development

The neglect of physiological objectives in the curriculum literature is symptomatic of the separation in schools of mind and body and of the general failure of educators to promote children's physical well-being. Physiological education and training tends to be provided in a haphazard way by the school and by such other agencies as doctors, dentists, parents, the media, health spas, and sports clubs. To date, there is little evidence that schools have a positive effect on physical development. The physical fitness of most children, in terms of their cardiovascular efficiency, deteriorates from the time they enter school (Bailey, 1973).

The development of salutary physical states in children requires the acquisition of knowledge and a favorable disposition along with involvement in exercise and appropriate activities. Specific forms of training appropriate to the development of certain physiological attributes, such as strength, suppleness, and oxygen consumption, can be provided in physical education programs; even if they cease when the student leaves school, they will have beneficial life-long effects (Saltin and Grimby, 1968). At the same time, schools can provide an environment in which, for example, the furniture encourages good rather than bad posture; pupils are not required to sit still for five hours a day; nutritious food is more readily available than junk food; and children are exposed to natural in preference to artificial light.

The ultimate effect of the schools on physical development and health would be greatest, however, if certain habits were ingrained during the school years. Teachers can model and reinforce habitual behavior (the physical education teacher who is a chain-smoker, overweight and

---

Alive and Well and Living Near Paris

After World War II, many French doctors and educators were concerned with the heavily overloaded intellectual program in the elementary schools. As a result, several experiments were set up in Vanves beginning in 1951, by the Ministry of Education. These were aimed at obtaining a better balance between the pupil's physical and intellectual activities, thereby arriving at a much more effective way of educating children. This was done by selecting certain classes, revising the daily program significantly, and then comparing intellectual, physical, social and other educational components with those of carefully paired control classes which continued under the traditional program. Essentially, the experimental classes did their academic work in the morning and devoted the afternoons to daily physical education, art, music and supervised study. The time spent on academic education was reduced to about four hours per day and that devoted to physical education raised to about eight hours a week.

The results of the experiments more than confirmed the hypothesis. Not only was the health, fitness, discipline and enthusiasm superior in the experimental schools, but the academic results surpassed those of the control classes.

—*D. A. Bailey (1973, p. 427)*

allergic to exercise is a significant model). Students can be given the opportunity in school to develop certain practices such as daily exercise that can become part of their normal life-style.

Good health is a state universally recognized as desirable. In principle, education can make as significant a contribution to health as can medical services (Carr-Hill and Magnussen, 1973). Yet schools still tend to be judged almost exclusively in terms of their academic effectiveness. The importance of physiological objectives suggests that the schools in which students spend the majority of their formative years should also be judged according to how effective they are in reducing illness and medical costs and increasing health, vigor, and longevity.

Dispositions

The development of attitudes toward learning, toward other people, and toward oneself is perhaps the most serious responsibility of the school. Once a disposition has been identified as sufficiently important

Listeners

to be an objective of a program, the curriculum developer is obligated to seek an effective strategy to bring it about. Verbal exhortation, probably the most widely used approach by teachers, parents, ministers, and others, appears to have little effect on people's attitudes. Four techniques have greater potential, particularly if used in combination: information, reinforcement, modeling, and involvement. These methods overlap to a significant degree.

Information   Almost all attitudes have a significant knowledge component. Your attitudes toward Nazis and rattlesnakes, private enterprise and progressive education, are based largely on what you know about them. Alteration of this informational base may change the attitude. "Personal causation training" is a largely informational process by which people come to recognize their own strengths and weaknesses, set personal goals, and identify criteria to assess their achievement. Personal causation training has proved effective in helping teachers develop a sense of control over their lives and careers, which in turn was passed on to their pupils (de Charms, 1972).

An interesting illustration of attitude change through information is provided by Silvern (1972) in a simulation of a curriculum developed to train factory workers in fire fighting. A contributing cause of extensive fire damage at an apparently hypothetical furniture factory was the lack of knowledge of emergency fire fighting on the part of some employees, and their tendency to stand by, enjoying the blaze as spectators, thereby affecting the efficiency and morale of those employees attempting to put out the flames. In the program aimed at training all employees in emergency procedures, the first two hours were to be spent on having each employee work out the consequences to himself and his family if the plant burned down and he lost his job. For example, he was to consider the financial cost of losing his salary and fringe benefits, of being transferred to another plant, of selling his home and moving to another city, and of being unemployed. It seems reasonable to speculate that this approach would induce a serious and cooperative attitude toward fire safety training among employees.

Attitudes important enough to be an objective of instruction should be given a firm informational base. Attitudes built on inadequate or false information, or on rhetoric or emotion, are vulnerable to manipulation by those who provide new rhetoric, play on stronger emotions, or supply new truths, half-truths, or untruths. No Western society can hope to build a firm commitment to democratic principles by exhorting the values of democracy and failing to illuminate its strengths and limitations, as well as those of alternative political systems. Some of the pain in American political life over the past decade must have been due to the collapse of the myths regarding the integrity of individuals and institutions that were so assiduously promoted by the schools and the media in the previous twenty years.

Information by itself, however, is often insufficient to change basic attitudes. The world is full of smokers who know the cancer risks, junk-food addicts who are experts on nutrition, and drivers who know that seat belts save lives but who do not use them. New information can usually be rationalized into the attitudinal framework, as a classic case cited by Allport shows. A psychiatrist was treating a woman who suffered from the delusion that she was dead. All rational arguments having failed, the psychiatrist asked her whether dead people could bleed. When she answered in the negative, he punctured her finger and squeezed out a drop of blood. "Well!" she said, "So dead people do bleed!" (Allport, 1954, p. 25).

Reinforcement   People tend to develop positive attitudes toward things that become associated with pleasant experiences. To develop favorable attitudes, whether toward topology, romantic painting, or cultural pluralism, it is necessary to ensure that the learner's experiences of the attitudinal objects are enjoyable or in some other way rewarding. Contact with members of another race may improve racial attitudes, but if this is a planned experience, care must be taken to ensure that the experience is a pleasant one; a competitive situation may serve only to increase antagonisms (Silverthorne, Chelune, and Imada, 1974).

Attitudes toward learning will tend to improve if teaching is in the hands of congenial rather than disagreeable people, is conducted in a cheerful rather than a drab environment, and uses interesting rather than wearisome methods, materials, and subject matter. Attitudes are also improved by curricula designed to produce as much student success as possible.

These strategies are intended to make the learning experience consciously agreeable. They are not to be confused with conditioning, which implies subverting people's will by establishing unconscious mental associations that will predispose them to act in certain ways. Any deliberate attempt to change students' attitudes without their knowledge is ethically highly suspect.

Modeling   Modeling has a powerful effect on attitudes. The models provided by parents, peer groups, and admired individuals can leave a permanent imprint on attitudes, beliefs, and behavior. Even the behavior modeled by characters in television cartoons can affect the behavior of young children, as Bandura and his colleagues showed in a series of experiments that began in the early 1960s (Bandura, Ross, and Ross, 1963). This insight has not been lost on the producers of television commercials.

An effective strategy for developing student dispositions is to pair or group learners so that an admired peer (e.g., an older or popular student) can model the desired attitudes. Successful use of peer models was demonstrated in an experiment by Csapo (1972) in the first grade of an elementary school. Disruptive children were paired with pupils who consistently modeled appropriate behavior. Within three weeks, disruptive behavior was reduced from a very high level almost to zero.

Involvement   A large-scale survey of research on attitude change in American colleges, conducted a generation ago (Jacob, 1957), observed that while almost every college professed a commitment to developing increased political awareness or efficacy, the only consistent attitude changes that occurred could be attributed to four years of maturation and changes in society at large during that time. The study noted, however, a few exceptional institutions, which were highly successful in developing a unique "community of values" with long-lasting attitudinal effects. In every case, these were colleges that provided real-life political experiences, in such forms as involvement in political campaigns, social surveys, or community projects. The effects of these programs in terms of such factors as voting record were still evident twenty years after the students graduated.

A well-known experiment with involvement as a means of developing attitudes was conducted by Jane Elliott with her elementary-school class in Iowa. Seeking a way to bring home to children the impact of discrimination, following the assassination of Dr. Martin Luther King, Ms. Elliott decided to distinguish between the pupils on the basis of eye color. For one day, the class agreed, the Brown Eyes would be superior; on the second day, the Blue Eyes would be superior. On the first day, the brown-eyed children were given various privileges and responsibilities and praised frequently; the Blue Eyes were often criticized, usually with some allusion to eye color. By the end of the day, the Brown Eyes were gloating, while the Blue Eyes were downcast and truculent. Exactly the same happened in reverse the following day. The discussion and compositions produced by the children at the end of the experiment showed that the experience had demonstrated to them the realities of discrimination and developed an attitude toward it that no amount of objective teaching could have done (Peters, 1971).

Although a simulation, this experience produced a high level of pupil involvement. Currently, a real-life experience is being provided to juvenile offenders in some American cities by having them visit penal institutions to be told and shown the realities of prison life by long-term convicts. The program, largely run by prisoners, appears to be having considerable impact on young offenders. In general, shock tactics, like showing movies of traffic accidents to careless drivers, or taking smokers through cancer wards, tend to have a fade effect, and it may be preferable to work on positive experiences. A positive but realistic attitude toward law and the police might be fostered by having students ride in a patrol car for one shift. A day spent in an executive's office could provide insight into the business world, which could be balanced by an extended visit to a consumer protection bureau.

In developing attitudes, as with other areas of the curriculum, designers need to exercise their imagination in selecting and recommending experiences that will be educative in the widest sense.

Experiences

This brings us to the last kind of objective: intrinsically valuable experiences. Above all else, our experiences make us the people we are. From school experienced as years of sitting at a desk listening to a teacher we could expect only the development of impoverished personalities.

Once a significant experience has been defined as a desirable educational objective, the instructional procedure is simple: provide it. However, it is easier to say what is to be done than how. It is one thing if the experience is visiting the zoo, and another if it is climbing Mount Everest.

An experience can be provided at three main levels: direct, simulated, and vicarious. Both impact and cost will vary directly with the level.

Many intrinsically valuable experiences can and should be provided directly by the school. These include experiences in the arts, both as participant (painting, sculpture, playing a musical instrument, acting) and as audience, and physical experiences involving body awareness and control, such as dance, gymnastics, yoga, and athletics. Many schools make intercultural experiences possible through sponsored travel and exchanges. Social experiences are provided through volunteer work in hospitals, old age homes, and the community. And outdoor education, with long canoe trips, hiking, and mountaineering expeditions, has introduced a new and compelling experience of the natural world.

In other areas, such as history, simulated experiences must be contrived. A few years ago I watched a re-creation of the Battle of Brill in Oxfordshire, originally fought in 1644 during the English Civil War. While spectators observed from one side of a valley, some three thousand participants refought the four-hour battle on the opposite hillside. Companies of infrantry, armed with sixteen-foot lances, advanced on one another, entangled, and withdrew, leaving the dead and wounded for the gray-caped nurses to attend. Smoke from the artillery drifted across a patchwork of buff uniforms of the Parliamentarians and the scarlet and black of the Royalists. Small groups of Royalist swordsmen dashed up the enemy ramparts, to be repulsed by the defenders, among whom, Bi-

A remarkable simulation was conducted by Beatrice Kleppner with her class of senior history students in Massachusetts. They lived for a January week as seventeenth-century Pilgrims at the reconstructed Plimoth Plantation. The students steeped themselves in the history of the period, made Pilgrim costumes, cooked on the open hearth, ate the meager food available in a pioneer winter, and relived the complex and ultimately tragic relations with the Wampanoag Indians. A realism was achieved which could not be achieved through books:

"In spite of the camaraderie there were irritations: our attempt at seventeenth-century realism was too successful; we itched and we smelled. The act of crowding at the hearth prevented everyone from being warm simultaneously. We relied on natural courtesy, but that wore thin during the week. And there were shirkers among us. Feeding the fire through the long cold night fell by default on three public-spirited members. We learned to feel for the Pilgrims; no wonder occasional discord broke out."

—*Beatrice Spencer Kleppner (1976)*

bles in hand, stalked black-robed clergy. The air was full of the shouting of orders, the yelling of soldiers, the beat of drums, the rattle of muskets, and the intermittent crash of cannon.

Those who learn most from such simulations are the participants. For the spectators, the experience is vicarious but can nevertheless be significant. Vicarious experience is provided in many forms; in Western culture, television and books are predominant. The value of the experiences that children normally receive from such sources is open to question—for example, the 18,000 violent killings that an average child sees on television by the age of eighteen (Winn, 1977). It may be that the trite and stylized treatment accorded by popular media to important events in fact dulls the sensitivity rather than sharpens it. The great novel or film, however, remains a potent source of meaningful and enriching experiences.

Conclusion: Only Variety Can Absorb Variety

Students vary in innumerable ways; so do teachers. The kinds of learning and the instructional context introduce additional variety into the classroom. Advocacy of any "one best method" is out of place in instructional design. Neither art nor science supports monolithic prescription. The field of science that studies the management of variety is cybernetics, and one of its laws is Ashby's Law: "Only variety can absorb variety" (Beer, 1974, p. 18). If variety enters a system, the system must respond with variety.

The role of the curriculum designer, therefore, is not to impose strategies on the teacher, but to help liberate the teacher from imprisonment within a limited range of conventional techniques; to suggest principles and possibilities that the teacher can apply creatively to generate new and more effective approaches. The structure and clarity of the scientist and the variety and imagination of the artist: these have been, and are likely to remain, the keys to instructional effectiveness.

ACTIVITIES

1. Observe a number of lessons, if possible at different levels of schooling. By making a note every thirty seconds, determine (a) the amount of time the class focuses on the subject of instruction; (b) the amount of time the teacher is talking; (c) the amount of time the focus of the lesson is on communication of information; (d) the number of different instructional strategies used. What are your findings? How do they differ from one class and level to another? What conclusions do you draw?

2. Individually or in a group think of as many ways and subjects as you can in which you could use any three of the following in instruction: cooking, crosswords, an exhibit, an interview, a poster, puppets, a scrapbook, a treasure hunt.

3. Choose a topic that you have taught at some time in the past. Select from Table 11–1 all the means you could possibly use in teaching it. Then select the ten that would be most productive. How much do they differ from the means used previously?

4. What main strategies would you use in a program intended to change people's attitudes towards (a) littering, (b) smoking, (c) speeding?

5. Examine your attitudes toward (a) Turks, (b) Hindus, (c) faith healers, (d) marijuana users. To what extent in each case are your attitudes based on (1) systematically studied information, (2) incidental or anecdotal information, or (3) personal experience? What kind of experience could cause your attitudes to change?

6. In teaching a geography or social studies unit, you want to provide your students with "a significant experience of Inuit (Eskimo) life." How would you do this?

QUESTIONS

1. Which of the following factors would be most likely to produce consistently high achievement from learners?

   a. competition and extrinsic rewards
   b. detailed instructional strategies in the curriculum

   c. knowledge that the lowest achievers in the class will fail

   d. cognitive prerequisites, motivation, and appropriate instruction

2. In centrally developed curricula, treatment of subject matter and instructional methodology is best

   a. omitted altogether

   b. spelled out in detailed lesson plans

   c. dealt with in special inservice training designed for teachers of the curriculum

   d. limited to suggestions with detail left to the judgment of the individual teacher

3. Presentation methods are most appropriate for the development in learners of

   a. skill

   b. knowledge

   c. experience

   d. disposition

4. A teacher is planning an introductory poetry appreciation course and wants to use the poetry of Geoffrey Chaucer, Robert Frost, Alfred Tennyson, and the lyrics of contemporary popular songs. The best sequence to introduce these works would probably be

   a. Chaucer, Tennyson, Frost, pop songs

   b. Pop songs, Frost, Tennyson, Chaucer

   c. Tennyson, Chaucer, Frost, pop songs

   d. Tennyson, pop songs, Chaucer, Frost

5. A general principle for teaching skills is

   a. provide appropriate practice, but avoid drill

   b. practice is the only procedure that should be used

   c. provide practice only if the skill has to be automatic

   d. first teach a cognitive understanding of the skill, then provide appropriate practice

6. A teacher says, "We are trying to get away from practice and drill." A likely result of this policy is

   a. lower level of skill achieved by students

   b. a curriculum better suited to student needs

   c. diminished understanding of concepts by students

   d. more favorable attitudes by students to instruction

7. It is most likely to be legitimate to require the student's physical presence at a given time and place when the objective of instruction is

   a. skills

   b. knowledge

   c. experience

   d. disposition

8. In developing student attitudes

   a. knowledge is irrelevant
   b. it is sufficient to provide correct information
   c. knowledge may be necessary but is rarely sufficient
   d. such methods as reading and lectures are inappropriate

9. Reinforcement, modeling, and presentation of information can help to shape student dispositions. Another appropriate technique is

   a. drill
   b. exhortation
   c. involvement
   d. conditioning

10. Which of the following statements about motivation is supported by the research?

    a. prior success is a stronger motivator than failure
    b. money is the most effective incentive for learning
    c. competition will stimulate better problem-solving than cooperation
    d. extrinsic rewards will have a more permanent effect than intrinsic motivation

Check your answers against the key in Appendix 2.
9 or 10 right: You understand the material presented.
8 or 7 right: Review the areas of uncertainty.
6 or less right: Reread the chapter.

Recommended Reading

Bligh, Donald, G. J. Ebrahim, David Jaques, and D. Warren Piper. *Teaching students.* Devon, England: Exeter University Teaching Services, 1975. Written to provide college teachers with some knowledge of curriculum and instruction, this book concisely summarizes the research findings of many aspects of teaching relevant to all levels of schooling.

Cronbach, Lee J. *Educational psychology.* 3rd ed. New York: Harcourt Brace Jovanovich, 1977. An encyclopedic work by one of America's leading educational psychologists. Especially valuable on instructional design; Cronbach's approach is eclectic, his writing interesting, readable, and well illustrated.

Hamilton, Darlene Softley, Bonnie Mack Flemming and Joanne Deal Hicks. *Resources for creative teaching in early childhood education.* New York: Harcourt Brace Jovanovich, 1977. A gold mine of ideas for primary-level teachers; teachers of older children could also benefit from the authors' creative strategies and humane approach.

Johnson, David W. and Roger T. Johnson. *Learning together and alone: Cooperation, competition, and individualization.* Englewood Cliffs, N.J.: Prentice-Hall, 1974. The authors admit a bias in favor of cooperative over competitive classroom structure, but draw together and analyze fairly the arguments and evidence surrounding the issue.

Joyce, Bruce, and Marsha Weil. *Models of teaching*. 2nd ed. Englewood Cliffs, N.J.: Prentice-Hall, 1979. Description, classification, and analysis of different teaching models, with their theoretical bases, rationales, and implications for classroom practice.

References

Allport, G. W. *The nature of prejudice*. Cambridge, Mass.: Addison-Wesley, 1954.

Ausubel, David P. *Learning theory and classroom practice*. Toronto: Ontario Institute for Studies in Education, 1967.

———. In defence of advance organizers: A reply to the critics. *Review of Educational Research*, 1978, 48, 251–257.

Bailey, D. A. Exercise, fitness and physical education for the growing child: A concern. *Canadian Journal of Public Health*, 1973, 64, 421–430.

Bandura, A., D. Ross, and S. A. Ross. Imitation of film-mediated aggressive models. *Journal of Abnormal and Social Psychology*, 1963, 66, 3–11.

Beer, Stafford, *Designing freedom*. Toronto: Canadian Broadcasting Corporation Publications, 1974.

Bloom, Benjamin S. *Human characteristics and school learning*. New York: McGraw-Hill, 1976.

Bogen, Joseph E. The other side of the brain II: An appositional mind. *Bulletin of the Los Angeles Neurological Societies*, 1969, 34, 135–162.

Bronfenbrenner, Urie. *Two worlds of childhood: U.S. and U.S.S.R.* New York: Russell Sage Foundation, 1970.

Bruner, Jerome S. *The process of education*. New York: Random House, 1960.

Carr-Hill, Roy, and Olav Magnussen. *Indicators of performance of educational systems*. Paris: Organization for Economic Cooperation and Development, 1973.

Csapo, Marg. Peer models reverse the "One bad apple spoils the barrel" theory. *Teaching Exceptional Children*, 1972, 5 (Fall), 20–24.

Davies, D. R. The effect of tuition upon the process of learning a complex motor skill. *Journal of Educational Psychology*, 1945, 36, 352–365.

De Bono, Edward. *Children solve problems*. Harmondsworth, England: Penguin, 1972.

De Charms, Richard. Personal causation training in the schools. *Journal of Applied and Social Psychology*, 1972, 2, 95–113.

Devries, David L., and Keith J. Edwards. Learning games and student teams: Their effects on classroom process. *American Educational Research Journal*, 1973, 10, 307–318.

Edwards, Judith, Shirley Norton, Sandra Taylor, Martha Weiss, and Ralph Dusseldorp. How effective is CAI? A review of the research. *Educational Leadership*, 1975, 33, 147–153.

Faw, Harold W., and T. Gary Walker. Mathemagenic behaviors and efficiency in learning from prose materials: Review, critique, and recommendations. *Review of Educational Research*, 1976, 46, 691–720.

Fitts, P. M. Factors in complex skill training. In R. Glaser (ed.), *Training research and education*. Pittsburgh: University of Pittsburgh Press, 1962, pp. 177–197.

Frey, Peter W., Dale W. Leonard, and William W. Beatty. Student ratings of instruction: Validation research. *American Educational Research Journal*, 1975, 12, 435–447.

Gagné, Robert M. *The conditions of learning*. 2nd ed. New York: Holt, Rinehart & Winston, 1970.

———. Learning and instructional sequence. In Fred N. Kerlinger (ed.), *Review of research in education 1*. Itasca, Ill.: Peacock and American Educational Research Association, 1973, pp. 3–33.

———. *Essentials of learning for instruction*. Hinsdale, Ill.: Dryden Press, 1974.

———, and Leslie J. Briggs. *Principles of instructional design*. 2nd ed. New York: Holt, Rinehart & Winston, 1979.

———, and Richart T. White. Memory structures and learning outcomes. *Review of Educational Research*, 1978, 48, 187–222.

Goodlad, J. L., Frances M. Klein, and Associates. *Looking behind the classroom door*. Worthington, Ohio: Charles A. Jones, 1970.

Harnischfeger, A., and D. E. Wiley. Teaching-learning processes in elementary school: A synoptic view. *Curriculum Inquiry*, 1976, 6, 5–43.

Hess, R. D., and M. D. Tenezakis. Selected findings from the computer as a socializing agent: Some socioaffective outcomes of CAI. *AV Communication Review*, 1973, 21, 311–325.

Hodgetts, A. B. *What culture: What heritage?* Toronto: Ontario Institute for Studies in Education, 1968.

Hughes, M. M., et al. *Assessment of the quality of teaching in elementary schools*. Salt Lake City: University of Utah, 1959.

Hunt, David E. Teachers' adaptation: "Reading" and "flexing" to students. *Journal of Teacher Education*, 1976, 27, 268–275.

Jacob, P. E. *Changing values in college*. New York: Harper, 1957.

Jacobson, E. Electrophysiology of mental activities. *American Journal of Psychology*, 1932, 44, 676–694.

Johnson, David W., and Robert T. Johnson. Instructional goal structure: Cooperative, competitive, or individualistic. *Review of Educational Research*, 1974, 44, 213–240.

Joyce, Bruce R. Selecting learning experiences: Linking theory and practice. Washington, D.C.: Association for Supervision and Curriculum Development, 1978.

Julian, J. W., and F. A. Perry. Cooperation contrasted with intra-group and inter-group competition. *Sociometry*, 1967, 30, 79–90.

Karlson, Alfred L. Curriculum practices in preschool and primary schools in the People's Republic of China. In Leonard Golubchick and Barry Persky (eds.), *Early childhood education*. Wayne, N. J.: Avery, 1977, pp. 390–393.

Kleppner, Beatrice Spencer. Playing pilgrim. *Times Educational Supplement*, January 9, 1976, p. 29.

Leithwood, K., J. Ross, D. Montgomery, and F. Maynes. An empirical investigation of teachers' curriculum decision-making processes and strategies used by curriculum managers to influence such decision-making. Mimeo. Toronto: Ontario Institute for Studies in Education, 1978.

Lepper, M. R., D. Greene, and R. Nisbett. Undermining children's intrinsic interest with extrinsic reward: A test of the "overjustification" hypothesis. *Journal of Personality and Social Psychology*, 1973, 28, 129–137.

Littauer, Raphael. Instructional implications of a low-cost electronic student response system. *Educational Technology,* 1972, 12 (Oct.), 69–71.

Madsen, M. C. Developmental and cross-cultural differences in the cooperative and competitive behavior of young children. *Journal of Cross-cultural Psychology,* 1971, 2, 365–371.

McLeish, John, *The lecture method.* Cambridge: Institute of Education, 1968.

Michaelis, James W. Classroom reward structures and academic performance. *Review of Educational Research,* 1977, 47, 87–98.

Murray, Henry G. Classroom behaviors of social science lecturers receiving low, medium, and high teacher ratings. *Ontario Universities Program for Instructional Development Newsletter,* no. 14, February 1977.

Newberry, Janet McIntosh. The beginning teacher's search for assistance from colleagues. *Canadian Journal of Education,* 1979, 4, (1), 17–27.

Novick, David. Long-range planning through program budgeting. In Erich Jatsch (ed.), *Perspectives of planning.* Paris: Organization for Economic Cooperation and Development, 1968, pp. 255–284.

Oxendine, Joseph B. *Psychology of motor learning.* Englewood Cliffs, N.J.: Prentice-Hall, 1968.

Partin, Ronald L. The instructional effectiveness of random, logical, and ordering theory generated learning hierarchies. Paper presented at the Annual Meeting of the American Educational Research Association, San Francisco, April 1976.

Peters, W. *A class divided.* New York: Doubleday, 1971.

Polanyi, Michael. *Personal knowledge: Towards a post-critical philosophy.* London: Routledge and Kegan Paul, 1958.

——— . *The tacit dimension.* New York: Doubleday, 1966.

Posner, George A., and Kenneth A. Strike. A categorization scheme for principles of sequencing content. *Review of Educational Research,* 1976, 46, 665–690.

Rickards, J. P., and F. J. Di Vesta. Type and frequency of questions in processing textual material. *Journal of Experimental Psychology,* 1974, 66, 354–362.

Rosenshine, Barak. *Teaching behaviors and student achievement.* London: National Foundation for Educational Research, 1971.

Salili, Farideh, Martin L. Maehr, Richard L. Sorensen, and Leslie J. Fyans, Jr. A further consideration of the effects of evaluation on motivation. *American Educational Research Journal,* 1976, 13, 85–102.

Saltin, B., and G. Grimby. Physiological analysis of middle-aged and old former athletes. *Circulation,* 1968, 38, 1104–1115.

Schleich, David. Creative writing in high schools. Mimeo. Kingston, Canada: St. Lawrence College, 1977.

Shackel, Denis S. J. "Imagineering": Some teachable techniques for creative thinking in the classroom. *Teacher Education,* 1976, 9, 42–49.

Silvern, Leonard C. *Systems engineering applied to training.* Houston, Texas: Gulf, 1972.

Silverthorne, C., G. Chelune, and A. Imada. The effects of competition and cooperation on level of prejudice. *Journal of Social Psychology,* 1974, 92, 293–301.

Slavin, Robert E. Classroom reward structure: An analytical and practical review. *Review of Educational Research,* 1977, 47, 633–650.

Smith, Robert G., Jr. *The design of instructional systems.* Alexandria, Va.: George Washington University, Human Resources Research Office, 1966.

Snow, Richard. Research on aptitude for learning: A progress report. In Lee S. Shulman (ed.), *Review of research in education 4*. Itasca, Ill.: Peacock and American Educational Research Association, 1976, pp. 50–105.

Taylor, Philip H., B. J. Holley, and R. Sretzer. Influences and constraints on the teaching of economics: A study of teachers' perceptions. Mimeo. Birmingham, England: University of Birmingham, School of Education, 1974.

Walker, Decker F., and Jon Schaffarzick. Comparing curricula. *Review of Educational Research*, 1974, 44, 83–111.

Winn, Marie. *The plug-in drug*. New York: Viking, 1977.

Wurman, Richard Saul (ed.). *Yellow Pages for learning resources*. Cambridge, Mass.: M.I.T. Press, 1972.

12

PRINCIPLES

- Aptitude is reflected primarily in a person's speed of learning, which may vary from one area of achievement to another.

- Obtaining consistently high achievement from a group of students who vary in aptitude may be conceptualized as a cybernetic problem.

- Minor learning difficulties should be detected and corrected before they produce major failure.

- Remediation should be rapid, motivational, and administratively unexacting.

- The marginal time of faster learners may be effectively used by enrichment, peer tutoring, or acceleration.

- The evidence suggests that conventional patterns of ability grouping on balance do more harm than good.

- Readiness, in terms of motivation, maturation, and prerequisites, may be the ideal criterion for grouping learners.

CONCEPTS

Aptitude	Marginal time	Acceleration
Cybernetics	Enrichment	Age grading
Set point	Peer tutoring	Readiness
Monitoring	Ability grouping	

12
Managing Aptitude Differences

I do not deny, Sir, but there is some original differ-ence in minds, but it is nothing in comparison of what is formed by education.

—Dr. Samuel Johnson

Student Diversity

A major challenge facing most teachers is to bring about a common body of learning in a class of students who vary widely in background, motivation, and aptitude. As every teacher knows, a typical classroom may contain children with a wide spectrum of IQs. Reading levels ranging from first to twelfth grade have been known within a single sixth grade (Gronlund, 1974). And the attitude of learners to a given subject may vary from passionate enthusiasm to ill-disguised contempt. How can the curriculum developer hope to design a program that will produce a consistent level of high achievement from such diverse students?

One solution is to individualize instruction completely. Then, instead of one class of thirty students, the teacher essentially handles thirty classes of one student, and the problem of diversity ceases to exist. Many teachers, using only their own resources of energy and imagination, are quite successful in providing for the individual progress of learners. The one-room schoolhouse, in which perhaps a dozen children represented eight or ten grade levels, while sometimes a disastrous educational environment, was in other cases a model of individualization. Sophisticated individualized learning programs exist today. Among the most widely adopted are PLAN (Program for Learning in Accordance with Needs), developed by Westinghouse Learning Corporation and American Institutes for Research; IGE (Individually Guided Instruction), developed by the University of Wisconsin Research and Development Center for Cognitive Learning; and IPI (Individually Prescribed Instruction), developed by the Learning Research and Development Center at the University of Pittsburgh. These three programs differ in several respects, but all of them allow the student to progress at his or her own pace. All of them also require the teacher to have help not usually available in the typical classroom: IPI and IGE call for teacher aides, and PLAN uses a computer that does most of the ordering of materials, test marking, daily reporting of progress, record keeping, and direction of the learner through the curriculum (Educational Products Information Exchange Institute, 1974).

These may well be the programs of the future. But, as was suggested in the previous chapter, it seems unlikely that individualization of school learning will replace group instruction as the norm much before the end of the century. The immediate problem for most classroom teachers is how group instruction can be designed to meet the varying needs of the learners.

The Nature of Aptitude

A number of characteristics on which students differ have been noted in preceding chapters. Personality differences can be accommodated by using a variety of subject matter and methods. Critical differences in background can be controlled by means of prerequisites. A variety of strategies

---

The necessity of leading in equal ranks so many unequal powers of capacity and application will prolong to eight or ten years the juvenile studies, which might be despatched in half that time by the skilful master of a single pupil.

—*Edward Gibbon, c. 1790 (1907, p. 29)*

can be used in the effort to achieve a common minimal level of motivation in students.

Aptitude—"capacity for learning" (Webster's, 1973)—is often considered to be a general trait, like height or eye color. Often little distinction is made between aptitude and intelligence or among different kinds of intelligence, in the belief that such characteristics are innate, inherited, and little influenced by the school experience. This position was maintained by the British psychologist Sir Cyril Burt:

> The innate amount of potential ability with which a child is endowed at birth sets an upper limit to what he can possibly achieve at school and in after life (1968, p. 17).

Such a conception of aptitude justified a general typing of students as of high and low aptitude. But the conception does not correspond to most people's experience or observation. True, some people seem able to turn their hand to anything—the all-rounders who inspire envy in the rest of us. At the other extreme are the unfortunates all of whose talents appear to be undiscovered. But these are exceptions. In most cases an individual is gifted in some areas, average in others, and devoid of talent in still others. Thus a child may be talented in verbal skills (which will often be interpreted as "general" ability), but relatively weak in mathematics and the arts. Another child may be gifted only in music, or in athletics, mechanics, leadership, or sense of humor. There are people with an aptitude for making money, and others with an aptitude for making friends. But the correlation between aptitude in different areas is generally low. The overlap between creativity and intelligence, for example, is so slight that a class selected from the 20 percent most intelligent students would omit 70 percent of the most creative, and vice versa (Torrance, 1965, p. 39). Consequently, general labels applied to learners, such as "gifted," "low ability," or "average," simply do violence to the variability of human characteristics. In this chapter, therefore, the terms "faster learner" and "slower learner" are used not to describe general characteristics of students, but only to denote speed of learning within a specific area.

This leads to the point that aptitude is manifested principally by speed of learning. Carroll, who is mainly responsible for promulgating this idea, concluded that the slowest 5 percent of students in a typical classroom will usually take about five times as long to master a given learning as the fastest 5 percent (1971). Anderson (1976) found a variation of 1:7 to 1:3 in the studies he reviewed. However, pupils do not concentrate or attend to their learning for 100 percent of classroom time. When we examine differences in learning speed in terms of "time on task," the typical variation is closer to 1:3 (Bloom, 1974). This suggests that the faster learners tend to spend proportionately more of their time concentrating on their work, while the slower learners are more easily distracted

---

Briton's Classic IQ Data Now Viewed as Fraudulent

The classic reports of the late Cyril Burt, the eminent British psychologist whose research had long been accepted by many as evidence that differences in intelligence were hereditary, are now widely considered to be without scientific value. . . .

Dr. Burt's research, unquestioned and highly influential before his death in 1971, has been criticized in psychological circles since 1972, when it was found to contain a number of virtual impossibilities.

In recent weeks, however, the basis for criticism has widened as a result of a report in *The Sunday Times* of London that Dr. Burt's two collaborators, cited in his published articles, may never have existed.

Further investigations by *The Sunday Times* and by Leon Kamin, a Princeton University psychologist, suggest many additional instances of questionable scientific thought, including biased language, favorably reviewing his own books, using pseudonyms in his own journal and fabricating data. . . .

His view that intelligence was predetermined at birth and largely unchangeable helped to shape a rigid, three-tier school system in England based on an IQ test given to children at the age of 11.

—New York Times, *November 28, 1976*

---

and spend more time woolgathering or daydreaming, a hypothesis recently confirmed by Roecks (1978).

Until recently it was widely believed that aptitude was a fixed characteristic, leading educators to the conclusion that rates of learning would always vary widely in the classroom. But recent research suggests that, given certain conditions, this variation can be radically reduced. The necessary conditions are (1) the students must have the necessary cognitive prerequisites (clearly a class will vary widely in the speed at which it masters division if some of the learners have not yet mastered subtraction); (2) the students must have an appropriate level of motivation (which depends largely on prior experiences of success in the subject); and (3) appropriate instruction must be provided. Experiments in which these three conditions were met suggested that the variation in learning speed could be halved (Block and Burns, 1976) and possibly reduced almost to zero (Anderson, 1976). It seems reasonable to conclude that speed of learning is an alterable and not a fixed characteristic of learners.

The previous experiences of learners, then, in terms of success and mastery of prerequisites, will greatly influence the speed at which they learn. However, most teachers can exercise little control over the learning experiences their students have before they arrive in the class. Consequently, curriculum designers should take variable learning speed into account. In practical terms, the designer must try to ensure that one group of learners is not held back and that another is not left behind. Thus the curriculum must specify the provision to be made for those students who learn particularly fast or slowly in that area of learning.

A Cybernetic Perspective

Before discussing specific strategies for dealing with differences in aptitude, it may be helpful to consider the question from a somewhat different perspective. The problem of maintaining consistently high achievement from a group of learners who differ in aptitude and other characteristics can be seen as an instance of the general question of how a system with variable input can be designed to produce stable output. Phrased in this way, the question lies squarely within the field of cybernetics, the study of self-regulation in systems.

Regulation of temperature in a building provides an illustration of a simple man-made cybernetic system. The environmental temperature varies with such factors as air temperature, solar radiation, and wind speed. The effects of variation in external temperature are moderated to some extent by the insulative value of the building. The air temperature inside the building is monitored continuously by a thermostat, which is set to switch a heating unit on and off when the temperature reaches certain predetermined levels. The effect is a continuous and regular oscillation of temperature inside the building within fairly narrow limits (Figure 12–1).

Human ingenuity has produced an enormous variety of self-regulating devices, from the flyball governor that James Watt perfected in 1769 to regulate the speed of his steam engine, to the boron rods and their driving mechanism that are used to maintain equilibrium in the neutron flux of a modern nuclear reactor. But the most elegant and complex cybernetic systems are found in nature. Temperature regulation in the human body may serve as an illustration.

Regulation of body temperature may be viewed as a cybernetic system that manages changing environmental and internal conditions to produce a stable output of 37°C. People moderate some of the effects of changes in external temperature by behavioral responses: wearing clothes, living in heated and insulated houses, and so on. The internal regulative system provides a much finer equilibrium than behavior can achieve. The body is equipped with sensors, mainly in the skin, which detect changes in temperature. This information is transmitted to the hypothalamus, a structure in the brain, which acts as a switching mechanism

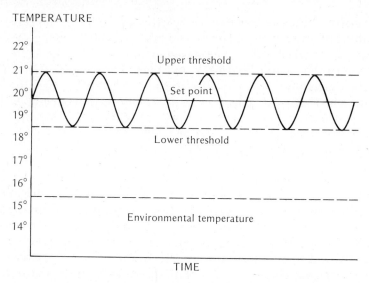

Figure 12–1   Thermostatic temperature regulation

to initiate certain responses to temperature change. When body heat begins to drop, heart rate and blood pressure are increased, peripheral blood vessels are constricted, "gooseflesh" raises the hairs on the skin, and shivering may begin. All these reactions serve to conserve or produce heat. If the body temperature begins to rise above normal, heart rate and blood pressure decrease, surface blood vessels dilate, and sweat may be secreted, the evaporation of which cools the skin. Figure 12–2 shows these effects in simplified form. The effectiveness of the system is such that humans can be exposed to temperatures from 5° to 50°C, either resting or exercising, without losing equilibrium of body temperature.

Let us now examine the characteristics of systems that succeed in regulating themselves in such a way as to produce stable output, and their implications for curriculum.

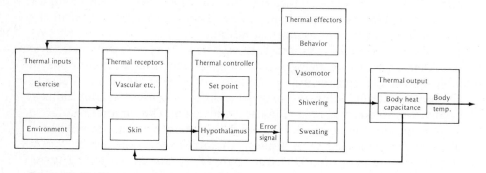

Figure 12–2   Human temperature regulation

Set point. All systems have a set point, an ideal or steady state to which the system returns after a disturbance in its equilibrium. The set point for a domestic heating system may be set at will. The set point of temperature of the human body is fixed at about 37°C. The more explicit the set point in the system, the more stable the system. The set point of a curriculum is the aim, the objectives, and the performance criteria. Evidence cited in earlier chapters indicates that the more unequivocally outcomes of instruction and standards of performance are recognized and accepted by instructors and students, the more likely they are to be achieved.

Exclusion of variety. All systems have boundaries or strategies for preventing extremes of variety from entering the system. This reduces the variety that must be managed within the system. Animals exclude some climatic variety by migrating, hibernating, building dens or nests, and by their fur, feathers, hide, or body fat. Human organizations such as churches and political parties exclude nonbelievers so that they will have to deal internally only with minor deviations from official doctrine, or heresies. Classrooms exclude variety primarily in terms of age of learners; some variety in ability, intelligence, background, and social class may also be excluded deliberately or unintentionally. However, much variety is allowed to enter the system. As mentioned earlier, high variety is found in classrooms in such significant variables as reading competence. In effect, the high-variety output of unstable systems in the lower grades provides the upper grades with high-variety input. In a curriculum, prerequisites perform the function of excluding extreme variety from the system. From a cybernetic point of view, a prerequisite is valid if it contributes to the stability of the system. If relevant prerequisites are ignored, the system will be able to maintain stability only by devoting considerable energy to managing the increased internal variety.

Sensing output. All systems have sensors that monitor the performance of the system. A motor skill such as walking is made possible by complex feedback systems with sensors in the muscles, joints, tendons, and skin, which monitor and compute changes in load, mechanical advantage, position, and rates of angular movement. The more sensitive the sensors and the more frequently they operate, the more stable the system. Formative evaluation, which monitors progress and diagnoses difficulties, constitutes the sensor mechanism in a curriculum.

Controller. The controller compares information from the sensors with the set point, and if there is a critical difference, signals remedial action. The hypothalamus is the controller for human temperature regulation and for several other body systems. A general in a military campaign compares information from reconnaissance units (sensors) with his strategic objectives (set point), identifies discrepancies, and orders action of the infantry or artillery. Decisions have to be made quickly, or the initiative may be lost. The more rapid the response of the controller, the more stable the system. If a student's achievement is falling seriously below the desired level, inordinate delay in deciding how to correct the situation exacerbates the problem. Hence remedial strategies must be predesigned by curriculum developers to help teachers act promptly.

Intervention of effectors. The controller orders or switches into operation effectors, or actuators, whose function it is to restore equilibrium to the system. Furnaces and refrigeration units are the effectors in a domestic heat regulation system. The thyroid, adrenal, and sweat glands are effectors in human temperature regulation, along with the heart, the vasodilator and vasoconstrictor centers, and the muscles involved in gooseflesh and shivering. The more rapid and effective the action of the effectors, the more stable the system. In the classroom, remediation must be sufficiently effective to return the underachieving student to the mainstream of the class, and it must do this before the other students have forged much further ahead.

The principles described above apply to all cybernetic systems: man-made, natural, and social. They provide a theoretical explanation of why the world does not dissolve into chaos. Chaotic education results from failure to apply these principles. The theory allows us to predict that instructional systems designed to follow basic cybernetic principles will be able to manage variety in pupil characteristics in such a way as to produce consistently acceptable levels of achievement in learning (Pratt, 1978).

Dealing with Underachievement

A stable instructional system must attend at the design stage to both aptitude extremes, the faster and the slower learners. We will deal first with strategies for dealing with those learners who tend to fall behind their peers. In both cases, it is instructive to examine strategies that have commonly been attempted in the past.

One response to underachievement is to ignore it. Figure 12–3 illustrates a system in which there is neither monitoring nor remediation. Children enter school at a fixed age and thereafter advance in lockstep year by year. The child who fails to master basic skills at any level is nevertheless advanced with the rest. This pattern used to be relatively common in English primary schools. It may account for the approximately one million English adults who, according to a recent government

Figure 12–3   No assessment, no remediation

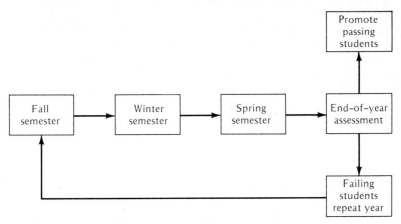

Figure 12–4   Annual assessment model

report, "cannot read simple recipes, 'social pamphlets,' tax return guides, claims for industrial injuries, national insurance guides for married women, and most of the Highway Code" (Bullock, 1975, p. 11).

Figure 12–4 shows the traditional pattern prevalent until recently in North America. The basic time unit is one year. Underachievement at the end of the year is treated by repetition of the year's work in one or more subject areas. This practice wastes the underachiever's time. The student repeats the whole year—often an ineffective form of remediation—although failure may have been only in part. If the failure occurred early and had been remedied then, the whole year might have been salvaged.

Figure 12–5 shows an attempt to overcome this weakness. Short units are followed by a test. Deficiencies in the class are remediated by devoting a lesson or two to remediation with the whole class. While this approach may be effective, it wastes the time of the successful students, who have to sit through remediation they do not need.

Figure 12–6 shows what appears to be a logical solution: identify the underachievers at the end of each unit, and give them remediation

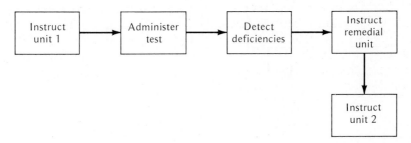

Figure 12–5   Group remediation

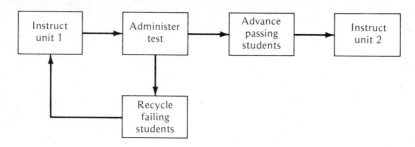

Figure 12–6   Unit repetition

while others proceed to the next unit. In practice this strategy will result in having multiple classes within each classroom. In one sense the effect is highly desirable: the class becomes increasingly individualized as the size of the subgroups approaches one. If one-to-one teaching is the intent, then the curriculum will need to be designed on an individualized model, with the necessary human and material resources provided to implement it effectively. The purpose of our discussion, however, is to identify a model that will work effectively on a group instructional basis.

Figure 12–7 shows a model that aims to avoid the shortcomings of the previous approaches. Units are relatively short; underachievers are given immediate remediation so that they can catch up with the rest of the group *before* it begins the next unit. Clearly the system will be easier to operate if there is some selection into the program (Figure 12–8). Failure to identify and redirect students who either lack prerequisites or have already mastered the objectives at the beginning of the course simply introduces additional variety into the system and means that greater resources, especially of the teacher's time, energy, and imagination, will have to be devoted to managing the differences among learners. In its simplest terms, there is a tradeoff between prerequisites and remediation. This hypothesis has recently been substantiated by empirical experiment (Pascarella, 1978).

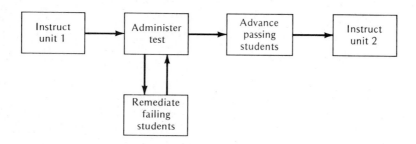

Figure 12–7   Immediate remediation

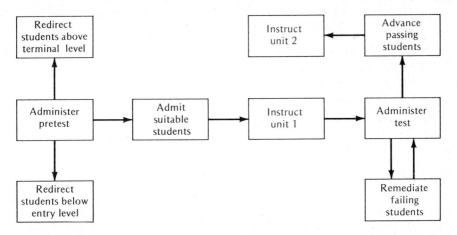

Figure 12-8   Optimal system

For the model to operate effectively, special care must be taken in the design of three factors: the length of the units, the nature of the unit tests, and the remediation.

Length of units

A unit may be defined as an instructional sequence having distinct objectives and separate assessment. Relatively short units enable the instructor to detect and remedy minor learning difficulties before they develop into major failures. Some European universities still have little or no serious testing until the final examinations at the end of the undergraduate's three- or four-year degree course; at that stage, remediation is impossible. Units of one year or one semester also present serious obstacles to effective remediation.

The "Keller plan," a mastery approach to learning now used with more than a million university students a year, calls for units containing as much material as can be tested on a fifteen-to-twenty-minute test: usually about one week's work (Keller and Sherman, 1974). Bloom recommends learning units of one to ten hours (1976, p. 22). Larger units increase the probability of failure in the intervals between tests and make both adequate testing and remediation problematic. On the other hand, excessively frequent testing erodes the time available for instruction. In most school situations, two to four weeks work, or ten to fifteen hours of learning time, seems to be an appropriate unit length.

If there is a danger that short units and frequent testing will fragment the learning and encourage only short-term cramming, a final course examination may encourage the students to integrate the learning from the course as a whole.

Michael Poole
Aged thirty-seven: orchard worker
Michael is one of Akenfield's some twenty or so bachelors, a good half
of which share his age group. They are simply waiting for a time which
suits them to marry but he waits in vain for any opportunity which will
take him from his parents' hearth. There are scarcely any words left to
describe him; the world has become a much kinder place where his sort
is concerned. "He is *simple* . . ." people will say, putting a wealth of
meaning into the description to make sure that it implies something quite
unalarming. Simple is exactly what he is not. He is illiterate and it is this
which cuts him off. He cannot read or write a single letter. "He couldn't
learn," it is explained. While the others thundered their way through the
multiplication tables, collects, Alfred Noyes's *Highwayman* and history
dates, Michael made rag rugs. He worked with incredible speed and
ingenuity, translating bundles of old coats, skirts and frocks into cosy
oblongs to lay along the side of beds, warm shaggy islands in the icy lino
seas. The women brought the rags and the school provided the time.
Nobody seemed to realize that a child who could work so hard and who
could make such good designs might have been able to learn if learning
had been a less rigid thing.

—*Ronald Blythe (1969, p. 226).*

Formative evaluation

The function of formative evaluation, as we have seen, is to monitor
student progress in learning. It is contrasted with summative evaluation,
which follows instruction and evaluates the achievement of objectives.
Airasian expresses the distinction succinctly: "Formative evaluation provides data about how students are changing . . . summative evaluation
is concerned with how students have changed" (1971, p. 78).

A test may be both formative and summative. For those students
who achieve the course objectives, the test is summative. For those who
do not, but are allowed an opportunity to repeat the test, it is formative,
indicating needed remediation. Scores on formative (qua formative) tests
should not affect the student's final grade, which should represent only
final achievement. If formative test scores are used for grading purposes,
students may reach a point where they cannot achieve a high grade for
the course, however well they ultimately master the objectives.

Most teachers practice very frequent formative evaluation by questioning pupils orally, observing them at work, checking notebooks, reading pupils' "body language," and so on. As Marion Blank points out (see
box), classroom groups make easy hiding places, and the designer is wise
to build into a curriculum some formative evaluation that will gather

fairly deliberate data on the achievement of individual learners. Many formal instructional approaches, such as computer-assisted instruction, systematically design formative evaluation into the program. Niedermeyer (1970) describes a reading program in which data on class achievement is gathered daily by systematic oral questioning of randomly selected pupils (Figure 12–9).

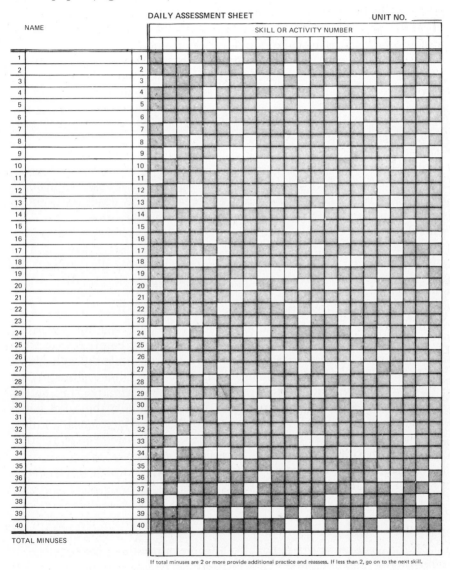

Figure 12–9   The instructor notes with a plus or minus sign the responses to oral questions by those children against whose names a blank square appears. (Niedermeyer, 1970, p. 12).

> The group-based structure of nursery school helps protect the child in his efforts to avoid learning. Because so many children are present, the child has opportunities for "appropriately" completing an activity even when he is totally unaware of the cognitive content of the task. This can occur through imitation, habit, or rote associations. For example, many disadvantaged children happily join in group singing by uttering nonsense syllables in place of the words of the song. The presence of fifteen other voices who are singing the appropriate words easily disguises the child's failure. The traditional group-based nursery school situation is thus perfectly designed to perpetuate the avoidance of learning in those children who have the most difficulty in learning.
>
> —*Marion Blank (1971, p. 3)*

The need for a rapid response to the results of formative evaluation requires that formative tests be self-marking or quickly marked. In some circumstances, students may mark their own or other students' work to expedite the marking process. Essay-type tests, which often require considerable time to evaluate, tend to be unsuitable for formative evaluation.

Although the purpose of formative tests is different from that of summative tests, the content will often be similar. Needless to say, the criteria of validity, objectivity, and reliability apply to formative evaluation just as they do to summative evaluation.

It is ideal if instructional units can be designed and tried out to ensure that not more than about ten percent of a typical group of learners fail to meet the minimum required standard at any point. A high incidence of learning difficulties suggests (1) an inappropriate difficulty level of the test, (2) inappropriate instruction, or (3) inadequate prerequisites or pretests. In other words, high failure rates at the formative stage imply a need for redesign rather than simply remediation. On the other hand, consistent success by all learners may not necessarily point to an ideal program; it may indicate either that (1) the tests are not assessing competence with sufficient rigor, or (2) a significant part of the instruction is redundant. The instructor should be alert to the design implications of both unusually high and low success rates.

Remediation

If the designer wants to develop a stable curriculum system—one in which individual students do not fall seriously behind their peers—then remediation must follow swiftly on the heels of identification of learning difficulty. In practice this usually means that remediation must be (1) predesigned, (2) unexacting for the teacher, and (3) relatively painless for the learner.

It may be sound practice to plan formative tests to take place before a weekend or holiday so that the student will have a day or two to complete the remediation. As the remediation is to be applied immediately, it is not usually possible for the teacher to start designing it only when underachievement becomes apparent. The exception would be the case in which an interview, tutorial, or special class after school is the appropriate form of remediation. Often it will be preferable to have a number of remedial "packages" ready, based on prediction or prior experience of the main areas of underachievement. The remediation might consist of a prerecorded cassette the identified students are to listen to several times over the weekend; a film they are asked to view in the school resource center at lunch time; a list of specific pages in the textbook they should reread; a few pages of programmed instruction they are to work through in their own time; an experiment or problem they can work on at home; or a visit to a remedial teacher specifically assigned to provide remediation to individual students.

Mere repetition of the original instruction is unlikely to be effective. If it didn't work the first time, there is no strong reason why it should the second time. The evidence of the effects of repetition of an entire year of school is not encouraging. In the United States alone, about one million students repeat a school year annually at a cost to society of close to one billion dollars (Jackson, 1975). Moreover, while some students improve, an equal number do worse the second time than the first (ibid.). The social and psychological trauma of repeating a year may be more significant than the fact that the experience is not designed to be remedial; repeaters tend to feel out of place and to be rejected by their classmates (Sandin, 1944). But even when feelings of rejection do not occur, there appear to be few academic benefits to repetition (Worth, 1959).

At the unit level, as at the grade level, the problem of underachievement may be one of motivation. If learners fail a course for which they have the prerequisities, the objectives of which are selected to meet real student needs, and the instruction in which is intelligently designed, the cause may be that they are not inspired to make the necessary effort. If possible, the reason for this should be ascertained, but in any event, as a general principle, the remedial work should be *more interesting* to the student than the regular instruction. This involves some self-discipline on the part of teachers, who naturally want to use their most spectacular instruction with the entire class.

An illustration   Ms. Rodriguez is teaching an intensive summer course in Spanish conversation. The course consists of five one-week units. The students, aged fourteen to seventeen, meet four hours a day, five days a week. The third week is devoted to basic tourist communication. At the end of the week, by way of a formative test, the students perform two-minute improvisations of tourist situations in small groups. Three students have not reached the required level of facility. The teacher calls them together at the end of the session and explains the need to achieve mastery before advancing to the next unit. Are they all free on Saturday evening? Two of them have dates. Sunday? Sunday is free. She arranges to obtain their parents' approval and to meet them at 7:00 P.M. at El Faro, the local Spanish restaurant. They will enjoy a leisurely Spanish meal and then listen to the Spanish folk singer for an hour or so. The single requirement is that only Spanish will be spoken during the evening. Furthermore, the cost will be assumed out of a cultural grant made to the program by the Spanish Embassy! Considerable progress can be made in oral language skills in three hours of conversation, especially with a teacher-pupil ratio of 1:3. The only risk entailed in such "painless" remediation is the "fatted-calf syndrome"—the danger that the class will begin to associate failure with pleasurable consequences.

Provision for Faster Learners

One purpose of designing effective formative evaluation and remediation is to ensure that slower learners do not waste their talents, their time, and their aspirations. This need is fairly widely recognized by educators, as is witnessed by the heavy investment in most jurisdictions in special education for the disadvantaged and disabled. In the United States, public willingness to invest in this area has been indicated by numerous items of legislation, such as the Education for All Handicapped Children Act of 1975, which appropriated $200 million annually for federal support of educational programs for the handicapped. Few would begrudge such an investment. Yet investment in programs for faster learners tends to be relatively slight. Without special attention to the needs of these learners, they, too, will be made to waste their talents, their time, and their aspirations.

Once again, it is necessary to insist that this discussion is dealing with students with above-average aptitude in specific areas, and not with

---

You can evaluate an educational system by the attention it gives to its extremes.

—*Lawrence Cremin, historian of education*

"In this class, young man, poetry rhymes.*"*

students holistically labeled as "gifted" or "talented." If the faster learners are arbitrarily defined as those whose learning speed is significantly
(say, one standard deviation) faster than average in a given area, then
almost all children are gifted in some way. And certainly it seems more
humane and socially functional to start from the assumption that every
child has particular gifts than that the gifted are a tiny elite who can be
distinguished in some general way from the rest of the population.

Traditional educational practice has treated student talent in one of
two ways. Elitist systems attempt to identify "the gifted," segregate
them, and give them superior educational resources. Egalitarian systems
attempt to bring everyone to a moderate level of achievement, often
frustrating those capable of higher attainment. The need is to develop
patterns of curriculum management that will allow all students to develop their talents to the fullest extent. This is the challenge facing the
educator who views education as a primary means of human development.

Six strategies for handling gifted students will be examined, some of
which are preferable to others: disregard, busywork, enrichment, peer
tutoring, ability grouping, and acceleration.

Disregard

Possibly the commonest response of all to the gifted is a nonresponse. It is almost inevitable if the student's aptitude is unrecognized. Studies have shown that teachers are often unaware even of exceptional aptitude in students whom they teach (Stanley, 1976). Constantly obliged to proceed at a pace far slower than their optimum, high-aptitude students may respond in one of two ways. They may resign themselves to marking time for much of their schooling, their boredom carefully controlled. In such cases, their talent may continue to go undetected, perhaps forever. Or, if an explosive frustration triggers disruptive behavior, they may simply be labeled troublemakers, their schooling perhaps prematurely terminated as a consequence.

Busywork

Susan is in third grade. The teacher has set the class twenty addition problems. Susan mastered addition in second grade. She finishes the problems well ahead of the rest of the class. Braving the glances of her peers, she takes her work up to the teacher. All twenty answers are correct, so the teacher gives Susan another twenty problems. Or she is asked to sort out the library books, wash the paintbrushes, or take a ten-minute break.

It does not take many such experiences for children to realize that working faster than their peers is rewarded by time-filling tasks. If this pattern is repeated over several years of schooling, it may have two main effects. One is that much potentially productive time is wasted. The other is that children may become so habituated to adapting to mediocrity that they actually become mediocre. In either event, the social costs are excessive.

Enrichment

The "problem" presented by fast learners is how to use the marginal time made available by their more rapid completion of work or attainment of objectives. Many teachers attempt to use this time to provide some kind of enrichment. Enrichment may take a number of forms: (1) greater breadth or depth in the same subject or (2) in another of the student's subjects; (3) remediation of underachievement in another subject; (4) the study of a new subject not presently part of the student's program; or (5) cultural enrichment.

The key question to be asked about enrichment is Is it enriching? Does it enrich a student's program, or a student's life, simply to add novels to the English requirements or assign extra research papers in social studies? If these activities are essentially "more of the same," then they are just as much busywork as cleaning out the hamster's cage or reorganizing the notices on the bulletin board. If, on the other hand, the enrichment activities are building breadth and depth in a student's knowledge of one of his or her academic fields, then sooner or later the student will have to be accelerated in that area. In Stanley's words,

> The more relevant and excellent the enrichment, the more it calls for acceleration of subject-matter or grade placement later. Otherwise it just puts off the boredom a while and virtually guarantees that eventually it will be more severe (Stanley, 1976, p. 235).

Using marginal time to remediate weak areas has obvious advantages. So does allowing the fast learner to spend time mastering new areas; the student who is ahead in mathematics may study astronomy, and the student ahead in French may begin German. Or faster learners may learn how to use a movie camera or to play the guitar. In designing enrichment, as in all curriculum, the essential criterion is that the experiences help to meet a significant human need.

The major problem in enrichment is logistical. The teacher is likely to feel that his or her primary responsibility is to the twenty-nine children who have not yet mastered the objectives of a program, rather than to the one who has. Little time can properly be spared to direct an individual project by the fast learner. As with remediation, enrichment must be preplanned. One way of doing this would be to have one teacher in every school, located in the library or resource center, whose major responsibility is to design and supervise individual projects for faster learners referred by the classroom or subject teachers. If budgets would not stretch that far, a teacher's aide or a team of volunteers could probably serve equally well. If even that were impossible, a filing cabinet of self-instructional projects remains an alternative. Leaving enrichment to the discretion of the student may not be ideal. A research project that was conducted in a Texas school system and eventually led to the discontinuance of daily free-choice enrichment periods reported that "one of our observers had observed a student wrap string around a chair leg repeatedly for 35 minutes as his choice of an enriching experience for that day" (Hester and Ligon, 1978, p. 17).

Peer tutoring

Older pupils were widely used in nineteenth-century schools as monitors assisting in the instruction of younger students. Much informal peer tutoring is carried on in most occupational and educational contexts, and most effectively among siblings in the home. Educational innovators and researchers are now turning their attention once again to peer tutoring as a structured part of the school program. Definitive studies have yet to be conducted, but some preliminary conclusions may be drawn.

> The gifted Joachim Fortinus used to say that if a student wished to make progress, he should arrange to give lessons daily in the subjects which he was studying, even if he had to hire his pupils.
>
> —*John Comenius (c. 1650)*

Studies of peer tutoring have been conducted in many curriculum areas. In reading, the subject in which peer tutoring has been most frequently reported, the effect on the tutored child's learning ranges from slight to substantial (Devin-Sheehan, Feldman, and Allen, 1976). Furthermore, peer tutoring appears to have consistent and significant benefits for tutors. Not only do they make academic gains, which usually outweigh those of their pupils (Lippitt, 1975), they also tend to develop an improved attitude toward school and an increased level of aspiration. Tutors gain the experience of helping others, of developing trust, patience, confidence, and responsibility, of being appreciated, of sharing resources, and of cooperating with teachers. "It gives you an absolute sense of accomplishment," one twelfth-grade student wrote after tutoring seventh-grade students for a year, "you are helping more than the children—you are helping yourself." "In order to gain a child's respect," wrote another, "you must win it or earn it, and when you have done that, it becomes a very precious, honored thing" (*Dimensions*, 1977, p. 2). Enriching for tutors, remedial for slower learners, peer tutoring is an ideal strategy for increasing the stability of the instructional system.

Faster learners are a natural choice as tutors; they have the aptitude and the extra time. But tutoring may offer even greater benefits to slower learners. Several studies have found low-achieving students effective as tutors for younger children. Tutors who are themselves retarded have been able to bring about significant improvement in the eating and dressing behaviors of other retarded children (Devin-Sheehan, Feldman, and Allen, 1976). After reviewing the evidence from several experiments using handicapped and learning-disabled children in helping and tutoring roles, McGee, Kauffman, and Nussen concluded that "it seems abundantly clear that children of all shapes and sizes can effectively participate as change agents" (1977, p. 464).

In passing, it may be noted that peer tutoring works as successfully with adults as with children. A U.S. Army training program for wiremen—soldiers who establish telecommunications facilities under battlefield conditions—found conventional training methods less than satisfactory with trainees varying widely in background and aptitude. An experiment was conducted in which officers trained a group of wiremen, each of whom then trained two others, and so on. Although 100 percent mastery was required at each stage, it was found possible to train men faster and at reduced cost. Furthermore, the training time unexpectedly declined for each "generation" of trainees. One aspect of peer tutoring was noted by a trainee: "It's a bit scary up there on that pole. But it helps to know that the guy who's telling you how to do it is just like you and went through the whole bit himself just two weeks ago" (Larkin, 1973, p. 21).

Peer tutoring does not have to be highly structured. Arranging learners in small groups for learning tasks can result in much informal tutoring (McGee, Kauffman, and Nussen, 1977). Having students complete formative tests in groups of two or three increases the likelihood that the test will constitute a learning experience. According to Bloom, "providing opportunities for small groups of students to help each other" is the most effective form of remediation (1976, p. 5).

Few general rules governing tutoring have yet emerged from the research, but three principles merit consideration: (1) the purpose and nature of the programs should be clearly understood by the tutors and those tutored and by their teachers and parents; (2) tutors should have mastered the basics of the subject to be taught; and (3) tutors should be rewarded for their work. In view of the academic gains usually realized by tutors, academic credit appears to be an appropriate reward, at least for high-school and college students (Keller and Sherman, 1974, p. 38).

Like any other practice, peer tutoring can be abused. The value of the experience to the tutor and the tutored student must be weighed against the cost of holding back the faster learner from proceeding at his or her own pace. Unless a benefit is being realized by both learners, peer tutoring can become exploitive. With this reservation, peer tutoring appears to be one of the more functional and creative strategies for dealing with faster learners.

Ability grouping

Ability grouping may be defined as organization of learners into groups for instruction on the basis of assumed or demonstrated intelligence or general or specific aptitude. In its most rigid form (known as streaming or tracking) students are segregated for extended periods into parallel but separate tracks, or streams, leading to different academic and career outcomes and life chances; the streams have a clear hierarchy of status, and upward mobility between streams is inhibited.

The gifted do not have special rights; they do have special responsibilities.

—*Dan Bitan, Israeli educator*

A study conducted in Sweden suggested that in heterogeneous classes teachers tend to direct their instruction at students who are between the bottom tenth and the bottom quarter of the class in terms of ability (Dahlöff, 1971). As a result, faster learners are held back, while the least able 10 percent are treated as expendable, and may fall behind and fail. Ability grouping is based on the intuitive or common-sense assumption that grouping students of approximately equal ability together will reduce the variance in learning speed within a class, prevent the faster learners being slowed down by the slower ones, allow greater attention to the needs of all learners, and increase the efficiency of instruction. As with so many common-sense beliefs about education, the empirical evidence indicates that it is not necessarily so.

The research literature on ability grouping is vast. It has probably been more extensively researched than any other organizational practice in schools. The bulk of the research has been conducted in Britain, Sweden, and the United States, and the only generalization that can safely be made about the results is that they are inconsistent. Space permits only a brief review of the research results in some of the major areas.

Effect on achievement   Analyses of the academic achievement of students in homogeneous ability classes show a generally random pattern, with the majority of studies showing no difference in average achievement of students in ability-grouped compared with ungrouped classes. The few studies where average and above-average students benefited from grouping are balanced by an equal number of cases where they achieved better in ungrouped classes. But the evidence shows consistently that ability grouping does not benefit slower learners academically and often reduces their achievement. Three major studies in England (Barker Lunn, 1970), Sweden (Husen and Svenssen, 1960), and the United States (Goldberg and Passow, 1965) showed no differences in the achievement of slow pupils under homogeneous and heterogeneous grouping. An equal number of studies in the same three countries showed slower students at a relative disadvantage in streamed classes (Daniels, 1961; Svenssen, 1962; Borg, 1965). As the main purpose of ability grouping is to provide academic benefits, it is a significant conclusion that it tends to produce no such benefit consistently but does tend to be detrimental to slower learners.

Effect on self-image   The effect of any educational practice on students' self-image must be given serious consideration, both because self-image is a major determinant of academic achievement and because it is integral to the development of the personality and the happiness of the individual.

Elder (1965) summarized the English research and concluded that a clear pattern emerged of a more negative self-image among lower-stream students. The practical effects of this may be inferred in such research as that of Douglas (1964), who found that elementary-school students of equal ability improved in achievement if placed in the "A" stream and deteriorated if placed in the "B" stream, making the selection process a self-fulfilling prophecy. Esposito (1973) reviewed the American research and concluded that the affective results of ability grouping were largely negative; while the practice sometimes inflated the self-esteem of superior pupils, it tended to reduce that of slower pupils, especially when they were taught by academically oriented teachers. In a large-scale study of two school districts in Utah, Borg found that the self-image of slow, average, and fast learners was "almost universally superior" in the ungrouped system (1965, p. 67).

Ability grouping restricts students' opportunities for social interaction. Fewer mixed-ability friendships occur (Barker Lunn, 1970, p. 276), and slower students cannot seek the help of faster learners. As lower streams are often used as "dumping grounds" for students with poor motivation, emotional problems, poor health, or minority backgrounds (Heathers, 1972), the least privileged and the least well adjusted are thereby prevented from associating with their more fortunate peers. Although lower-ability pupils have more chance of becoming "stars" in an ability-grouped classroom, it is in fact in such classes that lower aspirations and higher dropout rates develop (Elder, 1965). These tendencies are reinforced by a frequent pattern of providing more qualified and experienced teachers and better resources and facilities to the upper groups (Barker Lunn, 1967). It would be nothing short of astonishing if these practices, which are quite evident to students, did not adversely affect the self-image of slower learners.

Methods of selection   For ability grouping to operate as intended, the methods of selection would need to be highly valid, objective, and reliable. The evidence is generally discouraging in this regard. When ability is controlled, disproportionate numbers of middle-class children are

---

I felt good when I was with my class, but when they went and separated us—that changed us. That changed our ideas, our thinking, the way we thought about each other and turned us to enemies toward each other—because they said I was dumb and they were smart. . . . The girls that were in my class back in the sixth grade—they look at you—"You're in the basic section aren't you?" You know, all of a sudden, the guys you used to hang out with won't hang out with you no more.

—*Youth interviewed by Presidential Task Force on Juvenile Delinquency (Schafer and Polk, 1967, pp. 241–242).*

found in the higher streams, with a similar disproportion of lower-class children in the lower streams. This is a consistent finding of research in Britain (Barker Lunn, 1970), Sweden (Husen and Svenssen, 1960), and the United States (Esposito, 1973), and has also been noted in Canada (Porter, 1975). Table 12–1 shows the findings from one American study of two mid-western high schools in 1961. Studies in Britain have pointed to bias and inaccuracy in selection into streams (Yates, 1966; Davies, 1975). In American courts more than one judge has ruled against tracking in response to evidence that many black children capable of superior accomplishment had been placed in the lowest tracks (Samuda, 1973; Cuban, 1975). Detailed analysis of American data by Heyns (1974), however, indicates that social class per se does not have a large direct effect on placement in a curriculum track. It is rather the widespread use of verbal ability tests that gives middle-class children a substantial advantage over their less privileged peers.

Ability grouping: Conclusion   Ability grouping is practiced in the official belief that it helps the school meet the needs of individual learners. The mass of evidence suggests that it improves the achievement of few children and lowers that of many; that it damages children's self-esteem; that selection methods tend to be inaccurate and biased; that once initial grouping decisions are made, they tend to assign a stigma that is unalterable and self-fulfilling; and that it is based on erroneous assumptions regarding the validity and stability of intelligence measures and the concept of general aptitude. Before discussing alternative criteria for grouping learners, let us look at one further strategy for dealing with faster learners: acceleration.

Acceleration

There is an obvious logic in allowing faster learners to proceed more rapidly through school. But what often passes for acceleration is not so much allowing the student to proceed through the same steps at higher

FAMILY BACKGROUND	PERCENT IN COLLEGE TRACK	PERCENT IN NONCOLLEGE TRACK
White collar	81	19
Blue collar	50	50
White race	69	30
Black race	32	67

Table 12–1 Distribution of students in tracks by father's occupation and race, student IQ and previous achievement held constant (from Schafer and Olexa, 1971, p. 35)

speed, but "skipping," which allows the learner to miss certain steps, usually grades, altogether. If in the process the student misses learnings that are prerequisite to subsequent work, skipping may result in learning difficulties or failure.

There is a more significant reason why acceleration, as traditionally practiced, has limited effectiveness and can be damaging. The nine-year-old among a group of ten-year-olds is visibly different from the other children. The accelerated student can often handle social interaction with older children on account of greater interpersonal effectiveness and social maturity (Haier and Denham, 1976). But the other students may resent the arrival of a child a year younger and physically smaller than any of them. Unfortunately, this attitude may be reinforced by teachers (Haier and Solano, 1976). This aspect of acceleration is most frequently criticized by accelerated students themselves (Hayball, 1971).

The major obstacle to acceleration is that it runs counter to the traditional practice of organizing learning groups by age. Despite this obstacle, acceleration, even of the skipping variety (see box), is often successful. I once questioned a number of adults who had been accelerated in school, and between half and three-quarters of them averred that the benefits outweighed the disadvantages. From the available published evidence one can only conclude that the social and emotional problems resulting from acceleration tend to be exaggerated. The Study of Mathematically Precocious Youth at Johns Hopkins University has placed several dozen students in college in their early teens and as young as eleven and a half without encountering major problems of social adjustment (Stanley, 1976). Accelerated classes in that program have contained an age span of five years and great variation in physical size of children but report excellent social and academic interaction (George and Denham, 1976). Terman (1947) could find no evidence of social or emotional maladjustment resulting from acceleration among his group of highly intelligent individuals.

Too rarely considered in debates on acceleration are the costs of nonacceleration. First is the cost of frustration, boredom, and wasted time on the part of the faster learner forced to proceed at a slow pace. The tediousness of schoolwork may result in extended daydreaming, laziness, disruptive behavior, and even withdrawal from school. Second is the financial cost of keeping a student in school and college for more years than are necessary. Third is the cost of delaying the beginning of independent creative or professional work. To take a simple example: a physician who receives his M.D. at age twenty-seven and retires at sixty is a consumer of educational services for twenty-one years, and a producer of medical services for thirty-three years. But the physician who receives his M.D. at twenty-one and retires at sixty is a consumer for only fifteen years and a producer for thirty-nine years. Extrapolated throughout society, the cost of redundance in schooling is enormous.

Radical Acceleration

We first heard of this boy, whom I shall call Sean, in the fall of 1971. As a sixth-grader whose twelfth birthday came that December 4, he was rather old [for his grade]. . . . It was not until we formed our first fast-mathematics class in June, 1972, that he, then 12½ years old, began to get special educational facilitation from us. . . . The class continued until August, 1973, and Sean was one of its two stars. He completed 4½ years of precalculus mathematics well in 60 two-hour Saturday mornings, compared with the 810 45- or 50-minute periods usually required for Algebra I through III, plane geometry, trigonometry, and analytic geometry.

Sean skipped the seventh grade . . . and in the eighth grade took no mathematics other than the Saturday morning class. Also, during the second semester of the eighth grade he was given released time to take the introduction to computer science course at Johns Hopkins. . . .

While still 13 years old, Sean skipped the ninth and tenth grades and became an eleventh-grader at a larger suburban public high school. There he took calculus with twelfth-graders, won a letter on the wrestling team, was the science and math whiz on the school's television academic quiz team, tutored a brilliant seventh-grader through 2½ years of algebra and a year of plane geometry in eight months, played a good game of golf, and took some college courses on the side (set theory, economics, and political science). . . . This left time to prepare for the Advanced Placement Program in calculus and, entirely by studying on his own, also in physics. He won 14 college credits via those two exams.

During the summer after completing the eleventh grade, Sean took a year of college chemistry at Johns Hopkins—as usual, earning good grades. That enabled him to enter Johns Hopkins in the fall of 1974 with 34 credits and therefore sophomore status. . . . During the first semester he took *advanced* calculus, number theory, *sophomore* physics, and American government, making As on the two math courses and Bs on the other two courses. Also, he began to get involved in campus politics. He got along well socially and emotionally. As he told an Associated Press reporter who asked about this, "Either social considerations take a poor second to intellectual ones, or there are no negative social effects. . . . The most significant aspect of my life is having skipped grades."

—Julian C. Stanley (1976, pp. 235–236)

Grouping Learners for Instruction

This discussion of strategies for managing aptitude differences has touched at many points on the question of constituting instructional groups. Some limitations of ability grouping have been indicated, but an alternative has not been suggested. Before doing so, it is necessary to look briefly at the major criterion used to form instructional groups in schools: the criterion of age.

Age grading: An idea whose time has gone

Political and administrative considerations usually dictate that students enter school at about the same age. But after admission, why has age continued to be the main factor in school organization? Historically, students have been segregated by age, sex, and social class. We have, at least in theory, rejected the latter two criteria, but the first remains virtually unchallenged.

The argument in favor of age grading is that it ensures a common level of cognitive development and hence produces a homogeneous learning group. The contention is clearly fallacious. Homogeneous grouping involves other factors besides cognitive development. Furthermore, age does not consistently predict level of cognitive development. Girls at age thirteen have, on average, the intellectual maturity of boys at fifteen (Cornell and Armstrong, 1955). Hence if the goal is uniformity of maturation, it will require differential, not uniform, age grading.

Age grading has been the norm in schools for so long that it is generally considered to be "natural." (In the American South thirty years ago, racial segregation in schools was also considered "natural.") But is it natural? The first and most "natural" social environment experienced by the child is the family, which is characterized by variety in the age of the different members. Would family life be more enriching if all the children were the same age? Reflection suggests that the interaction of siblings and parents of different ages produces a uniquely rewarding experience. Placing the child with his or her age-peers throughout the years of schooling provides a model of social uniformity that is artificial and restricting. Informal evidence from schools that have persuaded adults to enroll in regular programs for adolescents suggests consistent salutary effects on class climate and interpersonal relationships.

This is not to say that age is never a valid criterion for grouping learners. A "home form"—a stable peer group and teacher with whom the student can identify over an extended period—has some merit and is apparently particularly welcomed by students who place high value on social relations (Fox, 1976). Sex education is unlikely to be most effectively taught to preadolescents and postadolescents in the same class, although here again maturation rather than age is the critical factor. In learning to ski or to skate, adults are shy of falling on their faces in front of children, and some age segregation may be desirable. And for legal reasons, age may be a criterion for a driver-education or wine-making course. But these instances do not seem to justify uniform age grading in schools. If age is dismissed as a general criterion for grouping, what should replace it?

Grouping by readiness

Consideration of the evidence reported in this chapter leads to the conclusion that the management of differences among learners will be most efficient, effective, and humane if the composition of instructional groups is generally determined according to the criterion of readiness for the learning.

Three kinds of readiness need to be considered: maturation, motivation, and prerequisites. As these have been previously discussed in the chapter on entry characteristics (10), only a brief review is given here.

The student's level of cognitive development must be sufficiently advanced that he or she can master the objectives and handle the subject matter and teaching methodologies used in the program. Thus, to study history successfully, the child must have acquired the concept of historical time; to usefully engage in a course on ethics, the learner must have reached the intellectual stage of formal operations.

It is a waste of time attempting to teach students anything if they are not motivated and if they refuse to develop any interest in the subject. Even carefully designed incentive programs often have little effect on children who hate school (Breuning, 1978). Potential motivation at least is necessary if learning is to take place.

Learning prerequisites are often critical to readiness. Students are not ready for calculus until they have acquired some basic concepts and skills in algebra and trigonometry. It will be recalled that cognitive prerequisites stated in terms of knowledge and skills are generally preferable to academic prerequisites stated in terms of courses, programs, or grades. In addition, prerequisites such as good health, eyesight, or hearing may be valid where their absence would endanger the learner or others in the group. Prerequisites imply maximum as well as minimum prior learnings. A student who has already mastered the objectives of a curriculum is no more "ready" for that curriculum than a person can be said to be ready to leave for the airport when he or she is already on the plane.

If these aspects of readiness are controlled, it should be unnecessary to base selection on age, aptitude, intelligence, verbal ability, teacher recommendation, academic grades, or any of the other criteria so frequently employed. But let us admit one exception. There may be valid grounds for grouping learners separately who have extremely high aptitude (the top 1 to 5 percent) in a particular subject. These learners master particular kinds of learning so much faster than the average that all the strategies of adjustment will not prevent them from being held back in a heterogeneous classroom. Enough highly successful experiments have been conducted with separate instruction in certain subjects for exceptionally talented children that some confidence is justified that the benefits exceed the risks. The same may be true with respect to the slowest 1 to 5 percent of learners. In some of these cases, learning disabilities may affect a wide range of curriculum areas, and the benefits of separation must be carefully weighed against the social and psychological advantages of mainstreaming.

Clearly the visitor to a school using readiness as the criterion for grouping learners would not see the familiar classrooms of pupils who are similar in age and size but widely different in interest and performance. More probably the typical classroom would contain twelve-year-olds, twenty-two-year-olds, and sixty-two-year-olds; students from elementary, secondary, perhaps college levels; homemakers, shiftworkers, and unemployed and retired people using their leisure time in self-development—all sharing an interest in the subject of instruction and a minimum basis of prior learning. In such a group, both the accelerated and the slower learner cease to be visibly distinct by reason of their age, thus removing a major difficulty that inhibits students from progressing at their own pace.

As Figure 12–10 indicates, the criterion for grouping learners determines the kind of adjustments needed in the curriculum to accommodate different speeds of learning. The evidence already available suggests that grouping by readiness reduces variation in learning speed. Consequently, it is less essential to make special provision for faster learners, because those who have already mastered the objectives are placed in a different group. However, it remains sound practice to plan formative evaluation and remediation.

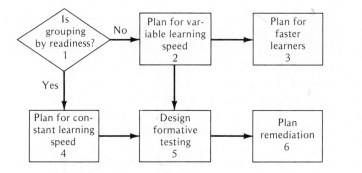

Figure 12–10   Management of aptitude differences

Immediate and Ultimate Possibilities

Pragmatic curriculum design must take account of constraints, some of which are imposed by patterns of school organization and administration. Many of the obstacles to managing differences in learner aptitude cannot be overcome by the curriculum designer single-handedly. Hence the question that is invariably posed at some point by students of curriculum design: How can we implement rational curricula in irrationally organized schools?

A realistic reply is that much can be achieved unilaterally by the designer and the teacher by intelligent use of the strategies of frequent formative evaluation, remediation, peer tutoring, and enrichment.

At the same time, it is intriguing to speculate on the potential of an educational system in which the curriculum, in its endeavor to meet the varying needs and aptitudes of learners, is supported rather than inhibited by the organizational structure of schools. One suspects that if a system were willing ruthlessly to question and revise its conventional assumptions and practices, to allow learners genuine control of their progress, it could produce results for all learners of which most practitioners have as yet not even dreamed.

ACTIVITIES

1. Three children in your fifth-grade class are falling behind in the unit on addition and subtraction of decimals. Design a remedial unit that can be completed during a weekend and that (1) reinforces the basic principles, (2) provides extensive drill, and (3) is fun for the learners.

2. Rank the students in a class in terms of their mastery of the subject. Then group the students into heterogeneous groups, e.g., students 1, 11, and 21 together. Have each group complete the next suitable formative test cooperatively. Observe the effects. Discuss the experience with the students.

3. Identify some slower learners who lack a strong academic self-image but are not severely alienated. Find an area in which they are competent. Give them some basic instruction in tutoring, and have them tutor pupils two or three grades younger who are having difficulty in the area. Observe the process and summarize conclusions.

4. Four pupils in an eighth-grade class are three weeks ahead of the others in a Spanish course. Design an enrichment unit that requires little teacher input and is genuinely enriching.

5. If during your own schooling you had been permitted and encouraged to proceed at your own best learning rate in every curriculum area, how would your education have been different? How would you now be different?

6. Suppose that you were asked to teach a class in your subject that contained students ranging in age from six to sixty-six. How would you alter the curriculum? What opportunities would this present? What problems?

QUESTIONS

1. Curriculum design ideally leads to the creation of stable instructional systems. In cybernetic terms, a system is stable if it

   a. produces unvarying output
   b. is not affected by changes in the environment
   c. produces fairly consistent output despite fluctuations in input
   d. produces output that, on average, is at approximately the desired level

2. Smaller units of instruction are generally more efficient than larger ones because

   a. most students' attention span is fairly limited
   b. they fit more appropriately within the conventional school year
   c. students can more easily grasp the total concept of the curriculum
   d. it is easier to correct minor underachievement before it becomes major failure

3. In which of the following courses would most resources probably have to be committed to remediation?

   a. a course that teaches skills and has no prerequisites
   b. a course emphasizing knowledge, with high prerequisites
   c. a course with largely experiential objectives and no prerequisites
   d. a course in biochemistry that admits only students who scored over 90 percent in a previous biochemistry course

4. Remedial work should be

   a. provided by the teacher in person
   b. a repeat of instruction that was not learned the first time
   c. more motivational to the remedial students than the regular content
   d painful enough to encourage underachieving students to do better next time

5. Annabel finishes her exercise on addition of decimals several minutes ahead of the rest of the class. Which strategy is likely to benefit her most?

   a. give her another exercise on addition of decimals
   b. ask her to pick up the litter in the classroom
   c. tell her she can go to the cafeteria for ten minutes
   d. ask her to help another student who is having difficulty

6. In providing enrichment for fast learners, the key question is

   a. is it critical?
   b. is it enriching?

    c. are the outcomes measurable?
    d. is it related to the subject?

7. For peer tutoring to be effective, it is necessary that

    a. the tutors have high aptitude or intelligence
    b. the tutor have mastered the basics of what is to be taught
    c. the tutoring has a detailed and clearly specified structure
    d. the tutor is approximately the same age as the child to be tutored

8. One of the effects of streaming into academic and nonacademic streams or tracks, is that as generally practiced

    a. the division tends to follow social class lines
    b. it improves the performance of less able students
    c. it provides an education more suited to individual needs
    d. one can safely predict a student's intelligence from his or her track

9. A major obstacle to acceleration is

    a. the financial expense
    b. the social immaturity of most gifted children
    c. the organization of schools on the basis of age
    d. the difficulty students below the age of eighteen have in coping with college

10. If a school wanted to increase instructional efficiency by teaching students in homogeneous groups, the most important factor to consider in grouping the learners would be

    a. age
    b. intelligence
    c. academic aptitude
    d. readiness for the learning

Check your answers against the key in Appendix 2.
9 or 10 right: You understand the material presented.
8 or 7 right: Review the areas of uncertainty.
6 or less right: Reread the chapter.

Recommended Reading

Allen, Vernon L. (ed.). *Children as teachers.* New York: Academic Press, 1976. Collection of articles on the theory and practice of children tutoring children. Necessary research still has to be done, but this book spells out the major benefits and costs, including the high effort needed to introduce the innovation.

Gallagher, James J. *Teaching the gifted child.* 2nd ed. Boston: Allyn & Bacon, 1975. A comprehensive survey by a recognized authority on the research and procedures related to education of the gifted. Deals with treatment of the gifted in general and in specific content areas. Interesting discussion of training teachers for the gifted and managing gifted underachievers.

Gronlund, Norman. *Individualizing classroom instruction*. New York: Macmillan, 1974. Written with Gronlund's usual clear and concise style, this book deals with several programs and approaches to individualization and describes general principles for individualizing instruction.

Glaser, Robert. *Adaptive education: Individual diversity and learning*. New York: Holt, Rinehart & Winston, 1977. Outstanding brief text relating instructional strategy to psychological theory. Deals with adaptation of curricula to pupils' background, interests, and learning styles, as well as to their aptitude.

Jackson, Brian. *Streaming: An educational system in miniature*. London: Routledge & Kegan Paul, 1964. Books on streaming can be classified as scholarly and polemic. This book is undoubtedly polemic, but the data and interviews presented are valuable for the vivid light they throw on the practices and results of streaming in English primary schools.

References

Airasian, Peter W. The role of evaluation in mastery learning. In James H. Block (ed.), *Mastery learning: Theory and practice*. New York: Holt, Rinehart & Winston, 1971, pp. 77–88.

Anderson, Lorin W. An empirical investigation of individual differences in time to learn. *Journal of Educational Psychology*, 1976, 68, 226–233.

Barker Lunn, Joan C. The effects of streaming and non-streaming in junior schools: Second interim report. *New Research in Education*, 1967, 1, 46–75.

——— . *Streaming in the primary school*. Slough, England: National Foundation for Educational Research, 1970.

Blank, Marion. The treatment of personality variables in a preschool cognitive program. Paper presented at the Hyman Blumberg Conference on Early Childhood Education, Johns Hopkins University, January 1971.

Block, James H., and Robert B. Burns. Mastery learning. In Lee S. Shulman (ed.), *Review of research in education 4*. Itasca, Ill.: Peacock and American Educational Research Association, 1976, pp. 3–49.

Bloom, Benjamin S. Time and learning. *American Psychologist*, 1974, 29, 682–688.

——— . *Human characteristics and school learning*. New York: McGraw-Hill, 1976.

Blythe, Ronald. *Akenfield*. Harmondsworth, England: Penguin, 1969.

Borg, Walter R. Ability grouping in the public schools. *Journal of Experimental Education*, 1965, 34 (2), 1–97.

Breuning, Stephen E. Precision teaching in the high school classroom: A necessary step towards maximizing teacher effectiveness and student performance. *American Educational Research Journal*, 1978, 15, 125–140.

Bullock, Sir Allan, Chairman. *Committee of inquiry: Department of Education and Science*. London: Her Majesty's Stationery Office, 1975.

Burt, C. Mental capacity and its critics. *Bulletin of the British Psychological Society*, 1968, 21, 11–18.

Carroll, John B. Problems of measurement related to the concept of learning for mastery. In James H. Block (ed.), *Mastery learning: Theory and practice.* New York: Holt, Rinehart & Winston, 1971, pp. 29–46.

Cornell, Ethel L., and Charles M. Armstrong. Forms of mental growth patterns revealed by reanalysis of the Harvard Growth Data. *Child Development,* 1955, 26, 169–204.

Cuban, Larry. Hobson vs. Hansen: A study in organizational response. *Educational Administration Quarterly,* 1975, 11 (2), 15–37.

Csapo, Marg. Peer models reverse the "One bad apple spoils the barrel" theory. *Teaching Exceptional Children,* 1972, 5 (Fall), 20–24.

Dahlöff, Urban S. *Ability grouping, content validity, and curriculum process analysis.* New York: Teachers College Press, 1971.

Daniels, J. C. The effects of streaming in the primary school: 1. What teachers believe. *British Journal of Educational Psychology,* 1961, 31, 69–78.

Davies, R. Peter. *Mixed ability grouping.* London: Temple Smith, 1975.

Devin-Sheehan, Linda, Robert S. Feldman, and Vernon L. Allen. Research on children tutoring children: A critical review. *Review of Educational Research,* 1976, 46, 355–383.

Dimensions. Students perform "adult" roles in credit course. *Dimensions,* 1977, 11 (1), 2.

Douglas, J. W. B. *The home and the school: A study of ability and attainment in the primary school.* London: McGibbon and Kee, 1964.

Educational Products Information Exchange Institute. Evaluating instructional systems: An in-depth report. *EPIE Educational Product Report,* 1974, 7, no. 58.

Elder, Glen H., Jr. Life opportunity and personality: Some consequences of stratified secondary education in Great Britain. *Sociology of Education,* 1965, 38, 173–202.

Esposito, Dominick. Homogeneous and heterogeneous ability grouping: Principal findings and implications for evaluating and designing more effective educational environments. *Review of Educational Research,* 1973, 43, 163–179.

Fox, Lynn H. Sex differences in mathematical precocity: Bridging the gap. In Daniel P. Keating (ed.), *Intellectual talent: Research and development.* Baltimore: Johns Hopkins University Press, 1976, pp. 183–214.

George, William C., and Susanne A. Denham. Curriculum experimentation for the mathematically talented. In Daniel P. Keating (ed.), *Intellectual talent: Research and development.* Baltimore: Johns Hopkins University Press, 1976, pp. 103–131.

Gibbon, Edward. *Autobiography.* London: Oxford University Press, 1907.

Goldberg, Miriam L., and A. Harry Passow. *The effects of ability grouping: A comparative study of broad, medium and narrow-range classes in the elementary school.* New York: Teachers College, Columbia University, 1965.

Gronlund, Norman E. *Individualizing classroom instruction.* New York: Macmillan, 1974.

Haier, Richard J., and Susanne A. Denham. A summary profile of the nonintellectual correlates of mathematical precocity in boys and girls. In Daniel P. Keating (ed.), *Intellectual talent: Research and development.* Baltimore: Johns Hopkins University Press, 1976, pp. 225–241.

Haier, Richard J., and Cecilia H. Solano. Educators' stereotypes of mathematically gifted boys. In Daniel P. Keating (ed.), *Intellectual talent: Research and development.* Baltimore: Johns Hopkins University Press, 1976, pp. 215–222.

Hayball, H. L. Acceleration: Effects, selection criteria, and factors associated with achievement. Scarborough, Ontario: Scarborough Board of Education Research Department, 1971.

Heathers, Glen. Overview of innovations in organization for learning. *Interchange*, 1972, 3, 47–68.

Hester, Joy, and Glynn Ligon. Where does the time go? A study of time use in public schools. Paper presented at the Annual Meeting of the American Educational Research Association, Toronto, March 1978.

Heyns, Barbara. Social selection and stratification within schools. *American Journal of Sociology*, 1974, 79, 1434–1451.

Husen, Torsten, and Nils-Eric Svenssen. Pedagogic milieu and development of intellectual skills. *School Review*, 1960, 68, 36–51.

Jackson, Gregg B. The research evidence on the effects of grade retention. *Review of Educational Research*, 1975, 45, 613–635.

Keller, Fred S., and J. Gilmour Sherman. *The Keller Plan handbook*. Menlo Park, Cal.: W. A. Benjamin, 1974.

Larkin, Timothy. Peer teachers: More than equal. *Manpower*, August 1973, 15–21.

Lippitt, Peggy. Cross-age helping programs. Paper presented at the Annual Meeting of American Educational Research Association, Washington, D.C., April 1975.

McGee, Charles S., James M. Kauffman, and Judith L. Nussen. Children as therapeutic change agents: Reinforcement intervention paradigms. *Review of Educational Research*, 1977, 47, 451–477.

Niedermeyer, Fred C. *Developing exportable teacher training for criterion-referenced instructional programs*. Inglewood, Cal.: Southwest Regional Laboratory for Educational Research and Development, 1970.

Pascarella, Ernest T. Interactive effects of prior mathematics preparation and level of instructional support in college calculus. *American Educational Research Journal*, 1978, 15, 275–285.

Porter, John. Equality and education. *Integrated Education*, 1975, 13, (76), 17–20; (77), 41–43.

Pratt, David. Cybernetic principles in the design of instruction. Paper presented at the Annual Meeting of the American Educational Research Association, Toronto, Canada, March 1978.

Roecks, Alan L. Instructional cost and utilization of classroom time for fifth-grade students. Paper presented at the Annual Meeting of the American Educational Research Association, Toronto, March 1978.

Samuda, Ronald J. Racial discrimination through mental testing: A social critic's point of view. *Institute for the Racially and Culturally Disadvantaged Bulletin*, no. 42, May 1973.

Sandin, Adolph A. *Social and emotional adjustment of regularly promoted and non-promoted pupils*. New York: Teachers College, Columbia University, 1944.

Schafer, Walter E., and Carol Olexa. *Tracking and opportunity*. Scranton, Pa.: Chandler, 1971.

Schafer, Walter E., and Kenneth Polk. Delinquency and the schools. In President's Commission on Law Enforcement and Administration of Justice, *Task force report: Juvenile delinquency and youth crime*. Washington, D.C.: U.S. Government Printing Office, 1967, pp. 222–277.

Stanley, Julian C. Identifying and nurturing the mathematically gifted. *Phi Delta Kappan*, 1976, 58, 234–237.

Svenssen, Nils-Eric. *Ability grouping and scholastic achievement*. Stockholm: Almqvist and Wiksill, 1962.

Terman, L. M. *The gifted child grows up. Genetic studies of genius*. Vol. 4. Stanford, Cal.: Stanford University Press, 1947.

Torrance, E. Paul. *Gifted children in the classroom*. New York: Macmillan, 1965.

Webster's new collegiate dictionary. Springfield, Mass.: G. & C. Merriam, 1973.

Worth, Walter H. Promotion vs. non-promotion II: The Edmonton study. *Alberta Journal of Educational Research*, 1959, 5, 191–203.

Yates, Alfred (ed.) *Grouping in education*. Report sponsored by the UNESCO Institute for Education, Hamburg. London: Wiley, 1966.

13

PRINCIPLES

- A complete curriculum requires detailed planning of all the means—human, material, and administrative—for the delivery of instruction.

- Many sources of critical information are available to help guide selection of instructional materials and equipment.

- Multiple criteria can be applied in selecting instructional materials.

- Teachers and students can sometimes benefit by developing instructional material themselves.

- Aspects of facilities to be considered by educators are flexibility, appropriateness, safety, spatial organization, noise, temperature, illumination, and aesthetic quality.

- The curriculum should describe the personal and professional qualities required of the teachers and outline any necessary inservice training.

- The total time commitment of all participants in a curriculum should be calculated.

- The curriculum should show the total expected financial costs of the program.

CONCEPTS

Logistics	Background noise	Spillover costs
Software	level (BNL)	Opportunity costs
Personal space	Thermal comfort	Cost-benefit analysis
	Shadow costs	

13
Logistics

He that would do good in this world must do it in minute particulars.

—William Blake

Curriculum Logistics

The details of an operation are known as the logistics. The term itself is derived from the Greek word for calculation, the stem *logos* meaning reason. While the grand sweep of the overall goals of a program captures the imagination, very often the more humble details make the difference between success and failure. It is proposed to use the term logistics to refer to the detailed planning of all the means—human, material, and administrative—for the delivery of instruction. This discussion will therefore include materials, equipment, facilities, personnel, time, and cost.

Materials

Curriculum materials include items such as paper, chalk, chemicals, electricity, and the kind of supplies used in courses like cooking and woodwork, about which most decisions are routine. More attention is necessary to those materials that are vehicles of communication, such as books, films, and audiotapes. Such materials are often called software.

The past decade has seen an explosion of curriculum software. The materials available to most teachers in the 1960s were largely limited to books, films, and filmstrips. Today's teacher must make a selection from a vastly increased range of books, 16-mm. films, 8-mm. film loops, audiotapes, videotapes, transparencies, simulations, work sheets, and multimedia kits. In 1973 the United States alone produced 17,230 new films and 5,270 filmstrips (Schefter, 1974). The range is so great that bibliographies are no longer adequate: there are now bibliographies of bibliographies of bibliographies! The problem of selection consequently requires gathering information and assessing the materials available.

Sources of information

Just as the ordinary citizen who fails to make use of product data provided by consumer publications deserves to be a victim of inferior manufacture and unscrupulous marketing, so the educator who selects materials by whim, by tradition, in ignorance of what is available, or at the insistence of importunate sales people is unlikely to make the best selection decisions. The cost of ill-informed choices by educators is ultimately borne by the learner and the taxpayer.

A wide range of bibliographies, annuals, and periodicals has developed in response to educators' needs for information about available teaching materials. A selected list of such sources is provided in Appendix III.

While there is no lack of published descriptive and evaluative data on curriculum materials, getting and digesting it is inevitably time-consuming. As with many other areas of information, the future may lie with automated data systems. A number of organizations are developing computer-based information systems to provide users with information and guidance on educational materials in specialized areas. One such system, providing information on materials for medical training, has been developed by the Division of Educational Resources of the American Medical Colleges (Johnson, 1976). Another system has been developed by the National Center on Educational Media and Materials for the Handicapped (Oldsen, 1976). It is at least technically possible that in the next decade each school could be equipped with a terminal on-line to a central educational materials information system. A teacher could enter the topics or skills he or she wanted to teach and receive within seconds a printout giving a description of the most appropriate print and nonprint teaching materials. The listing would be completely up to date and could include critical comment and feedback from users. Materials produced anywhere in the world could be included, and the process of rental or purchase of the materials could be incorporated into the system. For that matter, print, video, and audio materials could be transmitted electronically to a given terminal, yielding great savings in transportation costs and time.

Evaluating Instructional Materials

The variety of materials available means that it is essential for educators at every level to be able to make sound selection decisions. The criteria that need to be applied in the evaluation of materials are manifold, and a separate book would be required to describe them adequately. However, some of the most important questions that the curriculum planner needs to ask can at least be itemized. All kinds of materials may be evaluated with respect to producer claims and characteristics, cost, content, and instructional implications. Additional criteria apply specifically to print and to audiovisual materials.

Producer claims and characteristics   The production of educational materials is a multimillion dollar industry. The principle of "caveat emptor" (let the buyer beware) applies as much here as in any market sector. Significant questions that may be asked include the following:

- Are the materials described clearly, realistically, and honestly; or are claims made of magic solutions, panaceas, and breakthroughs, with excessive use of superlatives, jargon, and fad expressions?
- Are claims for appropriateness of materials for special groups, e.g., "learning disabled," substantiated?
- Are adequate details provided of development, field testing, and revision?
- Are there accurate and explicit data on user effectiveness and satisfaction?
- Are the credentials of the authors or producers shown? Are their education, experience, reputation, and previous works or products convincing?

Cost   Nominal costs of materials can be misleading, unless such factors as effectiveness and life of the materials are taken into account. Information should be sought on a number of questions:

- Is the total price clearly specified? Is it adjustable?
- Are the materials consumable? Can parts be replaced? Can ma-

terials or parts be repaired? Can they be repaired on site? What warranty do materials carry?

- What are the space requirements in use and storage? What is the shelf life?
- How many students can use the materials at once or consecutively?
- What is the per-student cost over the expected life of the materials?
- What supplemental materials, equipment, or facilities are required?
- What rights of reproduction does purchase convey?
- Are the materials compatible with other materials being used or considered?
- What maximum and minimum teacher-pupil ratio do materials require?
- How much time do the materials require of pupils?
- What total time demands do materials impose on teachers?
- What additional staff, aides, or volunteers are required?
- Are teacher prerequisites specified? Is teacher inservice training required? If so, are guidance, materials or training available in the materials or from the producer?
- What administrative backup is needed?
- Is backup, consultation, or trouble-shooting available from the producer?

Content   All other criteria are in a sense subordinate to the question of content. The first consideration must be the relevance of the content to the curriculum objectives and its likely effectiveness, especially with regard to motivation. Periodic attempts by community pressure groups to censor learning materials make it necessary for planners, when evaluating content, to be conscious of the potential audiences and critics beyond the classroom.

- Is the material relevant to program objectives?
- Is the material accurate, comprehensive, and realistic?
- Is the material interesting, challenging, and thought-provoking to students?
- Is the quality of the materials consistent?
- Is the content logically sequenced?
- Is the material up-to-date or easily updated?
- Is the material appropriate to the audience, the teachers, the program, and the school?
- Is the material acceptable in terms of school and community values?

- Do the materials avoid "talking down" to the audience?
- Is treatment of minorities, religion, politics, and women accurate, balanced, valid, and concrete?

The last question has special significance. The instructional materials that children encounter during their formative years have a strong potential for shaping their attitudes and values. A first-grade reader that repeatedly tells of Dick mowing lawns and delivering papers, and Jane washing dishes and playing with dolls, is teaching more than reading. Sex stereotyping has until recently been endemic in North American textbooks (Educational Products Information Exchange, 1973). Males are typically depicted as performing a wide range of active pursuits; females a small number of more passive and domestic activities. The role of women in history and their contributions in science, literature, and the arts tend to be given scant attention.

Many other attitudes are conveyed in curriculum materials. Numerous studies have shown an overall tendency toward negative treatment of nationalities, races, and ethnic backgrounds different from those of the textbook author and the expected readers. In one study of history textbooks used in Canadian schools, two out of every three value judgments relating to blacks or American Indians were found to be negative. The evaluative terms most commonly applied to blacks were, in order of frequency, *friendly, unfriendly, savage, faithful, kind, fierce, primitive, murder, violent,* and *backward.* The corresponding terms applied to Indians were *savage, friendly, massacre, skillful, hostile, fierce, great, murder, unfriendly,* and *thief.* The researchers came across numerous instances of more or less subtle prejudice toward these groups:

> In Britain, before the war, there was hardly any colored population, and therefore no problem.
> Champlain spent the winter with the Hurons, living in a longhouse swarming with Indians, mice, fleas, and lice (McDiarmid and Pratt, 1971, pp. 89, 98).

Racial groups and women are not the only objects of bias in teaching materials. "Ageism" is probably as serious a problem as sexism. Instructional materials also need to be examined before purchase with respect to their attitude toward different religions, political systems, and social classes.

Instruments exist for assessing expressed value judgments in verbal materials. One of them, ECO Analysis, is described on p. 375. It can be used fairly easily to determine the treatment of any subject on a positive-negative scale. However, positive or negative treatment of a group or subject is not in itself evidence of bias; criteria such as accuracy and balance should also be applied.

Instructional implications   New materials often imply new instructional approaches. The implications should be examined for their compatibility with the curriculum and the teachers.

- Are the objectives stated? Are they consistent with program objectives?
- Is the audience defined? Are materials suitable for a diverse audience? Are learner prerequisites defined? Do the materials challenge students at different ability levels?
- Is the role of the teacher defined? Is it appropriate? How onerous is it?
- Is the teaching methodology specified? Is it appropriate?
- Is there a variety of modes of presentation?
- Do the materials actively involve the students?
- Is the role of the students defined? Is the role appropriate?
- Can the materials be used for self-instruction?
- Are opportunities for practice and strategies for facilitation of transfer provided?
- Is there guidance for pacing of instruction and grouping of students?
- Is there frequent feedback for students and teachers?
- Are pretests, formative tests, and posttests provided?
- Are tests valid, reliable, objective, and diagnostic?
- Is the recording and reporting system described? Are materials provided? Are they comprehensible to parents and public?

Criteria specific to print materials   Print materials have an important place in most curricula. It is hard to find a more effective and versatile medium than a skillfully written, designed, and illustrated book. It is cheap and portable, usable in almost any environment, does not require electricity or the teacher's presence, and can be read, browsed through, skimmed, reread, and reviewed at will and at the reader's own pace.

Particularly important in print materials is that they be written at the appropriate level for the learners. The wide range in reading levels found in most classrooms means that text materials for use by a whole class should not greatly exceed half the grade level (i.e., fourth-grade level for an eighth-grade class) if they are to be comprehensible to all students (Bond and Tinker, 1973). A simple formula for estimating readability is recommended by McLaughlin (1969):

1. Identify 10 consecutive sentences near the beginning of the work, 10 near the middle, and 10 near the end.
2. Count the number of words of 3 or more syllables in the 30 sentences.

3. Calculate the square root.

4. Add 3. This is the reading grade level.

This formula, like others, is based on word length and sentence length, which are the two main contributors to reading difficulty. But it must be remembered that it provides only an estimate. The result would be the same, to take an absurd example, if the thirty sentences were written backwards. The appropriateness of the formula will depend on such factors as the familiarity or novelty of the subject matter, the com-

---

Measuring Attitudes in Texts

ECO Analysis was designed to measure positive-negative attitudes in verbal communications. There are five steps in the analysis.

1. Identify all the names or synonyms of the subject in the text (e.g., Indian, Amerindian, Redskin).
2. List all the evaluative terms (adjectives, nouns, adverbs, verbs) used in the text to refer to the subject.
3. Denote each term as positive or negative.
4. Count the number of positive terms and the number of negative terms.
5. Multiply the number of positive terms by 100 and divide by the total. This yields an evaluative coefficient between 0 (totally negative) and 100 (totally positive).

Example:
In a *daring* attack on the village of Deerfield, the Indians *ruthlessly massacred* fifty of the inhabitants. *Fearless* and *terrifying*, the *savages murdered* men, women, and children *without mercy*.

TERM	DIRECTION
daring	+
ruthlessly	−
massacred	−
fearless	+
terrifying	−
savages	−
murdered	−
without mercy	−

Positive terms 2 *Negative terms* 6 *Coefficient* $\dfrac{100 \times 2}{2 + 6} = 25.0$

For more detailed instructions, see Pratt (1971).

plexity of the author's style, and the way in which the text is handled by the teacher.

Some other questions to ask about print materials follow.

- Do chapters or sections provide an overview at the beginning and a summary at the end, or prequestions and postquestions?
- Is the text divided by suitable subheadings? Is the layout attractive?
- Do the spacing between words and lines and the line length provide maximum readability?
- Is the writing style economical, vigorous, and lucid?
- Is the concept level and language appropriate? Is complexity and obscurity avoided? Are unfamiliar words defined?
- Are there sufficient illustrations, figures, and tables? Are they helpful? Are they on the same pages as the reference? Is there adequate explanation of diagrammatic material? Are captions clear?
- Does the typeface and type size provide optimal clarity? Is page size appropriate?
- Is the quality of the paper and the binding satisfactory?
- Are references and bibliography adequate?
- Are the table of contents and index comprehensive?
- Is a glossary provided? Is it adequate?

Criteria specific to audiovisual materials   One of the findings of research into instructional materials is that elaboration and complexity do not necessarily add to the effectiveness of audiovisual media. Color materials are not always more effective than black and white, nor movies more effective than photographs, nor photographs than line drawings (Gulliford, 1973). In other words, color, motion, and detail are not automatically beneficial but should be justified in terms of their relevance to the instruction or their motivational value to the learners.

- Is the medium appropriate to the content and the objectives?
- Is the length of the materials convenient to instructional time blocks?
- Can the materials be conveniently subdivided for use at different times?
- Is the pace appropriate?
- Does the narration or audio commentary complement the visual image?
- Is background music appropriate and nondistracting?
- Is the visual focus on the point of interest?
- Are the color saturation, tone, light, and contrast satisfactory?
- Is the animation or acting convincing?

- Is the information presented at an appropriate speed and intensity?
- Are visual materials dated, e.g., by dress?
- Are titles bold, simple, and legible?
- Is there an instructor's manual? Is it adequate?
- Are the sound fidelity and volume at mid-range satisfactory?
- Are the materials durable? Is there a warranty? Is there repair service?
- Do materials pose high risk of theft?

The questions asked are drawn from the literature on the evaluation of instructional materials (especially Educational Products Information Exchange, 1974; Bleil, 1975; Niedermeyer and Moncrief, 1975; Krause, 1976; Hartley, 1978). They can help the planner make a comprehensive assessment prior to selection of instructional materials. What if no satisfactory materials exist?

Locally developed materials

Where suitable materials are commercially available, purchase is the first choice, because development costs are absorbed by a large number of users. But, bearing in mind that the curriculum should govern the nature of the materials and not vice versa, if no appropriate materials exist, it is worth considering local development. The time required may be substantial, but the benefit is in providing exactly what the curriculum requires, rather than depending on materials developed for more general purposes. While few teachers have the time or the means to make major films or write their own textbooks, it is not beyond their capabilities to produce simple 8-mm. films, 35-mm. slides, overhead transparencies, filmstrips, audio tapes, or videotapes. A more expensive option is to contract with a company to develop specific materials. Almost all the criteria that apply to published materials will apply to those that are locally developed.

A strategy used successfully by some teachers is to have students develop instructional materials. It is probable that the people who learn most from educational materials are the people who create them. Students can become deeply involved in producing a book of short stories, an anthology of poems, a film, a slide-tape presentation, a scientific model, a set of flashcards, or a multimedia kit. And their learning experience becomes a learning resource for subsequent groups of students.

Equipment

The equipment used in education ranges from projectors and microscopes to trampolines and globes; from slide rules and chalkboards to pianos and sewing machines; from radial arm saws to desks. In complexity instructional equipment ranges from the twenty-five-cent ruler to the multimillion-dollar flight simulators used in pilot training.

Research on instructional equipment and the criteria such research generates are less widely known than in the case of instructional materials. Manufacturers are still successfully marketing black chalkboards, although it has been known for forty years that it is easier to read dark lettering on a light surface than vice versa (Seymour, 1937). The seats and tables at which children work in classrooms often result in an angle between trunk and thigh of less than 90°, producing pressure on the lower back and the intestines (Scriven, 1975). School furniture can and should be designed to provide healthier and more comfortable posture.

Although a few large educational jurisdictions can commission furniture and equipment to their own specifications, most educators are limited to making an informed selection from what is commercially available. Many popular magazines review audiovisual equipment. Appendix III lists a number of specialized sources of evaluative data on instructional equipment. To find information on equipment specific to such subjects as science, music, physical education, or electronics, it is necessary to search the professional journals in the subject.

Evaluating instructional equipment

Some general criteria that can be applied in evaluating instructional equipment are listed below.

Physical characteristics

- Are specifications clear, accurate, and complete?
- What is its size and weight?
- Is it portable and transportable?
- What are its space requirements in use and storage?
- How much power does it consume?
- What is the effect of power failure?
- How sensitive, versatile, and flexible is it?
- How noisy is it? How stable?
- What are its safety features and hazards?

Operating criteria

- Are instructions clear and complete?
- How easy and convenient is it to use?
- Must operators be specially trained?
- Are instruments and controls easily manipulated?
- What are the user prerequisites?
- How acceptable is it to users?

- Is it suitable to the size and abilities of students?
- Can students use it without supervision?
- Can it be used continuously?
- How many students can use it simultaneously?
- How long does it take to assemble, set up, and take down?
- Is it compatible with existing hardware and software?

Costs

- What is the purchase price; the per-student cost?
- What additional hardware, software, and facilities does it require?
- What additional components or features can be purchased?
- What is its operational life?
- How soon will it be obsolete?
- How durable and robust is it?
- What routine maintenance is necessary; what is the time and cost?
- How susceptible is it to accidental or deliberate damage?
- What is the incidence and cost of repair?
- Can parts be replaced or repaired?
- Can repairs be made on site?
- What is the expected downtime?
- What warranty does it carry?
- What is the risk of theft and the insurance cost?

Facilities

Human beings, like all animals, are highly sensitive to their environment. Light, temperature, and noise affect our physical and emotional state in important, though often unconscious ways. Environments can be designed to promote or inhibit certain attitudes and behavior. The designers of schools should therefore have a clear perception of the activities and the curricula for which the school building will provide the setting. This implies that schools should be designed by educational architects in close collaboration with educators who are knowledgeable about curriculum and instruction. In fact, many schools are still designed by general architects in consultation only with school business officials.

The initial design of a structure places severe constraints on the kinds of environment, and hence on the programs, that can be developed in the building. For this reason, flexibility is an important criterion in modern school design. Ideally, schools need to be designed so that they can subsequently be extended upwards or outwards, and so that the interior spaces can be altered without major rebuilding. The least satisfac-

"It's always something. Now they claim the surroundings are so beautiful, they can't keep their minds on their work."

tory school buildings are those that make too many assumptions about the permanence of current conditions. Millions of dollars are currently being spent to replace single-glazed windows in buildings erected less than a decade ago by architects who assumed that the age of cheap energy for heating would never end. Schools designed in response to a temporary educational fashion can prove an even greater liability. Some school districts are now encumbered with buildings constructed in the 1960s on the assumption that team teaching would become the normal method of instruction. The same kind of embarrassment may in a few years face schools built with open teaching areas that cannot be easily modified.

The curriculum can recommend specific ways the teacher can modify the instructional environment to enhance the effectiveness of the learning. If a particular kind of environment is recommended, guidance should be provided to teachers as to how to use it most effectively.

All teachers and designers need to make safety a primary concern in the specification or modification of learning spaces. Hostile edges and corners are an unnecessary hazard. A sharp desk corner that can jab an adult's thigh could blind a kindergarten child. If heavy furniture or other objects must be moved or carried, it should be done only by people with adequate strength and knowledge of proper lifting techniques. Fire exits and precautions must be clearly shown and understood. Glass doors should be marked. Floors need to have nonslip surfaces. There should be sufficient well-placed electrical outlets to avoid trailing wires or over-loading of circuits. Flammable building materials can usually be avoided, especially substances such as polystyrene that produce dense and toxic smoke when ignited. Special safety requirements apply to such areas as shops, laboratories, darkrooms, and cafeterias.

Any special facilities that the program will require—a swimming pool, for example—should be specified in the curriculum. Specific in-structional methods, such as films or independent study, imply certain spatial organization, as well as special requirements, e.g., for blackout and power supply. The curriculum designer should pay serious regard to those aspects of the environment that can be manipulated independently by the teacher. These are more numerous and significant than many teachers assume. Almost any teaching environment can be modified with respect to six main variables, each of which is significant for learning: personal space, spatial organization, noise, temperature, illumination, and aesthetic quality.

Personal space

Schools are relatively crowded places. The most spacious schools allow up to 20 m² of floor space per pupil; the most crowded as little as 7 m² (Oddie, 1976). The individual classroom is more crowded than the school as a whole. In a typical classroom the child has an average of 2 to 5 m² of floor space—more than one has in a crowded train or theater, but much less than in an office or a home. Furthermore, the average is mis-leading, as the student's movement is often restricted to a desk or chair, while the teacher has free movement in the space at the front and throughout the room.

There is some uncertainty as to the effect of crowdedness on human behavior. It is known that crowdedness increases physical and behavior problems in rats, but it seems that among humans crowdedness will increase aggressive behavior only among people who are already prone to aggression (Drew, 1971). Other people tend to "cocoon" in conditions of crowding, much as people withdraw into themselves in a crowded elevator or subway train.

We shape our buildings, and afterwards our buildings shape us.

—*Winston Churchill*

People generally seem to prefer low rather than high population density and small rather than large social groups. Barker and Gump (1964) showed that pupils in large schools, as compared with their peers in small schools, were less likely to participate in extracurricular activities, student government, or district festivals and competitions, and more likely to become anonymous, forgotten faces in the crowd. Much the same forces appear to be at work in the large classroom. As class size increases, each individual plays a smaller role, receives less attention, has less opportunity to participate, and finds the experience less satisfying.

However, there is little consistent evidence that teaching or learning is more effective in smaller groups. One well-controlled experiment in class size, involving 62 fourth- and fifth-grade classes, showed that teachers found management, supervision, and evaluation much easier in classes of 16 and 23 than in classes of 30 and 37 and had more positive attitudes toward the smaller classes. But there were no differences in overall pupil participation, classroom atmosphere, or students' self-concept. In comparisons of achievement in art, composition, vocabulary, reading, mathematical concepts and mathematical problem-solving, the only significant difference was in mathematical concepts, favoring students in the smaller classes (Shapson et al., 1978).

In the absence of any conclusive findings on optimal class size, it would seem appropriate to use the maximum size of student group that is compatible with the instructional activity. In many schools, all that this would require is a modest increase in the amount of imagination brought to bear in the scheduling process. For presentation of information by lecture, film, or some other means, the size of the group is immaterial: several hundred students could receive the instruction at once. For supervision of practice, one teacher may not be able to work effectively with more than twenty students at a time. For discussions, five to seven is probably the optimal number, while diagnosis and remediation may

---

If the student-teacher ratio could be used as a measure of labor productivity (which I think it cannot), we would have the curious spectacle of an industry trying its best to worsen its productivity—and bragging about its success. . . .

Some time ago a colleague and I studied the matter briefly, and interviewed a good many teachers and other educators. We concluded that, according to our informants, the optimum size of any class is three less than are in it, and we came away with the impression that each teacher can name the three she wants out.

—J. A. Kershaw (1965, pp. 185–186)

require one tutor to one student. The conventional class size can be viewed as a reasonable compromise among the requirements of the various activities that often occur in a single class period. But it does not necessarily follow that every scheduled class should conform to the same norm. More diverse and flexible organization might result in greater effectiveness and greater recognition of each student as an individual.

It is helpful to teachers and administrators if curriculum writers indicate minimum, maximum, and optimal size of instructional groups. This in turn entails an obligation to suggest procedures for dealing with a shortfall or surplus of students applying for admission.

Spatial organization

In the early grades of schools, classrooms tend to be structured informally. Chairs are grouped around tables. There are specialized work areas throughout the room. Children can find comfortable corners to sit and read or work independently. At about the seventh-grade level, the small groupings of furniture give way to rows of desks. At the college level, the seats are often bolted to the floor. The grid pattern appears to be internalized by students. Robert Sommer attempted an experiment in the effects of classroom arrangement by having a collaborator move the seats in a number of college classrooms from rows into a circle. The experiment failed because in twenty of the twenty-five classes, as soon as they came in, the students on their own initiative rearranged the chairs back into straight rows before the class began (Sommer, 1974, p. 87).

In the grid pattern, what the student learns best may well be the shape of the head of the student sitting in front. The arrangement is an appropriate one for a parade ground; but why in hundreds of thousands of classrooms around the world is it considered so appropriate for a learning environment? A number of reasons suggest themselves: it allows a relatively large number of students to be fitted into a small space; it is suitable for a presentation mode of teaching; it limits eye contact among pupils and inhibits social interaction; it enables teachers to identify students more easily by reference to a seating plan; it facilitates checking of attendance; it isolates students from one another and facilitates control; its neat and symmetrical appearance appeals to a certain personality type; and it makes it easier for the cleaning staff to sweep the floors.

As a remedy for unthinking allegiance to conventional classroom patterns, unthinking adoption of "open area" organization does not seem to be much of an advance. There are open-area schools, notably in England, that model almost every physical and human quality one could desire by way of a learning environment. But these are often schools where the principal shared in the architectural design and handpicked and trained the teachers. In such schools the architecture is but one aspect of an educational philosophy embracing environment, program,

> We like standard shapes and sizes; as a result we live in a world of squares and rectangles. . . . It is a tribute to the intuition of teenagers that they look upon us as squares.
>
> —*Don Fabun (1967, p. 24)*

and teaching style. The attempt to transplant the architectural aspect to North America has not been universally successful. Frequently the innovation consisted of building schools with fewer interior walls, an environment into which teachers were introduced who had neither participated in, approved of, or been trained for the open environment. Continuing to teach in a conventional way, they found the absence of walls merely an audible and visible distraction. Bookcases, screens, and miniature palm trees were quickly turned into makeshift barriers between the teaching areas. Small wonder that the research evidence shows, at best, disappointing performance by students in open classrooms, not only in academic subjects but also in creativity, and an increased anxiety level (Bennett, 1976; Traub et al., 1976; Wright, 1975; Forman and McKinney, 1978).

Whatever its original intent, the open-classroom movement may turn out to have been an example of the overselling of a single variable under the aegis of an ideological position that the wide connotations of the term "open" imply. Summarizing the results of a large-scale experiment he conducted in two American schools, Wright stated that "it would appear from these data that the open school environment does not have a profound influence on either the cognitive or affective development of children," (Wright, 1975, p. 462). Bennett, author of the major British study, pointed to the wide variation in achievement among open classrooms. The architecture, he suggested, was not the critical variable. What mattered most was that the curriculum have some logical structure and that students spend a high proportion of their time actively engaged in learning (Bennett, 1976).

Louis Sullivan's dictum that "form follows function" is a useful maxim for the educator. The design of teaching spaces should depend on the nature of the subject, the activity, and the desired relationships among the participants. Straight rows are appropriate for presentation by lecture or film but not for group discussion, for which the first requirement is eye contact among all participants. King Arthur's Knights of the Round Table were probably not the first to recognize the symbolic and practical significance of physical design. Given that many different activities and programs will take place in most teaching areas, flexibility is a great asset in school design. Sound-proof movable partitions allow the size of teaching spaces to be altered. If a lecture theater is built in the round, it can be used either for presentation or for interaction. If floors are carpeted, students can sit on them comfortably. If furniture is light and maneuverable, it can be quickly arranged and rearranged in rows, groups, circles, or around the walls.

In specifying the most suitable environment for learning in a given curriculum, the designer might ask, What is the context in the world outside the school in which the learning will be applied? It is taken for granted that a science classroom will resemble a laboratory, an automotive classroom will be similar to an auto repair shop, and a home economics room will bear a resemblance to a kitchen. What, then, should an English classroom resemble? A theater? A newspaper editorial room? A library? A coffee shop? Perhaps something of all these. What it probably should not resemble is a conventional classroom.

Noise

Noise is a feature of the environment that in developed societies is almost never absent. Since it became known that excessive noise can contribute to a wide range of physical and mental ailments as well as to the more obvious loss of hearing acuity, noise has come to be recognized as a controllable environmental pollutant (Farr, 1972).

While noise as a health hazard is important in such school programs as industrial arts, the major interest of the curriculum designer is in specifying an environment whose acoustical characteristics will facilitate teaching and learning. Guidelines published by the Department of Education and Science for England and Wales summarize the concern of educational architects:

> The aim is to produce a building where, for example, discussion in class can be held in a normal conversational voice, where music can be enjoyed pianissimo or fortissimo, where one can use an electric drill or a vaulting horse without spoiling another's efforts to practice on the violin, to hear French verbs on a tape recorder or just to concentrate on a book. In short, the aim is to be able to hear clearly what one needs to hear, and not be distracted by other noises (Department of Education and Science, 1975, p. 1).

Generally the most significant acoustical feature of a learning environment is the background noise level (BNL). BNL is the kind of homogeneous sound produced by ventilation fans, air conditioning, or dis-

---

Architecture is a backdrop for worthwhile human activity.

—*Raymond Moriyama, architect*

tant traffic. Noise is measured in decibels, which indicate sound output on a logarithmic scale: 30 db. is ten times as intense as 20 db. and sounds twice as loud. The BNL must be high enough to mask distracting sounds but not so high as to interfere with communication. In the typical classroom the teacher must be heard clearly by a student seven meters away. With a BNL of 35 db. the teacher can communicate clearly in a quiet voice. Normal voice will carry well over a BNL of 40 db. The teacher will have to speak in a raised voice to be understood over 45 db. and in a very loud voice against 50 db. If the BNL reaches 55 db., the teacher can communicate only by shouting (Department of Education and Science, 1975). As the noise level rises, teachers and students must make more effort to communicate, and the level of stress, irritability, and fatigue will be raised on both sides. Intellectual performance deteriorates in the presence of distracting noise, and children work more slowly (Broadbent, 1958; Weinstein and Weinstein, 1978).

It does not follow that the quietest environment is necessarily the best for learning. A music room requires a very low BNL; it should also be free of echoes that confuse or distort the sound and have enough reverberation to give music a sonorous quality. On the other hand, libraries and study areas, where communication distances are typically one meter or less, are best designed with thick carpet, upholstered furniture, sound-absorbing structural materials, and a relatively high BNL

Hearing threshold	0
Still night in country	10
Normal voice at 9 m	35
Average home	40
Light traffic at 30 m	45
Normal voice at 1 m	55
Shouting at 2 m	65
Sixty preschoolers playing	70
Heavy traffic at 10 m	75
Hearing damage threshold	85
Train whistle at 75 m	95
Electric grinder on steel at 1 m	95
Disco with rock band	100
Pneumatic drill at 3 m	100
Woodworking shop	110
Powerful car horn at 1 m	115
Pain threshold	120
Jet plane taking off at 25 m	130

Table 13–1 Typical noise levels in decibels

> Doors and windows should be kept shut as far as possible to retain heat—ventilation is normally sufficient through cracks around windows and doors.
>
> —*From an Oxfordshire (England) County Council memorandum on fuel saving*

(about 45 db.), if necessary produced by "white noise" through loudspeakers, to insulate the learners from distracting sounds. The most inappropriate library environment is one with hard floors and furniture, reflective walls and ceiling, and big notices saying "Silence."

Temperature

People work efficiently and comfortably within a rather narrow temperature range. Learning rates can be significantly reduced by an increase in air temperature of as little as 1°C. While decisions regarding temperature in schools are often taken at an administrative level, many teachers can exercise some control by adjusting a thermostat or opening and closing windows. But in addition to air temperature and amount of radiation from heat sources, thermal comfort depends on humidity, air movement, clothing, and metabolic rate.

Humidity   High humidity makes cold air feel colder and hot air feel hotter, and encourages growth of mold in buildings. Low humidity causes shrinking and cracking of furniture, increases static electricity, and causes uncomfortable drying of skin and air passages. Relative humidity of 40 to 60 percent is ideal. Winter humidity levels of 12 percent have been measured in schools—lower than the humidity level in the Sahara Desert (Shaver and Company, 1968).

Air movement   Perceptions of "freshness" of the air tend to be related to warmth rather than air movement. But people will complain of drafts (i.e., unwanted local cooling effects) if air movement is too high and of stuffiness when it is too low. Radiation to a nearby cool surface, such as a window, will create the impression of a draft even if the air is still.

Clothing   Optimal temperature will also be a function of the amount of insulation provided by clothing. Wearing light clothing, an individual who is engaged in reading or writing at a desk will prefer an ambient temperature of about 23°C. Wearing heavy clothing, the same person will prefer about 19° (Wyon et al., 1975). In cooler conditions, however, people will feel uncomfortably cold if their feet are cold; hence, if energy is to be saved by reducing heating, attention must be paid to warm footwear and to floor temperature (McIntyre and Griffiths, 1975).

    Metabolic rate   Metabolic rate is the heat produced by the organism. This varies with the activity a person is engaged in. Walking at 3.4 km per hour produces a metabolic rate twice as high as being seated at rest; heavy manual labor produces a rate twice as high again. A sedentary person who is comfortable at 25° will be comfortable at 19° engaged in medium activity and 13° if performing strenuous activity (Fanger, 1970). For this reason, the recommended temperature of a teaching area will vary with the kind of student activity; a library will need to be warmer than a gymnasium. Children of elementary school age have a higher metabolic rate than adults, and as a result are comfortable in an environment 2° to 3° cooler (McIntyre, 1973).

    In the establishing of optimum temperatures for a learning environment, the comfort of students, efficiency of learning, and consumption of fuel must all be taken into account. There is not much point in reducing the temperature of the swimming pool from 25° to 20° if the result is that everyone takes three times as long to learn how to swim. For a classroom, 20° is often considered a lower limit, for people have become accustomed to wearing summer clothes indoors all year. But it seems likely that, if students and teachers could be persuaded to dress appropriately, it might be possible to heat classrooms only to 17° or 18° without reducing the efficiency of the learning. The savings would represent millions of barrels of imported oil a year.

Illumination

    Lighting consultants know that if bars are brightly lit and noisy, there will be a quick turnover of customers; if they are sound-absorbing and dark, customers will stay longer and couples will sit closer, making for more efficient use of space (Sommer, 1969). In designing a learning environment, the concern is the more prosaic one of ensuring that everyone can see what needs to be seen clearly and without strain. This will depend not only on the intensity of the light, but also on the source of the light and the reflective quality of interior surfaces.

    Glare is to be avoided in all circumstances. It is produced by gloss paints, reflective floor surfaces, polished wood or plastic furniture, bright colors, high contrast between light and dark surfaces, excessively bright lighting, and sunlight in rooms with windows facing south. Glare forces the eyes to keep readjusting, distracts the learners, makes it difficult for the teacher to see the students, makes gymnasium activities hazardous, and accelerates fatigue (Smith, 1974). Also undesirable is flat lighting, which makes it difficult to distinguish depth in three-dimensional objects. There is some evidence that children exposed for long periods to flat lighting tend to develop myopia (Shaver and Company, 1968).

Windowless classrooms, which are illegal in Britain and the Soviet Union, became popular in North America in the 1960s. They give greater control of lighting and blackout, save heating costs, eliminate a source of distraction, and reduce costs from vandalism. They also increase lighting costs, force total reliance on artificial light, reduce the escape routes in emergencies, and are apparently less congenial to the occupants (Karmel, 1965). Windowless schools have a fortress-like appearance, closed off from the surrounding community.

Light has significant and complex effects on biological organisms. No one is completely sure what are the effects on human beings, who evolved in natural light, of living for most of their waking hours under fluorescent lighting, which is deficient in a large part of the visible spectrum. Fluorescent lights are suspected of emitting small amounts of X-ray radiation and of triggering hyperactivity in certain children (Ott, 1976). Deprivation of the full spectrum of natural light (notably of ultraviolet) results in vitamin D_3 deficiency and impairment of the body's ability to absorb calcium (Wurtman, 1975). This is especially significant for people living in northern latitudes, who may receive very little exposure to sunlight during the winter months. It seems to follow that curriculum designers and teachers should seize every opportunity to get children out of doors in winter, especially in the middle of the day. Snowshoeing or cross-country skiing may be preferable to basketball in a mid-year physical education program.

Color is closely related to illumination. Red lighting appears to be associated with strong emotions, both of affection and aggression. Blue and green are more congenial to concentration and feelings of serenity. Under red lighting, blood pressure, pulse, and galvanic skin response increase; reactions are faster; and time, length, and weight are overestimated. The reverse effects are found under green lighting (Sharpe, 1974). Red might be suitable for a theater arts room, green or blue for a mathematics area.

In many environments the nature of the activity will require a specific color range. Blue-green is preferred for operating theaters because it is the complementary color to blood and facilitates vision into surgical wounds (Granville, 1962). Black laboratory benches make it easier to read instruments and check the cleanness of glassware. In a classroom the walls close to a chalkboard should not have so light a color that they provide excessive contrast.

Paint is a relatively cheap investment, but even this control over the environment is denied to some teachers. However, almost all teachers are free to alter the color hue of a room by covering walls with posters, hangings, or children's art work emphasizing certain hues.

Aesthetic quality

People tend to linger in a beautiful room but try to escape from an ugly environment. They are more likely to litter or damage an unsightly building than an attractive one. Pleasant surroundings also generate warm and positive feelings about the activities that take place in them. Maslow and Mintz (1972) placed students in a beautiful room, an average-looking room, and an ugly room, and asked them to rate photographs of human faces. When in the beautiful room, the students consistently gave the faces a higher rating in well-being and energy than they did when they were in the average room; and the ratings were higher in the average than in the ugly room.

Robert Sommer reported that in a long career in university teaching he had never taught in a classroom that initially had a single picture on the wall. When he introduced pictures and decorations into a classroom, the reactions of students and faculty were uniformly positive. The decorations were in fact so much appreciated that most of them were purloined within a few weeks (Sommer, 1974).

A teacher working in a drab and dingy classroom will have an uphill battle developing positive student attitudes toward the best-designed curriculum. Investment in carpeting, pictures, displays, and an attractive color scheme can only pay dividends in improved student response.

Personnel

A gifted teacher will transcend a mediocre curriculum, but an excellent curriculum is unlikely to be successful in the hands of an incompetent teacher. In other words, however well or badly the curriculum is designed, the teacher can make or break the program. How many people complete their schooling without being profoundly influenced, at at least one point, for good or ill, by a particular teacher? When the National Science Foundation asked a number of "breakthrough" scientists to identify the critical factor in their education, they almost uniformly answered, "Intimate association with a great, inspiring teacher" (Fuller, 1970, p. 82B). This crucial and widely acknowledged role of the teacher contrasts with the casual processes often followed in the selection and training of teachers. Few axioms are as telling in education as political scientist Leo Rosten's "First-rate people hire first-rate people; second-rate people hire third-rate people."

According to the conventional wisdom, what a teacher is is more important than what a teacher does; personality is more significant than skill; and hence good teachers are born and not made. But the evidence runs almost entirely counter to this notion. What a teacher is, at least as far as he or she can be assessed in terms of background, education, and personality, appears to have little consistent impact on student learning. On the other hand, what a teacher does, specifically such actions as showing approval, organizing and structuring instruction in a business-like way, communicating clearly, and teaching with variety and flexibility, has been shown consistently and significantly to affect student learning (Rosenshine, 1971).

Clearly a book could be written about the desirable characteristics of teachers, as many have. But most of the decisions in this area lie outside curriculum design. The curriculum designer must work with the human resources that are likely to be available. The competences required of the teachers should be stipulated parsimoniously and realistically, and their responsibilities outlined fully.

The principle of parsimony implies that minimal qualifications should be identified. The qualifications are better stated in terms of professional competences and personal qualities than as paper qualifications. If the required qualities can be found in a teacher's aide or a volunteer, there is no curriculum reason—although there may be legal or political reasons—for engaging a professional teacher.

The following illustrates the kind of description of teacher competences that might be appropriate in a curriculum.

> Outdoor Education: Teacher Competences Required
> *The teacher must be an experienced and enthusiastic outdoorsperson, committed to a conservationist philosophy. Skills in backpacking, camping, canoeing, and rock climbing are essential. High degree of competence in lifesaving, first aid, and emergency controls are critical. Organizational and group leadership abilities are important. The teacher must be sensitive to the needs of individuals and groups, and must relate well with children, adolescents, and adults in an informal educational setting. He or she must be able to maintain strict discipline together with high morale.*

Few things can undermine a curriculum at the implementation stage faster than the discovery by teachers that they have committed themselves to greater responsibilities than they were initially led to anticipate. For this reason, a complete and candid summary of the responsibilities of the teacher should be shown.

> Outdoor Education
> *Responsibilities of the chief instructor include the following:*
> *Instructing students of all ages in wilderness skills, in the classroom and in outdoor settings.*
> *Evaluating and reporting learner achievement*

Evaluating curricula and programs in outdoor education.

Purchasing supplies, and purchasing and maintaining equipment.

Maintaining accounts and preparing annual budget.

Making public presentations regarding outdoor education programs to teachers, parents, and public.

Planning and leading backpacking, canoeing, and mountaineering expeditions.

Arranging transportation.

Ensuring attainment of prerequisites and parental consent by students embarking on expeditions.

Notifying school authorities and lands and forests officials of itineraries of expeditions.

Training and supervising assistant teachers, aides, and volunteers.

Handling and reporting accidents.

In addition to the personnel directly involved, a program may require new or additional services on the part of people in or outside the institution. Will administators be needed to supervise, trouble-shoot, or handle community relations? Will the program require extra janitorial services? Does it make special demands on library personnel or media technicians? Will the services of professional evaluators be required? All such services should be itemized and described, so that the cooperation of appropriate personnel can be enlisted before the program begins.

The advance of knowledge and the changing needs of society sometimes require the development of curricula that few teachers have adequate academic background to instruct. New insights into learning and instruction may likewise suggest approaches to teaching that are unfamiliar to many instructors. This mismatch between the requirements of the curriculum and the repertoire of teachers may be resolved in a number of ways, including (1) replacing staff, (2) adding staff, (3) subcontracting the instruction, (4) developing "teacher-proof" curricula, and (5) retraining staff.

The first three options are often politically or financially impractical in contemporary school settings. The "teacher-proof package" was a device frequently tried out in the 1960s. The designers of certain new curricula, notably in the sciences, decided that teachers were not competent

---

There can be no such thing as curriculum development without teacher development.

—*Laurence Stenhouse, educator*

Short-term Planning: An Israeli Experience

They would tell our Minister of Education . . . You want to introduce a new program in the teaching of some subject, and he would ask them, How much does it cost? They'd say, Five million pounds, seven million pounds, whatever it was. The Minister, believing that for five million pounds, by introducing the "new math" they would have all these kids inventing new mathematical models: great. So he bought the program. . . . Then, six months after they introduced the program, they told him he'd have to retrain all the teachers. How much does that cost? That costs fifty million pounds. Well, why didn't you tell me that at the beginning? Well, we just thought of it. Then you talk about retraining the teachers, you have to readjust the other parts of the curriculum, because the new mathematics now takes more time. . . . Then all the supervisors are sabotaging the new program, so you have to retrain the supervisors. Then when you retrain the supervisors, the schools of education are conservative, you have to retrain them. . . . I think that had better be presented to the Minister at the beginning.

—Seymour Fox (1973)

---

to teach the subject. They therefore developed curriculum materials that required little or no teacher intervention. The packages contained the textbooks, films, and filmstrips; the scientific apparatus, materials, and directions for experiments; the tests, assignments, and marking guides; and a teacher's manual listing questions students commonly asked and the correct answers. The results were unimpressive. Teachers resented being asked to act merely as instructional letter carriers. Furthermore, the teacher-proof package provided no permanent solution to the problem of lack of teacher expertise.

Training or retraining is in most circumstances the best solution to this kind of problem. It enhances rather than threatens the teacher's self-image; it augments the human resources of the institution; and it provides a long-term rather than a temporary solution to the problem. Ideally, the teachers to be retrained will be those who have strong intrinsic motivation. However, extrinsic motivators can also help; two of the strongest incentives for inservice training appear to be credit toward a university degree and recognition of further training in the salary structure.

When a new curriculum requires retraining of teachers, it becomes an integral part of the designers' work to develop the retraining curriculum: a curriculum within a curriculum. The costs of retraining in time and money must also be calculated in detail and clearly presented.

Time

Time is a precious commodity, the disposition of which calls for skill and creativity. Yet the organization of time in schools has been characterized by rigidity and lack of imagination. Time is still largely distributed in uniform blocks of forty to sixty minutes and in unwieldy units of semesters and years. The traditional academic year is based on an agricultural model that has been anachronistic for half a century: a model that leaves the physical plant (and many students) idle for many weeks each year and radically limits the freedom of choice of children, families, and even industries in disposition of their time. In an institution dedicated to the promotion of learning, we should expect that the requirements of the curricula, rather than the influence of tradition or convenience of administration, would dictate the allotment of time.

In logistical planning, the main concern is with the amount of time needed for almost all the learners to achieve the objectives of a curriculum; this consideration will guide scheduling decisions. It is not enough to allot the average or expected amount of time for completion of a curriculum, because this will be insufficient in 50 percent of cases. Most designers would want to allow sufficient time for instruction to be completed nine out of ten times. Putting the same principle differently, we need to determine the amount of time needed for 90 percent of the students to complete the learning; a margin of 10 percent may be allowed to ensure efficiency, but it is assumed that these students will receive special attention and not merely be allowed to fall by the wayside.

By this stage in the design of a curriculum, the analysis of the objectives and the schedule of content should allow a fairly accurate estimate of time requirements. Where intuition or prior experience are considered inadequate guides, the procedure shown in the box may be used to estimate time requirements.

In addition to the total allotment of time, the planner needs to pay attention to the distribution of time. Table 13–2 shows estimates of the amounts of time needed to achieve various levels of proficiency in a foreign language, based on the experience of American government agencies training personnel in foreign languages during the Second World War. It is unclear how accurately the estimates apply to children, nor how much time is required to maintain a language at a given level. What the table does strongly suggest is that fluency in a foreign language, even with an easy language and high-aptitude learners, cannot normally be achieved within the conventional pattern of twenty to sixty minutes of instruction a day. Ree provides an explanation of why this may be so:

> No other subject is as handicapped as languages by the driblet method imposed by the school timetable. It is madness to habituate the muscles of the pupil's mouth, and all his brain cells connected with speech, to adjust

---

Time Calculation

A relatively simple procedure may be used for calculating the amount of time needed for completion of an activity. The formula shown is derived from procedures developed in *Program Evaluation and Review Technique* (Cook, 1971).

1. Estimate the *expected time* (E) that each activity will take under normal circumstances. If a curriculum task analysis was conducted earlier, this estimate will already be available.
2. Estimate the *pessimistic time* (P). This is the time the activity will take if everything that could reasonably (i.e., with a 1 percent or greater probability) be expected to go wrong, does so.
3. Calculate the mean ($\frac{E + P}{2}$) to yield the *allocated time*. This is an estimate of the time that will be needed for the activity to be successfully completed nine times out of ten.

Example:

A teacher is planning a unit that has four objectives or elements. Calculations are as follows (all figures are in hours):

ELEMENT	EXPECTED TIME	PESSIMISTIC TIME	ALLOCATED TIME
A	1	3	2
B	3	7	5
C	1.5	2.5	2
D	2	5	3.5
TOTAL	7.5	17.5	12.5

---

themselves for ¾ of an hour to hearing and making French noises—and then remove the child so that for the rest of his waking day and often for a whole weekend, his muscles and his brain cells are drilled and habituated to English noises repeatedly. So that by the time he is back in the French lesson, the whole process has to begin almost as though the previous lesson had never taken place (Ree, 1972).

This position receives substantial support from the Canadian evidence on the success of immersion programs in French as compared with conventional approaches to second-language teaching (Barik and Swain, 1976; Stern et al., 1976).

The question of general concern to the curriculum planner is whether intensive learning is necessarily more efficient than dispersion of learning time. If a subject is studied six hours a day, does it generate a momentum that is absent if the learning is fragmented into one-hour units? Hour for hour, does the learning develop more rapidly? Instructors in intensive courses often report high levels of enthusiasm among their students, but definitive research on this issue remains to be done.

HOURS PER DAY	LEVEL OF PROFICIENCY		
	Tourist	Moderate	Fluent
3 hours	4 months	never	never
6 hours	2 months	4 months	9 months
9 hours	1½ months	3 months	6 months

Notes:

1. The table refers to the time required for *high-aptitude* students to learn a *simple* foreign language, e.g., Italian, Spanish, French, or German.

2. "Hours per day" includes a minimum of two hours of drill and study for each hour of instruction.

3. "Never" means that it is impractical to attempt to achieve that level of proficiency given the number of hours per day indicated.

4. "Tourist" level of proficiency satisfies routine travel requirements. "Moderate" level is sufficient to conduct routine business within a particular field and to read simple material with the aid of a dictionary. "Fluent" meets ordinary requirements not involving unfamiliar technical subjects and includes the ability to read newspapers and documents with limited reference to a dictionary.

(Adapted from Cleveland, Mangone, and Adams, *The overseas Americans* pp. 250–251. Copyright © 1960 by McGraw-Hill. Used with permission of McGraw-Hill Book Company.)

Table 13–2   Time required to learn a foreign language

The estimation of time requirements of a curriculum should not be limited to the instructional time of teachers and students but should calculate all the time required of all the participants in the program. Like instructional responsibilities, the investment of time must be recognized prior to undertaking a program if it is not to be jeopardized at the outset. Table 13–3 shows an estimate for a hypothetical two-week unit, which includes a guest lecture and a Saturday field trip supervised by the teacher and two adult volunteers. It is only by providing a complete summary that the designer and the decision-maker can appreciate the total time consumption relative to the anticipated outcomes.

Cost

Almost all aspects of a curriculum carry cost implications. Consequently, as Figure 13–1 indicates, the cost analysis is the last design component to be drafted. The first question the administrator will often

PERSONNEL	ACTIVITY	TIME IN HOURS
Students (30)	Instruction	7.5
	Homework	5.0
	Field trip	4.0
	Total	*16.5*
Teacher (1)	Instruction	7.5
	Field trip	4.0
	Preparation	4.0
	Administration	2.0
	Remediation	2.0
	Marking	1.0
	Total	*20.5*
Volunteers (2)	Field trip	4.0
	Total	*4.0*
Guest lecturer (1)	Lecture	1.0
	Travel	1.0
	Preparation	3.0
	Total	*5.0*

Table 13–3 Estimate of time commitment

ask about a proposed innovation is What will it cost? and the designer needs to have a response ready. The sophistication of the response will depend on the needs of the administrator. For some, a simple budget will be sufficient; others will require a complete cost analysis. Whatever the level of complexity, the budget should conform to the accounting format used by the school or jurisdiction.

The simplest curriculum budget shows only the direct costs that are additional to existing expenses. Costs of instruction or use of school

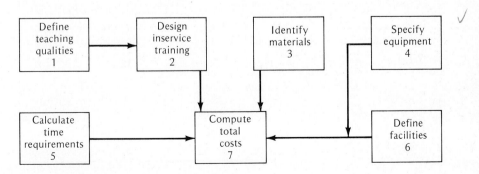

Figure 13–1 Planning curriculum logistics

facilities would not be shown in such budgets because these outlays are already assumed under other accounts. Table 13–4 shows a relatively simple budget for a driver-education program. The course is offered three times a year after school to classes of twenty students. It consists of thirty hours of in-car instruction (ten hours at the wheel) and thirty hours of in-class instruction. It is anticipated that seventeen students will be successful in each course and three will fail or drop out and not be replaced. The costs are shown both for the first offering of the course and for operation of the course over nine semesters. If the budget showed only the first-time costs, the course would appear to be relatively expensive because it would include capital or start-up costs that would not be repeated. If costs are projected over a period of years, inflation and salary increases must be taken into account. Income from specific grants or student fees is shown, and the net cost to the school, per student, and per successful student is calculated. These figures can then be used for comparisons among different programs.

In addition to direct costs, the educational planner should also consider the shadow costs, spillover costs, and opportunity costs. Shadow costs are largely invisible. When the New York State Office of Education surveyed sixty-seven driver-education programs in the schools, it found that those programs operating during the school day cost an average of

COSTS	1 SEMESTER	1 YEAR	3 YEARS
Instructor (½ time)	$2500	$7500	$25000
Dual-control car	7000	7000	7000
Car: Gas and maintenance	400	1200	4000
Insurance	150	450	1500
Films: purchase	1000	1000	1500
Films: rental	100	300	900
Other instructional materials	100	300	900
Total costs	11250	17750	40800
Costs per course	11250	5917	4533
REVENUE			
Government grant	960	2880	8640
Student fee ($75)	1500	4500	13500
Total revenue	2460	7380	22140
NET COSTS			
To school	8790	10370	18660
To school per course	8790	3457	2073
Per student enrolled	440	173	104
Per successful student	517	203	153

Table 13–4   Driver-Education curriculum budget

> A good budget won't make a shaky institution strong but a bad budget, in times like these, can make a strong institution shaky and destroy a shaky one.
>
> —*William G. Bowen, president, Princeton University*

$162 per pupil, while those operating out of school hours cost an average of $93 per pupil. (New York State Office of Education Performance Review, 1974). Thus the programs in school hours were incurring an average shadow cost of $69 per pupil. There is a shadow cost involved in having a $15,000-a-year teacher performing routine tasks such as playground supervision that could be performed by an $8,000 teacher's aide. (The shadow cost is not saved, however, by hiring a playground supervisor and having the teacher take a coffee break instead.) Professional incompetence always incurs shadow costs. Using library space for books that are never used or having an entire staff debate a decision that a committee of three could make are further examples of shadow costs.

Spillover costs are costs that a program incurs but does not pay. Parents experience the spillover costs of school programs by buying gym shoes, pencils, and hand calculators and by contributing to the cost of field trips. The cost of a business-education program that runs thirty electric typewriters and other office equipment spills over onto the school's electricity budget.

Opportunity costs are the costs of tradeoffs that are made whenever one must choose between mutually exclusive alternatives. One of the costs of marrying A is not being able to marry B. If a student may take either French or Spanish, one of the costs of learning French is the cost of foregoing learning Spanish. As time and money are always limited, any curriculum involves the student in opportunity costs.

Finally, cost-benefit analysis attempts to weigh the financial value of an endeavor against its costs. For such subjects as English or music, cost-benefit analysis would be fruitless and probably misleading. For other subjects, it provides interesting evidence that can be used in planning. The United States Department of the Budget, for example, calculated in 1967 that a breast-cancer screening program costing $22.4 million had a potential for saving 2,396 lives at a cost of $7,663 per life. Forty-seven million invested in an antismoking campaign could save 7,000 lives at an average cost of $6,400 per life. And $2 million put into a campaign encouraging the use of seat belts in cars could, it was estimated, save 22,930 lives at a cost of only $87 per life saved (*Business Week*, 1967).

Cost-benefit analysis is inappropriate for many areas of the curriculum. There are costs and benefits in developing a taste for Gothic architecture, eighteenth-century aquatints, and vintage port. While the benefits are, in the broad sense, economic, the attempt to express them in financial terms would probably be absurd. On the other hand, the financial benefits of some educational programs can and probably should be calculated. To take a simple example: If a program in dental hygiene can be predicted to reduce the incidence of tooth decay and gum disease by 20 percent, and if the average individual spends $50 a year on dental treatment, a private return of $10 a year can be expected. This is in addition to the returns in reduced pain and time spent in treatment and possibly reduced expenditure on tooth-decaying food and drink.

Educators sometimes adopt a cavalier attitude toward curriculum costs. This indifference is not justifiable. Money is primarily given in exchange for people's time and energy. Time and energy are not to be lightly dissipated, for they are life itself.

Logistics and the Curriculum Developer

A malfunctioning strap transducer at Edwards Air Force Base in 1949 elicited from one Captain Edward Murphy the immortal axiom that came to be known as Murphy's Law: If anything can go wrong, it will. Three other laws attributed to the same source are: (1) Nothing is ever as simple as it seems; (2) Everything takes longer than you expect; and (3) Left to themselves, things always go from bad to worse.

Most educators will vouch for the truth of these aphorisms. Curriculum developers are particularly vulnerable, because a curriculum consists of multiple elements, most of which are subject to failure. Logistical planning will not make everything go right, but it will prevent some things from going wrong.

Logistical questions are largely technical and hence lack some of the appeal of the lofty issues of educational policy in the abstract. But educational policies will remain abstract until educators are prepared to forge the fine detail that their implementation requires. High principle is the only right beginning for curriculum design, but it is an insufficient ending. If curriculum development is to be anything more than rhetoric, the "minute particulars" of logistics must receive the same dedicated attention that is merited by education in all its aspects.

ACTIVITIES

1. Conduct a complete analysis of a textbook you use or are familiar with. Refer to the criteria noted on pp. 371–376. Include a readability analysis and an ECO analysis of some such group as females, old people, or blue-collar workers. What is your overall judgment of the text?

2. Obtain the necessary resources, and have students make an instructional audiotape, videotape, filmstrip, or slide-tape presentation of a component of instruction; e.g., a short story, a scientific experiment, a physical-education demonstration, a geographical area study, a historical episode, or the life and work of an artist or musician.

3. Using a maximum/minimum thermometer, a hygrometer (for measuring humidity), and a noise meter, measure the range of temperature, humidity, and noise in several areas of the school or building where you work over a period of time. What conclusions would you draw about the efficiency of work in the building?

4. Observe pupil behavior in one classroom for at least one lesson. What aspects of behavior are influenced by such environmental factors as furniture design and arrangement, noise, lighting, and decor? What would be the ideal environment for the program you observed? How could the existing environment be modified to come closer to the ideal?

5. Identify the position you would like to be occupying five years from now. Write a complete description of the competences, personal qualities, and responsibilities the position requires. If possible, have a colleague assess the list for appropriateness, and revise your description accordingly. What does the process tell you about the training you need to acquire or the qualities you need to develop in the course of the next five years?

6. Select a unit of instruction of one month or less. Calculate the total costs, including the cost of instruction and use of facilities. Divide the dollar cost by 8 to give an approximation of the number of hours of work by taxpayers that the financial cost represents. Then calculate the time commitment of all participants. What is the total time consumption of the unit? What is the time commitment by students as compared with that of adults? Do the returns appear to justify the investment of time by the total community?

QUESTIONS

1. In the context of curriculum, logistics may be defined as
   a. a computer language
   b. a branch of philosophy
   c. sequential reasoning from assumptions and data to conclusions and decisions
   d. detailed planning of all the means—human, material, and administrative—for the delivery of instruction

2. Who is likely to learn most from instructional materials?
   a. the student who studies them
   b. the person who develops them
   c. the evaluator who assesses them
   d. the teacher who selects and uses them

3. A teacher analyzes a chapter on China in a geography textbook. She finds the Chinese referred to as artistic, barbarous, brilliant (twice), celebrated, civilized,

corrupt, cruel, distinguished, great (three times), renowned, skillful, weak, and wise. What is the coefficient of evaluation?

a. 45
b. 60
c. 75
d. 90

4. A teacher finds 49 words of 3 or more syllables in a sample of 30 sentences from a textbook. This suggests that the readability of the book is appropriate for a student who is reading at about

a. the fifth-grade level
b. the seventh-grade level
c. the tenth-grade level
d. the twelfth-grade level

5. For which instructional strategy is the conventional grid pattern of classroom seating most appropriate?

a. class discussion
b. individual research
c. small group activity
d. presentation of information

6. Which of the following learning environments needs to have the highest background noise level?

a. a library
b. a music room
c. a woodwork shop
d. a lecture theater

7. Which of the following statements about thermal comfort in classrooms is true?

a. children do not need as warm an environment as adults
b. air movement should be eliminated as it causes unpleasant drafts
c. an air temperature of 24°C. (75°F.) is appropriate for an elementary-school classroom in winter
d. relative humidity should be maintained above 65 percent to avoid drying out of skin and materials

8. Which aspect of logistics can most easily "make or break" a program?

a. time
b. budget
c. personnel
d. materials

9. A course is designed that contains three short units, expected to take 3, 5, and 7 hours to teach under average conditions. Under "worst likely" conditions, they

would take 6, 8, and 15 hours to teach. How much teaching time should the designer allow to ensure that the course is completed nine times out of ten?

a. 15 hours
b. 22 hours
c. 26 hours
d. 29 hours

10. A ninth-grade student has a choice between enrolling in art or in music, but may not enroll in both. The cost of this choice is most accurately termed

a. a shadow cost
b. a cost-benefit
c. a spillover cost
d. an opportunity cost

Check your answers against the key in Appendix 2.
9 or 10 right: You understand the material presented.
8 or 7 right: Review the areas of uncertainty.
6 or less right: Reread the chapter.

Recommended Reading

Department of Education and Science (England and Wales). *Acoustics in educational buildings.* London: Her Majesty's Stationery Office, 1975. Comprehensive overview of all aspects of sound control in schools; deals in a thorough and readable way with design procedures for optimal acoustics and listening conditions.

Gulliford, Nancy L. *Current research on the relative effectiveness of selected media characteristics.* Pittsburgh, Pa.: Westinghouse Electric Corp., Research and Development Center, 1973. ED 098 968. Good summary of the research on use of media in instruction.

Hall, Edward T. *The hidden dimension.* Garden City, N.Y.: Doubleday, 1966. Intriguing discussion by an anthropologist of the ways in which people use space in different cultures. Treatment of such topics as crowdedness and visual space are particularly relevant to questions of classroom design.

Hartley, James. *Designing instructional text.* New York: Nichols, 1978. This is an invaluable guide for the design of all kinds of instructional print material. Topics addressed include basic planning and layout, type size and spacing, illustrations and symbols, in texts, lecture handouts, worksheets, forms, and questionnaires.

Sommer, Robert. *Tight spaces.* Englewood Cliffs, N.J.: Prentice-Hall, 1974. Subtitled "Hard architecture and how to humanize it," Sommer's book treats the effects of physical surroundings on behavior with insight and style. Particularly valuable for its discussion of the architecture of schools and classrooms.

References

Barik, H. C., and M. Swain. Update on French immersion: The Toronto study through grade 3. *Canadian Journal of Education* 1976, 1 (4), 33–42.

Barker, Roger G., and Paul V. Gump. *Big school, small school.* Stanford, Cal.: Stanford University Press, 1964.

Bennett, Neville. *Teaching styles and pupil progress.* London: Open Books, 1976.

Bleil, Gordon. Evaluating educational materials. *Journal of Learning Disabilities*, 1975, 8 (Jan.), 12–19.

Bond, Guy L., and Miles A. Tinker. *Reading difficulties: Their diagnosis and correction.* 3rd ed. Englewood Cliffs, N.J.: Prentice-Hall, 1973.

Broadbent, D. E. Effect of noise on an "intellectual" task. *Journal of the Acoustical Society of America*, 1958, 30, 824–827.

Business Week. Putting a dollar sign on life. *Business Week*, Jan. 21, 1967, p. 87.

Cleveland, H., G. J. Mangone, and J. C. Adams. *The overseas Americans.* New York: McGraw-Hill, 1960.

Cook, Desmond L. *Program evaluation and review technique: Applications in education.* Washington, D.C.: United States Office of Education, 1971.

Department of Education and Science (England and Wales). *Acoustics in educational buildings.* London: Her Majesty's Stationery Office, 1975.

Drew, Clifford J. Research on the psychological-behavioral effects of the physical environment. *Review of Educational Research*, 1971, 41, 447–465.

Educational Products Information Exchange Institute. *Educational Product Report no. 57: Sex stereotyping in instructional materials.* December 1973.

Educational Products Information Exchange Institute. *Educational Product Report no. 62/63: Selecting and evaluating beginning reading materials: A how-to handbook.* May/June 1974.

Fabun, Don. *The dynamics of change.* Englewood Cliffs, N.J.: Prentice-Hall, 1967.

Farr, Lee E. Medical consequences of environmental home noises. In Robert Gutman (ed.), *People and buildings.* New York: Basic Books, 1972, pp. 202–211.

Fanger, P. Ole. Conditions for thermal comfort: Introduction of a general comfort equation. In James D. Hardy, A. Pharo Gagge, and Jan A. J. Stolwijk (eds.), *Physiological and behavioral temperature regulation.* Springfield, Ill.: Charles C. Thomas, 1970, pp. 152–176.

Forman, Susan G., and James D. McKinney. Creativity and achievement of second graders in open and traditional classrooms. *Journal of Educational Psychology*, 1978, 70, 101–107.

Fox, Seymour. Development and implementation of an educational program in Israel. Toronto: Ontario Institute for Studies in Education, Occasional Speakers Series, cassette no. 3402, 1973.

Fuller, R. Buckminster. *I seem to be a verb.* New York: Bantam Books, 1970.

Granville, Walter C. Color planning for hospitals and schools. Chicago: Mobil Finishes Co., 1962. ED 000 492.

Gulliford, Nancy L. Current research on the relative effectiveness of selected media characteristics. Pittsburgh, Pa.: Westinghouse Electric Corp., Research and Development Center, 1973. ED 098 968.

Hartley, James. *Designing instructional text.* New York: Nichols, 1978.

Johnson, Jenny. Appraisal of educational materials for AVLINE: An educational materials project in health education. *Audiovisual Instruction*, 1976, 21 (1), 22–27.

Karmel, L. J. Effects of windowless classroom environments on high school students. *Perceptual and Motor Skills*, 1965, 20, 277–278.

Kershaw, J. A. Productivity in schools and colleges. In S. E. Harris and A. Levensohn (eds.), *Education and public policy*. Berkeley, Cal.: McCutchan, 1965. pp. 185–191.

Krause, Kenneth C. Do's and don't's in evaluating textbooks. *Journal of Reading*, 1976, 20, 212–214.

Maslow, Abraham H., and Norbert L. Mintz. Effects of esthetic surroundings: I. Initial short-term effects of three esthetic conditions upon perceiving "energy" and "well-being" in faces. In Robert Gutman (ed.), *People and buildings*. New York: Basic Books, 1972, pp. 212–219.

McDiarmid, Garnet, and David Pratt. *Teaching prejudice*. Toronto: Ontario Institute for Studies in Education, 1971.

McIntyre, Donald. A guide to thermal comfort. *Applied Ergonomics*, 1973, 4 (2), 66–72.

McIntyre, D. A., and I. D. Griffiths. The effects of added clothing on warmth and comfort in cool conditions. *Ergonomics*, 1975, 18, 205–211.

McLaughlin, G. Harry. SMOG grading: A new readability formula. *Journal of Reading*, 1969, 12, 639–646.

New York State Office of Education Performance Review. Cost variations in driver education: A survey of 67 public school programs. Albany, N.Y.: New York State Office of Education Performance Review, 1974.

Niedermeyer, Fred C., and Michael H. Moncrief. Guidelines for selecting effective instructional products. *Elementary School Journal*, 1975, 76, 127–131.

Oddie, Guy. Building for educational change. *Organization for Economic Cooperation and Development Observer*, 1976, 80, March-April.

Oldsen, Carl F. The National Instructional Materials Information System. *Audiovisual Instruction*, 1976, 21 (10), 48–49.

Ott, John N. Influence of fluorescent lights on hyperactivity and learning disability. *Journal of Learning Disabilities*, 1976, 9, 417–422.

Pratt, David. *How to find and measure bias in textbooks*. Englewood Cliffs, N.J.: Educational Technology Press, 1971.

Ree, Harry. A license to learn languages. *Times Educational Supplement*, Dec. 8, 1974, p. 4.

Rosenshine, Barak. *Teaching behaviors and student achievement*. London: National Foundation for Educational Research, 1971.

Schefter, Joseph A. Guides to materials identification and selection. Washington, D.C.: National Institute of Education, 1974.

Scriven, Brian. Homo sedens: Theory and reality. *Times Educational Supplement*, Nov. 7, 1975, p. 38.

Seymour, W. D. An experiment showing the superiority of a light-colored "blackboard." *British Journal of Educational Psychology*, 1937, 7, 259–268.

Shapson, Stan M., Edgar N. Wright, Gary Eason, and John Fitzgerald. Results of an experimental study of the effects of class size. Paper presented at the Annual Meeting of the American Educational Research Association, Toronto, March 1978.

Sharpe, Deborah T. *The psychology of color and design*. Chicago: Nelson-Hall, 1974.

Shaver and Company. *The learning environment*. Salina, Kansas: Shaver Co., 1968. ED 021 434.

Smith, Peter. *The design of learning spaces*. London: Council for Educational Technology for the U.K., 1974.

Sommer, Robert. *Personal space: The behavioral basis of design.* Englewood Cliffs, N.J.: Prentice-Hall, 1969.

——— . *Tight spaces: Hard architecture and how to humanize it.* Englewood Cliffs, N.J.: Prentice-Hall, 1974.

Stern, H. H., Merrill Swain, L. D. McLean, R. J. Friedman, Birgit Harley, and Sharon Lapkin. *Three approaches to teaching French.* Toronto: Ontario Institute for Studies in Education, 1976.

Traub, Ross, Joel Weiss, Charles Fisher, Donald Musella, and Sar Khan. *Openness in schools: An evaluation study.* Toronto: Ontario Institute for Studies in Education, 1976.

Weinstein, Carol S., and Neil D. Weinstein. The effects of noise in an open-space school on reading comprehension. Paper presented at the Annual Meeting of the American Educational Research Association, Toronto, March 1978.

Wright, Robert J. The affective and cognitive consequences of an open education elementary school. *American Educational Research Journal,* 1975, 12, 449–468.

Wurtman, Richard J. The effects of light on the human body. *Scientific American,* 1975, 233 (July), 69–77.

Wyon, D. P., P. O. Fanger, B. W. Olesen, and C. J. K. Pedersen. The mental performance of subjects clothed for comfort at two different air temperatures. *Ergonomics,* 1975, 18, 359–374.

Part Five

IMPLEMENTING A CURRICULUM

14

PRINCIPLES

- Designers can often identify defects in a curriculum by rereading it some time after the first draft is completed.

- Appraisal by an outside expert can point to defects not perceived by designers.

- Confidential review enables designers to accommodate or anticipate criticisms from influential individuals.

- A pilot test is a small-scale tryout of all or part of a curriculum usually with individual students.

- A field test tries out a curriculum under conditions of typical use.

- Effectiveness and acceptability are usually the main features to be assessed in program evaluation.

- Implementation is primarily a political process.

- People tend to resist change if they are unmotivated, vulnerable, have inadequate resources, and are unclear about the change or sceptical of its value.

- It is judicious to approach decision-makers early, to observe proper channels, to allow them to take credit for the innovation, and to use appropriate language and arguments.

- It is important to reach teachers by personal contact and to provide resources, incentives, and clear directions.

CONCEPTS

Curriculum evaluation	Pilot test	Efficiency
Internal evaluation	Field test	Adoption
Expert appraisal	Program evaluation	Implementation
Confidential review	Effectiveness	

14

Validation and Implementation

I pondered all these things, and how men fight and lose the battle, and the thing that they fought for comes about in spite of their defeat, and when it comes turns out not to be what they meant, and other men have to fight for what they meant under another name.

—William Morris

Curriculum Evaluation

Challenging though the task of designing a curriculum is, the undertaking is not complete when the last word is written. The designer's work reaches fruition only when the curriculum makes an impact on the learners. Many an excellent curriculum has had insignificant results because its designers limited their horizon to production of a curriculum rather than implementation of a program.

Internal evaluation is the first step after the curriculum is written. The design team works through the curriculum with a fine-tooth comb. This is best done two or three weeks after completion of the first draft,

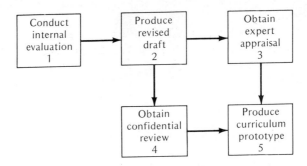

Figure 14–1   Main steps in curriculum evaluation

to allow a measure of objectivity to develop. This evaluation will almost invariably reveal numerous minor defects. Out of it emerges a revised draft.

The next stage is expert appraisal. The experts whose assessment of the curriculum is sought need to be knowledgeable about curriculum; they must also be willing, and encouraged, to deliver a candid judgment. Curriculum evaluators are too often forced to agree with Somerset Maugham that "people ask you for criticism, but they only want praise."

Whether evaluators should be expert in the subject matter of the curriculum is controversial. Worthen (1974) suggests that such expertise is rare in combination with the skills of curriculum evaluation and may serve only to introduce a particular disciplinary bias. According to Bloom, "A Nobel Prize winner in physics may be an expert on the nature and structure of the subject of physics, but he may have little competence in making judgments about what a sixteen-year-old student can learn about physics" (1977, pp. 88–89). There is something to be said for having an assessment by both disciplinary experts and curriculum generalists.

The criteria against which a curriculum is evaluated are implicit in the design principles described in the previous chapters. A checklist, which itemizes only the main criteria, is shown below. Items 11, 12, and 13 are discussed in detail in this chapter.

Figure 14–1 shows the five main steps in curriculum evaluation.

Curriculum Evaluation Guide

1. Aim
Is the overall intended outcome of the curriculum concisely stated?
Does the aim have prima facie significance?
Does the aim encompass all the main intents of the curriculum?

2. Rationale
Is the need for the program convincingly presented?
Are all the salient arguments for the program used?
Are they valid, sound, and rigorous?
Are objections anticipated and dealt with?
If a needs assessment was conducted, are the methodology and results adequately described?

3. Objectives
Are all the major specific intended outcomes identified?
Do they indicate how learners will be changed by the program?
Is the type and importance of each objective specified?
Is each objective relevant to the aim?
Are objectives precise, feasible, functional, significant, and appropriate?
If all the objectives were achieved, would the aim be realized?

4. Performance criteria
Is attainment of each objective evaluated by an explicit performance criterion?
Are performance criteria congruent, complete, objective, discrete, reliable, and efficient?
Are standards or cutoff scores appropriate?

5. Grading
Is the grading system clear and explicit?
Do grades reflect the priority among objectives?
Does the grading system ensure that critical objectives are achieved before credit is awarded?

6. Context
Is the social and community context described?
Is the institutional context explicit?
Is it clear how this curriculum fits, dovetails, or overlaps with the program of the student and of the institution?
Are the lines of authority clear?
Are other kinds of institution identified that could use the curriculum?
Is the impact on other courses, programs, and teachers identified?

7. Entry characteristics
Is there a description of the learners for whom the curriculum is intended?
Is the recruiting or selection process outlined?

Are prerequisites valid?
Are pretests appropriate?
Is there provision for students who are denied admission?

8. Instruction
Is the instructional schedule sufficiently detailed?
Is it viable?
Is the subject matter motivational?
Is it relevant to the objectives?
Are the teaching strategies appropriate, varied, and creative?
Are all objectives addressed by appropriate instruction?

9. Management of diversity
Is formative evaluation frequent, valid, and diagnostic?
Is remediation preplanned, appropriate, motivational, and efficient?
Is there provision for faster learners?

10. Logistics
Are minimum and maximum numbers of students and groups indicated?
Are there contingency plans for surplus or shortfall of students?
Are materials and equipment specified?
Do they meet all relevant criteria?
Are they available, or can they be obtained or produced?
Are they appropriate?
Are the required facilities identified?
Is total time consumption realistically calculated?
Are instructor qualities, competencies, and responsibilities specified?
Is the cost analysis complete?

11. Tryout
Is there provision for adequate pilot and field testing?
If tryouts have been performed, are results shown?

12. Program evaluation
Are there valid measures of effectiveness and acceptability?
Are other main aspects of the program subject to evaluation?
Is there provision for ongoing monitoring and revision?

13. Implementation
Is there a strategy and timetable for implementation?
Are roles and responsibilities clearly defined?
Are resources and incentives available to users?
Is the implementation strategy realistic?

14. Production

Is the curriculum free of stylistic and typographical errors, unsupported assertions, unnecessary jargon, verbosity, etc.?
Is it attractively and professionally produced?

Confidential review

Parallel with expert appraisal, it is judicious to obtain a confidential review of the curriculum by a small sample of teachers and influential persons in the community, such as members of the school board, who have not previously been identified with the project. There are few things more disappointing than seeing a good curriculum fail to win approval, or, having been approved, fail to be implemented in the classroom on account of misunderstanding of, or objections to, aspects of its content. With hindsight it is easy to see how the rejection of the Muskoka life skills curriculum (see box) might have been avoided by co-option of the leading critic as a developer or evaluator at an earlier stage.

A more celebrated case was that of *Man: A Course of Study* (MACOS). MACOS, based on Bruner's curriculum thought, sought to illuminate human nature and society by comparison of humans with other animals, and of American with Eskimo culture. The National Science Foundation and the U.S. Office of Education supported the project. The curriculum was attacked in Congress, notably by Congressman John B. Conlan, on the grounds that it depicted "abhorrent and revolting behavior by a nearly extinct Eskimo tribe," including adultery, cannibalism, infanticide, and murder. This controversy ultimately led to restrictions by Congress on the work of the National Science Foundation (McNeil, 1977). Had MACOS invited a confidential review from Conlan or other conservatives prior to dissemination of the curriculum, it is possible that the curriculum could have been modified at least to weaken the objections. Even if this modification were impossible, such a review could have made the developers more aware of the grounds of criticism and better able to defend the curriculum against them.

The outcome of this series of evaluations and revisions is the curriculum prototype, ready for developmental testing.

Curriculum Tryout

In any social system the costs of errors and defects tend to be passed downwards. Thus the costs of deficiencies in the operation of a hospital tend to be borne not by the medical staff or administrators, but ultimately by patients. The costs of defects in curricula will be passed down to the learners, where they will be translated into wasted time and

---

Curriculum Politics

In April 1977, the Board of Education for the County of Muskoka in Ontario, Canada, defeated by a vote of 8 to 7 a proposal to initiate a "Life Skills Program" in the Muskoka Schools.

A committee of teachers and administrators, with the general support of the Board of Education, had been developing the curriculum since December 1975. The Life Skills Program, to be implemented at all grade levels, would deal with numerous value issues, such as respect for property, the work ethic, manners and personal appearance, and use of alcohol, tobacco, marijuana, and junk food. The intent of the program was to produce graduates who would have a positive sense of self-worth, a commitment to personal development, a sense of identity, an understanding of the importance of the family, an ability to make rational choices, kindness, compassion, consideration, and respect for others, interpersonal skills, and a set of life goals.

According to the local newspaper (*Huntsville Forester,* 14 April 1977), defeat of the proposal was partly due to the "infuriated" opposition of one member of the board, who had been elected in 1976, after development of the program began. He felt that the program was indoctrinational, would be open to propaganda, and subverted the responsibility of the home. "This is how Hitler got his start!" he exclaimed. "I spent five of the prime years of my life fighting against such a doctrine!"

---

missed opportunities for learning. Developers therefore need to make every effort to eliminate weaknesses in a curriculum before it is introduced on a large scale. This is the function of pilot and field testing.

Pilot testing

Pilot testing is small-scale testing in which little emphasis is placed on reproducing the conditions of actual classroom use. It aims to obtain fine-grain data from intensive tryouts with a small number of individual learners.

The curriculum should be tried out in relatively small "chunks," starting with segments of five to thirty minutes of instruction at a time. Students who are engaged in the pilot test should be made aware that it is not they, but the curriculum, which is being evaluated. They should be encouraged to offer criticism and suggestions, which may be stimulated by inserting an obvious error near the beginning of the material. When they encounter difficulties, they should be encouraged to think aloud. Modifications can be made and tried out on the spot. Often the solution will lie in shortening and simplifying the instruction, rather than elaborating it. Until such problems arise, however, the instructor should avoid contaminating the trial by providing assistance to the learner over and above what is called for in the curriculum.

The material should be tried out with learners of both high and low ability. The less able students will provide more data in the form of errors; the faster learners may be more articulate in identifying difficulties and suggesting revisions (Branson et al., 1975, p. 298). After completion of the relevant test or performance criterion, an informal interview can be used to discuss difficulties in performance and to obtain feedback at the affective level.

Obtaining the students for pilot testing poses some practical problems. If the curriculum has popular appeal (jazz dance, revolver shooting, etc.), it will not be difficult to recruit volunteers on an extracurricular basis. Pilot testing of new curricula may also serve as a form of enrichment for students working ahead of their peer group. Summer school and evening classes present possibilities for pilot testing. Teachers who are parents may occasionally be able to try out instruction with their own children. One of the best solutions is to request funds in the original development proposal to hire pilot students. One hundred dollars would allow five consecutive individual trials of a ten-hour unit at two dollars an hour. In the absence of other alternatives, it may be necessary to try out a curriculum piecemeal in a regular classroom.

It is an advantage if students selected for pilot testing resemble the learners for whom the curriculum is designed, but it is inevitable that they will be somewhat atypical. This is not a serious problem. Typical learners will be used at the field-testing stage. Instruction in the first pilot tests will usually be conducted by members of the design team. But greater objectivity is attained by having the instruction in one or more pilot tests carried out by a teacher who is not associated with or committed to the design of the curriculum. The teacher can then be interviewed as to the problems he or she experienced or anticipates in the curriculum.

At the pilot-testing stage, the designers should not be perturbed if numerous problems become apparent. An absence of errors suggests that the instruction is not "lean" enough. It is relatively cheap and easy to detect instruction that is inadequate and develop additional material as needed. It is very difficult and expensive to identify areas where the instruction is inefficient or redundant and to remove material that has already been developed.

Throughout the tryout phase, the designer needs to maintain as far as possible the objectivity of an experimental scientist. Blaming the students or the designers is an inappropriate response to unmet objectives. Failure is merely evidence of the need for further revision. As Carl Rogers once said, "The data are always friendly."

Field testing

Pilot testing is continued, as Figure 14–2 indicates, until the program is ready for field testing. A field test is a dress rehearsal of a program. Field tests perform both experimental and political functions: they serve to evaluate the curriculum and to build support for it.

In the field test the final version of the curriculum emerging from the pilot testing is implemented under conditions as close as possible to those that will prevail when it is installed on a regular basis. Special administrative approval and support are usually required at this stage, as is the cooperation of teachers and schools involved in the field test.

From an experimental point of view, the teachers and classes chosen to field-test a curriculum should be as typical as possible. However, it could be fatal to select a teacher who is hostile to the new curriculum. Generally it is wise to enlist teachers who are open-minded and flexible and whose previous experience with innovation has been positive. The most typical class in any case becomes atypical when it is involved in an experimental program. This alone may produce significant gains in student enthusiasm and achievement—the so-called Hawthorne effect. The evaluators need to take this effect into account in interpreting the data on program outcomes.

The field test should allow participants "to try out the invention without substantial fear of failure" (Clark and Guba, 1967, p. 121). At the same time, it provides a semipublic demonstration of the innovation. If the preceding stages have been competently managed, the success of the field test should result in the new program being widely "talked up" among both teachers and students in the system. The interest generated helps create awareness and build support on the part of the system as a whole.

By this stage, the developers of the curriculum are heavily committed to it, and some objectivity may be preserved if one or more outside judges evaluate the field test. While the timetable for introduction of the new program will usually have been sufficient, lead time must be allowed

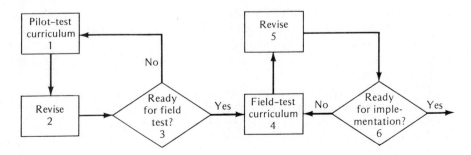

Figure 14–2 Curriculum tryout

for revisions that the field test reveals are desirable. If the earlier stages in the "debugging" process have been carried out effectively, only trivial defects should remain to be corrected. Major unforeseen problems arising during the field test may indicate the need for a second field test, if only to reassure users that the program really works before they adopt it.

Program Evaluation

The success of the program should be evaluated after the field test and after each offering of the course. The aspects of a program that require evaluation are numerous, and multiple criterion measures may be used to obtain information about them (Metfessel and Michael, 1972). It may be beyond the resources of the evaluators to gather all the available data on all aspects of a program. There are two program dimensions, however, that should always be evaluated: effectiveness and acceptability. Some attention should also be paid to the criterion of efficiency.

Effectiveness

In its most basic form, the crucial question to gauge the effectiveness of a program is Did the learners achieve the objectives? But as it is rare for a program to expect all students to achieve all objectives at the highest level, this question usually becomes Did the minimum expected number of students achieve the minimum stipulated objectives at the minimum level?

Where grades reflect achievement of objectives, the criterion level may be stated in terms of grades, with the exception of dispositional objectives, which do not usually enter into the grading system.

Such criteria imply precise definitions. Politicians and administrators are often reluctant to publicly state explicit criteria of effectiveness because they would then be answerable for nonachievement of program goals. Vague and diffuse goals allow more flexibility and scope for compromise (Carr-Hill and Magnussen, 1973). But the standards of curriculum evaluators are more rigorous than, or at least different from, those of politicians. In the absence of explicit criteria of effectiveness, there is the danger of making ex post facto (after the event) judgments—setting the criterion to match the results. Criteria help designers decide whether to revise the program or to maintain it unchanged; or, more properly, as even the best program can be improved, between "may revise" and "must revise."

A weakness of some contemporary research on program effectiveness is that dropout rate is not taken into account. It is clearly misleading to report a student success rate of 90 percent if the unreported dropout was 50 percent. Consequently, the criterion of achievement should either be stated in terms of students who begin the program, or there should be an additional criterion stipulating a maximum tolerable dropout rate.

Assessing student achievement at the end of the learning experience may be insufficient when it is sustained or lifelong performance that is the essential intent of the curriculum. In technical and vocational programs the measure of success should incorporate feedback from subsequent employers, managers, or supervisors. Skills that are likely to decay after the completion of training can be retested by delayed posttests to assess the effectiveness of overtraining and retention.

The judicious evaluator will take an interest in unanticipated as well as intended outcomes. The key question is not merely Did the program achieve its goal? but What effects did the program have? A narrow focus on targeted objectives may prevent the evaluator from noticing other outcomes. To overcome this problem, Scriven (1972) proposes "goal-free evaluation" as an addition to conventional evaluation. The goal-free evaluator is, as is the case in most rigorous program evaluation, independent of the program designers and remains ignorant of the program objectives until all the apparent results of the program have been assessed. This approach makes it more likely that unexpected effects, both salutary and unwelcome, will be detected; the program can subsequently be modified to incorporate or to eliminate them.

Effectiveness may also be considered in a relative light. Evaluators and decision-makers are often interested in whether a new program is more effective than its predecessor. In this case a time-series study may be most appropriate. Figure 14–3 shows the effect on school attendance of a hypothetical new extracurricular program. When presented in graphic form, the data from time-series analysis tends to have immediate impact. The chief weaknesses are oversimplification and lack of control over contextual differences between the old and the new program.

It is clear that a single criterion of program effectiveness will normally be insufficient. Let us suppose that a program in emergency first aid has been designed. The following might be proposed as criteria of program effectiveness:

The program will be regarded as effective if all the following criteria are met:

1. Ninety percent of those who enter the program achieve a passing grade (i.e., master all critical objectives).

2. Fifty percent of those who enter the program achieve a grade of Honors (i.e., master all objectives).

3. At least eight out of ten randomly selected graduates of the program achieve all critical objectives when retested without prior notice six to nine months after completion of the program.

4. The dispositional objectives are achieved.

5. No significant negative outcomes are identified.

6. In the twelve months following the course, no instance is dis-

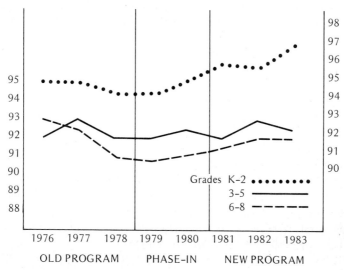

MEAN ANNUAL ATTENDANCE

Figure 14–3   Time-series study

covered of a graduate failing to take appropriate action in a first-aid emergency.

Acceptability

A program that achieves all its objectives may still be judged a failure if the people involved disliked the experience. For one thing, an unpleasant learning experience reduces the likelihood that what has been learned will be remembered or used. More fundamentally, if the ultimate purpose of education is to increase the happiness of individuals, then its components should also aim at this result.

The most widely used method for ascertaining student satisfaction is the course evaluation questionnaire. Such questionnaires have been extensively studied in postsecondary contexts. Some of the questions that consistently distinguish between most and least popular courses and instructors deal with the instructor's enthusiasm, organization, and teaching skill; the usefulness of assignments; the fairness of testing methods; the instructor's interaction with students; and the student's overall judgment of the course and the instructor (Marsh, 1977; Shingles, 1977).

The instructor should attempt to ensure that the evaluation is completed by a sufficient number of students to be representative of the total group and that the context in which students make the evaluation is not such as to bias the results (final examination or end-of-term party).

A target or cutoff may be set in terms of course evaluation results. Suppose that the evaluation calls for students to rate each of twenty aspects of a course as Poor, Fair, Good, or Excellent and that these four categories are weighted 1, 2, 3, and 4. (While such weighting is arbitrary, it will probably not do great violence to the results. Strictly, the weighting system should be based on empirical data on the perceived distances between points on the scale [Torgeson, 1958]). Responses can then be averaged question by question and student by student. The standard might be stated as follows: *The course will be considered acceptable if the average rating for each course aspect is at least 3.0, and the average rating by each student is at least 3.0.*

Open-ended comments on course evaluations allow students to express their feelings and make specific recommendations. They may be of direct value to the instructor, but it seems best that they be neither sought nor seen by anyone else. If administrators are gathering data on course acceptability, they will obtain the most objective picture by focusing on the broadly based quantitative results. The anonymous course evaluation, in exceptional cases, provides an opportunity for character assassination, and a single extreme statement, positive or negative, is likely by its very nature to have an effect greater than all the more representative numerical data.

Written course evaluations provide some general guidance to instructors, especially when they are used over several offerings of the same course. But they suffer from most of the weaknesses of questionnaires (see pages 84–85). Observation of voluntary choices made by students, especially those choices made weeks or months after the course ends, may be a more significant guide to student attitude. Attendance and dropout rates compared to norms in similar courses may be an indicator of acceptability but must be interpreted with caution. Registration by graduates of a course in subsequent courses in the same subject or taught by the same instructor may be relevant evidence. If an optional course is successful, its popularity will spread by word of mouth, often resulting in increased enrollments next time it is offered. In addition, there are all the incidental data in the form of spontaneous comments from students, their parents, and other interested individuals. Programs that generate positive student attitudes may also be responsible for a general increase in morale, as indicated by a decrease in disciplinary incidents and reduction of damage to school property. Few generalizations can be made about the use of such data for program evaluation; any criterion used must be specific to the program in question.

If a program is to survive, it must be acceptable not only to students, but also to teachers and as far as possible to everyone else who is in a position to undermine or injure it. A program that elicits enthusiastic student response will generally be popular with teachers. A structured interview is probably the best way to obtain teacher responses to such questions as Did you support the intents of the program? Was the program straightforward to implement? Did it involve extra work? Did you have adequate resources? Administrative response may also be obtained by means of interviews. Community reaction can be monitored by analysis of letters and phone calls concerning the program to teachers, administrators, elected officials, and the media.

Efficiency

Efficiency means production of output relative to input of energy and resources. A machine can properly be described in absolute terms as 50 percent or 80 percent efficient. But in social systems, judgments of efficiency are usually comparative: the relative costs of two equally effective solutions to a problem are compared, or a comparison is made of the relative effectiveness of two strategies equivalent in cost.

Valid assessment of the efficiency of an educational program is extremely difficult. What is required is a controlled experiment, but it is often impossible to control all the significant variables in a real-world educational context. In clinical trials of a new drug it is possible to set up "double-blind" experiments in which neither the patients nor the attending physicians know which subjects are receiving the drug and which the placebo. No such experimental purity can be obtained in the classroom: it is seldom possible to disguise from learners or teachers the fact that they are engaged in an experimental program. And while the financial inputs to different programs can be equated, it is not possible to control the inputs of time, energy, commitment, and enthusiasm on the part of learners and teachers. There is adequate guidance in the literature as to how to control such factors as differences in student aptitude between two classes (Campbell and Stanley, 1963), but little as to how to control teacher differences in instruction; even the imposition of detailed lesson plans does not guarantee equivalent teaching (Bellack et al., 1966). Finally, to compare the efficiency of two programs, they must be aiming at the same results and evaluated by tests equally appropriate to both curricula. Walker and Schaffarzick point out that this is not often the case:

> The advantage of groups studying from innovative curricula comes entirely from those studies in which the test content bias favors the innovative curricula. . . . Traditional curricula more than hold their own in tests biased their way (Walker and Schaffarzick, 1974, p. 97).

Nevertheless, the need for responsible use of resources requires the program evaluator to take some note of the costs of a program relative to those of other programs and to do so in the light of the achieved effects. Inputs of time and money should be quantified as far as possible: much other evidence will of necessity be relatively crude, impressionistic, and anecdotal. Glaring differences in the efficiency of programs will be apparent; so will gross underutilization or squandering of resources, redundant instruction, or waste of student time. Any absolute judgments that result will normally have to be made against the subjective criterion of reasonableness.

The evaluation of program effectiveness, acceptability, and efficiency is summarized on the opposite page.

Other criteria

While a program that is effective, acceptable, and reasonably efficient must be judged successful, several other aspects of a program may be evaluated if the maximum benefit from each trial is to be realized. The major aspects are itemized on pages 424–425. In most cases, the first question to ask is whether the program is operating according to the specifications outlined in the curriculum. If not, a judgment must be made as to whether the deviation represents a defect in implementation or an improvement on the curriculum. If it is the latter, then the curriculum should be revised to incorporate the modification.

The outcome of program evaluation

It should not be necessary at this point to stress the importance of program evalation in achieving the potential of a dynamic curriculum system. Without the kind of data that program evaluation provides, it is difficult either to justify or to improve what is being done in schools. In the absence of such evidence, the public's unwillingness to sustain escalating educational costs is understandable.

Program evaluation leads logically to one of four decisions regarding the future of a program: (1) maintain the program; (2) expand it; (3) revise it; (4) abandon it. Pressure is often strong to maintain even weak programs, on account of the time, training, aspirations, and sentiment that educators invest in them. To counteract this inertia, the evaluator should not hesitate to recommend scrapping a program when this seems appropriate: not when the program is devoid of merit, but when the resources it consumes can no longer be justified in the light of more significant programs that are being excluded for lack of space or resources.

Program Evaluation Guide

1. PROGRAM OUTPUTS

DIMENSIONS AND QUESTIONS	DATA SOURCES
Effectiveness What proportion of those registering for, entering, and completing the program achieved which objectives at what level, on completion of the program and in delayed posttesting? Do graduates perform adequately on the job, in subsequent educational programs, or in later life? What unanticipated effects did the program have? How could effectiveness be increased?	Analysis of program test results; interviews with graduates and dropouts; with employers, managers, supervisors, and subsequent teachers; interviews with teachers in the program; anecdotal reports of highly desirable or undesirable behaviors; standardized test results; goal-free evaluation; extramural awards, honors, prizes.
Acceptability Did students enjoy or appreciate the program? Did the program elicit positive responses from teachers? Did administrators approve? Did it have a good public image? How could acceptability be enhanced?	Analysis of course evaluation questionnaires; discussion with students, teachers, administrators; student dropout and transfer; disciplinary incidents; attendance data; damage to equipment, materials, or facilities; subsequent academic choices of students; subsequent course enrollments; analysis of public discussion and comment on the program; public attendance at open days, etc.; requests for and attendance at parent-teacher interviews; classroom observation.
Efficiency Do the outcomes of the program appear to justify the total resources it consumes? Does the program appear to be more efficient than corresponding programs? than the program it superseded? Is there any obvious wastage of student or teacher time, of materials or supplies? Are equipment or personnel underutilized? How could efficiency be improved?	In-class observation; analysis of time, cost, and outcome of different programs; depth of dust on expensive equipment; interviews with students and teachers.

2. PROGRAM ASPECTS

ASPECTS AND QUESTIONS	DATA SOURCES
Needs Is the need that the program was designed to meet still significant? Is a school program still necessary to meet the need? Is the program meeting the need? Is the need recognized by the learners? Are there prerequisite needs to be met? Are there related or additional needs the program could meet?	Review of needs assessment data; rerun of parts of needs assessment; interviews with learners, teachers, and others in community; data on program effectiveness.
Aims and objectives What aims and objectives are apparently being pursued in the program? Are they the same as those identified in the curriculum? Are needs, aims, and objectives recognized and accepted by learners and teachers? Are they functional, significant, and appropriate? Are there additional objectives that could usefully be introduced?	In-class observation; analysis of learning materials and tests; interviews with students and teachers.
Evaluation of student learning Are performance criteria, formative and summative tests, grading and reporting consistent with specifications in the curriculum? Are they providing necessary information to make decisions about students? Are measures congruent, complete, objective, discrete, reliable, and efficient? Is testing consuming excessive time? Is it promoting undue student anxiety? Do students regard tests as fair and useful?	Test analysis; data from guidance services; feedback from parents; discussion with students and teachers.
Entry characteristics Do student characteristics correspond to description of learners? Are prerequisites and pretests used as intended? Are any students out of place in the program?	Student complaints of difficulty or easiness of program; analysis of pretest data; student failure and dropout; student transfer; interviews with teachers.

2. PROGRAM ASPECTS *(continued)*

ASPECTS AND QUESTIONS	DATA SOURCES
Instruction Are the content and methods consistent with the curriculum? Are they appropriate to the objectives and the learners? Are they interesting? Do they engage student attention? Are they efficient?	Analysis of formative and summative test results; classroom observation; interviews with highest and lowest achievers.
Provision for aptitude differences Are students' learning problems rapidly recognized, diagnosed, and remediated? Is the marginal time of fast learners used productively?	Analysis of formative and summative test results; classroom observation; interviews with highest and lowest achievers.
Logistics Are materials and facilities that are specified in the curriculum available and being used? Are the materials effective? Are they unbiased? Are facilities appropriate? Are personnel competent? Is time consumption within specifications? Are costs in line with projections?	Classroom observation; discussion with teachers, students, administrators; examination of materials; complaints by teachers of difficulty, by students of teacher inadequacy; time calculation; analysis of expenditures.

Implementation: *The Great Barrier Reef*

The voyage from first identification of student need to eventual learner achievement is often stormy, but more good curricula sink without trace on the shoals of implementation than at any other point.

An important realization for curriculum workers is that the process of implementation is one of persuading people to make certain decisions. As such it is neither a curriculum process, nor an academic process, nor an intellectual process. Walker maintains that it is not even a rational process:

> I think it is time we dreamed a new dream about curriculum change. This time our ideal should recognize that curriculum changes are necessarily subject to the operation of enormously powerful social forces that cannot possibly be brought under the control of any technical procedure or systematically designed process (Walker, 1976, p. 299).

In a word, curriculum change is a political process, a question of "who gets what, when, and how" (Lasswell, 1958).

Perhaps because of its political nature, the question of implementation has often been ignored by curriculum writers and left to the administrative and management specialists, who have studied change and innovation extensively. There is much to be said for division of labor, but in this case one fears that it has led to the training of curriculum designers who do not know how to implement what they have designed, and of administrators who know how to implement changes but do not know what changes are worth implementing.

The educator who seeks to introduce innovation inherits a legacy of ill-managed efforts at change. Throughout the 1960s and early 1970s, the rhetoric of innovation often asserted that all that was necessary to implement educational reform was to provide the reality or the appearance of teacher involvement in designing the change. This belief, combined with the charismatic appeals of educational gurus and politically ambitious administrators, raised expectations that in the long run could only be disappointed. The confusion and frustration that resulted in many school systems, as inadequately equipped teachers attempted to plan and implement new curricula, add to the obstacles that must now be surmounted. Much resistance by teachers to change is solidly based on personal experience of manipulation and other kinds of assault upon their integrity. But this is only one of the barriers to change.

Barriers to change

Goodwin Watson suggested several years ago that few people welcome a totally unchanging environment. If people appeared to resist change, it must be because the natural human drive for newness and excitement was being counteracted by opposing forces. He concluded that such forces acted on both personality and institutional dimensions. The major personality factors antagonistic to change were: the tendency of any organism to return to equilibrium after a disturbance; to prefer the familiar and habitual; to stick with coping strategies previously found successful; to discount ideas that conflict with established attitudes; to emulate the values and behavior of past or present authority figures; to distrust one's own power to bring about change; to identify change with seduction and moral decay; to believe that imperfection is all we deserve; and to yearn for the good old days. Resistance in social systems appeared to Watson to rest on the conformity of groups to established norms; apprehension of side effects of the change; vested interests; commitment to deep-seated beliefs and loyalties; and rejection of "outsiders" who advocated change (Watson, 1967).

These phenomena are familiar to observers of all social organizations. The specific barriers that occur in educational institutions appear

Attitudes to Innovation

Everett Rogers, the rural sociologist, developed the idea of a continuum of dispositions towards innovation, based on the findings of numerous studies of innovation in education, agriculture, and medicine (Rogers, 1962; Rogers and Shoemaker, 1971). An adaptation of his ideas to curriculum innovation suggests the following model:

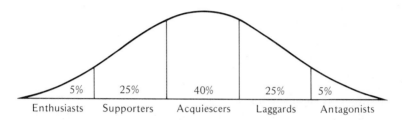

| 5% | 25% | 40% | 25% | 5% |
| Enthusiasts | Supporters | Acquiescers | Laggards | Antagonists |

The enthusiasts are characterized by vigor and independence of outlook. They need adventure, enjoy making changes and taking risks, and have high aspirations. They are gregarious and are likely to have contact with other change agents and sources of information from outside the organization. The enthusiasts are likely to participate in the design or testing of the innovation.

The supporters are respected members of the organization, who have a less radical image than the enthusiasts. Like the enthusiasts, they tend to be actively involved in professional associations and inservice training. They are knowledgeable about curriculum issues and are quickly persuaded of the value of an innovation once it has been thoroughly planned, justified, and tested.

The acquiescers are solid citizens, phlegmatic and deliberate in their approach to change. While prepared to consider change, they will not initiate it. Most of their contacts are with their peers within the organization. They tend to take the line of least resistance and hence will adopt a change, at least superficially, as soon as opposition becomes onerous.

The laggards tend to have a low profile in the institution and have few contacts outside their peer group. They are characteristically sceptical about changes. They tend to be dogmatic and fatalistic and have difficulty dealing with abstractions. They are fixed in a certain way of life and will not change until the majority of colleagues have done so.

The antagonists are loners. They resist changes for deep-seated psychological or philosophical reasons. They may work actively or passively to sabotage innovations that are proposed or introduced.

A general relationship can be perceived between personality type and attitude to change. But individuals may shift categories with respect to particular changes. An enthusiast for one change may be an antagonist of another. It is best therefore to consider the model as suggesting the spectrum of possible reactions. A strategy for change must work along the continuum, recruiting the first four groups and at least disarming the antagonists.

to have five main sources. The first is absence of motivation for change, and the other four are all related to the issue of motivation: vulnerability, inadequate resources, lack of clarity about the innovation, and scepticism concerning the value of the change itself.

Absence of motivation   People will not implement a change unless there are appropriate rewards for doing so. If the incentives attached to the implementation do not accord with the workers' own priorities, the most that can be expected is that they will adopt the appearance without the reality of the change.

The basic reward system of school teachers involves their relationships with learners in the classroom. Teachers are likely to resist any change that they believe will strain rather than enrich those relationships. For university faculty, on the other hand, classroom teaching plays little part in the reward structure, which is based primarily on publication (Tuckman, 1976). This may be why it is extremely difficult to reform university curricula other than to change content in response to the findings of scientific or scholarly research. The rewards that influence administrators are different again and concern public image and relations with superiors, colleagues, and subordinates.

Teachers and administrators who have had no input into a new curriculum will have no sense of ownership of the innovation. And where written memoranda from "absentee curriculum makers" are used as the chief means of communication, little commitment is likely to be built up at the local level.

The change agent must also be sensitive to the fact that the existing curriculum, however barren it appears, may be meeting important needs. A striking illustration of such a curriculum comes from Guyana. Curriculum specialists who examined the school curriculum in Guyana, which was a British colony until 1966, for three decades consistently deplored its academic bias, overemphasis on such subjects as Latin and English history, and neglect of the local environment and local vocational needs. What they failed to recognize was that passing the examinations in traditional academic subjects was the only means of entry into the local colonial elite. So long as Guyana remained a colony, the heaviest pressure to maintain the traditional curriculum came from Guyanese students and their parents. As a historian of education in Guyana comments, "Given freedom of choice, people are always likely to opt for the type of education which, however irrelevant it might be from an educator's point of view, will lead to the more rewarding jobs in the society" (Bacchus, 1975, p. 120).

Vulnerability   Schools are very visible places. Those who work in them have none of the screens of private ownership that protect corporations, nor can they engage in the bureaucratic stonewalling that obscures the workings of government from the public gaze. Particularly in times of slow economic growth, the public tends to cast a baleful eye on the schools. Community response to an innovation is consequently a

---

Antagonists of Change

Futilitarians maintain that every effort at change is futile, that "they" won't allow it, and that "you can't change human nature." They frequently cite research purporting to show that schools have few effects on children. Why they choose careers in education when they believe in the ineffectiveness of schools has not yet been explained.

Fainthearts are anxious and insecure. They view with alarm any potential disturbance of their fragile equilibrium. Novelty is a threat; they depend on established regulations, rituals, and patterns of authority.

The Old Regime may have designed the existing curriculum but more probably opposed it as newfangled when it was introduced. Now it "has done sterling service"; proposals to change it are "ill-timed and ill-advised."

Bureaucrats are interested principally in perpetuating their own existence. As they interact little with students, innovation offers them only disruption of their elaborate paper structures. As masters of obstruction and delay, they can generally outwit or outwait any innovation they choose to oppose.

Nostalgics look back with misty eyes to the golden age of education, which always coincides with the period when they were in school. The roots of nostalgia are escapism and self-pity; hence nostalgics are found in every age complaining that students are not what they were a generation ago.

Hard-core romantics devote their efforts to spontaneity and feeling. Anything related to planning or design is suspect; training, measurement, and technique are mechanistic and inhumane. Hard-core romantics are often dedicated and popular teachers, charming and vulnerable, but utterly inflexible.

major concern of many school people and will often lead them to resist a change to which public reaction is unpredictable.

Teachers are also vulnerable in terms of their roles and responsibilities. The more rigidly such roles are defined, as in highly hierarchical organizations, the greater the resistance will be to proposed changes. A curriculum innovation of modest proportions may involve a substantial commitment of teachers' time and energy, may require an unwelcome change in their mode of operation, and may pose the threat of long-term and undesired effects that have not been envisaged by the designers. In such circumstances, teachers and administrators strive to protect their small sphere of freedom, viewing what is to be taught and how as home territory and erecting "No Trespassing" signs as soon as it is endangered.

The antidote to vulnerability is not so much protection as trust. Decision-makers seeking to change teacher behavior must therefore work to develop trusting relationships among all those involved, including teachers, administrators, learners, and the public.

Inadequate resources   Almost any curriculum change, even one aimed at greater economy or efficiency, requires additional resources at least during the changeover period. The four main kinds of resource required are time, material resources, administrative support, and expertise.

Time is the teacher's most valuable resource, and the amount needed to implement curriculum change is almost always underestimated. This results in serious overload, especially when teachers find themselves required to implement four or five new curricula at once. Each new curriculum requires extra time for teachers to prepare lessons and materials, to become familiar with the concepts and skills to be taught, to prepare or administer new tests, and to gather reference sources. In addition, many new curricula impose extra time-consuming responsibilities on the teacher: for coordination or team teaching, for individualization or remediation, for greater amounts of evaluation and marking, or for inservice training. Administrators may also be obliged to spend time explaining the curriculum innovation to teachers or parents, organizing professional development, trouble-shooting the first-time problems, and working in liaison with the curriculum designers. It is incumbent on the curriculum developers to make accurate estimates of the new time commitments required, and on the decision-makers to clarify where the time is to come from.

Material resources present few problems, providing the curriculum designers make a thorough inventory of what is required and budget accordingly, and the institution provides the necessary funds, facilities, equipment, and materials. However, in the real world these requirements are often unmet.

Unequivocal commitment to the innovation by the administration

---

Futilitarians

When passenger service was first proposed on the newly invented railways, Dr. Dionysius Lardner, a professor and Fellow of the Royal Society, calculated mathematically that the force of gravity on acceleration on downhill grades would kill all the passengers. When Rowland Hill proposed the introduction of postage stamps in the 1830s, Lord Lichfield, the British postmaster-general, declared, "Of all the wild and visionary schemes I have ever heard or read of, it is the most extravagant." When Alexander Bell offered his telephone for development, it was turned down because "there was no real need for it." When Edison undertook development of the electric light, a body of distinguished experts agreed that his efforts were "unworthy of the attention of practical or scientific men." The professor of astronomy at the British Royal Institute said in 1956, "Space travel is utter bilge." The Xerox copying process was available for four years before a commercial sponsor could be found. And when the Swedish inventors of the heart pacemaker applied for a patent, they were rejected by the Swedish patent office on the grounds that the invention was not sufficiently significant.

---

is an essential form of support to school personnel. Halfhearted administrators can expect only a lukewarm response from teachers. When administrators engage in evasive waffling or prevaricative double talk about an innovation, they reward those teachers who resist the change. Wholeheartedness will be shown by provision of resources, moral support, and rewards and by clear evidence of intention to assess the degree and effects of implementation.

Regardless of the material and moral support provided, teachers will be unequipped to implement curriculum change if they lack the necessary expertise. They must have a competent grasp of the subject matter and of the approach to it adopted in the curriculum. Development of this expertise often requires specially designed inservice training. Without such training, teachers are likely to continue doing what they have done in the past with at most a few surface changes.

Lack of clarity about the change   Uncertainty about an impending change, when combined with personal insecurity, breeds rumors that can induce a state close to hysteria among those whose collaboration is essential to successful implementation (King et al., 1975).

Even the consent of teachers to an innovation does not necessarily indicate that they understand the change. It has been found that teachers who are supposedly implementing a new curriculum sometimes cannot even identify its main features (Fullan and Pomfret, 1975). The greatest difficulty is likely to be encountered when teachers are required to change their educational outlook or approach, as often happens with criterion-referenced, or mastery, programs. Rutherford reported such a case, where a system was attempting to implement a new commercially produced program in reading.

> All the reading teachers were attempting to use the criterion program; they were using parts of the program but few actually were using the program in a functional way. . . . It is pure fiction to assume that all teachers will use a criterion program just as it is intended. . . . The first and most difficult problem is that while criterion programs offer teachers a carefully designed and sequenced set of components, tests, teaching materials, record keeping systems, etc., they do not tell teachers how to take all these parts and make them work effectively for a classroom of children (Rutherford, 1978, p. 10).

Curriculum designers need to ensure that they describe in detail, and in language teachers will understand, all the significant changes in behavior, roles, and responsibilities that the curriculum requires. The written word may be insufficient for this task: face-to-face contact is likely to be more effective.

Scepticism   The barriers described above all contribute to user scepticism toward specific curriculum innovations and sometimes toward curriculum change in general. Clearly the credibility of those who design or promote curriculum changes is critical at this juncture, as is the plausibility of the new curriculum itself. Lortie (1975) argues that the recruitment, socialization, and work patterns of teachers attract and produce conservative individuals who are likely to distrust proposals for change from outside sources. But very often a teacher's scepticism is firmly rooted in previous experience. Educators have often become victims of magic formulas and panaceas that have been oversold by those with a commercial, political, or psychological investment in bringing about surface changes, and their reluctance to be taken in again is both understandable and justified.

Curriculum designers contribute to the scepticism of professionals in the schools if their own work is inadequately executed. Why should teachers and administrators accept on faith a curriculum unsupported by thorough needs assessment? Can they reasonably be expected to welcome the role of guinea pigs for a curriculum that has not been validated by adequate developmental testing?

While teacher scepticism is certainly a barrier to implementation, it does teachers more credit to take their scepticism for granted than to presume their credulity. Once doubt is assumed, the designer is forced to abandon rhetoric in favor of empirical demonstration of the value and effectiveness of the innovation.

> There is nothing more difficult to carry out, nor more doubtful of success, nor more dangerous to handle, than to initiate a new order of things. For the reformer has enemies in all who profit by the old order, and only lukewarm defenders in all those who would profit by the new order. This lukewarmness arises partly from fear of their adversaries, who have law in their favor, and partly from the incredulity of mankind who do not truly believe in anything new until they have had actual experience of it.
>
> —*Niccolo Machiavelli, c. 1520*

Obtaining Approval for an Innovation

The politics of innovation works in two directions: either a superior seeks to persuade subordinates to implement an innovation, or subordinates seek the approval of a superior. While discussion of curriculum change tends to focus on the problems of top-down implementation, major innovations will usually require approval from a level above that of the initiator: a superintendent, school board, state or provincial department of education.

Much significant curriculum change can be carried out in the classroom by an individual teacher on his or her own initiative. In fact, such curriculum changes have a greater chance of survival than those affecting other teachers and programs (Aslin and De Arman, 1975/76). It is sound practice not to seek approval unless it is required. However, if the change involves a departure from official policy, needs special resources, or is to be diffused beyond the initiating unit, experience suggests that individual teacher effort, however heroic, will not achieve much without substantial and continuous support from the administration (McKinney and Westbury, 1975).

The first thing to recognize is that administrators are likely to oppose many changes for at least five powerful reasons. First, their main aim may be to maintain the system in a steady state and hence to try to prevent the kind of disturbance that program changes represent. Second, the higher the position of officials in the hierarchy, the more visible and vulnerable they are, and hence the more reluctant to authorize any innovation whose effect on public opinion is uncertain. Third, innovations tend to cost money, and where this is not a reason for rejecting a change, it is often a convenient rationalization. Fourth, professional pride may suggest that if the innovation was worthwhile, the administration would have thought of it first. And fifth, a curriculum that targets specific measurable outcomes exposes decision-makers to double jeopardy: if it fails, its failure cannot be concealed, while if it succeeds, the public may demand that the same kind of accountability be applied to other programs.

Not surprisingly, we find that "conflict avoidance tends to be a salient orientation in the minds of school administrators . . . a leading theme in the ideology of the profession . . . reinforced through the nature of the typical recruitment and socialization process" (Boyd, 1979, p. 15). There are a number of ways in which change agents can help to reduce the anxieties of administrators.

Understand the decision-makers. Learn something about their interests and values. Identify the pressures they work under. Review their record. Find out what people they listen to, and enlist their support.

Approach decision-makers early. Let us suppose that you are planning a new curriculum in American history, which will require the approval of Mr. Dryasdust, the school board consultant in history. Don't wait until the curriculum is written and then seek his approval; his response will be "Why didn't you ask my advice earlier?" As soon as you have a clear conception of the innovation, make an appointment and ask him to give you the benefit of his experience in the subject. When writing the "Acknowledgements" in the curriculum, express your gratitude for his counsel.

Observe the proper channels. Don't try to end-run superiors by going over their heads or directly to the public, parents, media, or elected officials, unless you are extremely astute politically—or independently wealthy. At the same time, keep things as informal as possible, especially in the early stages. Raise the issue initially in a private setting. Administrators don't like surprises, especially in public, and if they turn down a proposal before witnesses, they cannot subsequently change their stand without loss of face. Don't seek an immediate yes or no answer, and avoid confrontation at all times.

Allow the administrator to take credit for the innovation. A Canadian advertising executive, Harry Foster, said, "If you don't care who gets the credit, you can accomplish anything." The higher in the hierarchy, the more political administrators become, and the more they need credit for successful innovations. Plant the seed of the innovation in the administrator's mind; surprisingly little time may need to pass before it becomes his or her own idea.

Use appropriate language. Detailed needs assessments or evaluation reports in technical language tend to be buried on administrators' desks. They receive low political priority because even if they were leaked to the press, the public would not understand them. Conclusions presented in the form of brief statements and simple figures or graphs comprehensible to the layman are more likely to receive a response from administrators (Hester and Ligon, 1978).

Use appropriate arguments. Remember that decision-makers pay more attention to messages concerning themselves and to messages that concur with their previous beliefs (Pool, n.d.). Arguments that an innovation will benefit students tend to have little impact at this level. More persuasive arguments are that the innovation is responsive to community feeling; will reduce vandalism, absenteeism, or dropout; will increase cost-efficiency; or will enhance the image of the institution. The arguments must match the ethos of the organization as well as that of the decision-maker. An innovative institution is more receptive to the argument that the change is in the forefront of educational thinking. A traditional organization prefers evidence that the innovation has been successfully instituted elsewhere.

Implementing and Diffusing Curriculum Change

Any curriculum that requires teachers to change methods of operation and modes of thought faces difficulties even without the many barriers to change discussed above. The complexity of educational politics and widespread uncertainty in educational institutions regarding roles and responsibilities does nothing to simplify the process.

The fallacy of the 1960s was that teacher participation was all that was necessary for successful innovation. It is doubtful that there was ever adequate evidence to support this belief. The experience of many school systems in the past two decades would lead many educators to concur with Leithwood and his colleagues that

> the unqualified assertion that teacher involvement in curriculum development will increase the commitment to, and effectiveness of, curriculum implementation leads to modes of work which are not only wasteful of time and human resources, but are counter-productive as well (Leithwood et al., 1976, p. 53).

Along with facile solutions, the change literature tended to promote a simplistic model of implementation, viewing "adoption" of the change by teachers as being the final stage in the process. Recently Hall and Loucks (1977) have shown that there are many stages in "levels of use," from total nonuse and ignorance of the change, through mechanical use, to refinement, integration, and renewal of the innovation. Perhaps the most important distinction is between "adoption" and "implementation." Adoption is the point at which users (school systems, schools, and teachers) express acceptance of the change. Implementation is the point at which the change is actually realized in the classroom. A considerable amount of time usually elapses between these two stages. Curriculum innovations often show few effects different from the conventional curriculum at the end of the first year of operation. The evidence suggests that in the first year following adoption, it is not the new curriculum

Completion of task: Unsystematic approach to restoring the belfry of a village church

that is being implemented in the classroom, but the old one slightly influenced by some elements of the new one (Rutherford, 1978). Change agents need to reconcile themselves to the fact that at least three cycles of the innovation will normally have to be completed before it is fully implemented. So long as schools adhere to the unwieldy one-year time unit, innovation can be expected to take three years from adoption to implementation. On the other hand, modules of nine or twelve weeks could reach full implementation within one academic year.

The task of implementation will be greatly facilitated if the organization and design stages have been carefully executed. Teachers and members of the public will have been consulted during the needs assessment and the political feasibility of the project confirmed. Credibility will have been a qualification for membership of the design team. Administrative approval will have been obtained, and the curriculum will have been developed in such a way as to produce a favorable student response and to affirm the professional self-image of the teacher. Completeness and explicitness will be the hallmarks of a systematically designed curriculum. Starting from this firm basis, those responsible for implementation can concentrate their efforts on four areas: personal contact with users, clear communication, furnishing resources, and provision of rewards.

Personal contact

Ernest House studied the research on innovation, not only in education but also in agriculture and technology. His conclusion:

> As the flow of blood is essential to human life, so direct personal contact is essential to the propagation of innovation. . . . Direct personal contacts are the medium through which innovations must flow. Innovation diffusion is directly proportional to the number, frequency, depth, and duration of such contacts (House, 1974, pp. 8, 11).

Apparently word-of-mouth promotion by a friend or colleague weighs more heavily than scholarly arguments written by unfamiliar experts or directives from remote school officials. Analysis of medical practice found similarly that "a major factor in the physician's adoption of new drugs was not the scientific literature but the personal influence of the physician's own colleagues" (Coleman, Menzel, and Katz, 1959). The mass media can impart knowledge of innovations, but face-to-face contact is more likely to change attitudes (Rogers and Shoemaker, 1971).

Who are the people to conduct this personal advocacy of innovations in the schools? One potential group is school principals. They are close to the teachers, and while not equal in status, are in the strongest position to dispense rewards. The evidence indicates, as might be expected, that elementary-school teachers view their principals as the primary influence on their teaching (Taylor, 1974). While principals can perform a critical linking role between developers and users and may effectively add advocacy of particular curriculum innovations to their other roles, there are advantages in the original curriculum designers assuming major responsibility for advocating the innovation. They are usually peers of the teachers; they are, or should be, influence leaders; they know the new curriculum best and have an enthusiastic sense of ownership over it. (These are all advantages that commercially produced curricula imported from outside the system can never have.)

The designers should start to develop personal contacts with the users even before beginning work on the curriculum. Contact should be maintained during design and developmental testing. Individual and informal contacts should not be overlooked: the ideal is to recruit advocates within each school. When the time comes for the finished and tested curriculum to be presented to teachers, the meetings should be carefully planned. A formal arrangement with the advocates on one side of a table and users on the other is less likely to be effective than an informal circle or round-table with advocates dispersed among users.

After adoption the exponents should be readily available for advice and support. They should hold further meetings to encourage exchange of ideas among users and to obtain feedback from teachers about the curriculum during and after its initial installation. If the curriculum is distributed in a loose-leaf binder rather than in bound form, it advertises the designers' willingness to make piecemeal changes as required.

Change agents must remember that classroom teachers determine whether or not an innovation is implemented. But parents and students are also participants in curriculum change. Effective contact with both groups can provide additional reinforcement for teachers in the implementation process and ensure the success of the innovation by developing community commitment (Fullan and Pomfret, 1975).

Clarity of communication

The problem of clarity has already been discussed. The solution boils down to the provision of clear descriptions of roles and expectations in language the users can understand.

As curriculum designers become involved and expert in their task, they begin to share a specialized terminology among themselves and with the curriculum community. The users have not participated in the same learning experience. When confronted with unfamiliar language, they may well misinterpret what is being said or react defensively with accusations of "jargon." Designers and change agents should therefore keep technical expressions to a minimum and ensure in as low-key a manner as possible that the specialized terms that are employed are plainly understood by the users.

Many new curricula are long on the rhetoric of goals and short on exact specification of means. Curriculum innovations often demand considerable changes in classroom behavior, instructional style, and even educational outlook. New and expanded forms of testing and record keeping may be required. Lack of explicitness on such issues will frustrate their implementation and may suggest an attempt to hoodwink the users. A negative reaction is likely if teachers find themselves without guidance or committed to unexpected responsibilities half-way through a program. To avoid this pitfall, change agents should repeatedly address themselves to the familiar interrogatives of who? what? when? where? why? and how?

This is not to imply that the curriculum must straightjacket the teacher in exact specification of every activity. It is rather that the curriculum must clearly specify the nature and range of the choices available to teachers at each decision point. Complete candor is also required regarding any novel responsibilities teachers are expected to assume and the resources on which they can rely. The experience of the Ford Foundation in its $30-million Comprehensive School Improvement Plan was that sharp definition of all aspects of innovations was a major factor determining the success of the projects it sponsored (Nachtigel, 1972).

A notable example of role clarification was provided by the Eastern Regional Institute of Education. In a project implementing *Man: A Course of Study*, the Institute required cooperating schools and teachers' colleges to sign a contract explicating the commitments and obligations on both sides. Cole (1971) reported that this made a vital contribution to the success of the project. While many educators would find such formality intimidating, the level of explicitness required in legal contracts may be a suitable standard for the definition of roles and responsibilities in implementing curriculum innovations.

Resources

Time is a recurring theme in curriculum, but at no point is it more critical than in implementation. It is rare to find adequate time estimates in curriculum proposals, and the oversight can be fatal. A basic rule of curriculum innovation is that *the total time required of all parties involved must be specified and provided.*

This rule has implications that need to be recognized in the first instance at the design stage. Procedures can be developed for provision of computer-based testing and record keeping, for employment of teacher aides or volunteers, and for use of students as peer tutors and proctors. Such strategies may enable a more effective curriculum to be introduced without a major increase in the teacher's time commitment. At the implementation stage, the alternative strategies for dealing with added time requirement are essentially limited to (1) reducing the teacher's workload in other areas; (2) providing additional help such as aides; and (3) providing monetary or other compensation for extra time committed.

Teachers also need to be given enough lead time to become familiar with the innovation before introducing it to their classes and time to make a gradual changeover from the old curriculum to the new, especially if they are introducing several new curricula at once.

Equally important is the provision of moral and political support from the administration, usually the principal. A conference of Canadian curriculum innovators in 1977 identified a number of ways in which school principals could support curriculum innovation: (1) by providing resources and time to facilitate and encourage innovation; (2) by challenging teachers to review and revise their curricula; (3) by monitoring curriculum and instruction; (4) by providing a personal example of effective curriculum design and teaching; (5) by establishing a climate of trust and security to reduce the threat implicit in innovation; and (6) by encouraging teacher participation in setting goals for the school and evaluating their attainment (Pratt, 1978).

Administrators and designers need to be sensitive to the fact that when teachers adopt an innovation, the results may be different from those intended. The first time through, the new curriculum may be less successful than the one it replaced. Teachers need a buffer against criticism at this point; they do not need a decision-maker prone to panic and abandon the program. At the same time, they should not be expected to teach in a mechanical and uncreative way. As a teacher integrates an innovation, the innovation itself undergoes change through adaptation to the particular needs of the teacher and the learners. This is not necessarily to be condemned as heresy. Differences in approach are not critical providing the objectives are met, and even a change in objectives or outcomes should be examined on its merits.

Obviously the material resources—textbooks, media software, equipment, tests, etc.—must be provided as specified in the curriculum. One of the reasons why professionally developed curriculum packages tend to survive longer (Aslin and De Arman, 1975/76) and be more effective (Nachtigel, 1972) than curricula developed in-house may be the convenient access they usually provide to needed materials.

The major remaining resource needed is knowledge and skill. The teachers who implement curriculum innovations need expertise in (1) the subject: what to teach; (2) the pedagogy: how to teach it; and (3) design: how to adapt the curriculum. The learning of these new behaviors and roles is a process that ranges from formal inservice training to informal socialization. There is no clear evidence as to how or by whom inservice training is most effectively conducted. But whether it is managed by the design team, by influential individuals in the system, or by outside experts or agencies, it requires adequate time and careful planning. It may be an advantage to invite users to participate in this planning. Needless to say, inservice training programs should be models of rigorous and reflective curriculum design.

Incentives

The teacher's perception of the reward system is a critical variable in educational innovation (House, 1974). But the identification of suitable incentives presents some problems. Salary and promotion are too circumscribed by political and economic factors to be widely used to reward innovation. Release time is welcomed by some teachers but may disrupt the schedule of others. Some teachers bask in public recognition; others take umbrage at the stream of classroom visitors that such recognition produces.

It is appropriate at this point to recall the evidence discussed in Chapter 11 that intrinsic is more effective than extrinsic motivation. Teachers who are innovative by nature will find the experience of successfully introducing a curriculum change a reward in itself. Others will be motivated by the value of the objectives pursued, by evidence of student success, and by overt student approval of the innovation. Herzberg's theory of job enrichment, referred to in Chapter 5, is essentially an argument for intrinsic incentives. Herzberg (1966) maintained that the most effective motivator of improved job performance was the opportunity to learn and grow by means of increased scope, challenge, authority, and responsibility in the job. Any worthwhile curriculum change can be introduced in such a way as to provide teachers with such opportunities.

A further advantage of intrinsic incentives is that they are likely to reward real change rather than merely its appearance. Supervisors, including principals, are often too remote from the classroom to judge how far an innovation has actually been installed and may consequently reward adoption rather than implementation. The reward system will itself become a disincentive if, as in some traditional institutions, it rewards resistance to change.

In an ideal world it would be unnecessary to expend effort to persuade teachers and schools to introduce changes that were manifestly beneficial to their pupils. In practice the merits of a curriculum change may persuade half of the potential users. Additional stimuli are necessary for others. A curriculum that is accompanied by school-wide or system-wide testing has an advantage in this respect. In addition to demonstrating the commitment of the administration, it allows teachers who disagree with the change the opportunity to show that their approach is equally productive. Low test scores, however, may result in attacks on the validity of the test rather than improvement in instruction.

Can teachers simply be ordered to comply with a curriculum change? A command strategy rarely seems to work so long as a substantial majority of teachers are unclear about the nature or value of the change and may alienate some potential supporters. There is evidence, however, that directives can be effective once the laggards are limited to a minority of isolated individuals surrounded by users of the innovation (Leithwood et al., 1976). Normally the change agents need to reconcile themselves to something less than 100 percent compliance. Unless children are being severely hurt, the task of converting antagonists is rarely worth the effort. In any case, the number of wrongheaded crusades education has experienced in recent years induces a good deal of tolerance for a measure of diversity in current practice.

Termination of Curricula

In a changing world there can be no such thing as a fixed curriculum. A curriculum is never more than an interim draft, pending the next evaluation. Evaluation, as Figure 14–4 indicates, should follow each operation. The primary criterion is that the curriculum continues to meet a significant learner need. Minor defects can be corrected by revision; but once the curriculum ceases to justify the resources it consumes, it should make way for other innovations. "Abandon" is the final function in the curriculum system, the point that all curricula will eventually reach.

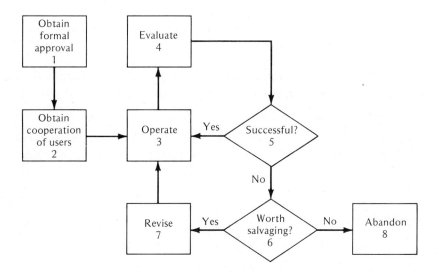

Figure 14–4   Curriculum implementation

Hesitation to abandon curricula that have outlived their value serves to render education moribund.

Design and Implementation

It has been argued in this chapter that to implement curricula successfully, designers must adjust to the fact that implementation is primarily a political process. By their nature, curriculum developers tend to be idealists. But however idealistic a curriculum, it must eventually enter and survive in the political arena. If the designers are unwilling to engage in political combat, they must rely on the political acumen of others. In so doing, they surrender control of the way in which their curriculum may be used. Persuading other people to approve, cooperate with, or implement a curriculum change is challenging and onerous. But the function of curriculum development is not to produce blueprints but to meet human needs. The responsibility of the curriculum developer begins with identification of a significant learner need and is fully discharged only when that need is satisfied.

ACTIVITIES

1. Using the Curriculum Evaluation Guide (pp. 410–413), evaluate a curriculum written at the school, district, or state level. What are the main omissions? What are the main defects?

2. Classify the attitudes toward innovation of a group of your colleagues. How well does Rogers' model (pp. 427–428) fit? Are their attitudes toward change consistent, or do they vary depending on the change? Where would you place yourself on the continuum?

3. Select a curriculum you are familiar with. Write criteria that would enable you to judge (a) its effectiveness and (b) its acceptability.

4. Identify a change you would like to see introduced into schools. Design a complete strategy for implementing the innovation.

5. "The politics of implementation are too unsavory for teachers to become involved in them." Discuss.

QUESTIONS

1. The purpose of "confidential review" of a curriculum is to

   a. obtain an expert opinion of the curriculum before tryout
   b. try out the curriculum with individual learners on a pilot basis

c. discover and resolve objections by people who could jeopardize its adoption
d. have the developers reread what they have written and make necessary revisions

2. Pilot testing is best conducted with

   a. both slower and faster learners
   b. average learners, as they are most typical
   c. slower learners, who will experience most difficulties
   d. faster learners, who can provide the most articulate commentary

3. It is desirable for curricula to be field-tested with typical students taught by

   a. typical teachers
   b. members of the design team
   c. teachers who are generally hostile to innovations
   d. teachers who are committed to the success of the curriculum

4. You want to find out what objectives are actually being pursued in a particular program. The most valid way to do this would be to

   a. read the curriculum for the course
   b. ask the students and their parents
   c. ask the teachers and administrators
   d. observe the lessons and analyze the summative tests

5. The people who are most familiar with and committed to a new curriculum, and in that respect most appropriate to advocate its adoption, are

   a. the users
   b. the designers
   c. the administrators
   d. those who give it official approval

6. Implementation of a curriculum innovation is accomplished when

   a. the curriculum innovation is adopted
   b. the users express acceptance of the change
   c. the intended change is actually realized in the classroom
   d. a new curriculum has gone through one complete cycle in the classroom

7. Evidence that a new curriculum is enthusiastically received by learners is likely to carry most weight with

   a. classroom teachers
   b. school administrators
   c. members of the school board
   d. writers of newspaper editorials

8. Which of the following incentives for innovation would gain most support from the theory of job enrichment?

a. praise and public recognition
b. increased scope and responsibility
c. more release time from the classroom
d. improved salary and working conditions

9. A curriculum design team should ideally continue to function

a. until the curriculum is adopted
b. after the curriculum is adopted
c. until the curriculum design is complete
d. until the curriculum has been field-tested

10. When a new curriculum has been developed, tried out, adopted, implemented, and found to be effective, it should be

a. frozen indefinitely
b. fixed for about five years
c. regarded as an interim design
d. changed each time it is offered

Check your answers against the key in Appendix 2.
9 or 10 right: You understand the material presented.
7 or 8 right: Review the areas of uncertainty.
6 or less right: Reread the chapter.

Recommended Reading

Doyle, Kenneth O. *Student evaluation of instruction.* Lexington, Mass.: D. C. Heath, 1975. A concise and comprehensive summary of the theory and practice of course evaluation by college students.

Guttentag, Marcia, and Elmer L. Struening (eds.). *Handbook of evaluation research.* 2 vols., Beverly Hills, Cal.: Sage, 1975. In this major resource for program evaluation, thirty-seven papers by evaluation experts provide a comprehensive guide to evaluation of programs in health and education.

House, Ernest R. *The politics of educational innovation.* Berkeley, Cal.: McCutchan, 1974. An important survey of the process of introducing change in schools. Particularly useful for its emphasis on the need for active advocacy of change by individuals by means of personal contact.

Rogers, Everett, and Floyd Shoemaker. *Communication of innovations.* New York: Free Press, 1971. Two authorities on innovation present conclusions drawn from review of hundreds of studies of adoption. Especially interesting is the authors' analysis of the characteristics of early and late adopters.

Taylor, P. H. (ed.). *Aims, influence, and change in the primary school curriculum.* Windsor, England: National Foundation for Educational Research, 1975. A number of studies of innovation in English schools indicate that even in a highly decentralized system many of the same principles apply as in the more centralized North American context.

References

Aslin, Neil C., and John W. De Arman. Adoption and abandonment of innovative practices in high schools. *Educational Leadership*, 1975/76, 601–606.

Bacchus, M. K. Secondary school curriculum and social change in an emergent nation. *Journal of Curriculum Studies*, 1975, 7, 99–121.

Bellack, A. A. et al. *The language of the classroom.* New York: Teachers College Press, 1966.

Bloom, Benjamin S. Tryout and revision of educational materials and methods. In Arieh Lewy (ed.), *Handbook of curriculum evaluation.* Paris: UNESCO, International Institute for Educational Planning, 1977, pp. 84–103.

Boyd, William Lowe. The politics of curriculum change and stability. *Educational Researcher*, 1979, 8 (2), 12–18.

Branson, R. K., G. T. Rayner, W. H. Hannum, and J. L. Cox. *Interservice procedures for instructional systems development: Phase 3-develop.* Ft. Monroe, Va.: U.S. Army Training and Doctrine Command, August 1975.

Campbell, Donald T., and Julian C. Stanley. *Experimental and quasi-experimental designs for research.* Chicago: Rand McNally, 1963.

Carr-Hill, Roy, and Olav Magnussen. *Indicators of performance of educational systems.* Paris: Organization for Economic Cooperation and Development, 1973.

Clark, David L., and Egon Guba. An examination of potential change roles in education. In Ole Sand (ed.), *Rational planning in curriculum and instruction.* Washington, D.C.: National Education Association, Center for the Study of Instruction, 1967, pp. 111–133.

Cole, H. *Implementation of a process curriculum by the campus team strategy.* Syracuse, N.Y.: Eastern Regional Institute of Education, 1971.

Coleman, James, H. Menzel, and E. Katz. Social processes in physicians' adoption of a new drug. *Journal of Chronic Diseases*, 1959, 91, 1–19.

Fullan, Michael, and Alan Pomfret. Review of research on curriculum implementation. Mimeo. Toronto: Ontario Institute for Studies in Education, 1975.

Hall, Gene E., and Susan F. Loucks. A developmental model for determining whether the treatment is actually implemented. *American Educational Research Journal*, 1977, 14, 263-276.

Herzberg, Frederick. *Work and the nature of man.* New York: World, 1966.

Hester, Joy, and Glynn Ligon. Where does the time go? A study of time use in public schools. Paper presented at the Annual Meeting of the American Educational Research Association, Toronto, March 1978.

House, Ernest R. *The politics of educational innovation.* Berkeley, Cal.: McCutchan, 1974.

King, A. J. C., J. G. Enns, J. W. Lockerbie, and W. K. Warren. *Semestering the secondary school.* Toronto: Ontario Institute for Studies in Education, 1975.

Lasswell, Harold D. *Politics: Who gets what, when, how.* New York: World, 1958.

Leithwood, K. A., J. S. Clipsham, Florence Maynes, R. P. Baxter, and J. D. McNabb. *Planning curriculum change: A model and case study.* Toronto: Ontario Institute for Studies in Education, 1976.

Lortie, Dan C. *School teacher: A sociological study.* Chicago: University of Chicago Press, 1975.

Marsh, Herbert W. The validity of students' evaluations: Classroom evaluation of instructors independently nominated as best and worst by graduating seniors. *American Educational Research Journal*, 1977, 14, 441–447.

McKinney, W. L., and I. Westbury. Stability and change: The public schools of Gary, Indiana, 1940–1970. In W. A. Reid and D. F. Walker (eds.), *Case studies in curriculum change*. London: Routledge and Kegan Paul, 1975.

McNeil, John D. *Curriculum: A comprehensive introduction*. Boston: Little, Brown, 1977.

Metfessel, Newton S., and William B. Michael. A paradigm involving multiple criterion measures for the evaluation of the effectiveness of school programs. *Educational and Psychological Measurement*, 1967, 27, 931–934.

Nachtigel, Paul. *A foundation goes to school*. New York: Ford Foundation, 1972.

Pool, Ithiel de Sola. Political information systems. In Erich Jatsch (ed.), *Perspectives of planning*. Paris: Organization for Economic Cooperation and Development, n.d.

Pratt, David. Local curriculum development in Ontario: State of the art. *Orbit*, 1978, 41 (Feb.), 20–23.

Rogers, Everett M. *Diffusion of innovation*. New York: Free Press of Glencoe, 1962.

———, and Floyd Shoemaker. *Communication of innovations*. New York: Free Press, 1971.

Rutherford, William L. Implementing criterion-referenced instructional programs: Truth or fiction. Paper presented at the Annual Meeting of the American Educational Research Association, Toronto, March 1978.

Scriven, Michael. Pros and cons about goal-free evaluation. *Evaluation Comment*, 1972, 3 (4), 1–4.

Shingles, Richard D. Faculty ratings: Procedures for interpreting student evaluations. *American Educational Research Journal*, 1977, 14, 459–470.

Taylor, Philip H. A study of the curricular influences in a mid-western elementary school system. Mimeo. Birmingham, England: School of Education Teaching Research Unit, 1974.

Torgeson, W. S. *Theory and methods of scaling*. New York: Wiley, 1958.

Tuckman, Howard P. *Publication, teaching, and the academic reward structure*. Lexington, Mass.: D. C. Heath, 1976.

Walker, Decker F. Toward comprehension of curricular realities. In Lee S. Shulman (ed.), *Review of research in education 4*. Itasca, Ill.: Peacock and American Educational Research Association, 1976, pp. 268–308.

Walker, Decker F., and Jon Schaffarzick. Comparing curricula. *Review of Educational Research*, 1974, 44, 83–111.

Watson, Goodwin. Resistance to change. In Goodwin Watson (ed.), *Concepts for social change*. Washington, D.C.: National Training Laboratories, 1967.

Worthen, Blaine. Content specialization in educational evaluation: A necessary marriage. Paper presented at the Annual Meeting of the American Educational Research Association, Chicago, April 1974.

15

Epilogue: Possibilities

The voice of the intellect is a soft one, but it does not rest until it has gained a hearing. Ultimately, after endless rebuffs, it succeeds. This is one of the few points in which one may be optimistic about the future of mankind.

—*Sigmund Freud*

Daniel Benor is an Israeli agricultural expert who works for the World Bank and who is succeeding where others have failed in showing farmers in the Third World how to grow larger crops. Teaching simple rules, he has found, such as good spacing of plants, can result in increased yields of 50 to 100 percent without any change in seed, fertilizer, or irrigation. "There are almost no new ideas," he says, "merely well-known principles applied systematically" (Rowen, 1978).

The reader who has persevered to this point will no doubt recognize two things. One is the truth of science fiction writer Poul Anderson's remark that "I have yet to see any problem, however complicated, which, when you looked at it the right way, did not become still more compli-

449

cated." The other is the relevance of Benor's observation to curriculum. Curriculum design has developed few radically new strategies. Most of the principles it draws from the study of education and from other fields are in themselves relatively familiar and straightforward. It is from their methodical application to curriculum that we may expect significant effects.

It is interesting to speculate on the implications of full-scale application in the schools of the principles of curriculum design that have been outlined in this book. Five of the main policies that are implied are: (1) the elimination of curricula that no longer meet significant learner needs; (2) the introduction of new curricula that do meet significant needs; (3) design of curricula so that almost all students will achieve mastery of critical areas; (4) design of curricula to allow students to learn as far as possible at their optimum pace; and (5) design of more efficient and effective instruction. What would be the results if all these policies were put into effect?

Ten or twelve years of schooling on this model should, without a real increase in educational costs, enable nearly all students to make substantial gains in literacy and numerical skills and in knowledge of science and the arts; to learn the basic survival skills, one or more foreign languages, and at least one marketable skill; to be freed from onerous, unrewarding tasks and have time to discover and explore their artistic and creative talents; to develop social skills and meaningful social and personal values; and to become more physically fit and committed to healthier life-styles. A positive self-image would, for most students, be the concomitant of a school experience of consistent, merited, and recognized success in worthwhile and challenging endeavors.

If these expectations are even partially justified, then the impact of "well-known principles applied systematically" would be revolutionary.

These possibilities have their roots partly in technology, partly in idealism. Many fads have come and gone, and huge resources have been invested in schooling. But the effectiveness of schools has not greatly increased (Harnischfeger and Wiley, 1976). Increased effectiveness is likely to be a result of the cumulation of a repertoire of principles and strategies that constitute an applied science or technology of education. As Jamison, Suppes, and Wells observed a few years ago at the conclusion of a major study of instructional media:

> The key to productivity improvement in every economic sector has been through the augmentation of human efforts by technology, and we see no reason to expect a different pattern in education (Jamison, Suppes, and Wells, 1974, p. 57).

Technology is value-free; it can determine the speed with which we move but cannot determine the path we take. While good will without technique is powerless, technique without good will is sinister. Curriculum design uses technology but must be guided by a vision of humanity and its future. That vision will be an individual one but, if education is to have a future, must almost certainly be optimistic, sharing in one way or another Camus' conclusion in *The Plague*, which was written in the shadow of the Nazi occupation of France: "To state quite simply what we learn in a time of pestilence: that there are more things to admire in men than to despise."

Curriculum designers, then, combine the scientific outlook of classic thought with the utopian ideals of the romantic. Almost two centuries ago Thomas Jefferson wrote:

> I know of no safe depository of the ultimate powers of society but the people themselves; and if we think them not enlightened enough to exercise their control with a wholesome discretion, the remedy is not to take it from them, but to inform their discretion by education.

The principle that Jefferson enunciated is pertinent to the role of those who work in the schools today. An enlightened and effective educational system will emerge as educators at every level develop the confidence and the ability to design and provide educational experiences that are effective and enriching. This does not call for outstanding dedication or intelligence, but for ordinary abilities methodically applied.

The educational system that relies on devotion or genius will not function in a world of ordinary men and women. Any design for the improvement of education must begin with the premise that those who work in the schools are ordinary people of good will and that they can master the professional knowledge and skill to make their intentions realities.

It is for educators of good will, who recognize that good will alone is not enough, that this book is intended.

References

Harnischfeger, Annegret, and David E. Wiley. Achievement test scores drop. So what? *Educational Researcher*, 1976, 5 (3), 5–12.

Jamison, Dean, Patrick Suppes, and Stuart Wells. The effectiveness of alternative instructional media: A survey. *Review of Educational Research*, 1974, 44, 1–67.

Rowen, Hobart. Making more corn to grow. *Manchester Guardian Weekly*, January 8, 1978, p. 16.

APPENDIX

I

Glossary of Curriculum Terms

The use of a new word, or of an old one in an unfamiliar way, will usually produce one of two reactions. Some people will ask for a definition or look the word up in a dictionary. Others will accuse the user of resorting to "jargon." The latter reaction seems especially common when unfamiliar terms are used in educational discourse.

Whenever people share a specialized interest, they develop a specialized vocabulary. The conversation of baseball fans is incomprehensible to most English people, whose discussion of cricket Americans find equally unintelligible. Nuclear physicists, rabbit breeders, and stamp collectors have their own technical language. So do economists and chefs, revolutionaries and spies, aircraft controllers and taxi dispatchers—the list is endless. Yet educators are expected to refrain from terminological exactness and converse in basic English.

It is tempting, but misleading, to interpret the charge of jargon as nothing more than a form of abuse leveled by those who do not understand a subject at those who do. To a point the charge is justified. It is in fact objectionable (1) to use terms that are not understood by a particular audience, (2) to use new words when old words are adequate, (3) to use long words when short words will serve, or (4) to camouflage intellectual poverty with verbal extravagance.

Many specialized terms have come into common use among educators, but this vocabulary has not always been accompanied by agreed-upon definitions. *Curriculum* is a case in point, a term for which many different and incompatible definitions are in current use. Consequently a great many educational disputes are semantic in origin. It is futile, for instance, to attempt to resolve an issue like "Is the function of the school education or training?" until the parties to the debate have agreed on unambiguous definitions of *education* and *training*.

This glossary provides stipulative definitions of most of the educational terms used in this text. They are not claimed as authoritative, nor are they necessarily the prevailing definitions. Although the general intent is to provide an exact statement of the essential meaning the terms convey as they are normally used in curriculum discourse, some of the definitions are idiosyncratic. The function of the glossary is not to provide a general dictionary of educational terms, but merely to enhance the clarity of communication between the author of this book and the readers.

ability grouping The organization of learners into groups for instruction on the basis of assumed or demonstrated intelligence or general or specific aptitude. (See also *streaming*)

academic self-concept The opinion an individual has of his or her aptitude for learning in general or within a specific area.

acceleration Progress through certain phases of schooling at a faster rate than normal.

accountability The disclosure and justification by an agency of the ends toward which resources committed to the agency have been applied, and the extent to which such ends have been realized.

adoption Overt acceptance of an innovation, with an implicit or explicit commitment to implement the innovation.

affective Related to attitudes, dispositions, motivations, preferences, tastes, or values.

age grading The grouping of learners on the basis of common age.

aim A general change intended to be brought about in a learner.

analysis The examination of a whole by separation into its component parts.

aptitude Capacity for learning (*Webster's*).

assessment An informal or general judgment.

background noise level (BNL) Ambient and generally consistent environmental sound such as produced by ventilation fans, distant traffic, or human movement.

behavioral objective An educational objective stated in terms of a specific or typical overt action to be performed by the learner following instruction.

brain hemisphere One of the two sides of the human brain: the left side controls verbal and logical capabilities; the right side controls spatial perception and nonverbal ideation.

brainstorming The generation of ideas or solutions to problems involving free-flowing creative thought and spontaneous noncritical expression of ideas; often conducted in a group.

client A person who engages or is served by the professional services of an individual or agency.

cognitive Related to knowledge or intellectual activity.

competency-based Designed so that demonstrated achievement alone determines learner progress and qualifications.

computer-based instruction (CBI) The provision of instruction by means of a computer.

concern Recognition that a need is not being met, without clear identification of the problem.

confidential review Scrutiny of a curriculum by individuals in a position to jeopardize its adoption, undertaken to discover and resolve their objections.

congruence The quality of being in agreement, conformity, harmony, or correspondence.

consensus A form of decision making in which all members of a group understand and share in a decision and either support or consent to it.

constraint A limitation on a system imposed from outside the system.

constructed-response test A test (usually written) in which the examinee writes the answers to questions in his or her own words.

controller A decision-making element in a system that compares performance of the system with a set point and initiates appropriate action.

cost-benefit analysis A calculation of financial returns of an undertaking and comparison with the costs.

criterion-referenced Judged against a fixed standard of performance.

critical Directly related to the success or failure of a system; a system component is critical if its malfunction jeopardizes the functioning of a superordinate component.

curriculum An organized set of formal educational and/or training intentions.

curriculum evaluation Judgment of a written curriculum against certain criteria, usually conducted prior to implementation.

curriculum prospectus A proposal submitted to an administration, consisting of an outline of a projected curriculum and the resources required for development.

cybernetics The study of communication, control, and self-regulation in systems.

design A deliberate process of devising, planning, and selecting the elements, techniques, and procedures that constitute some object or endeavor.

difficulty index An estimate of the percentage of examinees answering a question correctly.

discipline A structured area of knowledge characterized by a distinct configuration of subject matter, concepts, and methodology of inquiry.

discrete Individually separate or distinct.

discrimination The capacity to distinguish between categories or groups.

discrimination index Estimate of difference between scores on a test item of more and less knowledgeable or proficient examinees.

disposition The tendency to act in a certain way toward an object; attitude.

domain-exhausting test A test that examines every aspect of a capability.

domain-sampling test A test that examines a sample of behaviors to draw an inference regarding a general capability.

drill Repetitive practice.

ECO analysis A procedure for determining the evaluation of objects expressed in verbal communications by determining their location on a favorable-unfavorable scale.

education Development of an individual that includes exposure to significant experiences.

educational technology The development of a set of systematic techniques, and accompanying practical knowledge, for designing, testing, and operating schools as educational systems (Robert M. Gagné).

effectiveness Production of, or capacity to produce, a result.

effector A component of a system whose function is to restore the system to its steady state.

efficiency Production of output relative to input of energy and resources.

egalitarianism A social philosophy advocating the removal of special ecnomic, social, political, and educational privileges or inequalities.

elitism A social philosophy advocating leadership and/or privilege for a particular type or class of people.

enrichment An increase in the depth or variety of subject matter or activities in a student's program.

evaluation A process of judgment based on comparison of ascertained measurements against criteria.

expert appraisal Judgment of a curriculum by a specialist in curriculum design and/or the subject matter, usually conducted prior to pilot or field testing.

ex post facto judgment Judgment based on criteria that are not fixed in advance, but are influenced by the events judged.

extrinsic Not inherent in the nature of the object or event itself. Extrinsic motivation: motivation that arises from some factor unrelated to the learning itself.

feasibility The capacity to be successfully realized in the real world.

feedback A term commonly used as synonymous with negative feedback, viz., a method of controlling a system by reinserting into it the results of its past performance (Norbert Wiener). Negative feedback reduces system error to restore equilibrium to a system. Positive feedback magnifies system error, moving a system away from equilibrium.

field dependence A predisposition to perceive and judge objects, ideas, and people in relation to their field or context.

field test A tryout of a program under "typical use" conditions.

flow chart A graphic representation of a sequence of procedures and decisions by means of a diagram normally employing words and symbols.

formative evaluation Evaluation conducted for the purpose of diagnosis and correction; monitoring.

front-end analysis A series of analytical, administrative, and planning steps that follow identification of a need and precede design of a strategy to meet the need.

futilitarian A person who maintains that attempts to improve schools or society are futile.

goal A general term encompassing all types of learning outcome.

goal-directed Unconsciously pursuing an intrinsic goal; applied, e.g., to plant life.

goal-free evaluation Evaluation that examines the effects of educational programs without cognizance of the intended outcomes.

grading The process of classifying students on the basis of data from evaluation.

guessing correction An adjustment of student scores on selected-response tests according to a formula that endeavors to estimate the number of correct responses due to blind guessing.

hypothesis A tentative assumption made to draw out and test its logical or empirical consequences (*Webster's*).

impact analysis An examination of the predicted long- and short-term effects of an innovation.

implementation The realization of an intended change.

instruction The planned or deliberate systematic attempt of people to influence the learning of others (Merlin Wittrock).

instrumental activity An activity that is a means to an end.

interest A readiness to be concerned with or moved by an object or class of objects (*Webster's*).

intellectual development Maturation of cognitive capabilities.

internal evaluation A review of a completed curriculum by its developers, usually conducted prior to external review.

intrinsic Inherent in the nature of the object or event itself. Intrinsic experience: experience that is consummative or valuable in itself. Intrinsic motivation: motivation arising from the interest or recognized value of the activity.

intuition Insight, understanding, or apprehension by means of nonlogical, nondeductive thought processes that apparently operate mainly in the right hemisphere of the brain.

item analysis A formal technique for the evaluation of individual test items by examination of the pattern of responses.

job enrichment An approach to increasing employee motivation and sense of worth by providing the worker with greater scope, responsibility, authority, or expertise.

law A statement of a relationship among phenomena that so far as is known is invariable under the given conditions.

learning The process of acquiring new or changed knowledge, skill, or disposition.

logistics The detailed planning of all the means—human, material, and administrative—for the delivery of instruction.

marginal time The difference between the time needed and the time available for the completion of a task.

mastery The possession of a high degree of knowledge, ability, or expertise. Mastery learning: an approach to instruction aiming at the development of mastery in almost all learners.

measurement The assignment of numerals to entities according to rules (Daniel Stufflebeam).

model A simplified representation or analogy used to help visualize the structure of a more complex entity and the relation of its parts to one another and to the whole.

modeling Demonstrating a pattern of behavior with the intent or potential to influence the behavior of others.

monitoring Continuous or intermittent evaluation conducted to maintain quality or stability of output; formative evaluation.

need (1) Some thing or condition without which the state of an individual (or other entity) would be significantly less than satisfactory; (2) a discrepancy between an actual and an optimal state.

needs assessment An empirical and judgmental process for identifying human needs and establishing priorities among them.

norm-referenced Judged by comparison with the performance of others.

objective A specific change intended to be brought about in a learner.

opportunity cost The loss incurred by forgoing a certain choice in order to make an alternative mutually exclusive choice; tradeoff.

optimal Approaching the ideal as nearly as can reasonably be expected in the circumstances.

overtraining Training that goes beyond the point of competent performance to ensure long-term retention and/or automation of a skill.

parameter A constant or design characteristic of a system, whose value determines the nature or behavior of the system.

peer tutoring Instruction of one student by another student.

performance criterion A specified action or behavior on the part of a learner that the designer posits as indicating achievement of an objective.

personal space The physical space within which an individual may move freely.

pilot test A preliminary small-scale tryout of all or part of a program prototype under conditions that produce detailed evaluative data.

prerequisite A characteristic or experience stipulated as a necessary antecedent to another experience.

practice Systematic exercise for proficiency (*Webster's*). Guided practice: practice shaped by demonstration by and feedback from an expert.

problem A specific obstacle to the satisfaction of a need.

program Structured educational or training activities.

program evaluation Judgment against criteria of a program under trial conditions or in normal use.

purposive Consciously pursuing a goal or goals.

rationale An argument explaining the reasons for pursuing an aim, in order to justify the expenditure of resources required for its achievement.

readiness The capacity to engage in certain mental or physical activities by reason of maturation, motivation, or prior experience.

reinforcement The strengthening or encouraging of a response by association with a pleasant or rewarding stimulus or experience.

reliability The degree to which a test is consistent in measuring whatever it does measure (Bruce Tuckman).

rote learning Memorization of material that is meaningless to the learner.

selected-response test A test in which the examinee chooses an answer to each question from a given list of alternatives.

self-actualization The realization of potential; engagement in activities the individual finds intrinsically valuable.

set point The value or setting at which a system is stable or functioning as intended, and to which a system returns after a disturbance.

shadow cost A cost of a decision or program that is not readily apparent.

simulation A representation under controlled conditions of phenomena or events in the real world.

software Materials that function as vehicles of communication.

social indicator Data on the status or behavior of individuals that when aggregated and analyzed throw light on social conditions or trends.

spillover cost A cost that a program incurs but does not pay.

standardized test A test consisting of items refined by successive tryout, analysis, and revision, administered under clearly defined conditions, and allowing comparison of test performance with norms based on tests of extensive sample populations.

stereopathy A psychological disposition characterized by rigid dependence on rules and authority and by aversion for ambiguity and abstraction.

streaming An organizational pattern in which students are segregated for extended periods on the basis of assumed ability into parallel but separate tracks, or streams, leading to different academic and career outcomes and life chances; the streams have a clear hierarchy of status, and upward mobility between streams is inhibited.

summative evaluation Evaluation made subsequent to instruction to judge achievement of objectives.

system A complex of interacting and interdependent processes serving a common purpose and constituting a unified whole.

system error A discrepancy between the performance of a system and the set point.

table of specifications A detailed plan for the content of a test indicating the proportions of test items devoted to each main topic or capability.

task analysis The examination of an activity by decomposition into and description of its component elements and their interrelationships.

teaching point An individual fact, concept, subskill, or procedure introduced in instruction.

team competition A situation in which individuals cooperate within groups, while groups compete against one another.

temporary system A circumstance in which people act in concert for a limited time, disbanding once the task or activity is completed.

theory A plausible or scientifically acceptable general principle or body of principles offered to explain phenomena (*Webster's*).

thermal comfort The range of environmental conditions within which an individual feels neither too warm nor too cold.

time on task The time a learner spends consciously engaged in learning.

tracking See *streaming.*

training A deliberate process of developing in a person new or changed mental or physical states.

transfer The carry-over or generalization of learned responses from one type of situation to another (*Webster's*).

unobtrusive observation Method of studying typical or voluntary behavior by observing the actions of people who are unaware that they are being observed.

validity The extent to which a test actually measures the characteristics it is intended to measure. Derived validity: the extent to which the scores a test yields correlate with criterion scores that possess direct validity. Direct validity: the extent to which the tasks included in a test represent faithfully and in due proportion the kinds of tasks that provide an operational definition of the achievement or trait in question (Robert L. Ebel).

II

Key to
Chapter Questions

Chapter 3, pp. 72–73

1b	2a	3b	4c	5d	6c	7d	8c	9a	10d

Chapter 4, pp. 100–102

1b	2d	3d	4a	5c	6a	7c	8d	9b	10c

Chapter 5, pp. 132–34

1a	2a	3c	4c	5a	6b	7d	8c	9b	10d

Chapter 6, pp. 154–56

1d	2a	3b	4c	5d	6c	7b	8a	9c	10b

Chapter 7, pp. 188–90

1b	2a	3c	4d	5a	6d	7b	8c	9d	10c

Chapter 8, pp. 221–23

1d	2c	3b	4a	5a	6d	7b	8a	9b	10c

Chapter 9, pp. 260–62

1c	2c	3a	4d	5b	6a	7c	8d	9b	10d

Chapter 10, pp. 290–92

| 1b | 2c | 3d | 4a | 5c | 6c | 7d | 8a | 9d | 10b |

Chapter 11, pp. 322–24

| 1d | 2d | 3b | 4b | 5d | 6a | 7c | 8c | 9c | 10a |

Chapter 12, pp. 361–62

| 1c | 2d | 3a | 4c | 5d | 6b | 7b | 8a | 9c | 10d |

Chapter 13, pp. 401–3

| 1d | 2b | 3c | 4c | 5d | 6a | 7a | 8c | 9b | 10d |

Chapter 14, pp. 443–45

| 1c | 2a | 3a | 4d | 5b | 6c | 7a | 8b | 9b | 10c |

APPENDIX

III

Sources of Information
on Instructional Materials
and Equipment

General

Audio Visual. Monthly. Croydon, England: MacLaren.
Audio-Visual Communication. Monthly. New York: United Business
   Publications.
Audio-Visual Equipment Directory. Fairfax, Va.: National Audio-Visual
   Association, 1974.
Audiovisual Instruction. 9x a year. Washington, D.C.: Association for
   Educational Communications and Technology.
Booklist. Bimonthly. Chicago: American Library Assocation.
Canadian Training Methods. Monthly. Toronto: Chesswood House Pub-
   lishing.
Carter, Yvonne, et al. *Aids to media selection for students and teachers.*
   Washington, D.C.: U.S. Government Printing Office, 1971. (Supple-
   ment, 1973.)
Educational Digest. Monthly. Toronto: MacLean Hunter.
Educational Media International. Quarterly. London: International
   Council for Educational Media.
Educational Product Reports. Monthly. New York: Educational Products
   Information Exchange Institute.

Educational Resources and Techniques. Monthly. Mesquite, Tex.: Texas Association for Educational Technology.

Educators' Purchasing Guide. Annual. Philadelphia: North American Publishing Co.

EPIEgram. Twice monthly. New York: Educational Products Information Exchange Institute.

International Index to Multimedia Information. Quarterly. Pasadena, Cal.: AudioVisual Associates.

Learning Resources. Quarterly. Toronto: Chesswood House Publishing.

Limbacher, James L. *A reference guide to audio-visual information.* New York: Bowker, 1972.

Media and Methods. Monthly. Philadelphia, Pa.: North American Publishing Co.

Media Message. Quarterly. Toronto: Association for Media and Technology in Education in Canada.

Media Review Digest. Annual. Ann Arbor, Mich.: Pierian Press.

Perkins, Flossie L. *Book and non-book media.* Urbana, Ill.: National Council of Teachers of English, 1972.

Previews: Audiovisual software reviews. Monthly. New York: Bowker.

Rufsuold, Margaret, I., and Carolyn Guss. 3rd ed. *Guides to educational media.* Chicago: American Library Association, 1971.

Science Books and Films. Quarterly. Washington, D.C.: American Association for the Advancement of Science.

Update of nonbook media. Monthly. Los Angeles: National Information Center for Educational Materials.

Visual Education. Monthly. London: National Committee for Audio-Visual Aids in Education.

Westinghouse Learning Directory: Instructional Materials Index. New York: Westinghouse Learning Corp., 1971. (Supplement, 1973.)

Books

Book Review Digest. Annual. New York: H. W. Wilson.

Books in Canada. Monthly. Toronto: Canadian Review of Books Ltd.

Books in Print. Annual. New York: Bowker.

British Books in Print. Annual. London: Whitaker.

British Book News. Monthly. London: British Council.

Bulletin of the Center for Children's Books. Monthly. Chicago: University of Chicago Graduate Library School.

Canadiana. Monthly. Ottawa: National Library of Canada.

Canadian Books in Print. Toronto: University of Toronto Press, 1976.

Canadian Children's Literature. Quarterly. Guelph, Ont.: Canadian Children's Press.

Canadian Government Publications. Monthly. Ottawa: Ministry of Supply and Services.
Canadian Materials. Thrice yearly. Ottawa: Canadian Library Association.
Children's Books in Print. Annual. New York: Bowker.
Choice. Monthly. Middletown, Conn.: Association of Colleges and Resource Libraries.
Junior Bookshelf. Bimonthly. Huddersfield, England: Junior Bookshelf.
Kliatt Paperback Book Guide. Thrice yearly. Newton, Me.: Kliatt.
New York Review of Books. Biweekly. New York: New York Times Co.
Paperbacks in Print. Annual. London: Whitaker.
Paperbound Books in Print. Annual. New York: Bowker.
School Library Journal. Monthly. New York: Bowker.
Selected United States Government Publications. Monthly. Washington, D.C.: U.S. Government Printing Office.
The Reviewing Librarian. Quarterly. Toronto: Ontario School Library Assocation.

Films, Filmstrips, Transparencies, Videotapes

Ackerman, Jean Marie. *Films of a changing world: A critical international guide.* Washington, D.C.: Society for International Development, 1972.
Educational Broadcasting. Bimonthly. Los Angeles: Barrington Publishing Inc.
Educational and Industrial Television. Monthly. Ridgefield, Conn.: C. S. Tepfer Publishing Co.
Educators Guide to Free Films. Annual. Randolph, Wis.: Educators Progress Service.
Educators Guide to Free Filmstrips. Annual. Randolph, Wis.: Educators Progress Service.
Film Canadiana. Annual. Ottawa: Canadian Film Institute.
Guide to Foreign Government-loan Films. Annual. Alexandria, Va.: Serina Guides.
Guide to Free Filmstrips, Slides, and Audiotapes. Alexandria, Va.: Serina Guides.
Guide to Free-loan films. Alexandria, Va.: Serina Guides.
Guide to Government-loan Films. Alexandria, Va.: Serina Guides.
Index to Educational Overhead Transparencies. Los Angeles: National Information Center for Educational Media (NICEM).
Index to Educational Slides. Los Angeles: NICEM.
Index to Educational Videotapes. Los Angeles: NICEM.
Index to 8mm. Motion Cartridges. Los Angeles: NICEM.

Index to 16mm. Educational Films. Los Angeles: NICEM.

Index to 35mm. Filmstrips. Los Angeles: NICEM.

Landers Film Review. Bimonthly. Los Angeles: Landers Associates.

Library of Congress. *National Union Catalog: Films and other materials for projection.* Annual. Washington, D.C.: Library of Congress.

Limbacher, James L. *Feature films on 8mm. and 16mm.* New York: Bowker, 1974.

National Instructional Television Center. *Guide book.* Annual. Bloomington, Ind.: National Instructional Television Center.

Sight Lines. Bimonthly. New York: Educational Film Library Association.

Teachers Guide to Television. Biannual. New York: Teachers Guide to Television Inc.

Video Tapes. Annual. Toronto: Ontario Educational Communication Authority.

Audio Records and Tapes

Chicorel Index to the Spoken Arts on Discs, Tapes, and Cassettes. New York: Chicorel Library Publishing Co., 1973.

Educators Guide to Free Tapes, Scripts, and Transcriptions. Randolph, Wis.: Educators Progress Service.

Harrison Tape Guide. Bimonthly. New York: Weiss Publishing Co.

Index to Educational Audio Tapes. Los Angeles: NICEM.

Index to Educational Records. Los Angeles: NICEM.

Library of Congress. *National Union Catalog: Music, Books on Music, and Sound Recordings.* Biannual. Washington, D.C.: Library of Congress.

Directory of Spoken-voice Audio Cassettes. Annual. Los Angeles: Cassette Information Service.

Schwann Record and Tape Guide. Monthly. Boston: W. Schwann Inc.

Other Materials

Automated Education Letter. Monthly. Detroit: Automated Education Center.

Belch, Jean. *Contemporary games.* Detroit: Gale Research Co., 1973.

Collacutt, Ralph, (ed.). *Simulators: International guide.* Reading, Mass.: Addison-Wesley, 1973.

Graham, R. G., and C. F. Gray. *Business games handbook.* New York: American Management Association, 1971.

Hendershot, Carl. *Programmed learning and individually paced instruction bibliography.* 5th ed. Bay City, Mich.: Hendershot, 1977.

Lekan, Helen A. *Index to computer-assisted instruction.* 3rd. ed. New York: Harcourt Brace Jovanovich, 1971.

Zuckerman, David W., and Robert E. Horn. *The guide to simulations/games.* Lexington, Mass.: Information Resources, 1973.

IV

A Specimen Curriculum
Using the Dictionary:
A Curriculum Unit
in Communications

1. *Aim*

To enable students to use an English dictionary effectively.

2. *Rationale*

Language is words. It's bridges so that you can get safely from one place to another. And the more bridges you know about, the more places you can see.

—Arnold Wesker, playwright

Language is at the heart of a humane education, for a powerful and subtle language is a characteristic unique to humanity. Of primary importance in communications studies is the effort to develop in learners the capacity to use their native language articulately. The dictionary is one of the most valuable tools they can use in this lifelong learning

This curriculum is based in part on "Dictionary Skills", an unpublished curriculum by Mary G. McClung and Ralph D. Brown (Kingston, Canada: Queen's University Faculty of Education, © Mary G. McClung, 1978); adapted and published by kind permission of Mary G. McClung and Ralph D. Brown.

process, and as such merits a systematic rather than a casual introduction to students.

The dictionary is not in itself a passport to an eloquent style in written or spoken English; but it does provide a foundation on which students can build their skills in the use of words, particularly with regard to comprehension, word usage, spelling, and pronunciation.

Study of the dictionary is not restricted to a particular context or mode of presentation. While meeting community demands for emphasis on basic communication skills, the unit can be taught in such a way that students find it meaningful, interesting, and worthwhile.

3. Objectives and Performance Criteria

Knowledge

3.1 The student will know the kinds of information provided in a dictionary entry (critical).
P.C. When the student is asked to list five parts of a dictionary entry from memory, at least four of the student's answers will be correct. (Note: In this and subsequent performance criteria, it is not considered necessary to impose time constraints. Enough time should be allowed, within reason, for all students to complete the activity.)
3.2 The student will understand common dictionary abbreviations (important).
P.C. Given ten abbreviations commonly used in dictionaries, the student will give the correct meaning of at least eight.
3.3 The student will know what material is often provided in the "back matter" of dictionaries (desirable).
P.C. When the student is asked to list from memory five types of information often found at the back of dictionaries (e.g., forms of address, handbook of style), at least four of the student's answers will be correct.
3.4 The student will know the main kinds of specialized dictionaries available (desirable).
P.C. Formal assessment of this objective may not be necessary, but the teacher who wished to do so could design a simple true/false test, containing questions such as "The best source for detailed information on the origin of a word is a thesaurus: T/F."

Skills

3.5 The student will be able to use a dictionary to determine the meaning of words (critical).
P.C. Given a dictionary and a list of ten appropriate unfamiliar words, the student will write a sentence illustrating the correct usage of each. At least nine of the ten sentences must be judged acceptable by the

teacher (peer evaluation might be a practicable alternative); sentences must not plagiarize the examples provided in the dictionary.

3.6 The student will be able to determine correct spelling by means of a dictionary (critical).

P.C. Given a dictionary and ten orally dictated words (none of which have silent initial letters), the student will write the correct spelling for all ten words.

3.7 The student will be able to determine correct pronunciation from a dictionary (critical).

P.C. Given a dictionary and a list of ten nonphonetic and little-known words, the student will pronounce at least nine of the ten as indicated in the dictionary (if a language laboratory is available, it may be convenient to use it for this test).

3.8 The student will be able to use a dictionary to determine the correct plural or singular form of words (important).

P.C. Given a dictionary and ten words with irregular singular or plural forms (e.g., datum/data, criterion/criteria), the student will write the correct singular or plural of at least nine of the ten words.

3.9 The student will be able to use a dictionary to find information about the etymology of words (desirable).

P.C. Using a dictionary for reference, the student will answer correctly at least nine out of ten true/false questions, e.g., "The word 'holocaust' is derived in part from a Greek word meaning 'to burn': T/F."

Disposition

3.10 The student will develop the habit of consulting the dictionary (important).

P.C. Assessment of this objective requires unobtrusive observation of dictionary use by students for an equivalent period before and after the unit. This might be done by counting the number of times students are seen to use dictionaries in class or by means of some covert device, such as turning down the corners of pairs of pages in the class set of dictionaries and counting the number of pages separated at the end of a given period of time. Whatever measurement technique is employed, usage should at least double for the objective to be considered achieved.

4. Grading

The grading system will depend on the academic context of the unit and on its weight in relation to any course or program of which it constitutes a part. If completion of the unit earns an independent grade, the following might be considered as a model:

Student achieves all knowledge and skill objectives: Honors.
Student achieves all critical objectives: Credit.
Student fails to achieve all critical objectives: Incomplete.

5.   Context

The unit is designed for introduction at the intermediate, middle-school, or junior-high-school level; that is, for grades seven through ten or ages twelve to sixteen. The earlier it is taught, the greater its subsequent use and the less likely it is to be redundant.

The natural place for the unit is in the English or communications program. Dictionary skills will, however, be beneficial in many areas, and teachers of almost all subjects are likely to welcome these capabilities on the part of their students.

The unit is not dependent on any particular kind of educational or cultural context. With minor modifications, it could be adapted for older or younger students than those indicated above; for adult retraining, literacy, or English-as-a-second-language classes; in special education; in hospital and correctional settings; and in correspondence courses and distance education.

6.   Entry Characteristics

6.1 The learners

As indicated above, the unit may be taught to a wide range of learners. Great variety can be expected in verbal aptitude, background, and personality. The unit can be taught in such a way as to appeal to many different types of students. The precision and certainty of definition will appeal to students who tend to be "authoritarian" or insecure; the subtlety and ambiguity of language will attract the "open-minded" or independent student. Those learners who have high verbal ability can be expected to find the unit most congenial; consequently, the appositional or metaphorical element in words should be emphasized for the benefit of the more intuitive students. Adolescents in the twelve-to-sixteen age group, for whom the unit is primarily intended, are becoming interested in their own ability to manipulate abstract questions by means of words. In selecting the subject matter of the unit, the instructor should choose examples that will help to cultivate the cognitive development and the growing idealism of students at this age.

6.2 Prerequisites

The only necessary prerequisites are a firm grasp of alphabetical order and an ability to read and write English at a minimum level of about fifth grade.

6.3 Pretest

If the reading level of learners is not known, a brief reading pretest at or before the beginning of the unit will serve to identify students below the minimum required reading level. Such students should be provided with, or directed to, remedial reading instruction. Problems of alphabetization may be given immediate remediation.

A brief pretest may be developed that will assess students' initial status with respect to the unit objectives. This test will provide students with an overview of the unit. Careful analysis of the results will yield a summary of the present level of dictionary skills among the students and a base line with which performance at the end of the unit may be compared. It will identify objectives that are redundant and those that require emphasis. It will also serve to identify learners who have already mastered all or most of the objectives. Such learners, depending on the situation, may be accelerated to the next unit, provided with enrichment, or given the oportunity to help other learners in the dictionary unit.

7. *Instruction*

7.1 Strategies

Although the subject matter of the unit is precisely defined, the variety of potential teaching aproaches is limited only by the imagination and creativity of the teacher. The methods chosen will reflect the personality and preferences of teachers and students and the context of the unit. It is most important that strategies motivate students to learn. There are numerous ways of making the instruction interesting, but the unit could undoubtedly be deadly if taught in an uninspired manner.

Anecdotes, puns, and riddles based on word meanings abound and may easily be introduced by the teacher or collected by the students. A number of dictionaries of puns, anagrams, obsolete words, etc. are published, which are useful for teacher and student reference.

Bulletin boards may be used effectively to mount displays on themes such as definitions, spelling, etymology, or types of dictionaries. The value of bulletin boards for learning is enhanced if students are assigned responsibility for displays.

Debates. Once students develop some knowledge and interest in the subject, they may become quite involved in a formal debate on topics such as the following:

"English spelling should be standardized."
"The influence of Latin on English was pernicious."
"Dictionaries are a futile attempt to freeze a living language."
"A picture is worth a thousand words."

Prerequisites for successful classroom debates are a grasp of debating skills and procedures and respect for the opinions of others.

Epigrammatic definitions. Students find or invent epigrammatic definitions for report or display, e.g.:

Archaeologist: A person whose future lies in ruins.

Politician: Public figure who approaches every issue with an open mouth (Adlai Stevenson).

Prejudice: The reason of fools (Voltaire).

Games. There are innumerable word games that can be very valuable. They include pen-and-paper games such as crosswords and anagrams; group games, such as bingo, that can be imaginatively adapted; board games such as Scrabble; card games such as Foil and Password,* and performing games such as charades. The teacher should try to prevent excessive competition developing, which may limit the learning value of these games.

Guest speakers could be invited from a college department of English or linguistics, from a publishing house, or from the editorial department of a newspaper. It is wise to ensure in advance that people invited can communicate effectively and in an interesting way at the students' level.

Personal dictionaries. Students may be encouraged or required to maintain a personal dictionary of words encountered in English and in other classes, in private reading, and in out-of-school contexts. This encourages the practice of asking or referring to the dictionary for the meaning of unfamiliar words and provides insight into the construction of a dictionary. In addition, periodic review by the teacher of these dictionaries encourages students to maintain the practice, enables the teacher to check for correct spelling and definition, informs the teacher of the students' vocabulary level, and provides material for class discussion.

Research projects can be conducted by individuals and groups. Questions of etymology lend themselves to research. A group of students could make a glossary of special terms used in the school or the community. Another group could analyze word usage by local citizens, politicians, or school principals. Evaluation standards for research projects should be clearly understood. There is a danger of projects degenerating into busywork in which little learning takes place. Informal research leading to one-minute oral reports by students to the class is sometimes a more efficient use of student time.

Team competition is an effective way of stimulating interest and involvement. Contests can be held among teams in the classroom on spellings, meanings, syllabification, knowledge of the dictionary, or speed of dictionary use. The teams should preferably be differently constituted on each occasion, to avoid one team winning consistently and the others becoming discouraged.

7.2 Schedule

The schedule will depend on the particular context in which the unit is taught. Assuming that the unit is assigned about fifteen hours

---

* Scrabble, Foil, and Password are registered trademarks.

over a four-week period, the following sequence might be an appropriate guide.

Before the unit

In the month before the unit begins, unobtrusively analyze level of dictionary use, as indicated in objective 3.10. Conduct pretest preferably before the unit begins; analyze the present status of learners; redirect or make special provision for students who lack prerequisites or for whom the unit would redundant. If the pretest cannot be conducted before the unit, the first session may be used for this purpose. Prepare attractive exhibits, displays, or posters for the first day of the unit.

First week

Introduce the course and outline its purpose. Teach the topics that will be used throughout the unit: dictionary abbreviations and form of dictionary entries. Assess understanding and remediate underachievement. Assign projects and responsibilities that will continue throughout the unit. Ensure adequate challenge and high levels of success; use games, quizzes, puzzles, etc. to develop motivation.

Second and third weeks

Teach use of dictionary for determining meanings and usage, spelling, pronunciation, and pluralization. Teach topics thoroughly in the first instance, and refer back to them frequently to assist retention. Use numerous, varied, and interesting examples at every point. Monitor for underachievement or disinterest; take corrective action (self-remediation, individual help, peer tutoring, etc.).

Fourth week

Introduce students to use of the dictionary for tracing word origins, to the back matter in dictionaries, and to specialized dictionaries. These three topics lend themselves to high-interest activities. Provide further practice on topics dealt with earlier in the unit. The fourth week may be a suitable time for a guest speaker or a field trip. Assessment should be completed prior to the last lesson to allow time for final remediation and retesting.

After the unit

Take frequent advantage of opportunities to refer to the dictionary in succeeding weeks to reinforce skills and habits of dictionary usage. Some time after completion of the unit, conduct follow-up as indicated in objective 3.10 to determine development of dictionary habits.

8. *Provision for Slower and Faster Learners*

Extreme variety in background is best dealt with at or before the beginning of the unit, by identifying and making special provision for learners who lack prerequisites or who have already mastered the objectives. The remaining variety can be dealt with in a number of ways.

8.1 *Slower learners*

The activities of the first week will be designed in such a way that they are intrinsically interesting and all students experience substantial success. This is important in establishing a high level of motivation.

The pretest will allow ranking of learners. Groups can be chosen for activities and team competitions to include diverse aptitude. This will encourage a certain amount of informal peer tutoring.

Student learning will be subject to frequent monitoring; the teacher should watch for and correct minor misunderstandings as they become apparent during instruction. The steps represented by the performance criteria are small enough that few students should fail to meet the required standard, and it is therefore anticipated that little formal remediation will be necessary. Performance criteria may be marked by students working in pairs, so that there can be some immediate peer discussion of problems that arise. For underachievers who need additional practice, self-remedial exercises can be prepared for each objective. These should have high intrinsic interest. A crossword puzzle or interesting prose material might be appropriate. For some objectives, an audio cassette could be prepared, which a student would listen to in his or her own time, referring to the dictionary as instructed. At least one retest should be provided for each performance criterion; it may be desirable to conduct this on a Monday, so that the previous weekend can be used for remediation. If necessary, time can be diverted from desirable objectives to critical objectives to ensure minimal achievement in the unit.

There are few inherent intellectual difficulties in the unit. If substantial failure to learn is experienced, the teacher should examine (1) the validity of the pretest; (2) the rigor of the prerequisites; (3) the motivational quality of instruction; and (4) the general attitude of students towards learning. Steps must then be taken to remedy the underlying problem.

8.2 *Faster learners*

Lexicography is a rich enough field to challenge the most superior intellect: Activities and examples can be chosen at various levels of difficulty, so that interest is maintained for all students. A number of enrichment activities should be available, such as use of the dictionary for finding synonyms and antonyms, determining parts of speech and syllabification, or for research into etymology, comparative study of dictionaries, or composition of crosswords. Faster learners may also serve as formal and informal peer tutors for slower learners and as chairpersons of teams in competitions and in preparing research projects.

In some circumstances it may be possible to allow students who achieve the objectives of the unit rapidly or who "pretest out" of the unit to use their marginal time in other subjects where they need extra time, for private reading, or for other unrelated "cultural enrichment" activities.

9. Logistics

9.1 Materials

There should be a class set of an appropriate dictionary. In the United States *Webster's New Collegiate Dictionary* might be chosen; in Britain the *Concise Oxford Dictionary*; in Canada the *Gage Senior Canadian Dictionary*.

Several other reference works should be available in the classroom, including a thesaurus (e.g., *Webster's Collegiate Thesaurus*), an etymological dictionary, and one large-scale dictionary such as *Webster's Third New International Dictionary* or *The Shorter Oxford English Dictionary*. Some useful teacher references are J. S. Crosbie, *Crosbie's Dictionary of Puns* (New York: Harper & Row, 1977); W. R. Espy, *An Almanac of Words at Play* (New York: Potter, 1976); and Laurence Urdung (ed.), *The New York Times Everyday Reader's Dictionary of Misunderstood, Misused, Mispronounced Words* (New York: Quadrangle, 1972). Additional reference dictionaries may be borrowed from libraries as needed.

Several other materials that should be provided include:

A number of games of Scrabble, Password, Shake-a-word,* etc.

Books of crosswords and word games

Prerecorded audio cassettes, if necessary, for remediation

Posters focusing on dictionary use (obtainable from educational media suppliers)

Materials for bulletin board displays, handouts, etc.

Optional: a class set of daily newspapers (many newspaper publishers will provide papers to schools at nominal cost; discarded newspapers should be recycled)

9.2 Equipment

Three or four cassette players for remedial cassettes.
Overhead projector and screen as required.

9.3 Facilities

The unit could operate with a class of almost any reasonable size. A regular classroom would be satisfactory. It should be possible to ar-

* Scrabble, Password, and Shake-a-word are registered trademarks.

range the seating in both small and large groups. The more attractive the classroom, the more positive student reaction will be.

9.4 Personnel

In principle, this unit could be taught by any teacher, aide, or volunteer having the necessary skills. It could also be taught on a team basis by a group of teachers. The teacher(s) should have a strong interest in language and communication and be able to express and communicate this enthusiasm to the learners. The teacher should consistently model high standards of spoken and written English (but this does not mean using an artificial or alien vocabulary or enunciation). He or she should make a point of consulting the dictionary frequently during lessons, not only during this unit but as a matter of course. A background in languages, linguistics, English, or communications would be an asset. The teacher must be familiar with the major dictionaries and with basic principles of lexicography; this knowledge can be acquired if necessary by independent study. Good organizational skills will also be required, and an ability to relate to learners of the age and background expected in the class.

The responsibilities of the teacher will include the following:
—instructing
—diagnosing learner difficulties
—providing learners with individual help
—organizing activities
—negotiating arrangements with members of the community, e.g., guest lecturers, newspapers, and publishers
—obtaining approval for surveys, field trips, projects, etc. to take place outside the school
—preparing or having students prepare exhibits and displays
—ordering, cataloging, issuing, and organizing materials
—evaluating and grading.

Other personnel involved may include the principal in approving certain activities, and the school librarian in providing assistance in acquiring materials. Other teachers may be invited to reinforce dictionary use in their own classes.

9.5 Time

It is estimated that fifteen hours of instructional time and six hours of independent study will be sufficient for at least 90 percent of learners to achieve all objectives. The remaining 10 percent of learners may need to commit an additional one to four hours for practice or remediation.

The schedule (7.2, above) organizes the instruction on the basis of one forty- or forty-five-minute lesson a day for four weeks. But the time could be distributed according to the preference of the instructor and the context of the program. The unit could, for example, be completed in one lesson a week over a twenty-week semester. Or it could be taught to an evening class in one two-hour session a week for eight weeks.

Most of the evaluation, marking, and remediation is included within the instructional time. Time shown below for the teacher is for the first operation of the unit; this should decrease on subsequent occasions.

	ACTIVITY	HOURS
INSTRUCTOR	Instruction	15
	Preparation of lessons and materials	10
	Acquiring and organizing materials	4
	Designing, marking, and analyzing tests	6
	Preparing remedial materials	4
	Remediation outside class time	2
	General administration	2
	Total	43
STUDENTS	In class	15
	Out of class	6
	Remediation	0–4
	Total	21–25
OTHERS	Guest lecturer: preparation, travel, lecture	3
	Librarian, principal: as required.	

9.6 Cost

The main costs would be capital expenditures for the first offering of the unit, particularly a class set of good hard-bound dictionaries. But these should last for up to ten years. Minimum and maximum start-up costs and expected continuation costs are shown below.

	START-UP COSTS		CONTINUATION COSTS
	Min.	Max.	(Average)
30 dictionaries	$240	$360	$30
Reference dictionaries	0*	120	10
Word-game books	20	60	10
Games	20	40	10
Cassette tape	20	40	10
Posters	0†	20	5
Newspapers	0‡	30	15
Paper	10	20	10
Field trip: transportation	0§	50	25
Guest lecture: expenses	0″	10	5
Total	$310	$750	$130

* Rely on library   ‡ Obtain free   ″ No expenses
† Make   § Students pay transportation

10. Tryout

10.1 Pilot test

The unit could be pilot-tested with individual students as enrichment or remediation, during a summer-school program, or in an advanced English-as-a-second-language class. If funds were available for pilot testing, four students could probably be employed to try out the unit for a total of less than $100.

10.2 Field test

The unit should be field-tested with a typical class and teacher under normal conditions.

Particular attention should be paid during the pilot and field test to student interest and understanding.

11. Program Evaluation

11.1 Effectiveness

The program could be regarded as effective if:
—100 percent of the students* receive credit, i.e., master all critical objectives;
—50 percent of students* receive honors, i.e., master all objectives; and
—dispositional objective 3.10 is achieved.

11.2 Acceptability

The course could be regarded as acceptable if:
—on a course questionnaire requesting student opinion of the interest and value of the curriculum and the quality of the teaching, mean rating is at least "good" on a scale of poor/fair/good/excellent, and
—positive comments volunteered by parents and teachers during the unit and in the two months following it outnumber negative comments by at least 2:1.

11.3 Other dimensions

It would probably not be worthwhile to attempt to assess the efficiency of the unit in the absence of a control group. The program should be monitored, however, for possible underuse of time or materials. Instruction and classroom activities should be observed for relevance to

* Excluding students who commence the unit with less than fifth-grade reading level.

curriculum objectives, engagement of learners, and incidental learning. Formative and summative tests should be analyzed for validity, reliability, time consumption, student reaction, and technical quality. Use, non-use, or abuse of pretests and prerequisites should be observed. The quality of materials for student use should be examined. Students, teachers, administrators, and parents may be interviewed for in-depth reaction to the unit.

12. Implementation

In most cases, this unit would represent a course revision within the authority of the individual teacher. Approval might be required for expenditures and for activities outside the school. In the event that the unit was introduced as a discrete innovation requiring official sanction, formal channels should be followed. Whenever approval or cooperation is needed, the following points should be stressed: the care with which the curriculum has been developed; the extent to which the curriculum responds to current community concern for renewed emphasis on communication and language skills; and the real benefit the learners will realize from the program.

V

Model of a Curriculum Design System

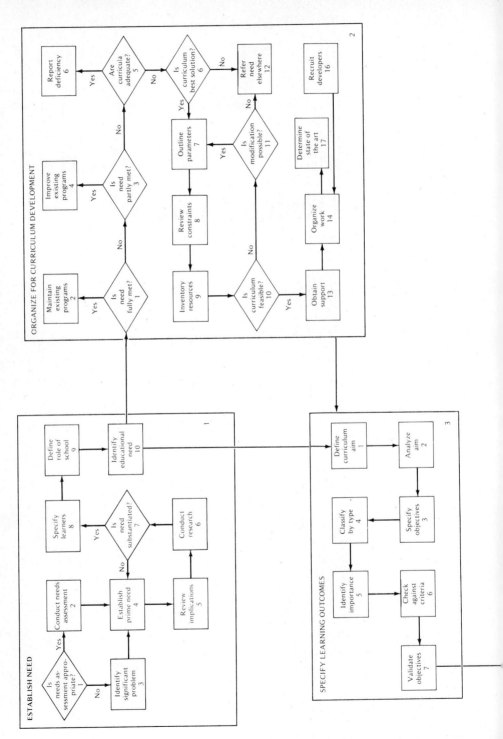

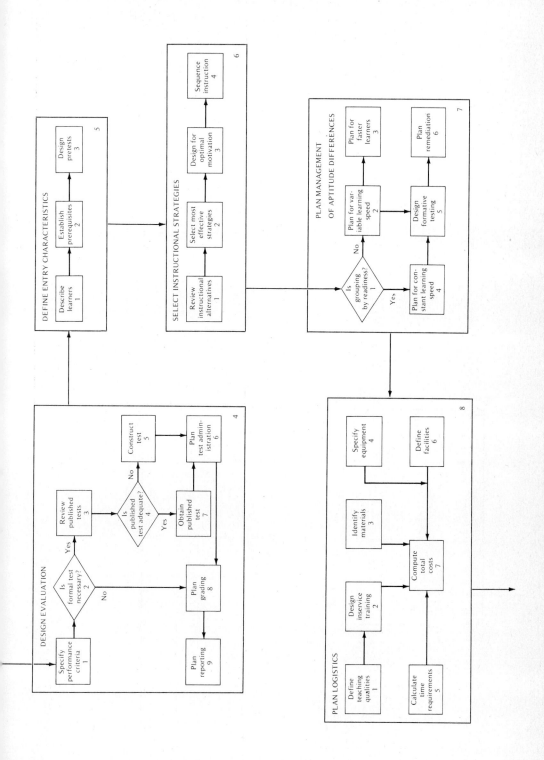

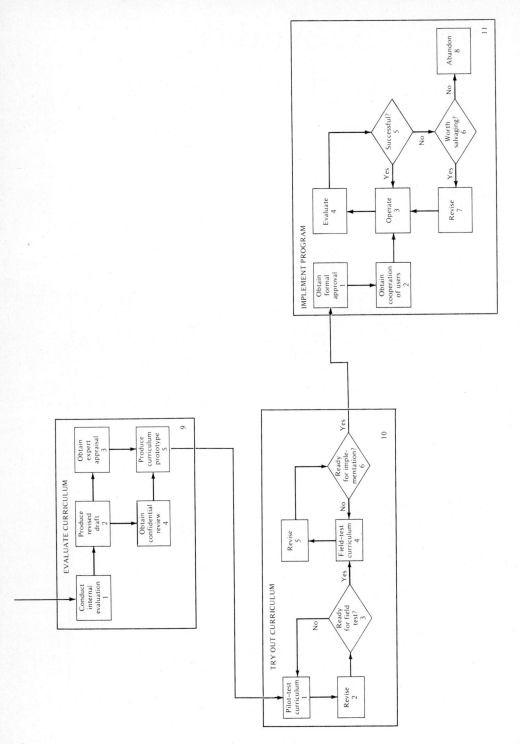

Copyrights
and Acknowledgments

Epigraphs

Page 3   Courtesy of The MIT Press from Simon, Herbert A., *The sciences of the artificial.*

43   Courtesy of Continuum Books and Sheed and Ward Ltd. from Freire, Paulo, *Pedagogy of the oppressed.*

79   Courtesy of The University of Chicago Press from Tyler, Ralph W., *Basic principles of curriculum and instruction.* Copyright © 1949 by The University of Chicago Press.

161   From Fanon, Frantz, *The wretched of the earth.* Reprinted by permission of Grove Press, Inc. Copyright © 1963 by Presence Africaine. Courtesy of Granada Publishing Limited.

195   Courtesy of the Frontiers of Science Foundation from Bloom, Benjamin S., Quality control in education, *Tomorrow's Teaching.*

269   From *Educational psychology: A cognitive view* by David P. Ausubel. Courtesy of David P. Ausubel.

297   Courtesy of Little, Brown and Company from Barzun, Jacques, *Teacher in America.*

Text

Page 162   Courtesy of *Audio-Visual Language Journal* from Harding, Ann and Page, Brian, An alternative model for modern language examinations, *Audio-Visual Language Journal*, 1974/75.

163–64   Courtesy of Arnold Lawrence.

Boxes

5   Courtesy of The Wilderness Society from Gunter, Peter A., *The living wilderness.*

12   From *The human side of enterprise* by Douglas McGregor. Copyright © 1960 by McGraw-Hill Book Company. Used with permission of McGraw-Hill Book Company.

31–32   Courtesy of National Society for the Study of Education from Rugg, Harold, The foundations of curriculum-making, *Twenty-sixth Yearbook of the National Society for the Study of Education.*

Figures, Tables, and Photos

Index

ability grouping: achievement affected by, 352; of curriculum aims, 151–52; defined, 351; selection methods in, 353–54; self-image affected by, 352–53

acceleration of faster learners, 354–56

acceptability in program evaluation, 419–21, 423

achievement, learner: ability grouping and, 352; determinants of, 298; reporting, 258. *See also* faster learners; underachievers

achievement criteria, *see* performance criteria

achievement reports, 258

achievement standards: academic credit and, 215–16, 220; on examinations, *see* cutoff scores; mastery learning and, 216–18

Ackoff, Russell L., 141, 147

activism, 11

administration, innovation and, 118–19, 430–31, 433–35, 440

adoption of innovation, 435

aesthetic needs, 59

aesthetic quality in instructional environment, 390

affective domain, *see* dispositions.

age grading, 357–58

aim(s), curriculum, 139, 410, 424; completeness of, 150–51; conciseness of, 149; curriculum rationale and, 152–53; exactness of, 150; intention in, 147; learner change as, 147–49; objectives and, 161–64, 184; public acceptability of, 151–52; task analysis and, 164–71

air movement in instructional environment, 387

alternatives to new curriculum, 107–9

American Red Cross First Aid Instructor's Manual, 151

analysis: of aims, 162–63; front-end, 105–9; impact, 117; item, *see* item analysis; of learning materials, 371–77; of tasks, *see* task analysis

Anderson, Lorin, 182

Appalachia Educational Laboratory, 89–90

applied science, curriculum design as, 9–10

appropriateness of curriculum objectives, 186

aptitude: of faster learners, 346–56; as general trait, 332–33; grouping by, 358–59; in program evaluation, 425; speed of learning as, 333–35; underachievement and, 338–46

aptitude-treatment interaction (ATI), 274, 299

Aristotle, 178–79

art: aesthetic education and, 59; design in, 6–7; education, evaluation in, 199

assessment, self, 201–2

Association for Supervision and Curriculum Development, 131

Astin, Alexander W., 277

Athens, ancient, education in, 16–18

ATI (aptitude-treatment interaction), 274, 299

attitude, public, in needs assessment, 88

attitudes, *see* dispositions

audiovisual instructional materials, 376–77; sources of information on, 463–67

Austria, curriculum constraints in, 112

Ausubel, David P., 269; on drilling, 312; on pretesting, 288–89

automation, in skill learning, 312, 314

Avis Co., 141

CURRICULUM

Design and
Development

Part One

FOUNDATIONS OF CURRICULUM DEVELOPMENT

Schmuck, Richard, 123
school, *see* instructional system
Schools Council (Great Britain), 129, 131
Schwab, Joseph, 37, 121; on curriculum teams, 122
science(s): applied, 9–10; behavioral, 34, 201; emphasis on teaching, Sputnik I and, 35–36
Science Research Associates (SRA), 219
Scriven, Michael, 62, 228; on goal-free evaluation, 418
selected-response tests, 233–34; "all of the above" answers in, 238–39; confusing questions in, 238; creativity in design of, 240–41; incorrect items in, 240; internal clues in, 236–37; item analysis in, 246–49; opinion in, 239–40; overlapping answers in, 237; reliability of, improving, 250–51; trick questions in, 239; triviality in, 239
selection, in ability grouping, 353–54
self-actualization, need for, 54, 56
self-assessment, by learner, 201–2
self-image: ability grouping and, 352–53; failure and, 217, 218
set point, 337
sexism, in instructional materials, 373
shadow costs, 398–99
significance, as criterion for aims, 147; for objectives, 186
skills: evaluation of, 210–11; teaching of, 312–14; as objective of education, 174–75
Snow, C. P., 23
social indicators analysis, in needs assessment, 87
social needs, 58–59
Society of Jesus, 19
Socrates, 16–17
software, *see* materials, instructional
Sommer, Robert, 383, 390
Sophists, 17–18
Southwest Regional Laboratory, 115, 129
spatial organization: form following function in, 384–85; grid pattern in, 383; open classroom approach to, 383–84
Sparta, ancient, education in, 16
Spearman-Brown formula, 251

specialists, academic, opinion of, in needs assessment, 82
Spencer, Herbert, 21–22
Sperry, Roger, 172, 174
spillover costs, 399
SRA (Science Research Associates), 219
staff, *see* teacher(s)
Stanley, Julian C., 349, 356
Starch, Daniel, 230
stereopathy, 273
stereotypes, in instructional material, 373, 375
streaming, *see* ability grouping
stress, reduction of, 9
students, *see* learner(s)
Study of Mathematically Precocious Youth (Johns Hopkins University), 355
subject matter, 4; choice of, and motivation, 307; classics as, 21; Committee of Ten on, 26–27; Latin as, in medieval Europe, 19, 20; survival skills as, 60–61; team curriculum development and, 121
success, as motivator, 309
summative evaluation, 228, 342
Suppes, Patrick, 449
survival needs, 60–62
Sweden, ability grouping in, 352; curriculum reform in, 83
system theory, biological, 8

table of specifications, 234–36
tacit knowledge, 311–12
task analysis, 164–66; elements of, 167–70; second-level analysis in, 170–71
task delay tolerance, 169–70
taxpayers, opinion of, in needs assessment, 81
teacher(s): acquaintance with learners of, 289; as constraint in curriculum development, 113–14; in curriculum design, 297–98, 321–22, 435; in curriculum teams, 121, 127; defining competencies of, 390–92; expectations of learners by, 219; goals and, 145; incentives for, 441–42; innovation and, 428–32, 439–41; instructional strategy control by, 297–98; learners as, 115, 349–51; opinion of, in needs